3rd Edition

PROBLEM SOLVING

in
Recreation
and Parks

Joseph J. Bannon &
James A. Busser

SAGAMORE PUBLISHING INC.
Champaign, Illinois

Production supervision and interior design: Susan M. Williams
Cover design: Michelle R. Dressen
Editor: Lisa Busjahn
Proofreader: Phyllis L. Bannon

Third Edition, 1992.

Printed in the United States of America

ISBN: 0-915611-50-3
Library of Congress Catalog Card Number: 91-68237

This book is dedicated to our families:

Anne, Joe, and Peter
and
Cynny and Katie

Contents

ACKNOWLEDGMENTS

The first and second editions of *Problem Solving in Recreation and Parks* were well received by students, teachers, and practitioners. This feedback provided the maturation needed to complete the third edition. Obviously, a book of this nature could not be possible without the involvement and participation of many individuals. Many students and practitioners, as well as participants in our workshops have contributed ideas and actual problem situations for the third edition.

We would like to extend our appreciation to the authors and publishers of journals and magazines who have permitted us to use their work to strengthen our ideas.

Sincere thanks is also extended to our colleagues in the Department of Leisure Studies at the University of Illinois who have shared with us their critical review of the problem-solving model and the case studies presented in this edition.

A special expression of gratitude is extended to Brad Wesner who spent many hours in the library searching for references for each case study. A special thanks to Lisa Busjahn for editing the manuscript, and to Susan Williams for an excellent job in following the edition through the production process. Thanks also to Michelle Dressen for her creative ideas for cover design and illustrations.

It is also important to recognize our mentors, George D. Butler, and Allen V. Sapora, who stimulated our thoughts, insisted we put our ideas into writing, and provided support and encouragement over the past two decades.

Joseph J. Bannon

ACKNOWLEDGMENTS

I want to acknowledge the efforts of several individuals who have been of assistance to me in this work. Deborah Wright conducted in-depth library searches, which have greatly enhanced the support of ideas presented in the book. Kathryn Ayers developed the background for two case studies, which broadened the variety of issues and professional settings depicted. Mauri Collins carefully reviewed the manuscript, and provided many valuable suggestions resulting in a clearer presentation of ideas. Most importantly, Cynthia Carruthers contributed much to the revision of this book. She was always available to discuss ideas, provide encouragement, and critically comment on the manuscript. It was again a pleasure to work with the Sagamore publishing staff, particularly Susan Williams, who provided much support and assistance in bringing the manuscript to completion. Finally, I'd like to express my appreciation to Joe Bannon for allowing me the opportunity to work with him on this manuscript, for being open to my ideas, and for demonstrating ongoing confidence in my work.

James A. Busser

FOREWORD

One of the features that distinguishes a profession from other occupations is the ability of its members to problem solve. That ability is predicated upon the individual's knowledge of the field of practice, the research that undergirds that practice, and a sensitivity to the dynamics that are involved in the creation of the problem situation, as well as those that aid in its resolution. Technicians are given to facts and specific applications. Professionals seek information based upon theoretical considerations, in an attempt to resolve problems in an optimal manner, recognizing there may be more than one satisfying approach to any given situation.

Problem solving requires practice. One develops skills in ascertaining potential solutions and in recognizing factors that condition choices through practice and experience. That skill can be enhanced through the use of case study materials and small group discussions utilizing the case method. Case studies provide simulation experience, and group discussions afford opportunities to measure one's observation and solutions against those of others. The process is enhanced considerably when probing questions are asked, and conceptual materials are identified as a source for understanding. The case method has been used most effectively by schools of business administration, law, and medicine. *Problem Solving in Recreation and Parks* by Joseph Bannon and James Busser affords our profession the opportunity to use the same method in improving our skills of analysis and decision making.

Unlike any other publication in parks and recreation, this text is grounded in the practice of park and recreation professionals. The authors have amassed a significant collection of case studies touching upon all facets of park and recreation: programming; personnel administration; budgeting and fiscal accountability; advisory and policy board relationships; planning and development; and publicity and public relations. For each problem there are references to the theory and experience that offer insight and direction for problem resolution. The relationship between theory and practice becomes obvious as one goes beyond technique to understanding. This contribution alone would be significant, but the work provides the reader with an additional dimension. It also offers a strategy for problem solving through the use of small group discussion techniques and decision-making strategies.

For students of group dynamics, *Problem Solving in Recreation and Parks* is ideal. The materials on decision making, and the use of brainstorming as a technique to stimulate creative thought are well developed. They enable the reader to become more familiar with the means by which groups can draw from the experience and knowledge of individual members in decision making. The case studies provide a focal point for the practice of that skill, and for the development of the professional. The human relations factor in problem solving is never understated. It is an obvious given, and the key to successful administration. The approach offered by Bannon and Busser helps one to understand and deal with individual value judgments, perceptions, and decision preferences. It also enables one to develop a more democratic style of leadership, and a true appreciation of democracy.

This text is a proven one. The mere fact that this is the third edition attests to its credibility and vitality. Those of us who have used it understand its usefulness. Those discovering it for the first time will realize very quickly its value and application. There are scores of new case studies included, updated critical references, and resources devoted to small-group concepts. Students, administrators, educators, and volunteers will find it an excellent resource, one that will hone their skills as decision makers and problem solvers. It also affords greater insight into the nature of park and recreation operations, and the myriad of situations that park and recreation professionals encounter in their provision of opportunities for meaningful leisure expressions. It is one of the cornerstones of my professional library.

H. Douglas Sessoms, Professor
University of North Carolina-Chapel Hill

PREFACE

The third edition of *Problem Solving in Recreation and Parks* introduces a second author to this work. This edition represents a transition as we integrate our theoretical orientations and attempt to articulate the ideas contained in this work with a common style. As we prepare this third, revised edition, the need for skill in solving problems in recreation and parks, or other fields for that matter, is no longer questioned. What is important is that the problems one is likely to encounter, and these are for the most part predictable, are those for which students and practitioners have been prepared. Preparation comes through experience, either practical experience in day-to-day operations, or intellectual and academic experience through formal education. A false dichotomy is often made between those who work and those who study. A student is often told that the "real world" awaits him, while a practitioner with years of field experience is content that he has nothing more to learn.

Both generalizations are false, in that the world of a student is as real as any other, while practical experience too often is a means for resisting innovation and change. Furthermore, many students obtain work experience while also attending school, whereas too many careerists see little value in taking courses and seminars once they are entrenched in professional positions. In this textbook, we attempt to combine practical with academic approaches to problem solving, offering both the theoretical and pragmatic viewpoints, combining these wherever possible. For these reasons, this book should be useful not only for teaching park and recreation students how to handle hypothetical problems systematically, but as an update and refresher for those involved with actual problems in agencies and organizations. Regardless of whether one is a student preparing for a career in parks and recreation or a related area, or one is a professional already working in the field (not to mention those who serve on advisory boards and commissions), the concepts and ideas presented in this book should: 1) increase one's problem-solving ability; 2) offer a systematic multi-idea approach to problem solving; and 3) improve one's performance as a student or a worker as the result of one's more effective problem-solving and decision-making skills.

In this edition, greater attention is given to creative thinking as an important aspect of effective problem solving. It does not suffice to say that one should be creative, or that all of us are potentially creative. As with any much-used word, creativity is not only misused as a concept, it is easily misunderstood as a personal quality. Creativity varies from person to person, and for each person, from situation to situation. Here is an instance where inherited ability and one's present environment both play an important part. While it is not the purpose of this book to scrutinize the factors that make one person more creative than others, it does seem important to clarify some aspects of creativity that are carelessly handled, or too readily misunderstood.

In addition to all the chapters being substantially revised, 75 new case studies have been added in Part III. These case studies represent a wide array of more current problems, since the issues facing park and recreation professionals change as rapidly as the times. Case studies included represent subjects such as the environment, tourism, user fees, youth at risk, crowd control, cost-cutting strategies, agency reorganization, protection of wildlife, and legal liability. All cases are drawn from actual situations collected from practitioners in the field, and news stories that have appeared in newspapers throughout the United States. Each case study is supplemented with up-to-date references for further study. These are all presented in case studies relating to park and recreation organizations, though they can just as well be modified for other human service organizations.

There is no need for this book to be confined to classroom use only. It can be readily used in staff development programs and inservice training, by park boards, or a wide variety of social and educational institutions. We have used the problem-solving model presented in this book for 25 years, not only as educators, but for staff development in problem-solving and decision-making skills. Since the first edition of this book in 1972, many useful suggestions and criticisms have been received from the vastly increased number of people using the model. For the most part, these suggestions have been incorporated into the present edition. It is hoped, therefore, that this edition will prove more useful and relevant for students both in the classroom and in the field.

INTRODUCTION TO PART I

Part I is intended to provide individuals with the framework needed prior to engaging in the problem-solving process. Chapter One attempts to highlight some of the issues facing students, educators, and practitioners in the field of leisure services. This discussion is certainly not an exhaustive treatment of the subject matter. However, the chapter is aimed at identifying the need for creative problem solving. In essence, problem solving is an important part of professional development, and a necessity for identifying and addressing crucial issues facing universities and leisure service organizations.

Chapters Two and Three delve into the use of case studies and role playing, respectively. These are aids to problem solving, and the discussion is meant to assist all who will engage in this process. It is our intention that the presentation of case studies and role playing will provide supporting information and facilitate the use of accompanying cases. These methods may be very beneficial in obtaining optimal results when training individuals in the use of problem solving.

Chapter Four examines the relationship of creativity to problem solving. This discussion sets the stage for problem solving in leisure service organizations. Two managerial practices; participative management and delegation, are also presented. These practices can play a vital role in facilitating employee creativity.

Chapter One

PROBLEM SOLVING: A PROFESSIONAL NEED

The Role of Education

Students in leisure studies curriculums are expected to learn basic information and skills, analyze theoretical constructs, and at the same time gain experience in dealing with the daily problems of their profession. While some students come to the university with practical experience, many students have limited exposure to the field. However, as graduates, they are expected to take on the demands and responsibilities of professional life. Education is becoming increasingly important for securing professional positions, particularly as certification plays a more prominent role in hiring decisions. Few curricula provide educational experiences that promote the development of problem-solving skills, trusting that they will be acquired elsewhere or are somehow instinctive. Research on university education (Fisher and Grant 1983) strongly indicates that college students have limited opportunity in applying higher-order thinking processes to subject matter. It was found that complex thinking processes were not promoted, and actually were severely limited as a result of overly controlled (e.g., lecturing) classroom sessions.

Ask educators, employers, or recent graduates what is lacking in education today. Their answers probably will be practical skills in reading, writing, and analytical thinking. Such skills are considered so fundamental that they are simply overlooked, especially on the college level. Most students are un-aware that they lack them. Educators are continually frustrated by students' lack of these basic skills, blaming previous teachers or schools. Employers, while expecting to have to orient and train new employees, cannot be expected to provide a new employee with fundamental information-gathering skills and analytical thought processes. And so the cycle continues.

As leisure service educators, we are interested in teaching and researching the theoretical aspects of leisure studies. How-ever, we also must be concerned with instructing students in the pragmatic skills needed for management in leisure service orga-nizations. If the student's problem is integrating philosophical issues with professional practice, the educator should incorpo-rate opportunities for skill development into the curriculum. For instance, a student with a degree in leisure studies may be required to perform administrative functions such as: conceptu-alizing, developing, and planning a summer camp program; identifying the comprehensive needs of the clientele; marketing programs and services; developing a master plan for the agency; and generating and managing the financial aspects of a leisure service agency. The newly graduated leisure service profes-sional will also be expected to deal systematically with common problems involving vandalism, labor negotiations, low atten-dance at agency programs, and poor community relations, as well as broader social problems directly affecting the profession.

Each of the issues facing the field, as well as day-to-day operational problems, cannot be addressed specifically or com-pletely within an educational curriculum. The student, first and foremost, must acquire the ability to think clearly and logically, and judge, select, and predict the outcomes of problems as they arise. Most importantly, they have to be able to make decisions and to transform them into successful solutions. These skills are all part of any problem-solving strategy. Voss and Means (1989) suggest that instruction in the social sciences provides opportu-nities for students to develop creative thinking habits. They offer four suggestions regarding this challenge:

1.   Students need to acquire knowledge of basic facts, con-cepts, principles, and theory in the field, and more impor-tantly, such learning must concentrate on explanation and rationale.

2.   As the acquisition of knowledge takes place, students need to solve problems. This process would help make knowledge accessible, as well as provide experience in the use of research methods.

3.   Students need to develop skills in evaluating arguments, both with respect to their own arguments, and those of others.

4.   Controversial issues need to be discussed and the various positions evaluated.

New and creative ideas will be necessary to solve the issues facing us in the 1990s. If leisure service professionals do not begin to work at systematically addressing the problems confronting the field, when we review our progress in the year 2000, we may still face many of the same problems.

Issues Confronting the Field

The future is not some unknown quantity over which we have little control, but a prospect we can do much to create, envision, or attempt to accomplish, as individuals or as part of a group. Even though the world may seem out of control, increasingly chaotic, and more complex, and the future appears likely to intensify these tendencies, we should not forget that each of us helps to create the future through either our passivity or activity, awareness or ignorance, defiance or apathy. Furthermore, we affect it through futuristic daydreaming, and working to realize these aspirations. In order to positively influence recreation and leisure education in the next century, we must plan now. By focusing on challenges that are already obvious and on those likely to occur, we can look at some situations to which our profession might respond.

One issue that will continue to confront the leisure service profession is very limited financial resources. Public and private enterprises will continue to emphasize containing the costs of goods and labor. We are not going through some aberrant financial phase that will pass, leaving matters as they were before. Instead, we are seeing the end of unquestioned public monetary support for our activities and services. It has been a major challenge for some time now, that we become more entrepreneurial in our approach to funding, rather than continuing to rely on an ever-decreasing public fund.

Many in our profession resist this trend toward entrepreneurship, not wanting to be even remotely associated with sales and marketing. Frankly, we have little choice about selling our services if we want to do more than survive. If you believe in what you are doing and genuinely feel leisure services are an active component of the best of communal and intellectual life, then you need to defend and sell that belief.

It will be our responsibility to earn money for the services we offer through fee enhancement. Leisure service enterprises such as the National Park Service are attempting to meet more of their direct expenses in this manner, and are becoming more oriented toward profits and costs. We will receive less support from public monies and will be forced to be more autonomous, or at least semi-public in our orientation. The demand for the services we provide is burgeoning, and the private sector is quickly meeting it with a much higher price tag. The private sector is infiltrating the leisure service profession because of our disinclination to be competitive, to change and forge our own future direction.

As resources shrink, it is imperative that our imaginations expand. While we bemoan the diminishing traditional sources of funds, it is amazing how much money is spent on leisure services. We only need to look at the large expenditures made in the private sector. Many of these services are provided by those who were formerly in the public sector, but who have moved to where the action is.

The need and demand for child care will continue to grow. This is another service taken on by private investors, or employers seeking to attract and retain workers. With a loss of public funds, and an unmet critical need at hand, what better juncture of need and skill than to enter the field of comprehensive day care services for children and the elderly? Of course, these services are already provided by us, partly through traditional programs from childhood into older age. But we do not have to confine ourselves to caretaking. More and more, services that were once public remain unfilled, making the opportunities for expansion enormous. We must resist becoming a backwater profession, unable to keep pace with the changing times.

We are all beneficiaries of a revolution in personal nutrition and health that began during the past thirty years. Health, wellness, and sport are becoming big business enterprises, and all have implications for the leisure service profession. Not only are our clients living longer, more active lives; they are healthier, have more leisure time after retirement, and seek outlets for this leisure for which they are willing to pay. As leisure time experts, we can help others use their time effectively, be they employed or retired, young or old. Health clubs and spas, health foods and dietary supplements, participatory sports and other cultural events are billion-dollar industries emerging without our involvement.

The population of the United States is aging. During this next decade, there will be 6,000,000 fewer teenagers in the nation. All of our intense concentration on youth programs will quickly need to shift to other age groups. The largest segments of our population will be post-youth, involving citizens who will physically age more slowly and continue to seek a wide variety of nontraditional leisure and recreational outlets. What will be our role in eldercare?

Our profession will have to enter an arena we have long avoided—politics. Since politics is primarily the formation of public policy and the dispersal of public funds, as both taxpayers and professionals, it behooves us to be more substantively involved. We are already active in public issues—land use, environment, the advent of national and state urban parks, cultural and natural resource management, housing and special communities, energy sources and uses, aging, and health policies. Many decisions that affect our profession are reached without our direct participation. We cannot use town halls and Congress merely for field trips; they should be field offices, where we are more than tourists or academic observers. Representatives of our professional interests should be involved in forming laws and legislation.

Generally, we need to work more with national and international organizations whose aims interact or overlap with ours: environmental groups, defenders of wildlife and animal welfare groups, ecological and land-use organizations, as well as senior citizen, ethnic and other community organizations. What should our relationship be with these groups in the future in order to advance our concerns?

More people now have leisure time than at any other period in history. No longer is leisure exclusive to the realm of the wealthy and privileged, or the sole domain of a particular race or class. The "wise" use of leisure time requires education (Brightbill and Mobley, 1977). The course of history prepared few of us for constructive use of leisure time. In fact, in the past, those who had an abundance of leisure were often bored and restless. In today's society, watching television, playing video games, and abusing mind and mood altering substances threaten both our relationships and our physical health. We have obviously not utilized our leisure time for the pursuit of health-enhancing activity. Through leisure education, we are interested in educating all ages, not only for a career of specific achievement, but for a fuller, more authentic existence.

Within the educational curricula there arises a perceived distinction between recreation and leisure. Teaching those who will in turn teach or guide others in refreshing and nonexploitive uses of leisure time is at the frontier of change. Some leisure service providers balk at the mandate to educate their constituents about utilizing leisure time and opportunities in ways that are rewarding and beneficial to personal growth and development, as well as immediately satisfying. The leisure service professionals of the future will have to determine not only their levels of responsibility, but how they will carry out the tasks that will meet their commitments to those levels.

Analysts predict the future better than fortune-tellers because they have a vested interest in the outcome, and thus strive to shape the future. Such a vested interest in the future of leisure and recreation education lies with those most likely to enjoy it—our students, and their children or students. We must continue to stretch and expand beyond the traditionally myopic view of parks and recreation, into areas that examine the impact of society on our profession, and our profession on society.

We have to be specific as well: do our programs and courses make a difference in enriching or enhancing people's lives? Do these programs and courses achieve what we believe they should? These have always been ambiguous issues in our profession, more often burdened with assumptions than evidence. These assumptions of worth, value, and impact need to be continually assessed. Specifically, we must concentrate on the research and study of human behavior in leisure settings, how people use their nonobligated time, changes in availability of free time, and so forth. This fascinating subtopic of leisure could offer invaluable insights into the ongoing study of human behavior. In fact, other disciplines such as economics, marketing, advertising, business administration, psychology, sociology, and library science research leisure issues far more broadly than our own profession. We need to continue to develop and maintain strong research programs in order to address the issues confronting leisure service professionals.

Our generation, and certainly those that follow, will have to come to terms with the consequences and actions of previous generations. At times, these consequences seem likely to overwhelm us. We must recognize the wide variety of options we actually have, and take advantage of them. It is, of course, difficult to maintain two visions simultaneously: we do indeed face many crises and opportunities and varied responses abound. There is a great deal of tension in thinking in this double-edged manner, yet our times require it if we are to reach our potential and ultimately flourish.

A Look Toward Problem Solving

As the exterior world becomes more complex, and at times bewildering, it is crucial that our imagination becomes richer, more flexible, and courageous. Remember, the future is not a fearsome unknown toward which we are hopelessly heading. It will be a composite of much that we decide to do now. We are not pawns of time, and we can actively engage in the decisions and changes that will make our profession a central part of that future.

Some argue that soon problem solving and decision making will simply be a matter of using a mathematical model with computers producing effective solutions. However, the leisure service administrator who must answer the question, "Is now the time to submit a bond issue referendum to the voters?" can do so only after he or she knows whether (1) people understand the need for the program; (2) how much the voters are willing to pay; and (3) whether enough community support can be raised to pass the bond. Mathematical models alone do not provide enough information or perspective to answer such a question. Some problems are so complex, and the amount of information about the problem may be so limited, that it is often impossible to use mathematical formulas. Such problems depend more on the administrator's judgment. Only through personal insight can an effective decision be made.

We do not minimize the importance of mathematical problem solving, but the individual problem solver will always be the most important part of the process. The solution to problems of the leisure service profession must be found within the profession. There can be no substitute for effective leadership. The responsibility is ours—shall we accept it or let it drop by default?

Past attempts at solving problems have not been successful. Just by reading newspapers, one can see that many of the problems of the leisure service profession existed ten to twenty years ago. Professionals must be able to solve problems and must be creative thinkers. College and university administrators and faculty must take a look at their curricula. Are they more concerned with information than with practical outcome? When hiring leisure service personnel, preference may well be given to those who consider creativity an important aspect of their work.

Many people can think more creatively if shown how to draw more effectively on their imaginations, and trust their abilities to do so. Most people were naturally quite imaginative as children, but because of various cultural pressures, including compulsory and formal education, they are too often taught to distrust the products of their own minds. Einstein once said, "Imagination is more important than knowledge, for knowledge is limited, whereas imagination embraces the entire world—stimulating progress, giving birth to evolution" (Holton 1971;p.103). Einstein is reported to have been unable or unwilling to speak until he was three. Einstein's comment on this was, "The words of the language, as they are written or spoken, do not seem to play any role in my mechanism of thought" (Holton 1971;

p.103). Thus, as an infant, Einstein had already learned to trust his "inner voice" more than authority and convention.

There is much teachers can do, particularly on the college level where education can be far more relaxed, to wean students from the habit of thinking as others do, to encourage their creativity, and to support the outcome of such efforts. It is through departure from more traditional methods of teaching and learning that people's imaginations can be freed. Only when students truly feel that their ideas will be valued, will they become more creative thinkers. New ideas are limited only by boundaries of individual skill, imagination, and the ability to grasp the complexity of information.

Conclusion

As this chapter has suggested, there is a real need for problem solving to address the issues confronting the profession as well as the concerns facing the practicing manager. Kotter (1982), in an examination of managers in a variety of organizations, found that the ability to solve problems was a key challenge associated with their responsibilities. At issue was not only the ability to identify problems, but the ability to deal with complex organizational and managerial problems. The dilemma for practicing managers is to analyze and resolve problem situations. The concepts and ideas in this text are designed:

1. to increase problem-solving ability;
2. to offer a systematic, multi-idea approach to problem solving; and
3. to improve individual, group, and organizational performance through more effective problem-solving and decision-making skills.

Bibliography

Bannon, J. J. (1990). Recreation in the future tense. *Parks & Recreation*, 25(1), 59-63, 69.

Brightbill, C.K. & Mobley, T.A. (1977). Educating for leisure - centered living, 2nd ed. New York: Wiley.

Fisher, C. & Grant, G. (1983). Intellectual levels in college classrooms. In C. L. Ellner and C. P. Barnes (eds.), *Studies of college teaching*. Lexington, MA: D. C. Heath.

Holton, G. (1971). On trying to understand scientific genius. *The American Scholar*, 102-104.

Kotter, J. P. (1982). *The general managers*. New York: The Free Press.

Voss, J. F. & Means, M. L. (1989). Toward a model of creativity based upon problem solving in the social sciences. In J. A. Glover, R. R. Ronning, & C. R. Reynolds, *Handbook of creativity*. New York: Plenum Press, 399-410.

Chapter Two

USE OF THE CASE STUDY METHOD IN PROBLEM SOLVING

The Case Study

The case study as an aid for management training was first developed in the 1920s at Harvard University's School of Business Administration. Based on the long-time practice of using actual court cases in legal training, the case study approach was one of the first teaching methods in the social sciences to depart from more traditional lectures, in which information was transmitted to, rather than elicited from students. Lovelock (1986) contrasts the case study and lecture styles:

> "Classes taught by the case method emphasize inductive learning, with conceptual frameworks and strategic guidelines being developed from the analysis of one or more real-world situations. This approach contrasts sharply with the deductive approach to learning used in lectures, where concepts and theories are taught directly.
> Although the lecture method is more efficient in terms of the instructor's ability to transfer a lot of knowledge in a relatively short period of time, the students' involvement in the learning process tends to be passive. Case teaching, in contrast, involves active participation by students as they seek to acquire the facility of learning how to act in the presence of new experience" (p. 25).

Although it is difficult to categorize many management problems, case studies are generally divided into one of the following three types, or into a combination of the three:

The individual problem - involves a specific person in an organization, and a difficulty that may be affecting his or her job, as well as the organization.

The isolated incident - involves something outside of usual occurrences in an organization, not covered by regulations and procedures, but disruptive to the organization.

The organizational problem - may be a labor relations conflict, or a sales or recruiting difficulty affecting the entire organization (Willings, 1968).

One limitation of using case studies is that too much is expected from it. As an aid to teaching, it is not meant to replace other methods of learning and obtaining information. However, case studies can successfully complement other teaching methods when used appropriately.

Case studies cannot be equated with actually working in an organization. Too many managers, after years of experience, are still mystified by problems and the best approaches to take, and often seek the help of consultants or take courses in management training. One purpose of the case study approach is to teach students indirectly how to solve problems and how to make specific decisions. Although a case study is intended to be realistic, it cannot include the wide variety of variables and contributing factors existing in most organizations. The case study should not be used, therefore, in more sophisticated management training programs in which qualified, successful managers are seeking more erudite techniques.

An instructor uses different case studies for different audiences. Undergraduates, new to the use of case studies, new even to the practice of problem solving, require simpler cases than do graduate students. If case studies are used with experienced managers, they must be given even more complex cases. Regardless of the audience, case studies should not be merely "filler" in a course of instruction, or as a form of entertainment. Such abuses only negate the material's possible advantages. Time is wasted; and everyone will feel cheated. There must be a reason for using case studies, and it should not be a trivial one. Key questions to be considered are:

- What do I want to achieve in this session?
- Which case, if any, will best aid me in this session?
- How can I best present the case?

If a particular case study is not appropriate to a topic of discussion or would not facilitate learning, it should not be used. There must be a good reason for its inclusion. The criticisms of case studies in teaching often stem from their inappropriate use, from a lack of seriousness in the instructor's manner of presentation, or lack of attention to their importance by the students.

Case studies are generally valuable in four types of management training:

Awareness training: Defining precisely those pressures and environments managers are likely to encounter and making students more aware of them.

Attitude training: Specifying various attitudes that enhance or detract from effective management in organizations, and expanding students' comprehension of them.

Technique training: Teaching specific skills, such as interviewing or being interviewed, and giving students practical experience in them.

Illustration of a specific point: Isolating a particular solution, such as reorganization, and revealing the pros, cons, and implications to the students (Willings, 1968).

Perhaps the greatest advantage of the case study is that it forces a student to think— first alone, and then with a group— because case studies presuppose a group environment. They also require concentration and introspection. To participate in generating solutions themselves, especially if a case is handled seriously, can be a far more successful experience for students than hours of note taking. For many students, especially if the instructor is well prepared with in-depth case studies, experiences in solving these cases can be a highlight of their education. Educational objectives of the case study have been identified by Matejka and Cossé (1981) and include:

- To provide an exciting educational experience
- To think like a manager
- To apply knowledge
- To give practice in making decisions

- To develop the skills required in order to use others as resources
- To learn to think analytically and objectively
- To develop initiative
- To gain skill in projecting outcome

Case Studies and Instruction

Both students and instructors must be prepared to use case studies in the classroom, because doing so changes the relationship among students, instructors, and the material to be learned. Although the instructor is no longer lecturing to a passive audience, he or she must still be in control:

"To the experienced instructor, the case method is not adequately described as a completely nondirective approach to teaching. Rather it involves direction in the most exquisitely subtle sense of the word. He must listen carefully to what students say — not only to words, but to meanings as expressed in feelings and attitudes" (Calhoon, Noland, & Whitchill, 1958 p.15).

In addition, the instructor should exercise thoughtful discussion involvement, encouraging reticent students to participate while curbing over-zealous individuals who monopolize the interaction (Charan, 1976).

This indirect mode of teaching requires that the instructor exercise some restraint and not force a solution, or pressure students who may be baffled by the obvious. Clues to a suitable solution may be given by the instructor, but the purpose of a case study is to encourage insight and self-direction. The atmosphere of the classroom should not resemble that of a quiz show, however. Case studies are noncompetitive and should not degenerate into contests or entertainment. If there are teams, there should be no form of cheerleading. Control over the atmosphere is entirely the instructor's responsibility. If unable to handle the students properly, the instructor should lecture instead. Table 2-1 suggests some limitations of the case method and inadvertent consequences that may be the result of an overly controlling instructor.

Table 2-1

Faculty Actions and Their Consequences

Faculty Behavioral Strategies	*Possible Consequences*
1. Get the topics introduced that the instructor feels are important *select responses *reinterpret student responses	Issues important to students may be ignored
2. Establish controversy *direct people with different opinions to resolve differences *misinterpret student positions to polarize *take votes	Leads students to select/distort information to be consistent with their position Maximize students' efforts to unilaterally control and/or produce solutions
3. Reveal principles at end of sessions *lecture at end *make sure principles do not get produced during session	Increases dependence on faculty member during the class session
4. Maintain control of interactions and topics discussed *cut off some lines of discussion *select whom to call on *inject comments to focus discussion	Little discussion of topics of interest to students but not to faculty
5. Induce students to generate incorrect solutions if someone gets the "best solution" early *ask for alternatives *bring up topics for discussion	Discouragement of good work Confusion among students Decreased probability that students will work for solutions

From Chris Agryis, "Some Limitations of the Case Method: Experiences in a Management Development Program," *Academy of Management Review*, 5(2), 1980, p.293. Reprinted by permission.

For the case method to be effective, the instructor must know his or her students fairly well, be a skilled and enthusiastic discussion leader (not just a lecturer!), and be well versed in the subjects of the case studies. The instructor must be able to anticipate the responses of students, ask the proper questions at strategic times, and maintain a relaxed atmosphere during discussions. Obviously, these qualities are not acquired quickly. An instructor who uses this teaching aid must be prepared for a great deal of study and practice; above all, he or she must have patience. Teaching with case studies is difficult, but it can be extremely rewarding for both students and instructors.

It is important for the instructor to carefully select the students who will participate in the problem-solving sessions. It would not be advisable, for example, to include students who have much experience in recreation and parks with those who have relatively little practical experience. This is not to say that inexperienced students should never be mixed in with experienced students; it is only to alert the instructor to potential difficulties in unintentionally mixing groups.

Students are important to the success or failure of using case studies. Those who come to the session unprepared, not having done their background homework, will not be good presenters or receivers of ideas. Students also must be prepared to discuss the case intelligently. For example, if a case deals with the development of a therapeutic recreation program, students must at least be aware of the planning principles, budgetary requirements, and administrative practices of operating such programs.

With case studies, students must develop their own rationale for decisions, accept responsibility for these decisions, and be prepared to defend them. This will make them more rigorous in problem analysis. Realizing that they may be judged by classmates, they will be more thoughtful of their final decisions.

Case studies not only encourage students to think independently, but also to work cooperatively in teams. Many decisions are the result of group discussions. For example, it is essential that a recreation and park board cooperate in formulating sound policies. A sound policy can be reached only by independent thinkers who recognize the importance of listening to other viewpoints. A recreation professional must work closely with boards, commissions, executive committees, advisory groups, and other community organizations. The recreation worker's success depends on the ability to think rationally, first as an individual, and then within a group.

Listed below are seven procedures to assist instructors and students in making case studies a productive teaching aid:

1. In presenting a case, it is recommended that the instructor ask students if there is anything about a particular case that is not clear. In each case certain assumptions are made; it is important that every discussant's analysis of a case be based on similar assumptions. For example, for a case on planning a comprehensive community recreation program, the problem solver makes certain assumptions about the amount of funds available for the program. If one discussant approaches the problem with the perspective that limited funds are available, and another that funds are no problem, the group discussion will be confusing, if not a waste of time.

2. The instructor must create an informal atmosphere for discussions; all ideas should be heard. No student should worry about the group's reactions to "inappropriate" ideas.

3. The instructor should not monopolize the discussion; otherwise, the students will quickly lose interest. The instructor's main responsibility is to help students build problem-solving abilities and effective thought processes, not to demonstrate that he or she has all the answers.

4. The instructor should keep the discussion focused on case details, their relationships, and implications.

5. The instructor should not anticipate the direction of the discussion or lead participants along predetermined lines of thought. To violate this rule denies students the responsibility they will need to gain if they are to become independent problem solvers.

6. The instructor should be alert to students who alter case facts. If overlooked, the discussion will drift from the principal aspects of a problem.

7.   If the instructor knows the outcome of a case study, he or she should not reveal it until students have had an opportunity to explore the case thoroughly. To do so would bias the discussion.

Conclusion

Case studies require that students become problem solvers. When students use a case study, they are required to (1) determine what the problem is, (2) analyze the problem in relation to all presented facts, (3) produce ideas for possible solutions, (4) select alternatives, (5) make decisions, and (6) develop actions for implementation. Obviously, this is demanding. Students are required to think, not as their instructor might wish, but as the employees confronted with an actual problem would. Creating such independence in students is one of the most constructive outcomes of case studies. It brings reality into the classroom by insisting that the students reach a decision and be responsible for its consequences. It also requires that they become deeply involved in problem solving, and therefore more successful decision makers.

Bibliography

Agryis, C. (1980). Some limitations of the case method: Experiences in a management development program. *Academy of Management Review, 5*(2), 291-298.

Calhoon, R. P., Noland, W. E. & Whitchill, A. M. (1958). *Cases on human relations in management*. New York: McGraw-Hill.

Charan, R. (1976). Classroom techniques in teaching by the case method. *Academy of Management Review*, 116-123.

Lovelock, C. H. (1986). Teaching with cases. In L. H. Lewis, (ed.), *Experiential and simulation techniques for teaching adults*. New Directions for Continuing Education, no. 30. San Francisco: Josey-Bass.

Matejka, J. K. & Cossé, T. J. (1981). *The business case method: An introduction*. Reston, VA: Reston.

Willings, D. R. (1968). *How to use the case study in training for decision making*. London: Business Publications Limited.

Chapter Three

ROLE PLAYING
AS AN AID
IN PROBLEM SOLVING

The Role-Playing Technique

Role playing involves acting out the problems presented in case studies, thus increasing the "real-world" quality of the various exercises. The techniques of role playing are widespread in management education because they enable the instructor to focus on the human side of the organization. Managerial problems in the leisure service organization often arise in the areas of:

- power and authority
- morale and cohesion
- norms and standards
- goals and objectives
- change and development
- interpersonal skills
- group development
- decision making

Using leisure service organization case studies that contain management problems provides students with the opportunity to practice interacting with others in certain roles (Van Ments, 1983). Role playing generally pertains to two areas of problems: those of individuals and those of groups. The value of role playing for education in these two areas includes the following:

- It requires students to act out a thought or decision, integrating the distinction between thinking and doing.
- It allows students to practice various actions, so that they realize that good human relations require as much skill as any other acquired talent does.
- It enhances attitude training by placing students in the positions (roles) of others, teaching them that attitudes are not merely the result of personality but also of situation.
- It helps students to become more aware of and sensitive to others, especially when relating to subordinates and groups.
- It can reveal students to themselves, notably behavior faults or emotions and feelings that disrupt decision making (Maier, Solem & Maier, 1975).

Two kinds of role playing are generally used:

1.   multiple-group
2.   single-group role playing

With multiple-group role playing, the entire audience participates in the role plays, and is involved in as many separate groups as necessary. In single-group role playing, one group acts while the remainder of the audience observes, much like in the theater, except that these observers then participate in discussions.

When the instructor wishes everyone to act in a case study, and when the objective of the case study does not focus on developing sensitivity to others, multiple-group role playing is a better choice. With the multiple-group method, the audience forms role-playing groups that role play the same case study simultaneously.

It is desirable to keep the groups sufficiently separated so that they do not disturb each others' discussion, but close enough so that the atmosphere stimulates the participants. There is no need to put groups in separate rooms; in fact, such separation might be detrimental. Finally, it is helpful to have written instructions, so that each group assumes consistent roles.

When using the multiple-group method, the participants are given a specific organizational situation and then are asked to react to a change in the situation. Details of a case are presented so that an emotional response can be elicited from the group. As the role playing progresses, additional information and actions are introduced into the case. This may cause a re-evaluation or a change of behavior by participants. This method of role playing is most effectively used for changing attitudes, but requires a skilled leader.

The more widely-used method is single-group. It is the preferred method when the purpose of a case study is to develop students' sensitivity to the feelings of others. The role play should be spontaneous and continue uninterrupted. However, the role-playing instructor can interpret the dialogue whenever there is a need for explanation or interpretation for the observers. An example is students who act out a recreation and park board meeting while other students observe the action and the individual roles.

The advantages of the multiple-group method are that everyone can role play and the groups can compare their results. For single-group performances, the advantage is that the actors are observed by interested outsiders. In later discussions these observers and actors can share their viewpoints, thus enlarging the experience for all students. Both participants and observers become more sensitive to the feelings and conflicts of the players, much as in a theatrical production. It is not necessary for someone to be an actor to role play effectively. If a student is excessively shy or reluctant, he or she should not be coerced. The required experience is for the students to act as the persons they are playing would behave, not as they themselves might behave. If a student is to play the part of a busy, preoccupied supervisor, he or she should not transform this role into an ideal supervisor and defeat the purpose of the case study.

Role playing requires students to be familiar with their assigned managerial roles. This approach is likely to bring out the interpersonal aspects of the situation more effectively than other methods (Charan, 1976). Role-playing situations are usually unrehearsed; therefore, the actors may not anticipate the spontaneous dialogue that occurs. This gives the case study a more realistic atmosphere. For both actors and observers, seeing a lifelike drama can be more effective than simply reading a case. The inclusion of role playing makes discussions livelier and more productive. Some of the cases presented in this book do not lend themselves to role playing, nor was it intended that they should. Many, however, represent a framework for excellent role playing. Therefore, it is suggested that students and instructors study them carefully and together select those that seem most appropriate.

The following advantages and disadvantages to role-playing are provided to better acquaint students and instructors with the benefits and hazards.

Disadvantages of Role Playing

- It is not an easy method to use, and it requires practice and the full cooperation of instructor and students.
- Students often place too much emphasis on their acting rather than on the problem.
- Unless the role players have been properly trained and coached, the results may be useless.
- It requires outgoing personalities. Persons who are shy, introverted, or overly sensitive may not be successful at role playing.
- Unless well planned, role playing allows little time for discussion. It is not advisable to use role playing unless ample time is scheduled for discussion.
- One person often may dominate the role-play exercise. As a result, only his or her viewpoint is presented. This can be corrected by preparation before presentation.
- If a person gets too deeply involved in a role, it may be difficult for him or her to drop it.
- If role playing is not introduced properly, it might be treated by students as a "child's way of handling problems."
- The method is often used by those with little study or training in its use.
- The instructor must guard against role playing becoming merely entertainment for the students.

Advantages of Role Playing

- It is a spontaneous method for putting an idea or discussion into action.
- It reveals feelings and attitudes toward organizational problems that might not otherwise surface in class discussions.
- It dramatizes the situation being discussed.
- It brings "real world" situations and behavior into the classroom.
- It is an effective method of achieving participation by all students.
- It aids in developing personal characteristics, such as poise, self-assurance, speaking ability, argumentative logic, and self-control.
- It puts the actor in another person's place, thus giving a better understanding of others' behaviors.
- It gives participants an opportunity to demonstrate how they would handle problems encountered on a job.

Conclusion

Because role playing is only an aid to teaching problem-solving skills, it should supplement other forms of training and educational experiences. As in using case studies alone, these aids are not intended to include the kinds of information needed by a student to recognize the demands of managerial problem solving. If used properly for achieving specific goals, for example, attitude or awareness training or increasing one's sensitivity to others, role playing of case studies will prove to be interesting, stimulating and effective. Often it will be the highlight of a student's education in leisure service management.

Bibliography

Charan, R. (1976). Classroom techniques in teaching by the case method. *Academy of Management Review*, 116-123.

Maier, N. R. F., Solem, A. R. & Maier, A. A. (1975). *The role-play technique: A handbook for management and leadership practice.* La Jolla, CA: University Associates.

Van Ments, M. (1983). *The effective use of role-play: A handbook for teachers and trainers.* London: Kogan Page.

Chapter Four

SETTING THE STAGE
FOR PROBLEM SOLVING

Introduction

There has been a great deal of interest in improving the creative contributions of employees, and this is certainly true in the leisure services field. As a result of this interest, researchers and trainers have advocated a variety of organizational training programs to accomplish this goal. "A nearly unanimous consensus is that such interventions should focus on reducing barriers to creativity, training in problem definition, problem solving, and improving communication skills and participative management styles" (Edwards & Sproull, 1985; p. 183). This chapter explores some of these interventions and their interrelatedness as a backdrop to engaging in problem solving.

Creativity and Problem Solving

Creativity and problem solving are inextricably linked. In fact, several researchers have viewed creativity as a component of problem solving. Newell, Shaw, and Simon (1962) wrote that creativity is "a special class of problem-solving activity characterized by novelty, unconventionality, persistence and difficulty in problem formulation" (p. 66). More recently, Hayes (1981) described creativity as "a special class of problem solving, that is the act of solving an ill-defined problem" (p. 199). Whether one accepts the above presumption that creativity is a special case of problem solving or creativity is a separate phenomenon, creativity is regarded as essential to effective problem solving.

There are a multitude of definitions of what constitutes creativity. Creativity has been described as the process of identifying a problem that was previously unrecognized and as a solution that is novel (Edwards & Sproull, 1985). It has also been viewed as the generation of ideas that result in the improvement of the efficiency and effectiveness of an organization (Matherly & Goldsmith, 1985). Amabile provides a general definition of creativity as the "production of novel and useful ideas by an individual or small group of individuals working together" (p. 126). Viewing creativity in this fashion enables us to incorporate creativity in the overall problem-solving model.

As the importance of creativity to organizations becomes more apparent, the question becomes "Can creativity be increased in this organization?" It should be noted that most creativity specialists today believe that creativity is not a special activity for which only some individuals have capabilities (Voss & Means, 1989). In fact, creativity is considered to be a common cognitive process that can be enhanced through training. A review of the research findings related to creativity training found that creative thinking is a skill that can be developed through a variety of teaching methodologies (Rose & Lin, 1985).

There are many research studies that have examined the personal attributes contributing to creativity in people, as well as the role of the environment in stimulating creativity. Amabile (1988) reports a study that she and a colleague carried out that is particularly relevant, because the subjects were employees and the environments were organizations. These researchers conducted interviews with three different groups:

1.   120 research and development scientists from over 20 corporations,
2.   16 marketing and development bank employees, and
3.   25 railroad marketing and sales employees.

Their findings provide insight into the qualities of environments and individuals that facilitate and constrain creativity.

Results of this interview study revealed nine qualities of the environment that served to promote or facilitate creativity:

1. *Freedom* - Autonomy in day-to-day work; freedom and control over task accomplishment and ideas;
2. *Good project management* - A management role model who is enthusiastic, communicates effectively, and provides clear direction without tight control;
3. *Sufficient resources* - Adequate resources in terms of facilities, equipment, information, funds, and people;
4. *Encouragement* - Ideas received with enthusiasm by management;
5. *Various organizational characteristics* - Organizational climate characterized by cooperation and collaboration;
6. *Recognition* - Creativity receives feedback, recognition and rewards;
7. *Sufficient time* - Openness to explore possibilities;
8. *Challenge* - Emanates from the type of problem, or its relevance to the organization;
9. *Pressure* - A sense of urgency stemming from a desire to accomplish something important.

The opposites of these environmental qualities existing in an organization were found to be constraints to creativity. For example, lack of freedom, resources, and recognition were found by interviewers to inhibit creativity. In general, these nine environmental qualities constitute important factors for managers to consider. In order to provide optimal conditions for creative employee effort, managers should consider eliminating any factors that would inhibit creativity while also enhancing those existing conditions that stimulate creativity.

The authors also reported several personal attributes common to good problem solvers that promote creativity. Three of these attributes are:

1. various individual personality traits such as persistence, curiosity, energy and honesty,
2. cognitive ability and expertise associated with their particular field, and
3. intrinsic motivation, being excited and engaged by the challenge of the problem and the work itself.

As a result of 12 years of study, Amabile has found that intrinsic motivation is central to creativity. She summarizes this work (1990):

"We find our results sufficiently compelling that we now refer to the intrinsic motivation principle of creativity: Intrinsic motivation is conducive to creativity, but extrinsic motivation is detrimental. In other words, people will be most creative when they feel motivated primarily by the interest, enjoyment, satisfaction, and challenge of the work itself - and not by external pressures" (p. 65).

Csikszentmihalyi (1985; 1988) supports this connection between creativity and intrinsic motivation. He suggests that individuals who enjoy engaging in problem solving for its own rewards will persevere and thus have a higher probability of developing creative solutions. For managers, the implications of these findings on the attributes of individuals that enhance creativity are related to the hiring of personnel, and the assignment of tasks to individuals. It is not only important to identify individuals who have knowledge, skills, and abilities in the field of leisure services, but also to consider their level of intrinsic motivation with regard to the problem-solving task at hand.

Although the position that extrinsic rewards are detrimental to intrinsic motivation is one supported by several individuals (e.g., Deci & Ryan, 1985), it is not without controversy as it applies to the work setting. There have been research results that have supported the perspective that extrinsic rewards have a negative effect on intrinsic motivation in the workplace (e.g., Jordan, 1986) and those that have refuted these findings (e.g., Staw, 1976). It has been suggested that intrinsic and extrinsic rewards interact in a complex fashion, that has yet to be fully explained (Szilagyi & Wallace, 1990). The distinction between intrinsic and extrinsic rewards, however, may be very important to creative problem solving.

Participative Management

There has been much discussion of the various styles of problem solving and decision making in organizations. These range from authoritarian to participative management and are illustrated as a continuum in Figure 4-1. This discussion will focus primarily on participative management as it would be the primary avenue for staff involvement in problem solving.

There has been a great deal of interest by organizational theorists regarding participativemanagement. This often philosophical orientation toward managing suggests that responsibility be shared by subordinates and managers. Because problem solving is a principal part of a manager's responsibilities, it follows that problem-solving tasks and responsibilities should also be shared.

Shaskin (1984) has defined participative management as a process in which employees are involved in:

- setting goals,
- making decisions,
- solving problems, and
- making changes in the organization.

Figure 4-1
Continuum of Leadership Behavior

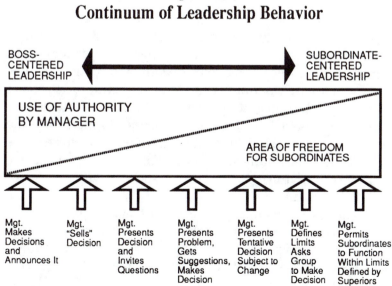

Source: Robert Tannebaum and Warren H. Schmidt, "How to Choose a Leadership Pattern," *Harvard Business Review*, March-April 1958, pp.95-101

He further suggests, as have many proponents of participative management, that as a result of this style occurring in an organization, employees will increase their level of commitment, satisfaction, performance, and innovation.

There have been several comprehensive reviews of the effects of participative management practices. Research results have consistently confirmed that participative management has a positive influence on employee satisfaction, but little or no effect on employee performance. In addition, participation in goal setting has not been found to enhance performance any more than goals assigned by managers. Participation may improve productivity; however, it does not necessarily have this effect and may be detrimental to performance (Locke & Schweiger, 1979; Yukl, 1981; Locke, Schweiger, & Latham, 1986).

Some employees may not react favorably to participative management practices. A group of 229 manager and subordinate pairs were surveyed to examine this issue. Findings indicated that subordinates with a great need for independence, those who were self-reliant or preferred to do tasks alone, performed better under participative management on tasks that were not repetitive. Subordinates with a low need for independence did not perform well under participative management (Abdel-Halim, 1983).

In addition to participative management contributing to satisfaction and performance under certain conditions, other positive effects have been reported. Jackson (1983) examined the effects of participation in decision making on occupational stress stemming from role conflict and role ambiguity. Role conflict exists when an individual is torn by conflicting performance demands. Role ambiguity is present when there is inadequate information about how the job is to be performed. In other words, there exists a lack of clarity regarding the performance of one's duties. The findings indicated that participative management was effective in reducing stress associated with role conflict and role ambiguity.

In a case study of the effects of participative management practices, several benefits were observed that accrued to employees and the organization. According to the authors (Margulies & Black, 1987), these benefits were attributable to the practice of participative management:

- "Cost savings due to members' analysis of problems and implementation of recommended solutions.
- Significantly improved attitudes, especially those concerning the level of trust in the organization, perceived quality of supervision, perceived human orientation of the organization, and the degree of involvement in decision making by employees.
- Increased abilities of employees and managers alike in work-related problem identification, analysis and resolution.
- Increased management awareness of the utility of participation in improving the communication channels between employees and supervisors.
- Increased abilities in conducting meetings, interpersonal processes, and the resolution of conflicts.
- Increased awareness throughout the organization of issues influencing the performance of the organization" (p. 406).

Many of these findings can be categorized as benefits or processes that contribute to creativity, problem solving, and decision making.

Plunkett (1990), in a related study, investigated the effects of increased participation in decision-making processes on creativity at work. The results indicated that individuals who experienced increased participation in the workplace also increased their creativity. This study suggests that when individuals have a choice with regard to task involvement, or are intrinsically motivated, increased creativity may result. In addition, the use of participative management practices to foster employee involvement in decision-making processes may be a positive method of increasing creativity.

Participative management cannot be used with every employee or in every situation. However, it may be particularly beneficial in regard to the problem-solving process. As stated by Locke, Schweiger, and Latham (1986),

"Good management is the result of intelligence, experience, and clear thinking and is facilitated by the results of relevant organizational research. With respect to participation, research results are clear. Sometimes participation is useful and sometimes it is not . . . Until we know more, executives must do what they have always done: Integrate what is known from research with their own good sense" (p. 79).

The following methods are suggested as guidelines for managers interested in facilitating participative management (Hamlin, 1986):

1.   Identify situations that provide appropriate opportunities for employee participation.
2.   Facilitate the participation of employees.
3.   Foster open communication.
4.   Openly share information with employees.
5.   Develop teamwork within the organization.
6.   Solicit different points of view.
7.   Acquire appropriate group resources to accomplish the task.
8.   Update employees regularly regarding plans.
9.   Provide employees with training in the problem-solving process.
10.   Reinforce employees for participating.
11.   Facilitate the process of getting group consensus.
12.   Actively listen to employees.
13.   Recognize the efforts of employees for participation and accomplishment.

Delegation of Authority

In studying successful organizations, Katz & Kahn (1978) found that effective leaders were more likely to delegate author- ity. Delegation of authority is a manager's assignment of a specific task or area of responsibility to an employee (Bannon, 1978). Delegation may be considered a form of job enrichment, as well as a method of developing subordinates. Increasing a subordinate's responsibility and authority is a means of making his or her job more interesting, challenging, and meaningful (Yukl, 1981). In addition, delegating may improve decision quality and acceptance by placing authority at the most appropriate level in the organization, i.e., where the decisions must be implemented.

Although many managers will admit to the value of and need for shared authority, few are able to delegate it. Delegation sounds simple, but managers that are used to running an organization often find it difficult to implement. They may believe they have delegated tasks and decision-making authority through organizational charts and detailed job descriptions, yet they still maintain restrictive control over the organization's daily activities. Even those managers who sincerely want to delegate a burdensome workload among competent and promising staff members, are easily confounded by what initially sounds so easy. Organizational theorists admit that few managers are able to put delegation of authority into practice.

The most common reasons why leisure service managers do not or cannot delegate the responsibility of problem solving are usually one or more of the following (Bannon, 1978):

- Lack of agreement among managers and workers on the specifics of delegation. Lack of standards and guidelines;
- Lack of training to accomplish delegated tasks;
- Lack of understanding of organizational objectives;
- Lack of confidence by managers in workers;
- Lack of confidence by managers in themselves. Unwillingness to take risks;
- Managers' fear that workers will outshine them;
- Fear of punitive action by managers;
- Failure at all levels to understand the advantages of successful delegation;
- Unwillingness of managers to delegate tasks they enjoy;
- A desire for nothing short of perfection; and
- A belief that things are going well enough as they are.

Although they should be concerned mainly with delegating responsibilities of problem solving, there are managers so bogged down in daily tasks and concerns that they never give much time or thought to problem solving in the first place! How can one delegate responsibility to another for a task that one does not have time for oneself, and all because one is too busy with minor details and deadlines?

Such a style of management becomes a relentless cycle of cease-less work with little or no time for reflection, and with no thought given to work delegation. Not only is problem solving neglected, such a manager gives little thought to long-range planning, coordination of work, or in-service training of employees, which can aid in effectively sharing work.

Overworked managers are not successful managers, al-though they may deceive themselves that ceaseless activity is constructive activity. Managers who cannot delegate effectively become more workers than managers. They work harder, yet produce less than those who delegate effectively. By limiting their effectiveness as managers, they limit their organization's success, though they are often too busy to see this.

The following guidelines will assist managers in establish-ing a climate favorable to delegation:

Set job standards that are fair and attainable. It is essential that managers and subordinates agree on standards for evaluat-ing performance. These standards should be understood before delegation of a task occurs.

Understand the concept of delegation. Delegation is not a technique for ridding oneself of responsibility, but for dividing it up. Successful delegation requires that both managers and subordinates know their duties. It is a continuing process in which managers participate as planners, coordinators, and allocators of responsibility. But managers must also accept that subordinates will do things in their own way.

Know subordinates' capabilities. Managers who know the characteristics and capacities of their staff, as well as the facilities and equipment they use, can delegate tasks more efficiently. Selecting the right person for a job is an important part of delegation. Delegating for the sake of delegating is always a mistake.

Develop goals and objectives. Subordinates must know not only *what* is to be done but also why, how well, when, with what resources, by whom, and according to what priority, for delegation to succeed.

Correct errors tactfully. Managers must use tact and discretion in correcting subordinates' errors. Organizations that have used shared goal setting have a distinct advantage over those that have not.

Reward subordinates for good work. The reward may be no more than an increase in the subordinates' self-esteem, but sometimes monetary rewards and promotions are more effective.

Be concerned. Show interest in what a subordinate does. This can be done in a variety of ways: personal interest in work problems, open discussion of problems, willingness to give support and guidance, and willingness to accept mistakes. Managers who snoop will be resented, but those who show a genuine interest in what is going on will be appreciated.

Evaluate performance. Subordinates expect evaluation of their work, even want it, but they have their own ideas of how the evaluation should be done, objecting to those that are pointless, unnecessary, or haphazard. There are many evaluation systems that require evaluation by both managers and employees.

Be aware of areas of "No Delegation." There are areas in which managers want things done precisely. They should make clear what these areas are and why such a position is taken.

Provide in-service training and development. Managers must provide appropriate training so that a subordinate has a reasonable chance of success. Training can be specific, particularly when special skills are required. Usually evaluation does not require formal training, but rather is a systematic attempt to see how well workers are doing. Managers can then plan an appropriate training program if needed.

Do not resume delegated authority. Making mistakes and finding and correcting them is a useful form of training. Good managers do not take away delegated authority because a subordinate makes a mistake.

Conclusion

Leisure service managers need to take an active role in facilitating the creativity of employees in their organization. In particular, barriers to creativity should be identified and eliminated. Further, individuals should be selected to work on creative activities in which they are intrinsically motivated. Participative management and the delegation of authority may well provide the opportunities for employees to engage in creative problem-solving endeavors.

Bibliography

Abdel-Halim, A. A. (1983). Effects of task and personality characteristics on subordinate response to participative decision making. *Academy of Management Journal*, September, 477-484.

Amabile, T. M. (1988). A model of creativity and innovation in organizations. In B. M. Staw and L. L. Cummings (Eds.) *Research in organizational behavior*, vol. 10, 123-167.

Amabile, T. M. (1990). Within you, without you: The social psychology of creativity and beyond. In M. Runco & R. Albert (eds.), *Theories of creativity*, pp. 61-91, Beverly Hills, CA: Sage.

Bannon, J. J. (1978). Delegation: A misunderstood management process. *Parks and Recreation*, March, 38-41.

Csikszentmihalyi, M. (1985). Emergent motivation and the evolution of the self. In D. Kleiber & M. H. Maehr (eds.), *Motivation in adulthood*. Greenwich, CT: JAI Press.

Csikszentmihalyi, M. (1988). Motivation and creativity: Toward a synthesis of structural and energistic approaches to cognition. *New Ideas in Psychology*, 6(2), 159-176.

Deci, E. L. & Ryan, R. M. (1985). *Intrinsic motivation and self-determination in human behavior*. New York: Plenum Press.

Edwards, M. A. & Sproull, J. R. (1985). Creativity: Productivity gold mine? *Journal of Creative Behavior*, 18(3), 175-184.

Hayes, J. R. (1981). *The complete problem solver*. Philadelphia, PA: The Franklin Institute Press.

Jackson, S. E. (1983). Participation in decision making as a strategy for reducing job-related strain. *Journal of Applied Psychology*, February, 3-19.

Jordan, P. C. (1986). Effects of an extrinsic reward on intrinsic motivation: A field experiment. *Academy of Management Journal*, 29(2), 405-412.

Katz, D. & Kahn, R. L. (1978). *The social psychology of organizations* (2nd edition). New York: Wiley.

Locke, E. A., Schweiger, D. M (1979). Participation in decision making: One more look. In B. M. Staw (ed.) *Research in organizational behavior*, vol. 1, 265-339.

Locke, E. A., Schweiger, D. M. & Latham, G. P. (1986). Participation in decision making: When should it be used? *Organizational Dynamics, 14*(3), 65-79.

Margulies, N. & Black, S. (1987). Perspectives on the implementation of participative approaches. *Human Resource Management, 26*(3), 385-412.

Matherly, T. A. & Goldsmith, R. E. (1985). The two faces of creativity. *Business Horizons, 28*(5), 8-11.

Newell, A., Shaw, J. C. & Simon, H. A. (1962). The processes of creative thinking. In H. E. Gruber, G. Terrell, & M. Wertheimer (eds.), *Contemporary approaches to creative thinking* (pp. 63-119). New York: Atherton Press.

Plunkett, D. (1990). The creative organization: An empirical investigation of the importance of participation in decision-making. *The Journal of Creative Behavior, 24*(2), 140-148.

Rose, L. H. & Lin, H. (1985). A meta-analysis of long-term creativity training programs. *Journal of Creative Behavior, 18*(1), 11-22.

Shaskin, M. (1984). Participative management is an ethical imperative. *Organizational Dynamics*, Spring, 5-22.

Staw, B. M. (1976). *Intrinsic and extrinsic motivation*. Morristown, NJ: General Learning Press.

Szilagyi, A.D., Jr., & Wallace, M.J., Jr. (1980). *Organizational behavior and performance*. Glenview, IL: Scott Foresman.

Voss, J. F. & Means, M. L. (1989). Toward a model of creativity based upon problem solving in the social sciences. In J. A. Glover, R. R. Ronning, & C. R. Reynolds, *Handbook of creativity*. New York: Plenum Press, 399-410.

Yukl, G. (1981). *Leadership in organizations*. Englewood Cliffs, NJ: Prentice-Hall.

INTRODUCTION TO PART II

Part II of this book provides an in-depth examination of each step of the problem-solving process. Chapter Five graphically introduces the problem-solving model and identifies each of the nine stages of the process. This brief overview provides the reader with a conceptual understanding of the problem-solving process, as well as placing each successive chapter in the context of its relevance to problem solving. Chapter Six is concerned with the identification of the real problem confronting the problem solvers. Often individuals do not address the problem, but only its symptoms. Obviously, of critical importance is the ability to correctly identify and articulate the problem. In addition, this chapter discusses a variety of methods that can be utilized to collect information related to the problem.

Once the problem has been clearly stated, short- and long-term objectives need to be established related to the solving of the problem. Chapter Seven presents a discussion of objective setting. Chapter Eight deals with blocks to problem solving that may occur, particularly from employees. An important aspect of this chapter is a discussion of dealing with resistance to change that may occur from the problem-solving process. Several methods for facilitating change in leisure service organizations are provided.

An important part of the problem-solving process is the application of creativity techniques, which are discussed in Chapter Nine. The use of creativity techniques encourages individuals to examine problems in unique ways and through this process to discover appropriate solutions. Chapter Ten presents a discussion of the process of selecting among the many alternatives that have been generated through creative thinking. Each alternative may have positive and negative consequences regarding its selection, and these must be considered and weighed.

Decision making is the ultimate responsibility of the problem solver, and Chapter Eleven examines some issues related to individual versus group decision making. There are some difficulties that may be encountered when using decision-making groups. Specifically, cohesive groups may develop groupthink, or riskier decisions may result. These group problems are discussed. In addition, some specific methods of facilitating group decisions are provided along with their advantages and disadvantages. Finally, Chapter Twelve addresses the strategies that may be used to get an idea accepted by those who make policy. The discussion centers around how individuals might react to new ideas and the presentation strategy to ultimately gain acceptance of the proposed plan.

Chapter Five

A STRUCTURED APPROACH TO PROBLEM SOLVING

Introduction

This chapter presents a simple problem-solving model that is appropriate for use in leisure services. This model can be implemented both systematically and creatively. Systematic thinking approaches a perceived problem through a linear step-by-step process, until some sort of solution is discovered. Creative problem solving, on the other hand, is more spontaneous, and is commonly called "a flash insight." Sometimes there is little difference between the two approaches to solving problems. That is, what appears to be a spontaneous solution to a problem may actually be the result of years of experience and knowledge systematically acquired by the problem solver.

Persons often compliment quick and perceptive problem solvers or those who respond creatively to problems, by telling them "it's easy for you." Such a compliment completely overlooks the variables that create the impression that it is easier for them to solve problems. Are they instinctive problem solvers, or do their experiences, patience, backgrounds, and personality traits affect their talent? What appears to be a flash insight is often revealed to be a very systematic approach to problems.

Although a line can be drawn between creative and systematic thinking, it should be a thin one. Chaos is not creativity, nor is plodding necessarily systematic. A problem solver, especially one encountering the types of problems facing the leisure service profession, may be simultaneously systematic and creative. It is inappropriate to classify persons as one type or the other, because most of us draw to the best of our abilities on a sort of systematic creativity.

The Problem-Solving Model

The model in this section includes a step-by-step approach to problem solving. As illustrated in Figure 5-1, there are nine steps to the problem-solving process:

1.   Defining the problem situation
2.   Defining objectives for a solution
3.   Identifying obstacles to a problem solution
4.   Observing change and conflict
5.   Identifying factors that influence change and conflict
6.   Facilitating creative solutions
7.   Selecting among alternatives
8.   Making the decision
9.   Generating strategies for implementing decisions

Although problem solving, as educator John Dewey (1910) first described it, is presented as a step-by-step process, one should not assume such a cookbook approach automatically leads to effective solutions. Although it is possible to analyze problem solving, to some extent it is complex and often uncertain. As the reader moves through each of the following chapters, it will become readily apparent why the problem-solving model depicted here actually requires much skill, insight and ingenuity to be successful.

Because there are many frustrating and unexpected obstacles in problem analysis, it is important that problem solvers, novice or experienced, understand that some problems have no acceptable solution. If there are any constraints on a problem solution over which they have no control, then the problem is either not solvable to their satisfaction, or they must compromise on a less than ideal solution. In fact, ideal solutions are seldom effective solutions.

Figure 5-1

Bannon's Problem-Solving Model

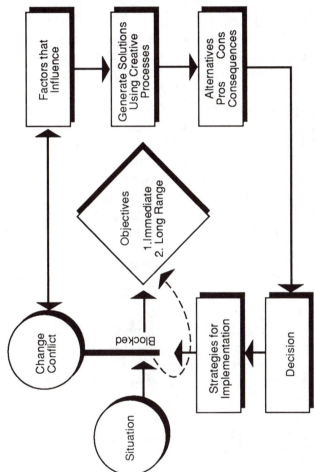

For example, leisure service specialists constantly face a common dilemma in land-use planning for recreation purposes. They wish to develop or maintain a natural, complex, semi-wilderness area for campers and other vacationers. But the more attractive the area the recreation specialists plan, the more campers it entices, leading eventually to the destruction of the very qualities for which the site was selected or designed. There is really no ideal solution to such a dilemma. Sometimes the problem is truly unsolvable and the area is entirely closed to campers in an attempt to forestall irreparable damage to the ecosystem caused by the destructive intrusion of nature lovers.

However, if students study and follow the problem-solving model presented here, they certainly will improve their mode of analyzing problems, their patterns of thinking about problems, and their personal and professional decision-making and problem-solving abilities. In simplest terms, a problem exists when a person encounters difficulties in obtaining a desired objective. According to Kepner and Tregoe (1976), a problem is an "unwanted effect—something to be corrected or removed. . . brought about by some specific event or a combination of events" (p. 17).

Conclusion

It should be kept in mind, however, as we follow the problem-solving model, that these steps need not be taken in a rigidly prescribed order, nor is one step necessarily separated from the others. They often can or should be simultaneous, though their order is based on what is used in most problem-solving approaches. These various steps are separated for discussion purposes here, but are usually part of an interrelated flow from start to finish.

Bibliography

Dewey, J. (1910). *How we think*. New York: D. C. Heath.
Kepner, C. A. & Tregoe, B. B. (1976). *The rational manager*. New York: McGraw-Hill.

Chapter Six

THE PROBLEM SITUATION

Problem Definition

The simplest definition of a problem is that something is wrong. A problem is a departure from some preferred or desired state that results in a need for change by an individual or group. If there is a deviation from some preferred state that is not of concern to anyone, then one can argue that a problem does not actually exist. A situation must be recognized and articulated as detrimental before it becomes a problem. As soon as someone notes the deviation, the problem definition can begin, no matter how intangible it might seem at first.

What seems an obvious deviation to us may not be the central problem at all, but symptomatic of a more critical problem. For example, we may consider the problem to be a poorly constructed dam, which leads to periodic flooding, when actually the artificial seeding of clouds to induce rain may be the real problem, or environmental abuses that initially produced excess runoff. Concentrating on dam repair (which is needed), to the exclusion of the larger variables that have brought this difficulty about leads to the eradication of the symptoms without solving the problem itself. The separation of the symptoms of a problem from the problem itself is an important skill of a talented problem solver, as is the determination of the level at which to concentrate efforts.

A problem solver must use self-restraint, for eventually all problems are related to larger issues. Problem solvers must be able to determine the level at which to concentrate efforts or they will be exhausted by the enormity of the situation, and will accomplish little. Thus, the administrator must establish which problems are more critical than others, and which can realistically be solved. Otherwise, an administrator is lost, gathering more and more facts, expanding his or her viewpoint to encompass larger and grander variables while the dike leaks. An administrator must decide at which level of awareness to begin defining and solving a problem, and at what point to cease defining solvable problems as symptoms.

Because analysis of the problem situation is the first step in the problem-solving process, it is also the most critical in determining how effectively a problem will be handled. Although individuals are usually impatient to get on with the problem-solving method once it has been determined that a problem does exist, sufficient time must be spent defining the problem situation. A rapid, generalized definition of a problem in the haste to find a solution should be avoided.

Problem Analysis

When considering problems, one must filter through the multitude of factors that influence situations to identify the key problem. The subsidiary problems are related to the key problem, or are symptoms that should diminish once the main problem is isolated and solved. Many individuals are tempted to solve simple problems or remove symptoms first, hoping that the larger issue will disappear in the interim. These interim solutions, except when done intentionally, are shortsighted and often confound the larger problem. A problem solver has to know how to isolate the root cause. Interim solutions, which are often incremental in nature, should be clearly identified as such and not treated as the problem solution.

Objectives

If the problem is defined as a deviation or departure from some preferred state, this departure is from an explicit or implicit standard. Most problems are deviations from a mixture of explicit, implicit, and normative standards. That is, standards are either clearly stated, understood but not stated, or they are what should be the desired state. The latter are normative standards or objectives.

If there is some measurable standard from which the leisure service agency has deviated and which causes a problem, then the objectives that the agency wishes to attain have to be stipulated during problem analysis. Objectives are closely related to problem analysis, for they are the measure against which alternative solutions will be gauged. Meeting objectives might not only entail correcting a deviation, it also often requires making the changes necessary to meet explicit standards in the future. Stating such objectives is not merely an attempt to catch up with the past, but is also necessary for forecasting and planning.

Viewpoint

The personal and professional viewpoints of those involved in problem solving or those likely to be affected by its outcome, must be anticipated and examined during the problem-analysis stage. The viewpoints of everyone involved or implicated must be considered when analyzing problems and solutions. Figure 6-1 illustrates this point.

Figure 6-1
Perspectives on Problem Solving

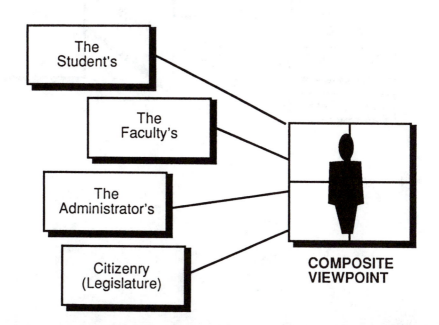

No one concerned about a problem, or likely to be affected by its solution should be excluded from problem analysis, no matter how encompassing our approach to problem solving appears. For example, as indicated in Figure 6-2, the perspectives on problem solving in an academic setting would include the viewpoints of students, faculty, administrators, and local and state officials. Any academic problem solving that does not reflect the viewpoints and involvement of these diverse groups in its problem analysis, and throughout the entire problem-solving process, is either dictatorial or doomed to fail in a democratic setting.

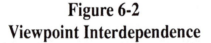

Figure 6-2
Viewpoint Interdependence

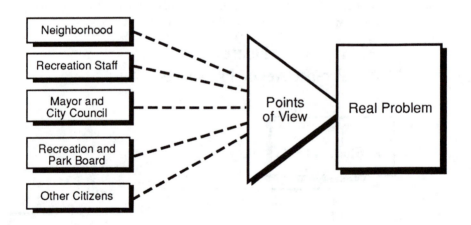

All viewpoints must be reflected and judiciously considered in analyzing a problem situation. If one seeks to solve a problem based exclusively on one viewpoint, without consideration given to all those involved, solutions will be ineffectual. For instance, when a leisure service agency board of directors attempts to provide a recreation program for young people, if the program is planned from the viewpoint of the board and agency staff alone, an ineffective program will most likely be the result. The program will be unsuccessful because those for whom it was "designed" had nothing to say about what went into its creation. No matter how well one believes they understand others; second hand points-of-view will not suffice.

Priorities

After listing the problem symptoms, they must be ranked. One will surface as more important than the others, though we do not know which one at this point. To help determine which is most important, three questions may be posed (Kepner & Tregoe, 1976):

- How urgent is the departure from the standard?
- How serious is it?
- What is the potential for improvement?

These questions adress which of these symptoms, if alleviated, would improve the situation, and which of these symptoms, if alleviated, would also have a positive effect on all the other symptoms.

Ideally, problem specification must be free of problem speculation, biases, and assumptions. We need to draw on as many relevant facts as we can. This is a somewhat systematic, mechanical action that requires discrimination as we decide what is to be taken into account and what is to be discarded. To do so, we must ask more specific questions (Kepner & Tregoe, 1976):

- What is the deviation?
- Where is it occurring?
- When does it appear?
- How large is the deviation?
- Whom does the deviation involve or affect?

The question *why?* is not asked at this stage, since we are not seeking the cause of a problem as much as its definition. *Why?* will be asked once we have isolated the problem and stated it clearly. To seek the cause of a problem before we have properly stated it is a dead end, no matter how good our hunches.

A legitimate problem statement is one that reflects the viewpoints of those who should be represented in any solutions considered. It is legitimate not only because it is equitable, but also because it is realistic, due to the input of all concerned. Furthermore, a problem statement is legitimate if it reduces biases or assumptions that result from one viewpoint dominating all others. A biased approach to problem definition limits the possibility of obtaining an accurate problem statement.

Once the problem solvers consider the various facets of problem definition — objectives, priorities, symptoms, and viewpoints — they are ready to make a tentative problem statement and begin gathering facts and information that appear relevant to that problem. The problem statement should be made in the most concise form possible. Because this statement will be conveyed to others, it is best to compose as precise a statement as possible before showing it to individuals who are external to the problem-solving process.

It is important to actually write down the problem statement. According to Hodnett (1955), "Unless you put a problem into words, you do not give it form. If it is formless, it does not exist in a manner that permits solution" (p. 19). Putting a problem statement into writing gives others a better opportunity to assist in finding a solution. It keeps the problem solvers focused on the actual problem and not on peripheral issues that continually arise.

Fact Finding

As the problem solvers continue to analyze the problem statement and situation, they immediately recognize that fact gathering is essential. Most problem-solving specialists agree, however, that gathering all the facts is almost impossible. The most difficult skill is to ensure that the facts gathered are relevant to the problem. The more relevant the facts one has, the better the chance one has to develop and write a logical problem statement. Problem solvers should be cautioned against simply looking for a quantity of facts, without regard to those that are most relevant. Relevance can be judged by four methods, which include:

1.   scientific investigation,
2.   opinions of experts,
3.   personal judgement, and
4.   demands of the problem analysis.

In addition, the facts considered should be measured and classified by three characteristics:

1.   the degree of confidence in the information accurately reflecting fact,
2.   the degree and effect of the fact on the situation, and
3.   the relevance of the fact to the problem situation (Schnelle, 1967).

Fact-Finding/Data Collection

There are many research methods available that can be utilized to collect data on problems. The use of research methods to support a problem analysis requires specific knowledge and skills in order to ensure that the data collected is valid and reliable. The validity of information refers to the degree to which the data collected accurately portrays the area of interest. For example, a leisure service manager may suspect that the agency's clientele are dissatisfied with the scope of programs and services. A questionnaire focusing only on satisfaction with special events is not a valid assessment of overall satisfaction with the agency's programs and services, and should not be used as such. A poorly conceptualized survey or data collection procedure may truly be measuring nothing well, and is therefore not valid.

Reliability relates to the consistency of the data. Consistency indicates that the information obtained through the assessment truly represents the individuals' perspectives and is not influenced by outside factors, which may vary. For example, a survey asking for overall program satisfaction may get different responses if conducted in the summer versus the winter, especially if the leisure service agency has a strong summer activities program and nothing in the winter. If what the manager wants to determine are comprehensive levels of satisfaction, the reliability of this assessment is doubtful as it produces inconsistent results.

While several methods of data collection are appropriate for gathering information about problems, this section will describe five that may be easily incorporated within the leisure service agency. Three of these methods, advisory boards, key informants, and focus groups are particularly useful in providing preliminary insights into issues, problems, and concerns of the leisure service agency. These insights may be investigated further through more in-depth types of data collection such as interviews and surveys.

Advisory Boards

An advisory board consists of approximately seven members who volunteer, are elected, or who are appointed to serve as representatives of the entire leisure service agency constituency. The functions of such an advisory board include:

- to provide an opportunity for constituents to participate in the decision-making process,
- assist in fund raising events,
- provide a source of volunteers, and
- assist the leisure service agency staff in aligning the programs and services provided with constituent needs (Kraus & Curtis, 1990).

For the purpose of problem solving and decision making, these individuals serve the function of providing input with regard to the problems and issues regarding service delivery. They can be utilized as a sounding board to discuss issues, bring suggestions from constituents, and assist in supporting the role of the leisure service agency. They also provide an additional vehicle to communicate with constituents.

Key Informants

Key informants are individuals who have the knowledge and ability to report on issues affecting the constituency. Key informants may be opinion leaders in the community who are aware of the problems and issues that are perceived as important by constituents (McKillip, 1987). Advisory boards may be utilized to identify ten to fifteen key informants who are able to express their perceptions of constituent issues (Gilmore, Campbell, & Becker, 1989).

Key informants are selected on the basis of:

- whether their views and actions influence others,
- their level of knowledge regarding the leisure service agency, and
- their level of knowledge about the community ("How to Use the Key Informant Survey Technique," 1985).

Information obtained from key informants may cover the broad range of general and specific issues. Information may be collected from key informants through an interview or survey. Key informants may be invaluable in providing information necessary for a thorough understanding of the problem.

Focus Groups

The use of focus groups is designed to provide general insights into the motives and behaviors of individuals through the use of unstructured interviews (Assael, 1984). The group consists of five to twelve individuals who have backgrounds or characteristics that are representative of the entire constituent base. A range of ages, males and females, and individuals with varying family configurations should be represented in the focus group, as they are represented in the community.

The focus group is directed by a leader who acts as a moderator to understand constituent issues or needs related to the provision of programs and services. The moderator directs the session by asking questions to solicit group reactions to issues of concern. Focus group sessions are approximately two hours in duration and may be taped for later analysis of the discussion.

The intent of the focus group is to generalize concerns and issues from the group to the larger constituent base (Dignan & Carr, 1987). The depth of knowledge, as well as the representativeness of information related to problem areas can be greatly enhanced through the use of focus groups.

Interviews

The personal interview is a face-to-face interpersonal situation in which an interviewer asks constituents questions designed to obtain answers relevant to the issue or problem (Nachmias & Nachmias, 1987). A scheduled interview with structured questions has the most advantages for gaining useable information. Structured refers to questions that are the same in wording and sequence for each interviewee. Questions are written prior to the interviews and remain identical for every individual.

The structured interview has several advantages over other methods of collecting data. Great flexibility can be used in the questioning process to probe areas of concern to the leisure service agency or constituents. In addition, the response rate is generally high with this method, as opposed to the mail or telephone survey. The disadvantage of an interview is the higher cost and time involved in collecting the information. Interviewers also have to be trained in the techniques of effective interviewing. One final obstacle to this method is its lack of anonymity for the respondents. That is, individuals who participate in the interview recognize that their identities are known by the interviewer. This may prevent the use of interviews if the information to be collected is sensitive in nature.

Surveys

Surveys provide the greatest opportunity to solicit constituent input and to generalize the findings from a smaller group of individuals to the entire clientele. Surveys require expertise from knowledgeable individuals in order to implement them successfully. The use of marketing departments could be extremely beneficial to most leisure service agencies conducting surveys. There are five steps in the survey process and these include:

- an operational definition of the purpose of the survey,
- design and pretesting of data collection instruments (i.e., the questionnaire or the interview guide),
- selection of a sample,
- data collection, and
- analysis of data (York, 1982).

The purpose of the survey has already been discussed in this chapter. Each of the additional steps in the survey process will be briefly described below.

The design of the questionnaire includes both the development of the specific questions to be answered by individuals, and decisions concerning their form (e.g., multiple choice, fill-in-the blank). In addition, the directions for completing the survey, the procedures for carrying out the survey, and the method of returning completed questionnaires are determined. Pretesting the data collection instrument is essential in order to uncover or eliminate any difficulties that may exist in the data collection procedure (Bannon, 1978). Pretests can be considered mini-surveys and are conducted with a small group of respondents. They are administered the questionnaire and identify any difficulties in understanding directions, questions, or the type of information solicited. Further, the survey process is actually tested to determine if there are any difficulties that require changes.

Sampling is the use of particular procedures that allow the generalization of findings from a representative small group of individuals to the whole clientele. By selecting individuals through a random process (e.g., selecting every 10th person from a random listing of constituents), the results of the assessment are likely to be representative of the needs of all individuals, even though all constituents were not surveyed.

In collecting the data from individuals, it is important that the cover letter of the questionnaire explain the purpose of the survey and indicate that this information is confidential. It is the ethical responsibility of those individuals conducting the survey to ensure anonymity for respondents. After the questionnaire has been sent to constituents, it is important to follow-up with phone calls, postcards or other methods to continue to solicit the return of surveys. To be considered sufficiently representative, at least 35% of the surveys must be completed and returned. Inducements are often used to increase the return rate. For example, the leisure service agency could offer respondents a discount on programs for completing and returning the survey.

Once the data has been collected and tabulated, the data can be analyzed. The frequencies and percentages of responses to particular questions may reveal significantly desirable information. The data should be carefully analyzed to answer the questions and purpose of the survey.

The quality and quantity of facts gathered will depend partly on the money and time available, as well as the assumptions for their evaluation. To review what kind of facts we can afford to obtain and what we cannot, we evaluate each grouping as follows:

1. Make a preliminary analysis of the situation on the basis of facts that are immediately available at the time one first becomes aware of the presence of a problem.
2. On the basis of one's personal judgment, from clues furnished by the preliminary analysis, list the specific additional facts one would like to have before undertaking a final analysis.
3. By application of the appropriate research techniques, discover as many of the desired facts as time and money will allow (Schnelle, 1967).

Collecting facts can be tedious and time consuming. Therefore, it is essential that the problem solvers not spend time collecting irrelevant facts. Gathering facts can also be frustrating because many are simply not available. The problem solvers must make every effort to secure all possible facts but should not become discouraged if these are not as precise as desired.

Conclusion

After gathering the facts, we have to evaluate them to ensure that we have not permitted false assumptions or biases to persist. Bias is a concern throughout the problem-solving process but is critical to gathering and evaluating data. Many facts are based on an assumption that things will not change and that they will remain fairly static into the foreseeable future. Such an assumption is frequently unfounded.

We have to anticipate, as much as possible, the probable changes that may occur in all factors affecting the problem. For instance, if we select objectives against which to measure our solution, will these be merely short-range objectives, or will there be long-range and interim objectives as well? Such questions are discussed in more detail in following chapters.

Finally, when we seek to involve others in problem identification and ultimately decision making, we have to involve them seriously and not just keep them informed of what happens. If we want to have the viewpoint of constituents, we will have to give them responsibility and power. Without a relinquishment of power and responsibility to the constituents, our desire for participation is shallow. Such power entails the appropriation of funds and other decision-making authority to others outside the leisure service agency.

Bibliography

Assael, H. (1984). *Consumer Behavior and Marketing Action* (2nd edition). Boston: Kent.

Bannon, J. J. (1978). *Leisure resources: Its comprehensive planning.* Englewood Cliffs, NJ: Prentice-Hall.

Dignan, M. B. & Carr, P. A. (1987). *Program Planning for Health Education and Health Promotion.* Philadelphia: Lea & Febiger.

Gilmore, G. D., Campbell, M. D. & Becker, B. L. (1989). *Needs assessment strategies for health education and health promotion.* Indianapolis, IN: Benchmark.

Hodnett, H. (1955). *The art of problem solving.* New York: Harper & Row.

Kepner, C. & Tregoe, B. (1976). *The rational manager.* New York: McGraw-Hill.

Kraus, R.G., & Curtis, J.E. (1990). *Creative management in recreation, parks, and leisure services* (5th edition). St. Louis, MO: Times Mirror/Mosby.

"How to Use the Key Informant Survey Technique" (1985). *How to Evaluate Education Programs*, 1-6.

McKillip, J. (1987). *Need analysis; Tools for the human services and education*. Beverly Hills, CA: Sage.

Nachmias, D. & Nachmias, C. (1987). *Research methods in the social sciences*, (3rd edition). New York: St. Martin's Press.

Schnelle, K. E. (1967). *Case analysis and business problem solving*. New York: McGraw-Hill.

York, R. O. (1982). *Human service planning*. Chapel Hill, NC: The University of North Carolina Press.

Chapter Seven

DEFINING OBJECTIVES

Introduction

After identifying and carefully articulating the problem, the second step is establishing the objectives that will be used for evaluating the various proposed solutions. Objectives are the specific, measurable, and intended outcomes of the implemented problem solution. It is important that problem solvers define target outcomes that would represent an optimal problem solution prior to the generation of alternatives from which the most effective will be selected. Identification of both short- and long-range objectives may be necessary, depending on the situation under deliberation. Theobald (1979) suggested the following guidelines when writing objectives: objectives are stated in terms of persons involved; objectives specify a behavior that can be counted, verified or measured; and objectives indicate a minimum level of accomplishment or performance.

To solve any problem and to know whether the solution has been effective, we must be able to measure or evaluate it. How are we to know whether we have good objectives? What guidelines or criteria can be used? We must be as disciplined in our formulation of objectives as in the scrutiny of assumptions and biases during the fact-finding stage. We must state precisely what we hope to achieve through our problem-solving efforts. This is one step in the model that requires precision.

If a problem statement has been well conceptualized in the previous stage of the problem-solving process, it will often provide general direction for the objectives, and may actually include viable objectives. For example, if the problem statement is: *The community center has had a 25% drop in youth attendance*, a possible objective may be, *After our recruitment effort, youth attendance will increase by 25%.*

Oftentimes, one objective alone will not be sufficient to fully represent the problem solution. A set of objectives may be more appropriate.

Congruence With Organizational Objectives

In order to be able to state, clarify, and rank objectives in terms that can be understood, first an analysis of the objectives of the organization as stated in the bylaws or policies must be conducted. That is, a determination must be made of the organizational objectives of the leisure service agency, and how these policies are related to the problem statement. If, for example, an attendance figure is low, we need to know if there is a policy — formal or otherwise — that states a percentage or degree of involvement from which the agency has deviated. Is there a policy that states an intention by the advisory board to achieve a degree of constituent involvement not now being reached? Such comparisons, with actual measures in mind, can yield specific, measurable objectives. The objectives generated by the problem-solver must be consistent with these organizational objectives.

The problem may be a deviation from a formal policy, from an implied or informal organizational policy, or may not be reflected in organizational policy at all. A simple discrepancy between formal policies related to optimal functioning and the actual situation reflected in a problem statement does not automatically translate into objectives. Many intangible factors, seemingly unrelated to the organization's formal policy, are also important. For example, even though recommended attendance figures in policy statements are not being met, they may not be far from the manager's expectations. He or she may have ignored formal policy and decided independently what is feasible and practical — based on what previous attendance has been, or on other factors.

If such intangible policies exist, and often they do, they must be reflected in any problem analysis of formal organizational policies. If they are not examined, their implications will be hidden and their impact may be unrealistically assessed. These are real concerns — political, organizational, and personal — that are important, no matter how intangible or concealed. This is especially relevant if the problem solver is an outside consultant who might waste many hours before discovering these unwritten policies.

So far, we have discussed organizational objectives as if they always provide a positive standard on which to base the problem-solving objectives. This may not always be the case. An organization's objectives have to change to keep pace with the needs of those whom it serves. There may come a point in the delineation of the problem-solving objectives that the policies and objectives of the organization themselves may need to be evaluated to determine if they may be a part of the solution or a part of the problem. It is not necessary to radically change policies if the objectives of the organization are still valuable. Change in and of itself is not always the best solution, especially before we have carefully analyzed the existing organizational objectives. We must carefully review the present objectives of the organization before formulating new or modified policies.

Interim and Long-Term Objectives

Some objectives are intentionally selected as steps leading to others and are called interim objectives. Interim objectives provide a means of obtaining longer-range objectives. Objectives are not meant to be final at this stage (though they may be), and may be modified or changed as they approach the problem's solution. For example, if we select the reduction of vandalism as an interim goal, we could implement a twenty-four hour security system at the recreation center. This interim objective is intended as a stopgap, until we can begin to deal with the problem that causes such vandalism. However, if we feel that eliminating vandalism alone will solve the attendance problem in the long run, we are misusing interim objectives. Vandalism is one symptom of the problem, not the problem itself.

Although the value judgments, opinions, and expertise of those concerned are important in setting objectives and cannot be ignored during problem solving, economic and analytic factors are also important. The investigators must consider the resources that are available, and what resources will contribute to the achievement of various objectives. For example, how many staff members would particular objectives require; is there enough money in the budget; or will a special appropriation be needed? In other words, the objectives must be realistic.

Another consideration when formulating problem-solving objectives is the long-range plans of the organization. For instance, a leisure service manager who is determining how to get a bond issue passed must also be concerned with the development of any community comprehensive plan that encompasses or affects his organization's community role. A problem-solving objective that represents an ideal solution to an immediate problem will fail if it does not support or contribute to the long-range plan of the organization. A clear set of objectives will largely determine how successful we are in solving a problem, and the direction in which these solutions are likely to lead the agency.

Problem solvers must decide whether the solution is merely a stopgap, or a lasting solution to a problem. By labeling objectives as to *intention, duration,* and *flexibility,* their aims are clarified before an attempt is made to select a solution. Interim objectives can be helpful in the attainment of the overall objective, but there must be a logical and linear progression established and understood.

Defining objectives is not simple. Problem solvers must know what they are attempting to achieve and how to do it. These concepts are best stated in both quantitative and qualitative terms, and as specifically as possible. Objectives help remind us where we started, where we are going, and what we hope to achieve. They are checkmarks along a route that must be rigorously stated from the start.

Values and Objectives

Objectives in leisure service agencies are often value laden, and this must be considered when formulating the objectives to be used in problem solving. Many objectives in leisure service agencies are based on value elements rather than on measurable, objective standards. Problem solvers must have some mecha-

as well as the value outcomes commonly agreed on by those solving the problem. For example, a problem solver may not only want to increase little league attendance (factual objective), but also decrease the competitiveness of the games (value objective). If at all possible, some tangible weights should be quantitatively assigned to these values.

Although the quantification of value statements can be challenging, these quantitative weights must be assigned before incorporating any value objectives into problem solving. The importance of these value positions to those affected by a problem solution, and the potential repercussions if they are ignored, must be considered during the problem-solving process. To recognize that problems have a value or ethical component does not diminish the factual elements of problem solving. Both are interrelated in any statement of objectives.

Values have to be a "given" in our stated objectives, but we should be careful:

"In administration, the mixed character of the ethical givens is usually fairly obvious. A municipal department may state as its objective the provision of recreation to the city's inhabitants. This aim may then be further analyzed as a means toward building healthier bodies, using leisure time constructively, preventing juvenile delinquency, and a host of others, until the chain of means and ends is traced into a vague realm labeled the good life. At this point the means-ends connections become conjectural (e.g., the relation between recreation and character), and the content of the values so ill defined (e.g., happiness), that the analysis becomes valueless for administrative purposes.

The last point may be stated in a more positive way. In order for an ethical proposition to be useful for rational decision making, the values taken as organizational objectives must be definite, and it must be possible to form judgments as to the probability that particular actions will implement these objectives" (Simon, 1965; 50-51).

Usually a fairly clear line can be drawn between factual and value objectives by labeling them as administrative/factual objectives and policy/value objectives, since this is how they are usually developed in practice. Administrative concerns are more often with factual information and objectives; whereas, policy often stresses values, broad social achievements, and long- term goals.

Both administrative and policy solutions (factual and value objectives) must be addressed in order to solve the problem satisfactorily. If we keep this dichotomy in mind, it will aid us in properly weighing and designating the objectives for what they are intended to represent. For example, in leisure services, when an executive director recommends policy decisions for board approval, these policies incorporate the executive director's value objectives. When the board approves these recommendations, it is assumed that they are aware of any values underlying the policy. Their concern is achieving value objectives, not factual objectives. The decision and carrying it out is the concern of the managers. They must formulate measurable objectives of what they will actually do to meet the value objectives of the executive director and the board.

Another example might be useful in clarifying factual and value objectives. If a manager's desire is to increase the involvement of the advisory board, an objective could specify an increase from 5 to 15 board members. This objective would reflect the fact that there is more work for the board to handle, as well as the value that the manager wishes to expand constituent involvement in the agency. Such factual objectives take into account the values that the agency seeks to represent. Both types of objectives combine and comprise the means by which the solutions are evaluated, as illustrated in Figure 7-1.

No matter how broad-ranging and inspiring the stipulated objectives, failure to meet them because of their ambiguity or generality also represents failure to solve the problem. Failure because we have tried to achieve too much may be consoling to some, but when it involves the setting of vague objectives for an organization, it is simply poor planning.

Gathering Input

Input should be sought from those affected by the problem under deliberation during the formulation of objectives. Any modification in objectives should be a compromise among those

Figure 7-1
Value and Factual Objectives

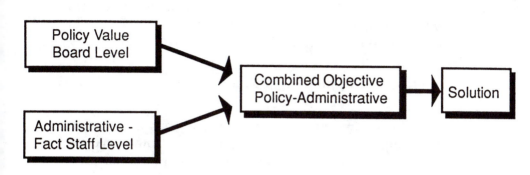

concerned about any previously stated and agreed upon objectives of the organization. For instance, the leisure service manager and staff, the neighborhood youth and their parents, as well as the city government officials, all might help formulate objectives. It is unlikely that they all would agree on similar objectives. Compromises must be made as those concerned seek to set equitable and constructive objectives for the problem.

When we begin to formulate factual objectives, we will ask questions such as:

- What kind of involvement in the agency program do we want from the local residents?
- How much involvement in the programs and activities do we want?
- When and where should this involvement be? How often?

Such questions aid in formulating objectives that are precise in time, place, and quantity. Thus, "We wish to increase attendance and community involvement in the program" can become "We wish to involve x number of youth and residents in our programs on a daily basis for x number of weeks of the year. We wish this involvement to be both in planning activities, as well as in participating in activities. This involvement is intended to include both administrative and policy matter. Such involvement should allow the residents to hire a community organizer or a detached roving leader to work with their youth on a personal basis." Since some objectives are likely to meet with resistance from officials, we should anticipate the need to have to "sell" our objectives to policymakers.

Evaluation of Alternatives

With objectives stated, the problem solvers can then begin to evaluate proposed solutions. At this point, some tentative solutions can be discarded simply because they do not meet objectives. For example, to attempt to alleviate the attendance problem by having a neighborhood meeting to announce a variety of new programs for the following season would not meet the objectives of serious neighborhood involvement. It would simply be announcing already concluded program plans, and not seeking the involvement of the residents in program design and implementation.

On the other hand, in an economically constrained situation, the objectives may require modification. Objectives come from two viewpoints—results that are expected, and resources that are needed to achieve results. If there is no possibility of obtaining additional money from the city to involve the residents in the center—by delegating power and money to neighborhood groups—it may be that a large neighborhood meeting announcing predetermined programs is the best solution that we can offer under the financial circumstances. It would not be considered an interim objective, since we know the next step of greater involvement will not be taken for some time.

Whenever possible, the solution should attempt to encompass the most important objectives. For example, even with economic constraints, the problem solvers might consider the value of involving a few key neighborhood representatives — which might be possible financially — in programming agency activities in lieu of designing programs without such involvement. A small but qualified involvement by the constituency may offer a better solution within the resource limitations. This is what is intended when the objectives and solutions are weighted and judged against one another.

After we have formulated, stated in measurable terms, and weighted objectives that we feel are important to the problem, we must classify and rank them by importance. This is a critical distinction, as it helps us to list our objectives in relation to different levels of resources. Kepner and Tregoe (1976) defined these classifications as the "MUST"and the "WANT" objectives. The MUSTS set the limits that cannot be violated by any proposed solutions. WANTS do not have absolute limits but express desired objectives.

After separating the MUSTS from the WANTS, the problem solvers can logically evaluate the objectives. These can be written out on a list or chart for easy analysis. With the MUST list as a guideline, the problem solvers can readily discard any solutions offered that do not, at the very minimum, meet the MUST objectives. The desired objectives—WANTS—should not be a catch-all for objectives that are simply difficult to rank. If objectives do not fit either list, they are most likely peripheral to the problem, and should be discarded.

To facilitate the accomplishment of objectives more effectively, all individuals concerned with the problem should be involved. If expanding the concept and role of recreation in the community is desired, this objective is not likely to stir the imagination of anyone but the director and staff. Its concern is too broad and not immediate enough to the community residents. This is a peripheral or WANT objective, because it is desirable, but not necessary to solve the problem.

This goal may be attained indirectly but should not be included on the MUST list. If the image of the center is improved through residential involvement in programming, the concept of recreation may be expanded beyond that of offering predetermined programs to citizens. Ultimately, community involvement in recreation planning and programming may indirectly increase the scope of recreation without stating it as a MUST objective. We might, therefore, solve our problem effectively without altering the perception of recreation at all. As mentioned, ambitious objectives do not necessarily lead to ambitious results. Sometimes they may even draw attention away from the real problem.

Problem solvers should be sure that the formulated objectives are not designed to be of personal value, or vindictive to other employees. For example, if they expand the role of recreation in the community simply because it will improve their chance for promotion or transfer, without regard for the impact on others, they are behaving unethically. An interesting comment on the effect of personal ambitions on the use of systems analysis in the U.S. government is the following:

An acquaintance, who has been deeply involved in analytic activities in one of the government departments, recently commented to me on his experience. Analysis, he felt, had been relevant in only a small proportion of the decisions. Half the time a decision had been foreclosed by high-level political involvement: a call from the White House, or interest expressed by key Congressmen or committees. In an additional 30 percent of the cases, the careers of immediate supervisors were involved. Analysis could not influence the recommendations: *it could only serve as an irritant.* [Emphasis added.] But, he argued, in something like 20 percent of the issues, analysis was unfettered and contributed to much improved overall results.

Personal and organizational goals can coexist, but they should be differentiated. Mixed goals are not necessarily incompatible, but should be distinguished. If we can honestly excite the group about a personal career goal that would promise organizational benefits to all involved, this is fine. Assuming, however, that a "good" ambition will lead to good objectives is specious reasoning. All organizations exist to meet both their own goals and those of their employees. Personal goals are an important stimulus for solving organizational problems, but their motives must be distinguished and understood.

While we are perhaps able to understand and recognize personal motives, we also have to be on the lookout for the personal goals of other participants — staff, residents, and city officials. For example, if one of the residents has ambitions to be a member of the advisory board, he or she may favor flamboyant objectives (however shortsighted) to make a good (and flashy) impression on the voters. He or she may want to totally ignore or downplay organizational objectives as of little concern. In such a case, the problem solver may support the organizational objectives if they are consistent with the intent of the problem-solving objectives.

The closer an objective is to a person's concerns, the more interested they will be in it. Neighborhood residents are not likely to be overly concerned with the budgetary concerns of the overall agency, nor with making every citizen physically fit. By delegating the initial formulation of objectives to those who are closest to the problem, the problem solver can many times get well-formulated and specific objectives to integrate with his or her broader objectives.

Conclusion

As we gather the various measurable objectives offered by those in problem solving, we must project, as much as possible, the effect of our objectives on the environment in which we operate. Many of the difficulties we will encounter come from changes in the environment that are not anticipated when objectives are set, or from our own mental blocks.

Bibliography

Kepner, C. A. & Tregoe, B. B. (1976). *The rational manager*. New York: McGraw- Hill.

Peterson, C. A. & Gunn, S. L. (1984). *Therapeutic recreation program design: Principles and practices*. Englewood Cliffs, NJ: Prentice-Hall.

Simon, H. A. (1965). *Administrative behavior* (2nd ed.): New York: The Free Press.

Theobald, W. F. (1979). *Evaluation of recreation and park programs*. New York: Wiley.

Chapter Eight

CHANGE AND PROBLEM SOLVING

Introduction

This chapter focuses on change as a factor that may precipitate problem situations, common resistance to necessary change, and the various techniques to overcome this resistance and implement needed changes. Most problematic situations have a complex interrelationship of causes, and it is difficult to pinpoint the cause. Through investigation, the problem solver becomes aware of a multifaceted set of causes, and the task becomes one of isolating those few that most significantly impact the situation. Change, both positive and negative, is often found to be one of the primary causes in problem situations.

Change as a Factor

If a problem has recently come to the attention of the leisure services manager, it is frequently because there has been some kind of change in the environment. A change, in its simplest form, is something different in an environment from that which had originally been perceived. Changes that can affect a situation can either be positive or negative, and can be complex or simple, radical or routine. Change can either evolve naturally, or be intentionally initiated. The leisure services manager may not become aware of a problem until a significant amount of change has occurred, sufficient to upset the environment's equilibrium. In problem analysis, individuals are often more interested in negative changes, although it is certainly possible for a positive overall change to create an unanticipated problem.

Isolating Causes

Before the causes of a problem can be found, one needs to distinguish it (Kepner and Tregoe, 1976). For example, a public leisure service manager may notice that fewer people overall are attending the recreation center, or that there are fewer youth or seniors involved. Optimal attendance has been stated as a quantitative objective for the center, so a drop constitutes a problem. Further investigation may lead to a concise problem statement such as: Monthly attendance figures were stable. However, over the past 3 months there has been a 40% drop in attendance. This may be further refined with the additional information that 25 percent of the decline was among seniors.

Once a problem has been distinguished, then the investigation of causes can begin. If a drop in program attendance is sudden and quite sharp, it would be reasonable to examine recent changes in the center's environment that may have precipitated this change. Possible factors to consider may be changes in public transportation schedules; the appearance of graffiti, indicating increased gang activity; increased police presence in an effort to curb drug dealing; a sharp deterioration in the local neighborhood; or internal changes in activities or staffing.

By examining these and other environmental factors as they have occurred during the time span indicated in the problem statement, it may be possible to draw fairly accurate conclusions as to relevant causes. Time, careful consideration, and input from both staff and community residents will be necessary to accurately state the most likely cause. Many problems have causes that cannot be addressed; for instance the relocation of a major traffic artery through a residential neighborhood, effectively cutting off access to a recreation center.

Once the immediate and accessible causes of change have been clearly identified, it becomes possible to formulate solutions based on ameliorating the negative effects of change. These solutions can address the nature of the relevant events precipitating the change, and/or the direction, duration and reason for such a change.

It is, of course, possible to solve a problem without knowing its cause(s). Randomly suggesting a variety of solutions to the problem, without investigation, could lead to an effective solution. This method has a high probability of failure, so conjectural solutions can be justified *only* if it is the best that can be accomplished after a thorough analysis of the situation, or if the potential impact of a wrong decision is not too great. For example, a problem solver could try some experimental solutions, such as increasing the budget or personnel for the center, better lighting near the center, or intelligent substance abuse posters in the lobby. But it must be realized that if these solutions address the causes of the problem, they may be costly. Although there is always an element of chance in problem solving, those taken should be realistic, not merely intellectual or experimental exercises.

Some speculation has a role in making distinctions and identifying causes in a problem situation. For example, individuals who speculate about the kind of changes that would affect attendance might find a much wider web of causes than anticipated. However, while speculation and imagination should be incorporated into this process, it should never replace more rigorous analysis.

If an idea seems valid, it should be tested as soon as possible to see if it is actually relevant to the problem. For example, if the problem solvers believed that a larger social change was precipitating the attendance drop at the center, such as a change in the ethnic make-up of the neighborhood, analysis might lead to more specific and accurate assessment that this was indeed the case. If, through speculation, managers are led into larger areas of concern, these areas should be pursued only if they seem relevant to the concerns of the recreation center. If it is discovered, for example, that recreation is no longer of interest to the community, problem solvers need to uncover the changes that have led to this opinion, which most assuredly does affect the recreation center's situation.

It should never be assumed that a larger or more complex change is usually the cause of a problem. For example, if managers believed that racial difficulties in the neighborhood may have affected the center's image and attendance, they might feel justified in pursuing improved community-police relations or community-center relations. However, the prime cause of the attendance drop may be as simple as a lack of locker space or change in activity schedules! Problem solvers must not be overly hurried in attempts to pinpoint causes.

As various changes in the situation are distinguished, the cause that is the nearest and most pertinent to the problem could be determined. For example, the cause of the problem at the recreation center may be social malaise, lack of resources, poor security for participants, or perhaps the suspicious attitude of staff toward youth. Managers must determine which, if any, of these causes is the key cause. As causes are discovered and analyzed, each should be ranked in terms of its likelihood of being the primary cause.

It is now clear why the problem situation was defined before seeking its cause. By having a clearly defined problem statement, the various causes can be compared with the problem statement, discarding those with no causal relationship. The process should begin by considering the most obvious causes. The most relevant or possible causes are dealt with at the start, for these are more likely to reveal the cause and thus end the search. "In short, the identification of the cause of any problem is not a matter of choice; it is a matter of systematically using the information and clues exposed through the specification of the problem" (Kepner & Tregoe, 1976).

The changes considered as probable causes are usually relatively few, and so the search need not be exhaustive. Changes uncovered previously will provide an excellent start for the investigation. It is not necessary to list endless changes in the environment, but only to examine those that are most evident and seem most closely related to the problem.

Whatever causes and changes are chosen for reexamination, they must be clearly stated in relationship to the problem. The change statement must clearly reflect the nature of the change that precipitated the problem. As with the problem statement, the more specific and rigorous the change statement, the easier it will be to select a solution to the problem. For example: Attendance figures started to decline after a particular date. The first gang fight in the streets of this neighborhood occurred on that date. Since that date we have had to clean gang graffiti off the center walls at least twice a week, and a group of young males has occupied the corner from the center at all hours of the day and night. Again, if more information is required to prepare a specific change statement, additional facts are gathered. Fact gathering does not have a definite cut-off point in the model, but continues throughout the problem-solving process.

As some of the more obvious causes are examined and hypothetical statements are prepared, other subtle or less evident causes may turn up. These may be aspects of change that no one wants to know about, such as a serious drop in the quality of programs offered by a recreation center, and the effect of this on attendance, or racism among the staff. Nonetheless, such analysis must be pursued if these changes are part of the problem.

Resistance to Needed Change

A major block in problem solving is the lack of receptivity to change. Hoffer (1963) discussed the entrenched human resistance to change, regardless of how obviously rewarding such change might be. Change often brings about conflict. The more common attitudinal blocks to change might include:

1. It's against policy
2. We've done it before
3. We've never done it before
4. It won't work
5. I know the kids won't like it
6. I know the supervisor is against it
7. It costs money
8. It might work for someone else, but not here

It must be recognized that most people are more comfortable with a familiar situation and resist the unknown, no matter how trivial the change. There has been much research on how to bring about necessary change in individuals and organizations. Such research has concentrated on changes that are desirable and planned. Random or chance changes were not considered. One of the difficulties of applying such research is how to introduce change effectively. No matter how much a change may benefit those involved in the problem, it can never be assumed that they will accept the risk of change. Nothing can be assumed about any openness to the positive aspects of any change.

In an organizational setting, changes are either radical or routine. Routine changes are those that occur frequently and cause little difficulty—minor changes in procedures, personal roles, or budgeting and other administrative details. Radical changes, on the other hand, are significant changes in organizational structure and management styles, shifts in personnel, relocation of facilities, or the cessation of activities (Ely, 1978). The ideal atmosphere for solving problems caused by changes is one in which management has reflected an open attitude and flexibility toward change. Such an attitude, over time, can help eliminate blocks to problem solving.

Mayhew (1976) outlines the following characteristics that led to successful and unsuccessful attempts to introduce change in institutions of higher education:

1.   Lack of relevant, persuasive evidence that the intended innovations or changes would produce results different from those obtained through more traditional ways is a significant deterrent.
2.   The lack of a clearly expressed purpose or reason for an innovation or change may be a significant condition for failure.
3.   If a given organizational system is overloaded with too many undertakings at one time, the chance for successful implementation and/or adoption of change decreases substantially.
4.   A possible condition for the failure of many innovations is the lack of collective memory or actual history of what has been tried before, and to what effect.
5.   Time and time again, attempts to innovate appear to be seriously affected by personal relationships, personality peculiarities, or changes in personnel.
6.   A major stimulus to innovation and change is the desire by institutions to satisfy their clientele (p. 40).

Various assumptions about problem analysis may cause serious blocks to reaching any solution. For example, if a leisure service manager wanted to involve residents in recreation center programs, this objective has various assumptions. The principal assumption of any proposed solution is that all those involved in the problem will appreciate the need for a solution. Because a group has been working earnestly on a problem does not guarantee that they will see the value of any one solution, especially one inducing substantial change. Lack of rapport or agreement about a solution can seriously block its implementation.

If changes are to be generally accepted, there must be continuing staff and administrative support for the ongoing involvement in the problem-solving and planning process by the program constituents. Lack of support for change from upper management will also create a major block to any lasting solution, if they do not approve and support the solution. Similarly, lack of involvement from front line staff will present a potentially serious block to any solution. Involvement by these various groups requires additional resources, which the problem solver has to consider. Lack of consideration of the various stakeholder interests is a strong deterrent to problem solutions.

The structure of an organization must be examined before making any changes in the relationship between those within the organization and their constituents. For instance, a leisure service manager may want to recruit some residents to assist in decision making and give them the authority to spend funds and recruit personnel. Before taking such an action, a structural review of the organization is mandatory. The problem solver needs to carefully evaluate how new personnel—volunteer or salaried—will function in the structure and context of an organization.

Simple questions, such as with whom the community residents will work at the center, what their tasks will be, and how much influence they will have on center programming are factors that must be determined through structural analysis. Everyone must have a clear idea of what organizational changes will take place as a result of resident involvement. Even with clear explanation of what is to take place, there may still be obstacles. However, such attitudinal blocks can be reduced by removing some of the ambiguity surrounding the problem.

Other blocks to meeting objectives that are related to attitudinal blocks, result in an inability to solve problems. These blocks can range from a mental set for or against a particular solution, to rigidity when confronted with change. Individuals develop a mind set for or against something, which then may hamper problem resolution. Mental blocks in individuals or groups of people are common and must be considered in problem solving. There are three common types of mental blocks inhibiting our creative ability to solve problems:

1.   perceptual blocks,
2.   cultural blocks, and
3.   emotional blocks.

To a great extent, these blocks are extensions of our value system.

Perception is not only how we objectively view our world, but also how we subjectively perceive events and activities intellectually, and what preconceptions enter into our analysis of events. Poor perception can result from poor training, a lack of education, or from outdated or inflexible values. Poor perception can become evident when an individual is presented with new data on a familiar problem. Because of prior perceptions or the lack of comparability among problems, the individual may reach conclusions unwarranted by more recent data.

Many persons exhibit perceptual blocks when they are unable to transfer expertise from one area to another. For instance, if a problem solver is capable of solving personal problems but is incompetent in business where comparable skills are needed, we could say that that person has a mental block. If an administrator sees the need for keeping detailed records of home finances but does not keep good business records, he or she is unable to perceive the need for maintaining good records in both places. The administrator has the necessary skill, but is unable to make the link between the two worlds.

One cause of poor perception of the value of change is the influence of culture on our problem-solving techniques. These values are standards for behavior to which group members conform to survive or succeed in a group. For instance, if racism is one of the central norms with which we have grown up, it may persist as an unspoken or assumed standard in an organization. Thus, if the problem solver at the recreation center wishes to involve members of the African-American community, there may be unexpected or unspoken resistance from the staff.

The same sort of implicit values can exist for personal ambitions within an organization. If a new staff member at the recreation center has innovative problem solutions, he or she may encounter resistance from other staff members. They may not want the new staff member to upset the status quo. Staff who have more years of experience may wish to overexert their influence, and cultural blocks may cause them to frown on anyone exceeding implicit norms of ambition in the group. The group is content: the new staff member should be also, if he or she wishes to get along with the group. A cultural block by others may also cause one to be seen as overly ambitious. Unless the individual is strong or willing to leave an organization, he or she usually succumbs to group cultural pressures, adopting group conceptions of what is acceptable behavior and accomplishment.

For example, if a problem solver has a particular affection for either a staff member or some community resident, this can be personally satisfying. However, if the problem solver lets his/ her decisions be overly affected by these feelings when these persons are factors in the decision, this can be a block. The highly-regarded community person may not be the best representative of the community. Thus, if the problem solver insists on having this person involved in the recreation center management, he may be satisfying his own needs at the expense of the community. The same, of course, applies to giving less talented staff members positions for which they are not qualified, simply because of an affection for them. The manager's feelings may cause an inability to view the individual objectively, and is therefore a block.

Fear is probably the greatest emotional block in problem solving regarding change. If individuals are fearful of setting innovative objectives, or of dealing with a problem because of expected repercussions, problem solving will be severely hampered. A common fear is that there is inadequate information to make a successful decision, and a great deal of anxiety surrounds having to make a decision. There is nothing wrong with emotions: they are usually healthy and necessary, but they must be evaluated as sources of potential blocks to dealing adequately with change.

As problem solvers attempt to reduce blocks that prevent problem resolution and needed change, they may realize that a change in values does not necessarily lead to a change in behavior. Individuals may appreciate the need for change, yet be unable to reduce the blocks necessary to bring about these changes. For example, people may sincerely see the need for more community involvement at the recreation center, yet be unable to work toward that goal.

Problems affecting leisure service organizations are not solved in a social vacuum. Managers are dealing with the attitudes and desires of others and have to anticipate blocks that are likely to occur with them. It is important to be realistic about which impediments can be impacted and which cannot. Not all blocks can be removed or circumvented. Not all problems have viable solutions.

Techniques for Change Implementation

Kotter and Schlesinger (1979) have identified in Table 8-1, six different methods for dealing with resistance to change. The variety and scope of the methods suggests that there is no one universal technique for dealing with individuals who resist change. The method chosen by a leisure service manager is dependent upon an analysis of the situation and the individuals involved. These strategies provide for a variety of approaches, some of which may be incompatible with time constraints, cost effectiveness and risks involved. However, knowing the advantages and disadvantages prior to implementation provides a basis for selecting a strategy that is compatible with a manager's needs.

Tactics for Implementing Planned Change

There are also several methods or tactics that are similar to those in Table 8-1 that can be utilized by leisure service managers to implement a planned change. In a study of 91 managers who

Table 8-1
Methods of Dealing with Resistance to Change

Approach	Commonly used in situations	Advantages	Drawbacks
Education & communication	Where there is a lack of information or inaccurate information and analysis	Once persuaded, people will often help with the implementation of change	Can be time consuming if lots of people involved
Participation & involvement	Where the initiators do not have all the information they need to design the change, and where others have considerable power to resist.	People who participate will be committed to implementing change, and any relevant information they have will be integrated into the change plan.	Can be time consuming if participants design an inappropriate change.
Facilitation & support	Where people are resisting because of adjustment problems	No other approach works as well with adjustment problems	Can be time consuming, expensive, and still fail
Negotiation & agreement	Where someone or some group will clearly lose out in a change, and that group has considerable power to resist	Sometimes it is a relatively easy way to avoid major resistance	Can be too expensive if alerts others to negotiate for compliance
Manipulation & co-optation	Where other tactics will not work, or are too expensive	It can be a relatively quick and inexpensive solution to resistance problems	Can lead to future problems if people feel manipulated
Explicit & implicit coercion	Where speed is essential, and the change initiators possess considerable power	It is speedy, and can overcome any kind of resistance	Can be risky if it leaves people mad at the initiators

Reprinted by permission of Harvard Business Review. An exhibit from "Choosing strategies for change," by J.P. Kotter and L.A. Schlesinger, March/April, 1979. ©1979 by the President and fellows of Harvard College, all rights reserved.

implemented significant change in their service organization (e.g., government, nonprofit agencies), Nutt (1986) observed four planned change tactics. These tactics were found to be in common use by managers, and included: edict, persuasion, participation, and intervention. Table 8-2 indicates the percentage of managers using each tactic and its success. Each of these four tactics will be briefly described below.

Table 8-2

Implementation Tactics in Nutt's Study

Tactic	Managers Using Tactic	Success Rate/ Effectiveness
Edict	23%	43%
Persuasion	17%	73%
Participation	42%	84%
Intervention	20%	100%

Edict. The edict tactic is one in which the manager uses his or her personal power to implement change. Change in this case stems from an authoritarian perspective that was previously illustrated in Figure 3-1. French and Raven (1959) have identified five types of power:

1. *reward power*, which is based on the manager's ability to reward individuals,
2. *coercive power*, which provides the manager with the ability to issue punishment,
3. *legitimate power*, which stems from a manager's right to influence subordinates due to position authority,
4. *referent power*, which stems from the interpersonal feelings that contribute to individuals liking and being attracted to the manager, and
5. *expert power*, which is based on the level of knowledge attributed to the manager.

Managers who used the edict change tactic had the lowest success rate of the four types.

Participation. The participation tactic involved the use of key stakeholders in a process similar in nature to the nominal group technique (presented in Chapter Nine). The manager fostering the change process identified the needs or opportunities, and then delegated the specific process to a task force. The task force in turn made recommendations to the manager. This method suggests that those involved in the change take part in addressing change issues.

Although Chapter Four discussed participative management, its specific value as a method of overcoming resistance to change is also relevant here. There are three reasons participatory management is beneficial for change. First, individuals involved in the change process become more committed to the change, and thereby invested in its successful implementation. Second, being engaged in the change assists in structuring its elements in a way that is desirable to the individuals affected. In this way, many of the negative consequences of change are ameliorated. Third, increased communication aids in acceptance and understanding of the change. This aids the reduction of any negative impact from the change that would have been due to lack of understanding (Lawler, 1986).

Participative management may also be facilitated by informal involvement of employees. Informal, in this context, does not have the connotation of a haphazard involvement of employees, but rather that formal structured systems are not utilized. Participation is facilitated through the interpersonal relationships between managers and employees. Informal participation may be very beneficial to employee satisfaction (Cotton, Vollrath, Froggatt, Lengnick-Hall & Jennings, 1988). This may have a positive effect on change.

Persuasion. Managers using this tactic were minimally involved in the change process. There was a propensity to utilize consultants and staff experts to develop, recommend, and document changes, and then sell the change to others. Managers used in-house staff experts when the knowledge and skill of these individuals was apparent. Consultants were employed when managers did not have knowledge or expertise in the area.

Persuasion is discussed further in Chapter Twelve.

Intervention. This tactic, which had the highest success rate, is characterized by key managers justifying the need for change. This is accomplished in several ways. Key managers created rationales for change with other key personnel. Rationales included comparison with similar organizations that had better performance and, in that way, created new standards to strive for. In addition, methods to improve current practice were described and demonstrated to be attainable.

Many managers using this implementation tactic were aware of the value of program or service users as a source of ideas and identifiers of poorly designed or inefficient procedures. As a result, task forces or key informants were employed to generate ideas and comment as changes evolved. This is an analogous situation to the prevalent use of advisory boards by most public leisure service organizations. Key managers also retained veto power over any recommendation by constituents. Managers using the intervention tactic have a high degree of involvement in the change process.

This intervention tactic is similar to the change process of Kurt Lewin that was elaborated upon by Schein and Bennis (1965). This well-accepted model of change consists of three stages:

1.   **Unfreezing.** This phase consists of recognizing dissatisfaction with the current state of operation. It is identified by gathering information about the problem and confirming its existence. It is critical to involve employees and convincingly focus on the current unacceptable state. In addition, managers minimize the negative consequences of the change, while the positive aspects are emphasized.

2.   **Moving or Change.** In this stage, the change is actually implemented and monitoring takes place in order to evaluate the change against prior goals.

3.   **Refreezing.** This is a critical step that managers often neglect. Refreezing consists of providing feedback about the positive consequences of the change. In addition, individuals who implement the change receive reinforce-

ment and rewards. In this way the change becomes a part of the norm. It is important for managers to provide the support for the change to be effective.

Conclusion

Change may best be thought of as an ongoing process in an organization, and one that fosters a transition to a more desired state. The discussion in this chapter can be subsumed under a larger scheme of planned change that consists of nine steps:

1. involve all employees in planning for change,
2. provide opportunities for open communication and feed-back,
3. consider change effects on work groups,
4. inform employees about the change effort prior to imple-mentation,
5. build employee trust throughout the organization,
6. use problem-solving techniques to assist change,
7. involve employees in the implementation of change,
8. ensure that the early aspects of change are successful, and
9. quickly stabilize and spread the change throughout the organization (Lippit, Langeth, & Mossop, 1985).

It is imperative that leisure service managers monitor the effect that change may play in the problem-solving process. In order to deal with change, potential blocks should be recognized and methods for handling resistance to change identified. Particular tactics may be utilized by managers to assist in facilitating change. The tactics presented have varying degrees of success and the advantages and disadvantages should be taken into account.

Bibliography

Cotton, J. L., Vollrath, D. A., Froggatt, K. L., Lengnick-Hall, M. L. & Jennings, K. R. (1988). Employee participation: Diverse forms and different outcomes. *Academy of Management Review*, 13(1), 8-22.

Ely, D.P. (1978). Creating the conditions for change. *Changing Times: Changing Libraries.* Urbana, IL: University of Illinois.

French, J. R. P. Jr., Raven, B. (1959). The bases of social power. In D. Cartwright (ed.) *Studies in social power*: 150-167, University of Michigan, Institute for Social Research.

Hoffer, E. (1963). The ordeal of change. New York: Harper & Row.

Kotter, J. P. & Schlesinger, L. A. (1979). Choosing strategies for change. *Harvard Business Review*, March-April, 106-113.

Lawler, E. E. III. (1986). *High-involvement management.* San Francisco: Jossey- Bass.

Lippitt, G. L., Langeth, P., & Mossop, J. (1985). *Implementing organizational change.* San Francisco, Jossey-Bass.

Mayhew, L.B. (1976). *How colleges change: Approaches to academic reform.* Stanford, CA: ERIC Clearinghouse on Information Resources.

Nutt, P. C. (1986). Tactics of implementation. *Academy of Management Journal*, 29(2), 230-261.

Schein, E. H. & Bennis, W. G. (1965). *Personal and organizational change through group methods: The laboratory approach.* New York: Wiley.

Chapter Nine

FACILITATING CREATIVE THINKING

Introduction

Leisure service managers who desire to increase employee creativity can utilize two methods. First, as previously discussed in Chapter Four, barriers to creative thinking can be eliminated or reduced. An organizational culture can be fostered that encourages employees to contribute new ideas. Second, managers can focus on developing and training employees to tap into their own creative talents (Zemke & Gordon, 1986). A recent meta-analysis of the impact of training programs on creativity found that training does affect creativity. While training and practice contribute to an increase in creativity skills, it should also be noted that some individuals have more innate ability for creative thinking than others (Rose & Lin, 1985). Creative thinking is an important component of the problem-solving process. This chapter will highlight some techniques that may facilitate creativity and thereby stimulate ideas and potential solutions to the problem under investigation.

Synectics

Synectics comes from the Greek word for the joining together of different and apparently irrelevant elements. This group creativity technique was developed by Gordon (1961) in 1944 and is guided by two underlying principles:

1.   making the strange familiar, and
2.   making the familiar strange.

Through the use of analogy, individuals generate familiar comparisons to a novel situation. Because creative problem solving also requires the ability to move into unfamiliar territory, participants are also encouraged to develop novel comparisons to what is currently familiar. Synectics problem-solving sessions use four types of analogies for making the familiar strange. These include: personal, direct, symbolic, and fantasy analogies.

Gordon believed that a limitation of brainstorming was that solutions were arrived at too quickly. In order to alleviate this, synectics group leaders are the only individuals who know the precise problem under consideration. The problem is intentionally left vague in order to allow freedom in the generation of all potentially relevant ideas. This technique was believed to increase the creativity of group members, particularly novices, to the synectics process. When the group was close to the best solution, the exact nature of the problem would be revealed (Arnold, 1962). Although no systematic research is available regarding the benefits of synectics as an overall creativity enhancement training program, some evidence exists that the use of personal analogy enhances the effects of a typical brainstorming session (Amabile, 1983).

Brainstorming

Alex Osborn (1963) developed the technique of organized ideation in 1938 while employed as an advertising executive. Participants involved in Osborn's organized ideation coined the phrase "brainstorm session," meaning the application of the brain to storm a problem. Brainstorming is perhaps one of the most widely known and utilized creativity training techniques, and is a method for generating ideas that may serve as potential problem solutions.

There are two important principles of brainstorming. First, ideas are generated with deferred judgment. That is, group members may not criticize an idea during idea generation. It is suggested that people are more creative in a group if they are sure that their ideas will not be attacked or criticized. Second, it is desirable to generate as many ideas as possible. This principle rests on the premise that quantity breeds quality. That is, the more ideas that are generated during a brainstorming session, the higher the likelihood that some of the ideas will be valuable.

There are four rules of brainstorming that also serve as guidelines for implementing a group session:

1. *Critical judgment is ruled out.* It is suggested that education and experience have trained most adults to think critically rather than creatively. As a result, they tend to impede the fluency of ideas by applying their critical power too soon. By deferring judgment during the generation stage, it is possible to think up substantially more and better ideas. Although open criticism and evaluation is not allowed, individuals may very well censor their own ideas before sharing. Therefore, it seems better to assume that judgment is not completely ruled out, but minimized.

2. *Freewheeling is welcomed.* The wilder the ideas, the better for creative thinking; it is easier to tone down than to think up.

3. *Quantity is wanted.* The greater the number of ideas, the more likelihood of achieving a new and effective solution to the problem.

4. *Combination and improvement are sought.* In addition to contributing ideas, participants are urged to suggest how their own and others' ideas can be turned into better ideas; or how two or more previous ideas can be joined into still another idea (hitchhiking).

Brainstorming sessions consist of approximately 6-12 participants who are at the same level in the organizational hierarchy. The session begins with the leader presenting the problem statement, as simply and specifically as possible. This is followed by group members contributing anything that comes to mind as a possible solution to the problem. Although brainstorming is considered an informal group process, the above four rules are generally followed and reiterated as necessary. The group leader records all ideas that are generated. Group members are encouraged to piggyback, elaborate, and combine other group ideas. The leader encourages participants to create radically new ideas.

Brainstorming has received a great deal of investigation. For example, Osborn's contention has been that individuals are stimulated by group brainstorming to produce more ideas than individual brainstorming. Findings by Dunnette, Campbell and Jaastad (1963) did not support this premise. In fact, these researchers found that individuals produce a greater number of high-quality ideas when working alone than in a group. "Placing a moratorium on all criticism is a good idea. However, the best bet for creative thinking in attacking problems seems, therefore, to be the pooled individual efforts of many people with perhaps an initial group session to serve simply as a warmup to their efforts" (p. 37).

Forsyth (1990), summarizes the research findings on brainstorming and provides several recommendations for its implementation.

- Group members should be trained to follow Osborn's four rules. Individuals new to brainstorming generate lower-quality ideas.
- The results of brainstorming can be improved by recording ideas individually, at the conclusion of the session.
- Talking should be halted on a periodic basis in order to provide group members the opportunity to think. Pauses and silences result in higher-quality ideas.
- Ideas should be recorded in the presence of group members. Ideas should also be shared by group members one at a time, by taking turns.
- The use of a skilled discussion leader may facilitate creativity, particularly when using synectics techniques.

These recommendations can also be effectively incorporated in the nominal group technique process.

Nominal Group Technique

The nominal group technique (NGT) was developed by Van de Ven and Delbecq (1974). The specific objectives of this process include:

- assuring different processes for creative activity,
- providing for balanced participation among group members, and
- incorporating voting techniques to determine overall group judgment.

The NGT has been embraced by administrators and planners in developing, revising, and implementing human service programs under complex or particularly challenging circumstances. This includes the need of managers to utilize effective methods of involving individuals who possess a variety of backgrounds and perspectives in the problem-solving process (Van de Ven & Delbecq, 1974). Some of the opportunities and situations in which group input may be solicited for optimal results to the organization are described by Delbecq, Van de Ven & Gustafson (1975):

- "Obtaining early review of the planning intent, and a clear mandate from top-level decision makers concerning the general approach followed in developing the program.
- Involving clients or consumers in problem exploration meetings to document unmet needs.
- Involving outside resource people (both scientific and technical) to help explore components of an appropriate program to solve those needs.
- Involving administrators, funding sources, clients, and professionals in an early review of program plans.
- Involving appropriate personnel in developing designs for implementation and evaluation.
- Involving other personnel, from other organizations who will be later adopters of the new program, as participant observers in a demonstration program, to prepare the way for technological transfer or diffusion of innovative programs" (p. 3).

NGT is a structured group meeting intended to address the processes of:

- problem exploration,
- knowledge exploration,
- preliminary review,
- design and implementation, and
- evaluation and review.

Each of these processes is posited to be enhanced by the sharing of critical judgments by participants in the group. The NGT has both advantages and disadvantages. The benefits of this procedure include the ability of this process to be concluded in a short period of time. In addition, it increases individual participation because all ideas are free from group influence. Two drawbacks of the process include the need for a trained leader to facilitate the group and the requirement that only one problem be considered (Delbecq, Van de Ven & Gustafson, 1975). The six stages of the NGT are briefly described below.

Leading a Nominal Group Technique Session

The first task of the nominal group leader once a NGT session begins is to welcome the participants and to impress upon them the importance and relevance of the task to be undertaken. It is essential that the leader create an atmosphere in which every member will be motivated and comfortable while actively participating in the NGT session. Once the members have been introduced to the NGT purpose, the leader follows a series of steps to implement the session. These steps and their benefits will be discussed below.

Step 1: Independent Written Generation of Ideas

The purpose of this first step is to generate a large number of ideas or solutions related to the problem statement. The group process begins with the participants brainstorming independently. This serves to reduce competition and need for conformity, as well as providing the time necessary for reflection.

The group leader presents the problem statement in a question format by both reading it aloud and by providing a written copy of the question to each group member. Working independently, each person generates a list of sentences or phrases that represent his or her ideas or responses to the problem statement. The leader provides time limits, such as five minutes, for this step. It is important that the leader curtail interaction or distracting behavior between group members. The leader should also engage in the silent generation of written ideas along with session participants and refrain from providing content-related feedback to participants. The leader should serve as a role model for participants.

Step 2: Round-Robin Recording of Ideas

This step involves writing the responses of group members on a flip chart. Round-robin recording consists of asking sequentially each group member for one response from their list. If an individual has the same item on her list as another member, it should not be restated unless it is considered somehow unique. The leader should encourage "piggybacking," which is the building upon or expanding of ideas presented by another group member, throughout step two. A group member may pass on her turn to present an idea, while not losing the opportunity to reenter the next cycle of the round robin.

The round-robin recording guarantees that all members have the opportunity to contribute their ideas, disassociates ideas from the individuals who presented them, and provides a written record of the group's efforts or problem solutions. The round robin is strictly limited to the sharing of solutions from participants' initial lists or piggybacking; discussing or debating ideas is prohibited at this step of the NGT process. This concludes the nominal phase of the group process.

Step 3: Serial Discussion for Clarification

In step three, each response that has been recorded on the flip chart is discussed in order by the group members. The leader points sequentially to each item, reads it aloud and asks group members for clarification, questions, and agreement or disagreement. The purpose of this step is to ensure that all group members understand the intent and nature of the proposed solution, and to openly discuss different perspectives. The leader must be careful that a balanced discussion is maintained and to move on, once the salient points have been made. It is important that all the proposed solutions be discussed without an inordinate amount of time being dedicated to any single solution. The discussion and clarification should not be allowed to degenerate into partisan debate on the merits or drawbacks of a particular solution.

Step 4: Preliminary Vote on Item Importance

In this step, the judgments of the individual group members are solicited in order to determine the relative value of the proposed solutions. The leader asks each group member to rank a specified number (e.g. five) of priority solutions from the list generated by the group round-robin process. The group members write each of their priority solutions on separate index cards. Then, each group member ranks five index cards in order, from the most to the least desirable solution. Taking all members' votes into consideration, a mean value is calculated for each solution. The item with the highest mean value would be considered the priority group solution. The NGT may be concluded at this point if the prioritized solutions have only minor disagreements, in terms of ranks, among group members. However, if there is great diversity among ranks, the following two additional steps may be warranted.

Step 5: Discussion of the Preliminary Vote

The purpose of this step is to discuss any dramatic inconsistencies among members' rankings. For example, if three participants ranked an item as the most desirable, and it was omitted from the list of the other group members, the discrepancy should be explored. It may be the case that certain group members have relevant information that others do not, or biases exist that may impact their reaction to a solution.

It is important that this step focuses on clarification, rather than attempting to persuade other members to change their positions. However, it is acceptable for members to change their ranks after clarification or additional information is provided.

Step 6: Final Vote

Once again, as in step four, the intention of a vote is to translate individual votes into a group decision. The same procedure of choosing priority solutions and ranking them on index cards may be used. The final vote will result in the selection of the problem solution, provide group members with a sense of accomplishment, and serves to document the decision-making process.

Individual Training

A different approach to improving group problem-solving effectiveness is offered by Bottger and Yetton (1987). These researchers studied the effects of group performance when members were individually trained to use their task knowledge effectively. The training consisted of informing problem solvers of four types of obstacles that can limit problem-solving ability and providing strategies, behaviors, or reflective actions to address the obstacles. The findings of this study revealed that individual task training in the four areas improved group problem-solving performance. These four training areas include:

1. *Hypervigilance*, which is characterized by flitting from one idea to another without reflecting long enough on any one solution to adequately evaluate it. Often the problem solver experiences high levels of anxiety and pressure, and will make a quick decision in an attempt to reduce those feelings. This results in poor decisions. The training solution to this obstacle is for problem solvers to assure themselves that they have adequate time, as well as the necessary expertise, to generate a good solution.

2. *Unconflicted adherence* is characterized by locking into one of the first ideas, and ignoring the value or potential of other solutions. At this point, problem solvers may ignore

important or additional information in an attempt to quickly solve the problem. In order to avoid this behavior, problem solvers should systematically double check the information, and look at potential difficulties and consequences associated with their priority solutions. They should refrain from minimizing the importance of the decision to be made until the risks of making an improper decision have been fully examined.

3. *Unconflicted change* is the practice of uncritically changing one's mind in response to alternative problem solutions. Again, the problem solver is not fully examining each problem solution on its own merits. The problem solvers should be willing to spend as much time evaluating alternative problem solutions as they did on the initial solution, and again judge all of the consequences and risks. Any alternative problem solutions should be measured against the first solution that was considered attractive.

4. *Defensive avoidance* consists of three different behaviors. *Procrastination* results in the inability to address and resolve the problem. While it is important that adequate time be dedicated to reflection within the decision-making process, it is also important to ultimately move towards problem solution. Problem solvers must be able to spread their time over a task in such a way as to maximize effort. *Disowning responsibility* occurs when the problem solvers do not demonstrate a commitment to the problem-solving process, and resist personal involvement. The problem solvers must recognize that their involvement is necessary for a successful problem solution, and be willing to attempt new behaviors. *Selective inattention* to corrective information is the ignoring of potentially valuable information due to lack of confidence in the proposed solution, and a desire to have the process completed. The problem solver must be willing to stay with the problem-solving process and to address remaining doubts as much as is practical or beneficial, in order to arrive at the best possible solution. It is always important that problem solvers be willing to thoroughly evaluate the robustness of their decisions.

Conclusion

There are many creativity training programs, some of which have merit, and some that are questionable in terms of their techniques and value. Zemke & Gordon (1986) summarized some of the findings related to creativity training techniques. These include:

- Participants gain self-confidence and judge themselves as more creative after their involvement in creativity training programs.
- Participant knowledge about creativity theory is important to long-term success.
- Providing participants with examples of solutions or outcomes improves creative efforts.
- Participants who like their co-workers perform better than those who have poor working relationships.
- Warm-up sessions improve the quality and quantity of problem-solving solutions.

This chapter has described some techniques that may have value for the leisure service manager attempting to increase creativity in the problem-solving process, or from employees generally. The creativity techniques discussed have undergone empirical testing and have enhanced creativity under specific conditions and with knowledgeable leadership.

Bibliography

Amabile, T. M. (1983). *The social psychology of creativity*. New York: Springer-Verlag.

Arnold, J.E. (1962). Useful creative techniques. In S.J. Parnes and H.F. Harding,(eds.), *A sourcebook for creative thinking*. New York: Charles Scribner's Sons, 251-268.

Bottger, P. C. & Yetton, P. W. (1987). Improving group performance by training in individual problem solving. *Journal of Applied Psychology*, 72(4), 651-657.

Delbecq, A. L. & Van de Ven, A. H. & Gustafson, D. H. (1975). *Group techniques for program planning: A guide to nominal group and delphi processes.* Glenview, IL: Scott Foresman.

Dunnette, M., Campbell, J. & Jaastad, K. (1963). The effect of group participation on brainstorming effectiveness for two industrial samples. *Journal of Applied Psychology, 47,* 30-37.

Forsyth, D. R. (1990). *Group Dynamics* (2nd edition). Belmont, CA: Wadsworth.

Gordon, W.J.J. (1961). Synectics: *The development of creative capacity. New York: Harper & Brothers.*

Lincoln, J. W. (1962). Developing a creativeness in people. In S. J. Parnes & H. F. Harding, (eds.)*A Source Book for Creative Thinking,* New York: Charles Scribner's Sons, 269-275.

Osborn, A. (1963). *Applied imagination: Principles and procedures of creative problem solving* (3rd edition). New York: Charles Scribner's Sons.

Rose, L. H. & Lin, H. (1985). A meta-analysis of long-term creativity training programs. *Journal of Creative Behavior,* 18(1), 11-22.

Training Manual for Nominal Group Technique Meetings. Office of Recreation and Park Resources, University of Illinois at Urbana-Champaign.

Van de Ven, A. H. & Delbecq, A. L. (1974). The effectiveness of nominal, delphi, and interacting group decision making processes. *Academy of Management Journal,* 17(4), 605-621.

Zemke, R. & Gordon, J. (1986). Making them more creative. *Training,* 23(5), 30-45.

Chapter Ten

SELECTING ALTERNATIVE SOLUTIONS

Idea Classification

This chapter focuses on the various solutions obtained from the "Facilitating Creative Thinking" stage of the problem-solving process. The ideas suggested during the previous stage are evaluated both creatively and judiciously. The consequences of each solution are projected and evaluated. The criticism suppressed during brainstorming, for example, is now allowed to surface. If a problem is simple and a good solution is evident, there is no need to exhaustively analyze alternative solutions or to conduct an elaborate search for another solution.

The step following the generation of creative potential solutions is a judicious evaluation of the various solutions suggested during the creative sessions. Throughout the problem-solving process, there has been some evaluation of the various solutions as they have been developed. Now the problem solver concentrates on evaluating the ideas developed in these sessions, as well as those from other sources.

As already discussed, brainstorming is only one method for generating ideas. Others come from many sources. There is no one best or proven source. Ideas can be offered by leisure service administrators, staff, a consultant, or consumers. Whatever the source of ideas, the number must be reduced so a few key solutions can be analyzed in depth. Before evaluating ideas obtained from the idea generation sessions, the first step is to list and classify these ideas by type of solution. This editing task combines similar ideas, eliminates those that do not meet the problem objective on first examination, and adds any last-minute suggestions.

The problem solver begins screening and classifying these ideas on the workday following the creative session. Before doing so, however, it is advantageous to ask the group members for any additional thoughts on ideas suggested at the creative session. The group members have had the opportunity to sleep on the problem, and many times offer excellent ideas during the next few days. Thus, it is not necessary to cut off a session at its formal ending. One simple method of collecting these follow-up ideas is to have the problem-solving coordinator call each group member the next day to obtain any additional thoughts they may have had. This procedure should be as informal as possible, and not in any way pressure the individual for last-minute ideas. Only ideas that have occurred after the session, and which the group members feel have worth, should be recorded.

The manager then incorporates all the ideas into one list, classifies and edits them according to similarity, relatedness, and applicability. This editing can be by any classification desired, such as similarity of ideas, by the resource most needed to attain it, and by time to carry out the solution. For example, a list of solutions could be classified by those involving people and those involving methods. This latter method, using a worksheet, can be helpful for making comparisons between possible solutions.

"This worksheet . . . is where you now begin to assemble the various factors that can help you toward your problem solution. Copy in the statement of the problem you have been working with . . . copy in the most important criteria for measuring your ideas . . . select the best possible ideas and group them by categories . . . Categories will usually be related groups of ideas; different approaches to the problem; cost, time, or manpower groupings" (Parnes, 1969; p. 13).

Solution Selection

If an idea is not clearly stated, the problem solvers can reword it more clearly. Next, problem solvers review the list, selecting those ideas that appear most promising for a solution. Those directly responsible for implementing the problem solution usually evaluate the ideas. For example, if a leisure service superintendent and managers are the problem solvers and are responsible for finding a solution, they may have the staff or others generate ideas. Then the superintendent and managers (who had not participated in idea generation) would evaluate the ideas. For most group members, their function ends with the session, except to monitor progress on the problem and the final solution.

While evaluating and selecting promising ideas, the problem solver also can restate and combine ideas for better formulations of related ideas. The solutions evaluated should be closely related to the objectives set earlier for the problem. For example, if the chief objective of the problem solution is an increase in attendance at a recreation center, and an improvement in the center's image and security measures, then the various solutions must be compared with these objectives. Objectives are, therefore, the first and constant measurement for screening and evaluating problem solutions. Objectives should not be changed because a solution, which does not meet the objectives, appeals to us. The objectives, if well stated, should remain fairly constant.

The solution may consist of the implementation of one action or a combination of necessary actions. The problem solvers must select carefully among the various solutions, evaluate their known and conjectured consequences (both pro and con), state the risks of implementing or not implementing each one, then be prepared to make a final selection.

Evaluation of Pros and Cons

It is also possible to again use a creative group process to elicit possible pros and cons for each solution, and to examine the risks in not implementing each particular solution under consideration. An idea generation session is needed on both positive and negative consequences of the solutions; what might result if each solution was implemented or not implemented. An example of such a process might be represented by the following:

> "Write down all of the known and suspected advantages and disadvantages. Do it as rapidly as possible. Especially, don't try to judge whether the advantage or disadvantage being listed is important or cogent. Don't even worry about whether the item being listed is really an advantage, or whether it might turn out to be a disadvantage. Just list the ideas as they pop into mind" (Schnelle, 1967; p. 71).

The pros and cons that were suggested could then be edited and evaluated just as the solutions were. The session on pros and cons would be conducted exactly as any other selected creative idea generation session that incorporated suspended judgment. Pros and cons should be freely generated, even though the problem solvers are closer to solving the problem and presumably have better hunches about the ultimate solution.

Evaluation of Consequences

Whether nominal group technique, brainstorming or another method is used at this stage, the evaluation and elimination of various solutions ranges from an intuitive rejection of some ideas, to in-depth research on, and analysis of others. Selecting a final solution requires a candid evaluation of the possible consequences and risks of doing or not doing something about the problem. Evaluation of most ideas requires a simple screening process. For instance, problem solvers can evaluate the idea of holding more citywide sports events at a community recreation center. If this solution is compared with the objective of increasing long-term attendance, we can see that attendance may be increased for the period of the event, but will not be increased on a daily basis. This solution is also not likely to have a lasting positive effect on the center's image. Therefore, it is discarded.

However, suppose that one consequence of holding the citywide event might be a lasting positive effect on the attendance and image of the center. Other alternatives must still be considered and evaluated, for no solution has only one consequence. The event could be too costly, or it could overstrain the staff who are not familiar with citywide events, and so forth. Even a solution that at first appears to solve a problem has to be examined further to ensure its tractability for a particular situation. All the known consequences must be anticipated or controllable to some extent.

Once the possibilities of known consequences are listed with each solution, the problem solvers must search for latent or probable consequences. These are as important as the obvious anticipated consequences. Figure 10-1 illustrates the types of consequences that can be considered when evaluating a proposed solution. In addition, some questions that may be relevant to this solution may be:

Figure 10-1

Consider the Consequences

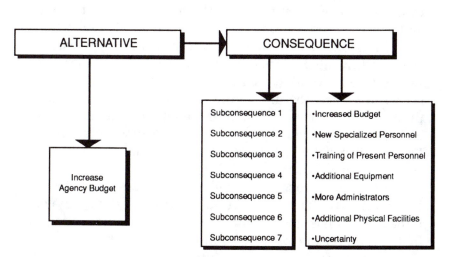

- Will the staff have the ability to enact the solution?
- Are enough funds available to sustain the implementation?
- Will the solution be what is desired by constituents?
- Will it require changes in existing programs and services?
- Will it fit into the long-range plan of future program and service provision?

Other Criteria

Osborn (1965) also suggests judging the proposed solution on whether the idea is:

- simple enough,
- compatible with human nature,
- timely, and
- possible.

These criteria are not used to prevent an idea from being considered, but indicate how a potential solution must be evaluated. Criteria are different from objectives: the former are a desired framework within which to judge ideas, and the latter are a constraint against which to measure solutions. As each idea is evaluated, the problem solvers use both their desires (objectives) and means (criteria) as determinants of the solution's worth.

Ideas can be classified and reclassified in many ways as they are evaluated: those that would cost money, those that would require additional staff, those that can be applied in the short run, or those that are more long range. For example, are the problem solvers seeking an immediate solution with long-range effects, or are they willing to wait for a longer-range solution with few interim benefits? This is something that must be decided for each problem solution.

If the main concern is money, then ideas that meet our objectives and criteria should be classified and evaluated by cost. If the constraint is staff, classification uses a personnel category first. Whatever the focus is, it must be the determinant of our classification: Is an expensive solution or a quick one required? Is money attainable while qualified staff are not? If the problem solvers are willing to strive for additional resources to implement a satisfactory decision, then the classification will remain the same, and the problem solvers can begin to think of ways of selling the idea to others.

Another way of evaluating ideas is to test them. This method, of course, does not apply to all ideas. However, if the problem solvers believed that increased newspaper coverage or publicity might be an answer to poor image and low attendance at a recreation center, the idea could be tested. If it fails, the idea could be discounted as the best solution. The idea may still have merit as part of a solution, but perhaps not as the entire solution.

Historical Evaluation

In addition to the use of criteria, objectives, and consequences, problem solvers have to be aware of what solutions may have been tried in the past, or how comparable problems have been alleviated. For example, if extensive press coverage and publicity for the recreation center has occurred in the past, with no discernible increase in attendance or image improvement, this idea can be eliminated. It is important to choose a few practical alternatives that clearly have a good chance of solving the problem.

It is important, therefore, for either the problem solver or an assistant to know the history of an organization, the community, and the experiences of other agencies in comparable situations. Outside consultants are valuable too, because they are not overly enmeshed in the inner workings of the organization, personal politics, or seemingly insoluble constraints. They can bring a much needed objective viewpoint. They are also aware of the experiences of similar agencies with related problems. Outside consultants are not essential, however, especially if the problem solver is familiar with existing literature related to both the field and the problem, and has a wealth of experience in the field.

During the fact-gathering stage, if the problem solvers did not solicit information from other organizations with similar problems, they should do so now. In addition, the problem solvers should consider field observations or a constituent survey, if this was not done during fact gathering. Although the process of evaluation is well underway, it is still appropriate to conduct further research at this point. In fact, the problem solvers are probably better equipped now to analyze facts than before, and better able to design a comprehensive and well-formulated research approach. Resources might be better spent on quality research now than previously, as the solutions to be investigated have been greatly reduced and more clearly defined.

The problem solvers should research solutions that are innovative, as well as more traditional solutions. If a similar situation has been satisfactorily resolved elsewhere, its precepts should be reflected in the current evaluation of options. Just as successful resolution of the problem would help others in comparable situations, the reverse is true. Solutions that have been tried and failed in similar situations should be approached cautiously. Problem solvers should draw on available research and experience other than just their own to avoid treating their situation as novel or atypical. Problem solvers cannot accept the judgment of another's experiences blindly, but they must carefully consider the conditions under which others handled a problem and its outcomes. An old solution may be useful for the current problem, but the problem solver must also be careful about oversimplifying the similarities between environments and problems.

It is important to reduce the number of ideas considered, perhaps by having a problem solver select from no more than four or five ideas. "Taking both the practical and theoretical considerations into account, but also relying, in large measure, on the reported experience of many analysts, we recommend selection of neither fewer than three nor more than seven alternative courses of action. Five frequently seems to be the best number of alternatives to investigate" (Schnelle, 1967; p.65).

Using the example of an underattended recreation agency, the problem solver has narrowed the possible solutions to four. This screening may have used any or all of the above evaluation steps. The following four ideas or combinations of these have been proposed as possible solutions:

1.   Convert the center to include adult-education programs.
2.   Provide free transportation to the center.
3.   Employ a roving recreation leader.
4.   Balance cultural and athletic programs.

Solution Viability

The problem solver then evaluates the viability of each solution. Adult education is good in that it would increase attendance at the center by expanding current programs (now athletic activities for youth). Such programs would actively involve adult residents in the center. The suggestion of free transportation was kept because it may have an immediate practical value for the problem. By offering free buses each afternoon at local schools to bring youth to the center, the problem solvers hope to increase attendance. A roving leader in the community has appeal because it might offer a way of increasing attendance and improving the center's image. Finally, the combined cultural and athletic program has potentially the same value as an adult-education program, offering arts, crafts, and other cultural activities for residents.

Then the problem solver begins to focus on selecting the most likely solutions to the problem. They must remain critical of those that do not match the criteria and objectives. Even if all four solutions appear to meet the objectives, they must be analyzed in relation to the consequences that their implementation might have. For example, if the problem solvers selected adult education programs because this appeared to be a good way to increase attendance by increasing the center's appeal, they must still anticipate all the consequences of each solution (See Figure 10-1).

The idea of modifying center programs to include adult education activities did meet the "must" objective on first analysis. Its appeal is broader than merely recreation programs, as it offers adults an opportunity to learn some useful vocational skills. But as the consequences of this decision are considered, the problem solvers find that such a revision would require, at the least, a change in the center's programs and facilities, as well as increased staff and budget needs. From these consequences they then consider subconsequences: the need to modify the present facility and purchase equipment for new uses, to hire educational staff and administrators, and to retrain present staff.

There are other consequences and risks whose influence is uncertain because the problem solvers have not anticipated them, or have no way of influencing them even if they knew of their existence. For example, what would be the effect on other educational institutions in the area if such a program were offered? Where would the youth of the community receive adequate recreation services if the agency reduced available opportunities? How would the school board react to the recreation commission's acquiring an educational function?

As the criteria and objectives are reviewed, it becomes obvious that in addition to being an expensive proposition, revision of the agency's programs will not increase youth attendance. If parents are concerned about their children and the agency's recreation programs are targeting youth and young adults, then adult education programs might not meet the criteria, even if they did increase total attendance.

The problem solvers apply the same analysis to the other three solutions and come up with as complete a scenario of their probable consequences as possible. A good method for analyzing the consequences of various alternatives is to pretend that the solution is already in effect, or, if possible, to test the solution in the community as was suggested for newspaper coverage. Sometimes the test itself requires the same amount of preparation as the final solution, and is not easy to achieve. It is more than likely that the analysis or consequences, or a test of their effects, will remain largely conjecture.

When the evaluation has been concluded (or the problem solvers feel it is no longer worthwhile to continue), they should create a detailed graph or list of the four solutions that they feel have the best chance of solving the problem. They can attach some weights to how closely each meets the main and supplementary objectives: A simple list of pros and cons, dollars and cents, and short- or long-range outcomes should suffice. How closely each solution takes into account and meets the more pressing criteria should be noted. Finally, the problem solvers have some indication of the resources needed and the changes each solution would require of those involved.

Conclusion

Prior to making the final decision, the problem solvers should have:

*   a set of different solutions,
*   their known and unknown consequences,
*   the risks of undertaking each, and
*   the risks of not undertaking each.

It is up to the decision maker to consider each of these before selecting the best one.

Bibliography

Osborn, A. (1963). *Applied imagination: Principles and procedures of creative problem solving* (3rd edition). New York: Charles Scribner's Sons.

Parnes, S. J. (1963). *Student workbook for creative problem-solving courses and institutes*. Buffalo, NY: University Bookstore.

Schnelle, K. E. (1967). *Case analysis and business problem solving*. New York: McGraw-Hill.

Chapter Eleven

DECISION MAKING

Introduction

Many believe decision making to be the essential task of an executive.

"Decision making is only one of the tasks of an executive. It usually takes but a small fraction of his time. But to make decisions is the specific executive task . . . Only executives make decisions" (Drucker, 1966; p. 113).

Decision making may be discussed as a skill in itself, apart from problem solving, because it may be used to reach a conclusion on a matter for which no problem analysis has been used or is needed. Many books have been devoted to decision making without any discussion of problem solving. The reverse is not possible, since a necessary step in problem solving is deciding on a solution. Many writers use decision making and problem solving (and at times policy making) interchangeably to indicate that the same skills are used in these processes. In fact, making a determination of the most pertinent problem to solve has been considered the most important act in decision making (Kolb, 1983). For the purpose of examining the problem-solving model, decision making is separated to indicate the distinctly different roles or processes that a manager undertakes.

Although we want to avoid a rigid, step-by-step approach to solving problems, for teaching purposes we must delineate the steps that an effective problem solver follows. Decision making is one of them, and in this model represents the point at which the major decision is made. However, smaller decisions may have been enacted throughout the process. If, as Drucker says, decision making is the specific executive task, selecting a solution to the problem is the specific administrative decision in problem solving. To make a final decision, it is necessary to know something about decision making.

The leisure service manager, as decision maker at this stage, has to draw on all the available expertise and information to determine which of the possible solutions is most likely to succeed. One of these solutions, or perhaps a combination, must be selected. Before discussing how decisions are made, some background is provided regarding the individual who makes decisions.

Individual Decision Making

Research and experience have presented the pros and cons of personality influence on decision-making skills. Although we shall concentrate on the personal attributes believed necessary for making decisions, it should be noted that many decisions are made without a strong, personally integrated decision maker, through means of analysts or computerized programs and models. Various quantitative aids, though successful, do not in themselves meet the goal of practicality for many problems faced by leisure service managers. Thus, the discussion of personality is important because the personal idiosyncrasies of the decision maker have greater bearing than they would if there was more reliance on quantitative tools. This is not to deny that the choice to use every mathematical model or computer program is influenced by the personality of the person involved.

The problem solver is primarily a problem analyzer. The manager as a decision maker goes beyond analysis into choice of, risk in, and responsibility for the consequences of a solution. The skills needed for decision making are comparable to those for problem analysis, with exception of a far greater amount of risk. The decision maker is the one who assumes ultimate responsibility for a solution. Even if the decision is made by a group, the risk and responsibility are borne by one person, perhaps two, in the organization. It is possible to delegate problem analysis, but we cannot delegate decision making, no matter how democratic our methods. We can share problem solving with staff and others, but unfortunately, responsibility and risk are entirely with the administrator.

In many large organizations, the problem analyzer and the final decision maker often are not the same person. One might be responsible for defining a problem and offering specific solutions to a decision maker for final selection. The decision maker then attempts to solve the problem by selecting one of the solutions offered by the analysts. Often our image of a decision maker is that of an executive who delegates problem analysis, then rapidly synthesizes the information received and reaches a decision. This decision then is quickly implemented and, without fail, is a success!

Unfortunately in many organizations, especially public service organizations, decision making and the people involved are somewhat less glorified. For example, municipal leisure service agencies usually do not have the financial resources to afford separate persons to operate as problem analyzers and decision makers. More likely these tasks will be performed by one person or group working on the problem from start to finish. To separate these two functions of problem solving for these organizations would be expensive and somewhat arbitrary. Most staff members are involved with organizational problems and would have much to contribute to any problem resolution.

The problem-solving model not only reflects today's problem environments, but also seeks to include the kinds of problems that might be encountered in the future. The type of decision maker needed will be one who can adapt to rapid change. The future decision maker will be more dependent on others, understand computers and other quantitative technologies, and be aware of changes in the more immediate and larger environments. An effective decision maker is well informed not only about agency concerns, but also about society and the world, especially as they affect professional decisions. Nothing is more valuable for decision making than broad, eclectic knowledge.

If the decision makers are unable to adapt to change because of the personal and cultural blocks already discussed, skill in decision making will be greatly curtailed. Leisure service managers must be aware of the changes in society and adapt to these changes. Understanding these changes should include a willingness to modify personal and organizational behavior to reflect modern realities. It is not enough to sympathize with demands for changes in program and service delivery; action should be undertaken.

If leisure service managers make decisions without considering the psychological and social forces within themselves and in society, they are simply being naive about the impact of these factors on decisions. All the blocks that were previously discussed rise again. Decisions are not necessarily made objectively: they are made by people, and are often subjective. Emotions play a large role in decision making, no matter how strong the attempt at rationality. To be a rational decision maker requires that positive emotions be permitted to surface, and negative emotions are dealt with confidently.

The first step toward achieving an emotional-rational balance is to examine ourselves and others in decision making. Introspection will be most beneficial, not only in this phase in the decision process, but later when the solution is implemented. The more time spent now on understanding the probable barriers to decision making, the better equipped the decision maker will be to handle any objections that might arise during implementation. A complete analysis of personalities is not suggested, but a candid appraisal of individual shortcomings of those bound to affect the decision is needed. Being aware of potentially troublesome emotions will reduce their interference in the efforts to make a decision.

When objectives were first set for solving the problem, these objectives were developed to be realistic under known constraints. Decision makers must comprehend what personal drives, needs and compulsions are motivating individuals, especially when decisions are crucial to professional interests and the well being of a community. An emotional response to a solution should not preclude the selection of an effective solution. Figure 11-1 suggests an individual's reaction to an initial solution.

In discussing barriers to decision making, Agryis indicated that interpersonal relationships provided the greatest source of frustration for managers. In his study of six companies, in which

Figure 11-1
Reaction to a Problem Solution

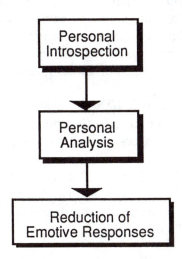

nearly 300 group decision-making meetings were observed, the major findings were:

1. "The actual behavior of top executives during decision-making meetings does not jibe with their attitudes and prescriptions about effective executive action.

2. The gap that often exists between what executives say and how they behave helps create barriers to openness and trust, to the effective search for alternatives, to innovation, and to flexibility in the organization.

3. These barriers are more destructive in important decision-making meetings than in routine meetings, and they upset effective managers more than ineffective ones.

4. The barriers cannot be broken down simply by intellectual exercises. Rather, executives need feedback concerning their behavior and opportunities to develop self-awareness in action. To this end, certain kinds of questioning are valuable; playing back and analyzing tape recordings of meetings has proved to be a helpful step; and laboratory educa-

tion programs are valuable" (Agryis, 1966; p.90).

In most cases Agryis found that executives seldom: took risks or experimented with new ideas and feelings; helped others to be open and take risks; used a behavior style that encouraged individuality and trust; or expressed any feelings. He suggested that the use of a solitary decision maker was over and stressed the need to handle group decision making carefully:

> "No one man seems to be able to have all the knowledge necessary to make an effective decision. If individual contributions are necessary in group meetings, it is important that a climate be created that does not discourage innovation, risk taking, and honest leveling between managers in their conversations with one another. The value of a group is to maximize individual contributions"(p. 441).

An effective decision maker is one who is willing and able to take risks and to encourage others to do so. Because of the politics of decision making, the viewpoints of all those involved in the problem must be taken into account. At times political skill may detract from the willingness to take risks. Decision makers may concentrate more on reducing conflicts and strengthening the esprit de corps, only to lose sight of the need to take a chance, regardless of group harmony.

Limits to Individual Decision Making

A rational approach to decision making closely follows the problem-solving steps presented in Chapter Five. It assumes that managers go through each stage until the best solution has been determined. Herbert Simon (1976) has presented a theory of administrative decision making that suggests that managers are not rational decision makers. He posits that a rational decision maker would select the best alternative from a range of available solutions. This would be considered an optimal solution. However, Simon has suggested that managers are "satisficers" instead of "optimizers." That is, while managers are seeking solutions, they choose alternatives that are good enough to deal with the problem. In this way, the selection of decisions rests on one of the first alternatives that meet the criteria of acceptance. Satisficing stems from bounded rationality, or limits to the cognitive abilities of individuals to process information regarding decisions. For the leisure service manager, who will often be dealing with complex problems, limited information processing capabilities may result in biased decisions (Dirkin, 1983).

Another example of managers' difficulty with rational decision making was reported by Soelberg (1967). In studying the decision-making processes of job searches of MIT students, he found that early in the decision-making process, students identified an implicit favorite. At this early stage, a decision has essentially been rendered by the individual, and the decision process becomes one of self-justification regarding the favorite. Following the identification of an implicit favorite, individuals identify a confirmation choice alternative. This is followed by a search for information to assist the decision maker in a selection. Information is gathered that supports the implicit favorite and disconfirms the alternative. This study is illustrative of a decision-making process that is very subjective and intuitive in nature, rather than one based on rational choice or even on persuasive information.

Groups and Decision Making

It is recommended, if possible, that a group rather than just one person be assigned to handle problem analysis. If this task is limited to one person, it is likely to result in an overburdened staff member and a poorly perceived problem. In the past, when problems were perhaps simpler to solve and the environment not so complex or dynamic, the sole problem solver/decision maker was undoubtedly effective. Such solitary action is no longer prevalent in most organizations. Even simple problems affect many persons, and have a multitude of consequences. Expertise and the insights of others are necessary for effective solutions. Making decisions alone may be simpler, but the solution may not be as good as one reached cooperatively.

Many of the "situation variables" in measuring good decisions reflect the need for others (Vroom and Yetton, 1973).

Situation Variables

1. *Rational Quality Requirement* - Does it make a difference which course of action is adopted?
2. *Adequacy of Information* - Does the manager now have the adequateinformation to make a quality analysis?
3. *Structure of Situation* - Does the manager know exactly what information is missing and how to get the information?
4. *Commitment Requirement* - Is commitment to the solution by others critical to effective implementation?
5. *Commitment without Participation* - Will they commit to a decision made by the manager without their active participation?
6. *Goal Congruence* - Is there goal congruence between the subordinates and the organization?
7. *Conflict about Alternatives* - Is there likely to be conflict about alternative solutions among the subordinates?
8. *Subordinate Competency* - Do the personnel in the organization have the skill and know-how to implement the idea suggested? Note: Subordinates refers to those people whose information is needed or whose commitment is required for effective implementation of the solution.

Several advantages to group decision making have been suggested. Huber (1980) identified three benefits to group decision making as compared to individual decision making. First, the availability of information and its processing are enhanced and more complete when groups are utilized. Second, the acceptance and understanding of the decision by those who must implement it is greater when individuals participate in the decision-making process. Third, subordinate information and skill can be enhanced through inclusion in the decision-making process.

Although there are many advantages to group decision making, disadvantages to group decision making have also been identified in the literature. Five general disadvantages to group decision making of which a manager should be aware are provided below.

1.   "A greater amount of personnel time tends to be consumed in group decision making.
2.   Goals other than those considered most important by top management are more likely to be involved in group decision making.
3.   Unwanted expectations that future decisions will involve group participation may be a consequence of previous participation.
4.   Disagreement among members may result in the group's being unable to reach a decision" (Huber, 1980; p. 148).
5.   Groups tend to make more extreme decisions than individuals. That is, once a decision direction is accepted, members shift their views to the extreme end of the originally favored position. The result may be highly risky or conservative decisions (Myers & Lamm, 1975).

One significant problem that has been identified with group decision making has been identified by Janis (1971) and termed "groupthink." The concept of groupthink emerged from in-depth analysis of poor policy decisions by government leaders.   Janis examined documents and historical reports about formal and informal meetings and conversations of policy makers that led to disastrous decisions such as the blundered Bay of Pigs invasion, unpreparedness for the attack on Pearl Harbor, the Korean War stalemate, and the escalation of the Vietnam War.

Janis (1971; 1983) has described groupthink as a mode of thinking that individuals engage in when they are deeply involved in a cohesive group. Members of this group strive for unanimity and override their motivation to objectively evaluate alternative courses of action. Group norms are developed that support concurrence with group members at the expense of critical thinking. One of the main features of groupthink is that social pressures are brought to bear on those members who take a dissenting position. Social pressures result from group norms that serve to keep group members tied to positions or decisions that have already been formulated even when the group position is unworkable or disturbs the conscience of members. Groupthink, fosters "a deterioration of mental efficiency, reality testing, and moral judgment that results from in-group pressures" (Janis, 1983; p.9).

Eight characteristics of groupthink have been identified and are described in Table 11-1. Janis (1983) has suggested several specific methods for preventing the occurrence of groupthink. Of the various tactics discussed, one may be particularly beneficial for success. It is important for each member of the group to play the role of critical evaluator and thoroughly examine the strengths and weaknesses of proposed solutions. Group leaders can foster this evaluation by encouraging members to openly air any objections and doubts. Providing an atmosphere that does not inhibit members from expressing their views can do much to facilitate the expression of opposing viewpoints. Further, it is vital that group leaders do not influence members by indicating their preferences or biasing individuals in some manner. In essence, being aware of the possibility of groupthink and facilitating full participation of group members may play a significant role in alleviating this problem.

Types of Decision-Making Groups

There are five different group decision-making procedures that are widely recognized and utilized. These decision-making processes include ordinary, brainstorming, statistical aggregation, nominal group technique, and delphi. Brief descriptions of each are provided below (Murnighan, 1981).

Ordinary Group: A committee structure with a chairperson characterizes the ordinary group. Usually a very unstructured process, the meeting is open-ended and the discussion is free flowing. The meeting often becomes fatiguing for members, and as a result, the last solution offered may be accepted in order to move on to other issues. Benefits do arise from close interpersonal contact. This procedure may be useful when group members know and respect each other.

Brainstorming: This technique was described in Chapter Nine. One limiting feature of this group process is that it does not include a decision rendering procedure. Another mechanism must be employed to reach a decision after brainstorming has been concluded.

Table 11-1

Symptoms of Groupthink

Invulnerability	Members share an illusion of invulnerability that provides some degree of reassurance about obvious dangers, leading them to become over-optimistic and willing to take extraordinary risks. It also causes them to fail to respond to clear warnings of danger.
Rationale	Members rationalize their behavior, discounting warnings and other forms of negative behavior.
Morality	Members ignore the ethical or moral consequences of their decisions, believing in the inherent morality of the group.
Stereotypes	Members view opponents as evil, weak, or stupid, and therefore attempts at negotiating differences are not warranted.
Pressure	Members apply pressure to individuals who express doubts or question the validity of a perspective shared by the majority.
Self-censorship	Members keep silent about any questions or misgivings about the group's decision.
Unanimity	Members believe that individuals in the group share the same perspective.
Mindguards	Members protect the leader and other group members from adverse information that might affect the groups consensus.

Adapted from Janis, I. L. (1971). Groupthink. *Psychology Today*, June.

Statistical Aggregation: Statistical aggregation is limited to dealing with quantitative problems. The process consists of gathering information from individuals without any actual group interaction. Individuals provide estimates of their best judgment about a problem. These are collected and measures of central tendency employed such as the median (the midpoint of a range of scores) or the mode (the most frequently occurring score) to quickly arrive at a solution.

Nominal Group Technique: The NGT and the six stages of the group process were also described in Chapter Nine. One of the features of the NGT is the emphasis on independent consideration of the problem and solutions by group members. There is little interaction among group members, which greatly limits the influencing effects of opinionated individuals as well as the potential for groupthink.

Delphi: This group procedure has three important features: 1) anonymity, 2) controlled feedback, and 3) statistical group response (Dalkey, 1969). This procedure uses experts from a variety of geographic areas to react to issues or problems through a mail survey. First, a questionnaire is developed that addresses the problem, and is sent to participants. This provides delphi members with the opportunity for individual brainstorming to identify solutions to the problem. When the questionnaires are returned, the information is summarized and presented again through a questionnaire through which individuals prioritize solutions.

Table 11-2 contrasts each of these five decision-making procedures against several important evaluative criteria. Notable among the criteria evaluated are the high ratings for the NGT and Delphi methods with regard to the quantity and quality of ideas produced, as well as the task orientation of group members. In support of the value of these two methods, Van de Ven and Delbecq (1974) concluded that the NGT and Delphi are superior to the interacting group when a fact-finding problem that requires the pooled judgments of a group is needed. The NGT should be utilized when individuals can be easily assembled, and the problems that are faced require immediate attention. The delphi technique is preferred when it is not cost effective or too inconvenient to bring individuals together in one location, and the problems do not require a quick solution.

Table 11-2
A Comparison of Decision Processes

Criteria	Ordinary	Brainstorming	Aggregation	NGT	Delphi
Number of ideas	Low	Moderate	NA*	High	High
Quality of ideas	Low	Moderate	NA*	High	High
Social pressure	High	Low	None	Moderate	Low
Time/money costs	Moderate	Low	Low	Low	High
Task orientation	Low	High	High	High	High
Potential for interpersonal conflict	High	Low	Low	Moderate	Low
Feelings of accomplishment	High to low	High	Low	High	Moderate
Commitment to solution	High	NA*	Low	Moderate	Low
Builds group cohesiveness	High	High	Low	Moderate	Low

*Not applicable

Reprinted, by permission of publisher from MANAGEMENT REVIEW, February 1981©1981. American Management Association, New York. All rights reserved.

Conclusion

Decision making is of central importance to the work of the leisure service manager and, in particular, the problem-solving process. Managers in the field are faced with determining if a particular decision should be made individually or through group efforts. Although the previous discussion has identified the benefits and potential problems involved in group decision making, a final caveat is offered. In a comprehensive review of the literature that compared group versus individual performance in decision making, Hill (1982) determined that group performance was qualitatively and quantitatively superior to the performance of the average individual. However, group performance was often lower than the best individual in a statistical aggregate. Further, one exceptional performer is superior to that of a committee, especially if the problem is complex, and the committee has a number of low-ability members. Leisure service managers then, may greatly benefit from group decision making when members involved in the group have expertise in the problem under deliberation.

Bibliography

Agryis, C. (1966). Interpersonal barriers to decision making. *Harvard Business Review*, March, 84-97.

Dalkey, N. C. (1969). *Delphi*. Rand Corporation.

Dirkin, G. R. (1983). How free from bias are our decisions? Problems of information overload. *Journal of Park and Recreation Administration*, 1(2), 13-20.

Drucker, P. F. (1966). *The effective executive*. New York: Harper & Row.

Hill, G.W. (1982). Group versus individual performance: Are N+1 heads better than one? *Psychological Bulletin, 91*(3), 517-539.

Huber, G. P. (1980). *Managerial decision making*. Glenview, IL: Scott Foresman.

Janis, I. L. (1971). Groupthink. *Psychology Today*, June.

Janis, I. L (1983). *Groupthink: Psychological studies of policy decisions and fiascoes* (2nd edition). Boston: Houghton-Mifflin.

Kepner, C. A. & Tregoe, B. B. (1976). *The rational manager.* New York: McGraw- Hill.

Kolb, D. A. (1983). Problem management: Learning from experience. In S. Srivasta and Associates, *The executive mind: New insights on managerial thought and action,* San Francisco, Jossey-Bass.

Myers, D. G. & Lamm, H. The polarizing effect of group discussion. *American Scientist, 63,* 297-303.

Murnighan, J. K. (1981). Group decision making: What strategies should you use? *Management Review,* February, 55-62.

Simon, H. (1976). *Administrative behavior,* (3rd edition). New York: The Free Press.

Soelberg, P. O. (1967). Unprogrammed decision making. *Industrial Management Review,* 8: 19-29.

Vroom, V., H. & Yetton, P. W. (1973). *Leadership and decision-making.* Pittsburgh: University of Pittsburgh Press.

Van de Ven, A. H. & Delbecq, A. L. (1974). The effectiveness of nominal, delphi, and interacting group decision making processes. *Academy of Management Journal,* 17(4), 605-621.

Chapter Twelve

STRATEGIES FOR IMPLEMENTATION

Ideas and Action

Professionals in the leisure services field are usually idea people. They spend a great deal of their time thinking up new ideas, but only a limited amount of time bringing them to fruition. Although suggestions for solutions to problems may be quickly formulated, the development and implementation of these solutions require considerable commitment. The need for the development of implementation strategies is often ignored, because it is considered an automatic part of problem solving. However, ideas in leisure services are advantageous on a practical level only if they are fully conceptualized, developed and implemented. Leavitt (1963) states this situation clearly:

"A powerful new idea can kick around unused in a company for years, not because its merits are not recognized, but because nobody has assumed the responsibility for converting it from words into actions. What is often lacking is not creativity in the idea-creating sense, but innovation in the action-producing sense, i.e., putting ideas to work" (p. 73).

Organizational innovation has been referred to as the successful implementation of creative ideas within the organization (Amabile, 1988).

The generation of ideas is often considered a creative act. Yet, it is one-step thinking when time is spent conceiving ideas, but nothing is done to make them a reality. This inability to put a decision into practice may be due to a lack of awareness regarding the organizational and political pressures needed to implement an idea successfully. The inability to implement a solution may also be due to a lack of substantive facts. In cases in which all the necessary facts have been compiled, a failure to implement a solution is more likely an inability to plan the tactics necessary for selling the ideas to others. That is, individuals are not aware of how to make their ideas acceptable.

Implementation Planning

When business firms have a product to sell, their salespeople persuade or condition the consumer to buy it. A sale is always made in the mind of the buyer. Most books on persuasive communication in business do not confine themselves to the field of marketing. They stress that all managers, regardless of their profession, should be consumer oriented (Tillman and Kirkpatrick, 1972). Leisure service agencies provide programs or a service offered and delivered to consumers, much the same as any commercial product. Textbooks and other materials from marketing, business administration, advertising, and communications can be extremely relevant to leisure service professionals.

Before an idea can be implemented, tactics must be planned to achieve the objective. One or several of these tactics can be combined as a strategy for implementation. Whether the idea is simple or novel, planning and thinking about how an idea will be carried out is crucial to successful idea implementation. The implementation of tactics usually requires several steps:

1.   Informing others
2.   Persuading others
3.   Convincing others
4.   Fighting resistance to change
5.   Anticipating all blocks to acceptance of the idea.

Once an idea has been selected, it is necessary to plan the presentation of the idea carefully. If approval for the idea is pushed through without considering the attitudes of others involved in the problem, unnecessary barriers are likely to be encountered. The question to be answered is: How can we sell the idea to the staff, community, and the leisure service agency board of directors? As mentioned previously, the word "sell" is used intentionally, for this is precisely what must be done, especially if there is likely to be any resistance to the idea. Selling is suggested not as deception or pressure, but as enthusiasm for and knowledge of the "product" and the desire to sell it to others.

Recent research findings on persuasion can be compressed into four guiding principles (Cutlip, Center & Broom, 1985).

1.   *Identification Principle.* People will ignore an idea, an opinion, or a point of view unless they can clearly see how it affects their personal fears, desires, hopes or aspirations. The implication is that the message must be stated in terms of the self-interest of the audience.

2.   *Action Principle.* People seldom embrace ideas that are separated from action. The immediacy of the action to be taken contributes to the idea's perceived merit. The implication of this principle is that people tend to shrug off appeals to do things unless a means of action is provided.

3.   *Principle of Familiarity and Trust.* People endorse ideas only when they are presented by individuals that are regarded as credible. Without confidence in the presenter or institution, the audience will not be likely to listen to, or believe the message.

4.   *Clarity Principle.* The situation must be presented clearly and without any confusion. What is observed, read, or heard that produces impressions in the audience must be clear and not subject to several interpretations. Individuals tend to see things as either black or white. For communication to be effective, words, symbols, and stereotypes should be employed that the audience comprehends and is responsive to.

Illustration 12-1 summarizes, in model form, the steps in obtaining support for an idea that may result in the solution of a problem. As is evident, it is not a simple matter.

Figure 12-1

Establishing a Climate for Idea Acceptance

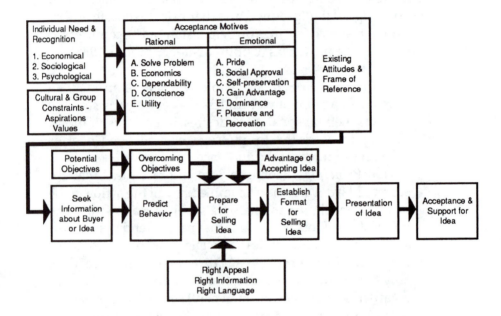

If the initial analysis of all the persons and factors in the problem situation has been thorough, the implementation of the plan will be greatly facilitated. For instance, whatever information we obtained earlier about staff, community, or board needs and expectations can be reexamined for use in planning the implementation.

As shown in Figure 12-1, individual needs or desires can be economic, sociological, or psychological. These needs can pertain to, among other things, job security, cultural pressures, or attitudes and beliefs in conflict with the proposed solution.

These needs must be anticipated and fulfilled, or countered in some way. Ignoring them will only hinder the attempts at idea implementation. There is no way to avoid personal and cultural blocks when planning to carry out an idea. In fact, these blocks could be most powerful at this phase, because a change is being sought. Any block encountered may have the power to derail or stop the implementation of the plan, whereas before it may have been merely annoying or frustrating. It is often necessary to apply political skill in order to circumvent or mitigate these blocks. Ultimately, blocks must be anticipated and preparation undertaken to alleviate their potential impact.

Objections to Ideas

There can be numerous types of objections to any new idea, the most common of which can be referred to as the "negative eleven":

The Negative Eleven

Causes of Negative Responses:

1. Idea costs too much (actual situation)
2. Idea costs too much (perceived)
3. Unable to make decision (sense of urgency not created)
4. Fear of making wrong decision (inadequate presentation or weak closing)
5. Client dissatisfied with idea (poor presentation)
6. Idea not practical (poor background and analysis of problem)
7. Idea not practical (poor presentation - failure to handle objections)
8. Strongly committed to own idea (lack of knowledge about new idea)
9. Did not properly process the idea (poor planning)
10. Cannot commit to future action (poor presentation - urgency not created)
11. Client not convinced of idea value (Lack of study on motivations)

As indicated in Figure 12-2, an individual's objections to any concept can be based on a variety of frames of reference. The information that serves as the foundation of their objections can be rational or emotional, organizational or individual. Problem solvers can respond to these facets by attacking them, evading or retreating from them, agreeing with them, submitting to them, or negotiating with them. One of these responses is required when encountering the objections of those involved in the problem solution.

Figure 12-2

Frames of Reference

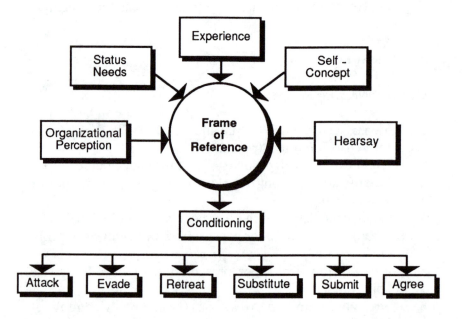

From: F. Russel, F. Beach, & R. Buskirk, Textbook of Salesmanship, New York: McGraw-Hill, 1974. p.113.

The best way to meet such objections is to anticipate another's objections, and to address them fully within the implementation plan. When an idea is presented to the staff, the community or board, it is important to include answers to possible objections as part of the presentation. This will achieve more than ignoring the objections or hoping they will not arise. Many of the likely objections to an idea should be understood, and dealt with, in advance.

Preparation is necessary in the identification of possible objections. Listing every conceivable objection to the idea before it is presented is essential to its implementation. The presenters should determine the most advantageous appeal for the audience, provide correct, persuasive information, and frame it in the appropriate language.

The problem solvers should ask themselves the questions, What information will be required to translate this idea into one that fulfills the identifiable needs of the audience? What words and phrases should be used to communicate so that the 'buyer' will understand the idea? The best methods of handling objections include:

- agreeing with the criticism, and then turning the objection into a selling point,
- requesting the reason for the objection,
- admitting the objection is valid, and
- denying the objection by countering it with facts.

Once all the different objections to the proposed problem solution have been considered, the next step is to establish specific, concrete objectives for implementation. At this point, it is necessary to identify all variables that must be incorporated into a step-by-step implementation plan. Specific objectives for securing implementation should be formulated and documented. The problem solvers should prepare for a compromise in the implementation plan, should one become necessary. This willingness to compromise on implementation objectives differs from the previous discussion of establishing objectives. We were not willing then to modify our problem-solving objectives. These objectives would remain constant regardless of the means specified for their attainment. At this point, the problem solvers are willing to compromise on how or when they will carry out the idea, but not with the need to solve the problem itself.

If the discussion of objections gets bogged down, the problem solvers may consider assigning the matter to a study committee for further investigation or to present additional information at a specified later meeting. The policy-making authority should be informed if resistance is encountered, of the other supplementary objectives that have been formulated. If the problem solvers offer the option of assigning this idea to additional study; it is important that the policy-making authority arrive at that decision. If the policy-making authority recommends solutions other than those proposed, the problem solvers may not be prepared to meet them. All that can be done by problem solvers in such a situation is to be honest about their reactions and request additional time to review the other solution. It is important to realize that the alternative being proposed may be a better solution, and resistance should not stem from the idea originating from outside the professional staff. What should be resisted is rejecting the idea outright, without substantive objections to the solution. Hard feelings and embarrassment can be averted by giving solutions a courteous and considered appraisal, and by including representatives of all stakeholders from the beginning of the process as previously suggested.

To return to the analogy between presenting the problem-solving solution and selling, the proposed solution is vying with competitive products. The competitive products would be the other solutions considered, or any offered when the solution is presented. When the problem solvers introduce their idea to the policy makers, they should summarize the other concepts that have been rejected and explain why. Many of the objections that may arise can be deterred by a summary of the other solutions' drawbacks. If the presenters are comprehensive, yet brief in their summary of the shortcomings of the other products, they can move closer to making a sale.

Selling tips that can be useful in selling an idea include:

- Make the advantages of the product obvious to the purchaser.
- Satisfy the needs of those who should benefit from the solution.

- Indicate the economy of the idea vis-a-vis other solutions or no solution at all.
- Appeal to the ethical or moral concerns of those involved by showing how well funds would be allocated for this idea.
- Enlist the support of those already in favor of the idea when presenting it.
- Use audiovisual or other aids for selling the concept.
- Make the change acceptable to all concerned.
- Be convinced of your own decision before selling it to others.
- Back up your decision with research.

Besides anticipating objections, the timeliness of presenting an idea to the policy-making authority must be considered. For instance, if the policy-making authority is short of funds or near the end of the fiscal year, it may be best to wait until a new fiscal year begins. Or if advance notice for appropriations is mandatory, it may be wise to present the budget request near the end of a fiscal year, when projects are reviewed and surplus funds are pooled, rather than earlier in the year.

The problem solvers must be aware of the other concerns of the policy-making authority, and how the request fits in with the budget and policy concerns. More than likely, they will have other equally pressing problems to handle. The problem solvers should not overemphasize their request for time and money. If they neglect to acknowledge the policy-making authorities' preoccupation with other business, they might end up with nothing.

One can readily see why most of the work in strategies for implementation is done before submitting the idea for consideration. This is perhaps the most intense, behind-the-scenes preparation in the entire model. The problem solvers have to be alert to as many contingencies as possible to meet them effectively. This preparation indicates to others that the idea and its successful implementation has been given a great deal of thought. Enthusiasm alone will not suffice, although it is essential. The problem solvers should thoroughly understand the idea that is being suggested, why it was suggested, how objections to it can be countered and resolved, and how they intend to carry it out in the community. Without this preparation, they might come off as a tricky salesperson trying to sell a poor product to the seemingly uninformed.

The Presentation Strategy

There are also several obstacles to selling that suggest specific actions to avoid when making a presentation:

- Do not criticize those who object to the idea.
- Do not get over-excited.
- Do not be emotional in presenting the idea if the group becomes antagonistic or resistant.
- Do not debate the idea—sell it.
- Do not distort the value and impact of the solution. Be realistic about what it can achieve.
- Be ready to compromise on the implementation of objectives.
- Avoid empire building by the leisure service agency.
- Avoid pushing for approval—be willing to wait.

The kind of presentation designed should be reflective of the intended audience. One presentation method could be oral communication. However, when more detailed background information is required, a written report may be developed. The report could utilize the basic problem-solving model, reporting on the analysis of the problem, closing with the suggestions for addressing the problem, and finally, implementation strategies. A written report requires clarification of thinking. In addition, many of the questions will be addressed in the report itself. The report could also be utilized as a reference document to complement the presentation.

A written report using the problem-solving model could be outlined as follows:

I. Problem Situation and Background (a discussion comparable to that presented in a case study)
II. Problem Definition (what the problem is believed to be)
III. Problem Objectives (what is hoped to be achieved by implementing this idea)

IV. Barriers to Implementation (a tactful discussion of the more likely objections to be raised)

V. Other Implementations (various tactics for carrying out the idea can be listed)

VI. Selected Implementation (a discussion of why a particular strategy for implementation has been chosen)

VII. Decision (a request for what is wanted from the group, e.g., funding)

VIII. Implementation (what action is planned if the idea is approved)

Whatever report style is utilized; written or verbal, detailed or summarized, it can be complemented with illustrations, graphs, films, statements from constituents, statistics, and other support material.

Many ideas are rejected because they are weak. Such judgment of even a cherished solution must be anticipated. Someone other than the problem solvers may be better able to judge whether an idea is appropriate and has value or worth. The problem solvers must be able to drop the idea or hold it for another time when it might be more acceptable to those who must be convinced. The proponents of a plan must know when to stop trying to sell a solution. There is little to be gained from being persistent with a group that will not be persuaded. It will only cause bad feelings and antagonism, which may impede later presentations of other ideas.

If the problem solvers' idea is accepted, a final implementation strategy for the plan must be developed. According to Parnes (1963), the following questions should be addressed in the implementation strategy:

1. What are the various ways the idea could be implemented?
2. Who should do each one?
3. Where should it be done?
4. Where is the best place to do it?
5. How should it be done?

Conclusion

It should be remembered that many ideas fail not because a concept is weak, but because the manner in which they are presented is poor. For example, it will never be known how many bond issues have failed because of lack of forethought, publicity, or planning by those responsible for the bond proposal. The same criticism applies to projects to attract federal and state funds for local recreation projects. Many of the challenges that face leisure service professionals require creative thinking and anticipation of the difficulties that have to be faced when an idea must be carried out. More and better planning by recreation personnel can yield not only better ideas but also more effective implementation and successful solutions to the problems facing the field of leisure services.

Bibliography

Amabile, T. M. (1988). A model of creativity and innovation in organizations. In B. M. Staw and L. L. Cummings (eds) *Research in organizational behavior*, vol 10, 123-167.

Cutlip, S. M., Center, A. H., & Broom, G. M. (1985). *Effective public relations*, (6th edition). Englewood Cliffs, NJ: Prentice-Hall.

Leavitt, T. (1963). Creativity is not enough. *Harvard Business Review*, May-June, 72-83.

Parnes, S. J. (1963). *Student workbook for creative problem solving courses and institutes*. Buffalo, NY: University Bookstore.

Tillman, R. & Kirkpatrick, C. A. (1972). *Promotion: Persuasive communication in marketing*. Homewood, IL: Irwin.

INTRODUCTION TO PART III

Part III of the third edition presents seventy-five new case studies that represent the contemporary problems facing leisure service professionals. Because individuals work in various kinds and sizes of organizations, we chose cases that represent problems in administration, programming, personnel, finance, public relations, human relations, the environment, youth at risk, public policy, and facility management. The case studies allow the student and the practitioner to gain a better understanding of the difficulties in applying concepts and principles to solving operational problems. They also will give the student an opportunity to apply the problem-solving model discussed in Part II. The case study method lends reality to the study of leisure service management, improves analytical ability, and increases the potential for learning.

At the end of each case is a list of questions designed to provoke interest in and discussion of problems mentioned in the case. It is not suggested that these are the only questions related to the case; each student may perceive the case in a different way. A list of key words and phrases has been suggested to assist the student and instructor in their search for information pertaining to the case studies. These references represent only a partial listing; a complete listing would be considered a "never-ending" project. The case studies are based on actual experience, and thus are incidents that must be faced by recreation and park professionals. The cases have been drawn from many sources: from practitioners and students in the field of leisure services who have willingly shared their experiences, and from many newspaper accounts of stories related to the field. All names are disguised to avoid identification of organizations and individuals.

We wish to express thanks to the many administrators, supervisors, leaders, friends, and students who have contributed to this section of the book. Without their assistance, these cases could not have been included.

The cases in the first edition were numbered 0-100, the second edition cases were numbered 101-200, and these cases are therefore numbered 201-300.

201
Building the Ideal Boys' Club

Situation

Over the past decade, the directors, board members, and friends of the Boys' Club have spent considerable time, money, and energy pursuing the goal of building the "ideal boys' club." This extraordinary effort has been justified not only in terms of the obvious needs in the community, but also in the belief that their success could and would serve as an inspirational model for other boys' clubs to follow. To a great extent, the club has attained its goal of providing the "ideal club" when applying the criteria of success used within the boys' club system. On the other hand, it is clear that the club has not provided a "model" widely embraced by other boys' clubs in the metropolitan area.

The club is surrounded by one of the most complex diversified neighborhoods in the city. It is frequently referred to as a major melting pot of social, cultural, economic, ethnic, and racial conglomerations. It is similar to, but unlike, any other neighborhood of its size in the city of Chicago.

The club is a well-equipped modern facility, which has the outward appearance of a bank or medical building. It is a well-financed organization with the largest budget of any boys' club in the city. Although most of the board members of the organization live outside of the neighborhood, many have their places of business in the area. For the most part, these are men who are very influential leaders; they not only contribute large sums of money toward the financial support of the club, but they also take a serious interest in the problems of the community.

The present and former directors of the club must also be considered key elements in the organization. Although both men are highly skilled boys' club workers, their greatest strength is in their charismatic personalities. They have been successful in getting many people to follow them even when there is frequent disagreement with their methods. Also both men have been generally successful in maintaining continuity in staff over the years and this has contributed to the steady growth of the organization.

Another strength of this club has been the ability of the professional staff to maintain personal interest and concern for individual boys while conducting mass recreational programs. Sometimes, however, this individual interest in the boys is carried to the extent that the workers begin seeing themselves as counselors or "therapists." Although they seem to perform the role of counselor well, the time demands required to adequately perform their roles have a deleterious effect upon their other roles. Consequently, they do not have sufficient time to devote to the supervision of part-time employees and junior staff. This tends to contribute to a general deterioration in the quality of recreation programs, and low staff morale.

Some of the things that have been pointed out as strengths of the club might also be considered weaknesses. For example, the increased emphasis on developing the "ideal club" has resulted in the displacement of some goals considered primary in terms of boys' club philosophy. This has resulted in the downgrading of importance of the recreational programs in the club and has tended to subvert the democratic social group work principles upon which boys' club leadership is usually based.

As the club has become more like a comprehensive caretaking service agency, the staff has tended to move more toward professionalism and the structure of the organization has become more rigid and formal. Regimentation has resulted in increased emphasis on conformity. Children have less involvement in the decision-making process, which affects their interest in the life of the club.

As the club director became more aware of the problems the club was facing, he tended to become more autocratic in his style of leadership. The more autocratic the director, the less his subordinates are able to make decisions that might improve the situation at the program level. Their frustrations have led to job dissatisfaction and some staff departures. Even though this club has all the outward appearances of success, there are some early signs of organizational deterioration.

Problem

The club is showing major signs of organizational deterioration. Recreation programs are no longer as much fun as they once were. Staff roles are conflicted between recreation and counseling. Three of the five professional staff members have quit to take other jobs in the boys' club system. Community support is decreasing. The club director is fired by the board of directors and you are hired as the new administrator to come into this situation and bring it back to its former position. How would you proceed to improve the situation?

Suggested Key Words and Phrases for
Literature Search for Case 201

Autocratic management	Board
Boys' club	Community center
Democratic management	Job analysis
Job design	Job enrichment
Morale	Motivation

Selected References for Case 201

Elizur, D. (1987). *Systematic job evaluation and comparable worth.* Brookfield, VT: Gower.

Hampton, D., Sumner, C., and Webber, R. (1987). *Organizational behavior and the practice of management.* Fifth ed. Glenview, IL: Scott, Foresman.

Herman, R., and Til, J., (eds.) (1989). *Nonprofit board of directors: Analyses and applications.* New Brunswick, NJ: Transaction.

Huntington, S. (1985). *Planning a community center.* Ames, IA: North Central Regional Extension Publications.

Ibrahim, H., Banes, R., and Gerson, G. (1987). *Effective parks and recreation boards and commissioners.* Reston, VA: American Alliance for Health, Physical Education, Recreation, and Dance.

Kleinbeck, U., Quast, H., Thierry, H., and Hacker, H., (eds.) (1990). *Work motivation.* Hillsdale, NJ: Lawrence Erlbaum.

Knights, D., Willmott, H., and Collinson, D. (1985). *Job redesign: Critical perspectives on the labor process.* Brookfield, VT: Gower.

Manese, W. (1988). *Occupational job evaluation: A research-based approach to job classification.* New York: Quorum.

Morf, M. (1986). *Optimizing work performance: A look beyond the bottom line.* New York: Quorum.

Morf, M. (1989). *The work/life dichotomy: Prospects for reintegrating people and jobs.* New York: Quorum.

Nash, M. (1985). *Making people productive.* San Francisco: Jossey-Bass.

Olson, V. (1983). *White collar waste: Gain the productivity edge.* Englewood Cliffs, NJ: Prentice-Hall.

Schappi, J. (1988). *Improving job attendance.* Washington, D.C.: Bureau of National Affairs.

Stoops, J., and Edginton, C. (1988, April). Needed: Effective park and recreation boards and commissions. *Parks and Recreation*, 51-55.

202
Is 26 Percent Representative?

Situation

The Planno Associates have recently completed an attitude, interest and opinion survey in your community, which has a population of 13,000. The purpose of the survey was to determine the scope of opportunities available for use in the community; the kind of recreation activities in which adults and youth participate; the recommendations of adults and youth for additional park facilities and programs; and the sufficiency of programs and facilities according to adults and youth. The method employed to undertake this survey was a systematic random stratified sample of all adults and junior and senior high school students. Questionnaires were delivered to 600 homes and 417 were returned. This represented a 70.16 percent response. A total of 1,000 junior and senior high school student questionnaires were distributed, with 679 returned. This represented a 67.9 percent response.

As a result of the survey, the recreation and park board is submitting to the voters a referendum that will decide whether or not the board will build an indoor-outdoor swimming pool facility. You and the board feel that this issue will get a favorable response, since over 26 percent of those surveyed indicated the desire for such a facility when asked, "What recreation facilities and programs do you feel are needed in the community?" You have been quoted in the newspaper as saying that this 26 percent is a "significant response," and that the citizens will support the construction of a swimming pool.

While attending a public meeting, a number of citizens who are vigorously opposed to the passage of the referendum make the following comments: "It is not possible for only 417 adults and 679 youths to be representative of the entire community." "How do we know that those surveyed came from a cross section of the community?" "The percentage of 26 is not 'significant' and represents only a few people in the community." "It is impossible to get a representative sample." "If the 26 percent were a fair reading of community support, they still represent a resoundingly unimpressive minority."

Problem

What is a systematic random stratified sample? Is it possible to get a representative sample? Is a percentage of 26 significant in predicting the community interest for the construction of a swimming pool? Did Planno Associates give everyone in the community an opportunity to fill out the questionnaires? Is the percentage of 70.16 for adults and 67.9 for youth a high or low return? What is the normal return in surveys such as the one conducted in your community? What would be the best way for you to explain to the community the meaning and interpretation of the survey figures? Write a press release that might provide clarification to the questions raised at the public meeting.

Suggested Key Words and Phrases for
Literature Search for Case 202

Behavioral research   Needs survey
Probability   Research vs. practical
Research methods   Sample
Sampling technique   Significance level
Social research   Survey research
Systematic random
  stratified sample

Selected References for Case Study 202

Baker, T. (1988). *Doing social research.* New York: McGraw-Hill.

In Bell, C., and Roberts, H., (eds.) (1984). *Social researching: Politics, problems, practice.* London: Routledge and Kegan Paul.

Berdie, D., Anderson, J., and Niebuhr, M. (1986). *Questionnaires: Design and use.* Second ed., Metuchen, NJ: Scarecrow.

deVaus, D. (1986). *Surveys in social research.* London: Allen & Unwin.

Ewert, A. (1986, March). What research doesn't tell the practitioner. *Parks and Recreation,* 46-49.

Hudson, S. (1988). *How to conduct community needs assessment surveys in public parks and recreation.* Columbus, OH: Publishing Horizons.

Johnson, D., Meiller, L., and Summers, G. (1987). *Needs assessment: Theory and methods.* Ames, IA: Iowa State University Press.

Kalton, G. (1983). *Compensating for missing survey data.* Ann Arbor, MI: Institute for Social Research, University of Michigan Press.

Kraus, R., and Allen, L. (1987). *Research and evaluation in recreation, parks, and leisure studies.* Columbus, OH: Publishing Horizons.

Mann, P. (1985). *Methods of social investigation.* Second ed. New York: Blackwell.

McNeill, P. (1985). *Research methods*. London: Tavistock.

Mishler, E. (1986). *Research interviewing: Context and narrative.* Cambridge, MA: Harvard.

Sckaran, U. (1984). *Research methods for managers: A skill-building approach*. New York: Wiley.

Shafer, E., and Moeller, G. (1987, Oct.). Know how to word your questionnaire. *Parks and Recreation*, 48-52.

203
The Special District —Should One be Established?

Situation

You have been director of recreation and parks for the City of Olsenville for five years. During this time, you have found it difficult to get the mayor and council to provide enough funds to offer adequate recreation and park services. The long-range program for land acquisition and development has also suffered because of lack of funds. A number of citizens in the community recognize this deficiency, and have urged the establishment of a special district that would have the power to levy a tax for the purposes of operating and maintaining a recreation and park service. A separate board would be elected, and this board would control the affairs of the special district. The mayor has stated that he will lead the fight against such a district because, "it would saddle us with another taxing body, which once established would be next to impossible to do away with." Furthermore, it is his opinion that this would not only have an immediate effect on the tax structure, but would also cause the mayor and council to lose control of the recreation and park service. He cited examples of two nearby recreation and park districts in which taxes had been collected but whose actual expenditures were not in proportion to the proposed budgets. He also pointed out that other districts had ignored a state law requiring that all expenditures be published and filed annually with the county clerk. One of the councilmen stated that there are already enough tax districts in the community and another one would surely confuse the taxpayers. Another councilman stated that for the past year efforts had been made to educate people concerning the operation of local government, hoping that they would get involved in solving the city's problems. As more special tax districts are established, the more confused people become; therefore, the less interested they are in citizen participation. The League of Women Voters has not taken a position, but encouraged   intensive dialogue among the citizens of Olsenville concerning the issue.

As director of recreation and parks, you have a particular interest in this issue, and you have been asked to express your views.

Problem

Should a special district be established? What are the advantages and disadvantages of a special district? Would it be advisable for you to publicly take a position on this issue? Why? Do special districts tend to confuse people as to government operation? On what basis do you think special districts should be established?

Suggested Key Words and Phrases for
Literature Search for Case 203

Citizen participation	Enabling legislation
Feasibility study	Funding
Land acquisition	Municipal government
Public authorities	Public land
Public relations	Special district

Selected References for Case Study 203

Board of Economic Development, State of Illinois. (1962, Feb.). *Illinois enabling legislation for municipal planning and zoning as amended by the 72nd Illinois General Assembly.* Springfield, IL: Board of Economic Development, State of Illinois.

Culhane, P. (1981). *Public lands politics: Interest group influence on the forest and the bureau of land management.* Baltimore: Johns Hopkins University.

Hawkins, T. (1988, May). Parks: For the people, by the people. *Parks and Recreation*, 39-43.

Haworth, J., (ed.) (1979). *Community involvement and leisure.* London: Lepus.

Kelsey, C., and Gray, H. (1986). *The citizen survey process in parks and recreation.* Reston, VA: American Alliance for Health, Physical Education, Recreation, and Dance.

Klemens, M. (1990, Feb.). Property tax: Hot potato between local and state politicians. *Illinois Issues*, 11-13.

Lewis, Jr., S. (1984). *Taxation for development: Principles and applications.* New York: Oxford.

O'Bama, B. (1988, Aug.-Sept.). Why organize? Problems and promise in the inner city. *Illinois Issues*, 40-42.

Perrenod, V. (1984). *Special districts, special purposes: Fringe governments and urban problems in the Houston area.* College Station, TX: Texas A & M University.

Porter, D., Lin, B., and Peiser, R. (1987). *Special districts: A useful technique for financing infrastructure.* Washington, D.C.: Urban Land Institute.

Stevens, R., and Sherwood, P. (1982). *How to prepare a feasibility study.* Englewood Cliffs, NJ: Prentice-Hall.

Tindell, J. (1987). "Grass Roots" community development of leisure opportunity. In *Current issues in leisure services: Looking ahead in a time of transition.* J. Bannon, ed. Washington, D.C.: International City Management Association, 159-167.

Toalson, R., and Herchenberger, P. (1985). *Developing community support for parks and recreation.* Champaign, IL: Champaign Park District.

Urban Land Institute. (1985). *Working with the community: A developer's guide.* Washington, D.C.: Urban Land Institute.

204
The Tennis Association Monopoly

Situation

For the past eight years, the Owensville Tennis Association has leased a tennis-club complex that includes sixteen tennis courts and a clubhouse with showers, snack bar, and lounge area from the city for one dollar per year. The upkeep and maintenance is the responsibility of the city recreation and park department. In order to use these facilities, residents in the community must pay a membership fee to the tennis association. These fees are retained by the association to employ personnel to supervise the area. The personnel employed are directly responsible to the board of directors of the association. The department of recreation and parks has no jurisdiction over the operation of the tennis association or its program. The president of the association also serves as chairman of the recreation and park advisory board and because of his position he has been able to influence other members of the recreation and park board not to "disturb the administration of the tennis association."

Since you have been on the job as director of recreation and parks only a few months, you have not had the opportunity to review all existing lease agreements. However, while you are attending the Northend Civic Association meeting, a citizen informs you that he attempted to use the tennis-club facilities but was turned away because he would not purchase a membership. He indicated that this was unfair, since these are publicly-owned facilities. He was told by the attendant on duty that he was required to fill out a membership application that would then need approval by the board of directors of the tennis association before he would be permitted to play. In reply, you indicate that you are unfamiliar with the details of the tennis association, but that you will look into the matter.

You immediately contact the chairman of the recreation and park advisory committee and request an opportunity to discuss this situation. Upon hearing your concern, he becomes quite defensive and tells you that the association has operated this way for years and that he can see no reason to change it. He further informs you that he wants the matter dropped and that he does not want you to discuss it with other board members. You tell him that the present operation of the tennis association is not in the best interest of all the citizens in the community, and that you feel obligated to make your views known to the board at its next meeting. He informs you that if you are wise, you will not bring this to the attention of the board and if you do, there will be repercussions.

Problem

What should be the policy regarding the leasing of public facilities to private groups? Will you bring it up to the board? Is it acceptable to charge a membership fee for the use of the facilities? Under what conditions is it acceptable? If you decide to bring this situation to the attention of the board, what strategy will you use? Would you discuss this situation with the mayor and council before you bring it to the attention of your board? Would you attempt to get public support for your position? If so, how would you do it?

Suggested Key Words and Phrases for Literature Search for Case 204

Advisory council	Charges
Leases	Membership fee
Private groups	Public facilities
Revenue facilities	

Selected References for Case Study 204

Bierman, Jr., H. (1982). *The lease versus buy decision.* Englewood Cliffs, NJ: Prentice-Hall.

Bovaird, A., Tricker, M., and Stoakes, R. (1984). *Recreation management and pricing: The effect of charging policy on demand at countryside recreation sites.* Brookfield, VT: Gower.

Crompton, J. (1987). How to establish a price for park and recreation services. In *Current issues in leisure services: Looking ahead in a time of transition.* J. Bannon, (ed.) Washington, D.C.: International City Management Association, 93-107.

Crossley, J. (1986). *Public/Commercial cooperation in parks and recreation.* Columbus, OH: Publishing Horizons.

DeHoog, R. (1984). *Contracting out for human services: Economic, political, and organizational perspectives.* Albany, NY: State University of New York Press.

Fitchard, R., and Hindelang, T. (1980). *The lease/buy decision.* New York: AMACOM.

Greenberg, B. (1988, May). Contract management can help your golf course. *Parks and Recreation*, 28-30, 59.

Hatry, H. (1983). *A review of private approaches for delivery of public services.* Washington, D.C.: Urban Institute.

Herman, R., and Til, J., (eds.) (1989). *Nonprofit board of directors: Analyses and applications.* New Brunswick, NJ: Transaction.

Herst, A. (1984). *Lease or purchase: Theory and practice.* Boston: Kluwer-Nijhoff.

Heydt, M. (1986, Feb.). Ten principles for contract administration. *Parks and Recreation*, 48, 51.

Hipps, S. (1990, March). Partners in profit. *The Leisure Manager*, 14-18.

Ibrahim, H., Banes, R., and Gerson, G. (1987). *Effective parks and recreation boards and commissioners.* Reston, VA: American Alliance for Health, Physical Education, Recreation, and Dance.

Marlin, J. (1984). *Contracting municipal services: A guide for purchases from the private sector.* New York: Wiley.

McMullen, J. (1987, Dec.). Public recreation managers on thin ice: Maintaining a professional image. *Parks and Recreation*, 56-61.

Moore, B., (ed.) (1983). *The entrepreneur in local government.* Washington, D.C.: International City Management Association.

More municipal public fee courses as golf boom continues in '90s. (1990, June). *Park Maintenance and Grounds Management*, 3.

National Center for Policy Analysis. (1985). *Privatization in the U.S.: Cities and counties.* Dallas: National Center for Policy Analysis.

Stoops, J., and Edginton, C. (1988, April). Needed: Effective park and recreation boards and commissions. *Parks and Recreation*, 51-55.

Walters, J. (1987). Fees and charges: Underutilized revenues. In *Current issues in leisure services: Looking ahead in a time of transition.* J. Bannon, (ed.) Washington, D.C.: International City Management Association, 88-92.

Wood, A. (1990, May). Golf and government: A partnership that works. *Parks and Recreation*, 48-51.

205
Hiring the Architect

Situation

As a result of a recently passed bond issue, the recreation commission will embark on a major construction program. This program will include the development of three recreation centers, four swimming pools, and twenty-five tennis courts at a cost of $3 million. Naturally, the commission is interested in securing the services of a qualified architect to plan and design these new facilities. The board asks that you determine the top three architectural firms in the state and recommend one for their consideration.

As a member of the state recreation society, you contact a number of your colleagues to get the benefit of their experience. One of your board members, John Snyder, is also interested in giving you advice. He has indicated that the firm of Brown and Son has done an outstanding job for other recreation commissions, and their firm is well qualified to do your project. He also mentioned that the owner is his personal friend, and he has been informed that if Brown and Son are awarded the contract, a substantial gift will be forthcoming to the recreation commission. Other board members are not aware of this information. Mr. Snyder has put a great deal of pressure on you to hire Brown and Son.

Since you feel that this decision is extremely important and one that could mean the success or failure of the construction program, you decide to conduct a survey of recreation commissions throughout the state concerning the competing three firms that have been suggested. Over forty recreation commissions are contacted and a 100 percent return is received. The following are the results of the survey.

Concern	Brown and Son		Olympic, Inc.		Walker	
	Accept-able	Unaccept-able	Accept-able	Unaccept-able	Accept-able	Unaccept-able
Original design	22	18	20	20	16	24
Cost of service	16	24	23	17	19	21
Reliability of project estimates	19	21	15	25	23	17
Ability to work with contractors	21	19	20	20	17	23
Ability to work with boards	16	24	22	18	18	22
Supervision of project	23	17	15	25	16	24
Completion of deadline	24	16	17	23	23	17
Efficiency of design	18	22	23	17	19	21
Qualified personnel	17	23	22	18	21	19
Overall evaluation	18	22	20	20	21	19

Problem

What firm would you recommend to the recreation commission? How would you handle Mr. Snyder? Would you tell the other board members about Mr. Snyder's remarks? What is the most efficient way to select an architect? What other information would you have included in the survey?

Suggested Key Words and Phrases for
Literature Search for Case 205

Bidding   Board of directors
Conflict of interest   Consultant

Ethics   Gifts
Kickback   Networking
Survey

Selected References for Case Study 205

Allen, G., Bastaiani, J., Martin, I., and Richards, J., (eds.) (1987). *Community education: An agenda for educational reform.* Philadelphia: Open University.
Bar-El, R., Bendavid, A., and Karaska, G. (1988). *Patterns of change in developing rural regions.* Boulder, CO: Westview.
Board of Economic Development, State of Illinois. (1962, Feb.). *Illinois enabling legislation for municipal planning and zoning as amended by the 72nd Illinois General Assembly.* Springfield, IL: Board of Economic Development, State of Illinois.
Bradley, T., and Lowe, P. (1984). *Locality and rurality: Economy and society in rural regions.* Norwich, England: Geo.
Browne, W., and Hadwiger, D. (1982). *Rural policy problems: Changing dimensions.* Lexington, MA: Lexington.
Cloke, P. (1988). *Policies and plans for rural people: An international perspective.* London: Unwin Hyman.
Davis, D., (ed.) (1981). *Communities and their schools.* New York: McGraw-Hill.
Hawkins, T. (1988, May). Parks: For the people, by the people. *Parks and Recreation*, 39-43.
Haworth, J., (ed.) (1979). *Community involvement and leisure.* London: Lepus.
Hudson, S. (1988). *How to conduct community needs assessment surveys in public parks and recreation.* Columbus, OH: Publishing Horizons.
Johnson, D., Meiller, L., and Summers, G. (1987). *Needs assessment: Theory and methods.* Ames, IA: Iowa State University.
Kamberg, M. (1989, Sept.) *The three R's in Overland Park, KS: Reading, 'riting, and recreation*, 92-93.
Kelsey, C., and Gray, H. (1986). *The citizen survey process in parks and recreation.* Reston, VA: American Alliance for Health, Physical Education, Recreation, and Dance.
Lewis, A. (1986). *Partnerships connecting school and community.* Arlington, VA: American Association of School Administrators.

Long, P. (1989, Sept.). Reaching rural communities with recreation. *Parks and Recreation*, 82-86.

Mulford, C. (1984). *Interorganizational relations: Implications for community development*. New York: Human Sciences.

Potter, E., (ed.) (1986). *Employee selection: Legal and practical alternatives to compliance and litigation*. Second ed. Washington, D.C.: National Foundation for the Study of Equal Employment Policy.

Russell, C., and Nicholson, N. (1982). Public choice and rural development. Washington, D.C.: Resources for the future.

Shelby, B., and Heberlein, T. (1986). *Carrying capacity in recreation settings*. Corvallis, OR: Oregon State University.

Stevens, R., and Sherwood, P. (1982). *How to prepare a feasibility study*. Englewood Cliffs, NJ: Prentice-Hall.

Tindell, J. (1987). "Grass Roots" community development of leisure opportunity. In *Current issues in leisure services: Looking ahead in a time of transition*. J. Bannon, (ed.) Washington, D.C.: International City Management Association, 159-167.

Tobin, G., and Peacock, T. (1981). *Problems and issues in comprehensive planning for a small community: The case of Soldier's Grove, Wisconsin*. Iowa City, Iowa: Institute of Urban and Regional Planning, University of Iowa at Iowa City.

206
What Kind of a Program for Downsville?

Situation

You are presently serving as a state recreation and park consultant. You have just received a request from the community of Downsville (population 31,500) asking that you assist the city's recreation committee in improving recreation opportunities. Downsville is located in the west central part of the state. It is the center of an agricultural area about forty miles in diameter. The economy of the area is generated in three main areas: agriculture, manufacturing, and retailing. The annual median family income is $8,000. About 20 percent of the population is black. Below is a chart describing the population.

Age	1970	Percentage	1980	Percentage
Under 5	4,171	9.7	4,770	9.7
5-19	11,200	26.0	12,340	25.0
20-44	13,000	30.3	16,990	34.6
45-64	8,753	20.4	8,957	18.3
65 +	5,867	13.6	6,103	12.4

Downsville founders were conscious of the need for open space and planned Laken Park and Woodworth Park in the original layout of the community. Realizing the need to maintain these park areas, Downsville citizens created the post of park director nearly fifty years ago. During this 50-year period, eleven new parks were established and park acreage increased from 10 acres to 690 acres. Other facilities in the city of Downsville include:

1. Municipal indoor swimming pool operated jointly by the city and the Y.M.C.A.
2. Lake Sagamore and Lake Vinton—these are two country clubs owned by the railroad. The man-made lakes serve a large segment of the Downsville population.
3. Camp WA-NO-ME—this area is also owned by the railroad and is located across from Lake Sagamore. It is the only resident camp within twenty miles of Downsville. The camp provides an area in which school camping could be established. All buildings would need to be winterized.
4. Sun Lake—this is a small private lake built by Sun Products for its employees. The area boasts family picnicking, swimming, and playground facilities. However, presently only sixty residents of Downsville have access to it.
5. Rainbow Swim and Tennis Club—this facility is located on the south side of the community and is only open to members. Approximately 400 families pay a fee of $300 per year to use this facility.
6. Rod and Gun Club—this facility is located on ten acres of undeveloped land two miles outside the city limits.

7.   Downsville Country Club—this area provides an 18-hole golf course, tennis courts, and a swimming pool for its members. Family membership fees are $1,200 per year. This club serves only a very few of the citizens of Downsville.
8.   School facilities located in Downsville are ten elementary schools, two junior high schools and one high school.

At present the city provides no funds for conducting a recreation program. The Downsville Citizens' Recreation Committee is very concerned about this and has asked you to assist in organizing a program that might be proposed to the mayor and council for funding.

Problem

What kind of a program would you recommend for the citizens of Downsville? How would you assess the needs of the community? Does the population chart reveal any significant characteristics that would be helpful in planning the program? What kind of relationship should be developed with the schools? Do you think the school facilities would provide good playground locations? What kind of staff would be required to implement your program? Would it be possible to apply for federal grants that would assist in implementing the program? What would be the total cost of implementing the recommended program? What state enabling legislation would you recommend for administering the program? How would you involve the citizens in the planning of the program? Is citizen involvement important? To what extent would you allow the citizens to become involved in the decision-making process? Be specific. What additional information would be helpful in solving this problem?

Suggested Key Words and Phrases for
Literature Search for Case 206

Citizen involvement   Enabling legislation
Feasibility study   Needs assessment
Planning   Public-private relations

Rural community   Rural development
Rural recreation   School relations
Staffing

Selected References for Case Study 206

Allen, G., Bastaiani, J., Martin, I., and Richards, J., (eds.) (1987). *Community education: An agenda for educational reform.* Philadelphia: Open University.

Bar-El, R., Bendavid, A., and Karaska, G. (1988). *Patterns of change in developing rural regions.* Boulder, CO: Westview.

Board of Economic Development, State of Illinois. (1962, Feb.). *Illinois enabling legislation for municipal planning and zoning as amended by the 72nd Illinois General Assembly.* Springfield, IL: Board of Economic Development, State of Illinois.

Bradley, T., and Lowe, P. (1984). *Locality and rurality: Economy and society in rural regions.* Norwich, England: Geo.

Browne, W., and Hadwiger, D. (1982). *Rural policy problems: Changing dimensions.* Lexington, MA: Lexington.

Cloke, P. (1988). *Policies and plans for rural people: An international perspective.* London: Unwin Hyman.

Davis, D., (ed.) (1981). *Communities and their schools.* New York: McGraw-Hill.

Hawkins, T. (1988, May). Parks: For the people, by the people. *Parks and Recreation, 39-43.*

Haworth, J., (ed.) (1979). *Community involvement and leisure.* London: Lepus.

Hudson, S. (1988). *How to conduct community needs assessment surveys in public parks and recreation.* Columbus, OH: Publishing Horizons.

Johnson, D., Meiller, L., and Summers, G. (1987). *Needs assessment: Theory and methods.* Ames, IA: Iowa State University.

Kamberg, M. (1989, Sept.) *The three R's in Overland Park, KS: Reading, 'riting, and recreation, 92-93.*

Kelsey, C., and Gray, H. (1986). *The citizen survey process in parks and recreation.* Reston, VA: American Alliance for Health, Physical Education, Recreation, and Dance.

Lewis, A. (1986). *Partnerships connecting school and community.* Arlington, VA: American Association of School Administrators.

Long, P. (1989, Sept.). Reaching rural communities with recreation. *Parks and Recreation*, 82-86.

Mulford, C. (1984). *Interorganizational relations: Implications for community development*. New York: Human Sciences.

Potter, E., (ed.) (1986). *Employee selection: Legal and practical alternatives to compliance and litigation*. Second ed. Washington, D.C.: National Foundation for the Study of Equal Employment Policy.

Russell, C., and Nicholson, N. (1982). Public choice and rural development. Washington, D.C.: Resources for the future.

Shelby, B., and Heberlein, T. (1986). *Carrying capacity in recreation settings*. Corvallis, OR: Oregon State University Press.

Stevens, R., and Sherwood, P. (1982). *How to prepare a feasibility study*. Englewood Cliffs, NJ: Prentice-Hall.

Tindell, J. (1987). "Grass Roots" community development of leisure opportunity. In *Current issues in leisure services: Looking ahead in a time of transition*. J. Bannon, (ed.) Washington, D.C.: International City Management Association, 159-167.

Tobin, G., and Peacock, T. (1981). *Problems and issues in comprehensive planning for a small community: The case of Soldier's Grove, Wisconsin*. Iowa City, IA: Institute of Urban and Regional Planning, University of Iowa at Iowa City.

207
A Program for Clearwater, USA

Situation

Clearwater is a community of approximately 8,900 people. Its per capita wealth is relatively high, much of it being derived from the oil industry. The community maintains two small parks, a swimming pool, and it has the usual minimum indoor and outdoor sports and recreation facilities for use by the schools.

During past summers two playgrounds have been operated for school age children, the funds having been provided by the city. Up until recently, through the efforts of the Citizens' League (consisting of representatives from the different civic services and fraternal organizations, and patriotic organizations), a youth center was operated for students of the junior and senior high schools. Due to overcrowding of the schools, facilities formerly used for recreation center purposes were returned to the school board for use as classroom space. Aside from the school program and the boy scout and girl scout activities, there is presently no organized recreation program for young people available in Clearwater.

At a public meeting sponsored by the Citizens' League, most of the discussion revolved around the plans for developing a recreation center. Clearwater is thinking seriously of building two new elementary schools and one junior high school. In this respect proper attention was given to the feasibility of designing the schools so that they could be used by the community as well as for educational purposes. Nevertheless, the league wasn't too optimistic about the chances for using the school buildings for both purposes, particularly because the current population center of the teenage group does not coincide with the suggested location of the new schools, which will mainly serve the elementary school population.

A careful check of existing facilities in the community revealed absolutely no available space, resulting in the serious intentions of the Citizens' League to construct an entirely new center. Land has been deeded to the league upon which a center might be built. It is located adjacent to the present senior high school, not too far from the school's athletic facilities and overlooking the Rankin River. There seems to be little doubt in the community about the possibility to raise as much as $50,000 or perhaps $75,000 to build the center. Many firms and organizations have already agreed to make large contributions in work, materials, or money, and some thought has been given to maintaining and operating the building through contributed funds. The pros and cons of financing the work in this manner as well as the potentials of securing funds through taxation were discussed at great length.

The civic leadership in Clearwater apparently realizes the importance of employing trained leadership to direct the program. At the meeting it was agreed that the following action would be taken:

1.   The Citizens' League representatives would meet with the members of the board of education to consider the possibility of using the new school facilities for recreational purposes.
2.   A committee would be appointed to explore the state enabling legislation for the establishment and operation of a recreation system.

Problem

What state enabling legislation is available that will permit municipalities to establish and operate a recreation and park system? What would be the purpose of meeting with the board of education? How can the civic and fraternal organizations play an effective role in promoting the establishment of a recreation and park system? Should the Citizens' League embark on a fund drive to construct a recreation center? Why? State the pros and cons of financing a facility in this manner. Should the mayor and council play an active role in promoting the recreation and park program? Why? Should a teen center be located on or near school grounds? With the current emphasis on education, is a teen center really necessary? What type of programs should be offered? Who should supervise the program? How can the establishment of a recreation and park agency stretch school tax dollars? Usually only the recreation and park agency benefits from park-school cooperation: how can benefits be equalized?

Suggested Key Words and Phrases for
Literature Search for Case 207

Board of directors	Citizens League
Citizen participation	Civic organization
Community recreation	Enabling legislation
Facility construction	Fraternal organization
Pooled facilities	Recreation center
School facilities	

Selected References for Case Study 207

Allen, G., Bastaiani, J., Martin, I., and Richards, J., (eds.) (1987). *Community education: An agenda for educational reform.* Philadelphia: Open University.

Allen, S. (1979). *Private financing in public parks: A handbook.* Washington, D.C.: Hawkins.

Badmin, P., Coombs. M., and Reyner, G. (1988). *Leisure operational management volume one: Facilities.* Essex, England: Longman.

Board of Economic Development, State of Illinois. (1962, Feb.). *Illinois enabling legislation for municipal planning and zoning as amended by the 72nd Illinois General Assembly.* Springfield, IL: Board of Economic Development, State of Illinois.

Castaldi, B. (1987). *Educational facilities: Planning, modernizing, and management.* Boston: Allyn and Bacon.

Crossley, J. (1986). *Public/Commercial cooperation in parks and recreation.* Columbus, OH: Publishing Horizons.

Crowley, K. (1988, Aug.). Teamwork: Resorts and the forest service. *Parks and Recreation,* 38-40.

Davis, D., (ed.) (1981). *Communities and their schools.* New York: McGraw-Hill.

Evans, T., (ed.) (1984). *Facilities management: A manual for plant administration.* Washington, D.C.: Association of Physical Plant Administrators of Universities and Colleges.

Fogg, G., and Shivers, J. (1981). *Management planning for park and recreation areas.* Arlington, VA: National Recreation and Park Association.

Kamberg, M. (1989, Sept.) *The three R's in Overland Park, KS: Reading, 'riting, and recreation,* 92-93.

Lewis, A. (1986). *Partnerships connecting school and community.* Arlington, VA: American Association of School Administrators.

Mulford, C. (1984). *Interorganizational relations: Implications for community development.* New York: Human Sciences.

Ruffin, Jr., S. (1989). *School-business partnerships: Why not?: Laying the foundation for successful programs.* Reston, VA: National Association of Secondary School Principals.

Williams, M. (1989). *Neighborhood organizing for urban school reform.* New York: Teachers College Press.

208
Is the Union Request Reasonable?

Situation

You are the director of parks and recreation in a city with a population of 120,000 in the southeastern part of the United States. Five years ago, the employees of the department formed Local Union 791 and became affiliated with AFL-CIO—American Federation of State, County, and Municipal Employees. During the past four years, you and the board have been able to negotiate an agreeable contract. However, the demands made by the union this year will be difficult to meet. Due to a large increase in the tax rate for the school building program and because of increased welfare costs, the mayor has restricted all city departments to a 2 percent general increase in budget appropriations. It is your opinion that with this restriction it will be almost impossible to negotiate a contract with the union. You request a meeting with the mayor to discuss the union demands and to work out an equitable agreement. The following are the union demands:

1. That a $60 per month increase in salary for all employees be made. (Note: this represents an 8 percent increase in salaries and would require an overall budget increase of 12 percent. Union officials have indicated that this demand is not negotiable.)
2. That minimum and maximum in all salary classifications be increased by $60.
3. That any employee who is presently not at the maximum of his rate range shall receive an automatic 25 percent salary increase. However, this increase shall not exceed the dollar amount received in request number one.
4. That an employee who is temporarily assigned to a higher-paying classification shall receive the rate of pay of that classification if he works over a four-hour period (Example: a laborer who is temporarily assigned to equipment operation).

5. That no employee shall work on his birthday—if the employee's birthday falls on a Saturday, Sunday, or holiday, then another day shall be substituted.
6. That there shall be a differential of $.20 per hour for any employee who works the night shift.
7. That negotiations for a new agreement shall begin three months prior to the end of the present agreement. (Note: prior to this time negotiations began thirty days before termination of the agreement.)
8. That all employees shall receive two weeks vacation after one year of continuous employment. (Note: present policy: one week vacation upon completing one year of continuous employment.) That all employees receive three weeks vacation after three years of continuous employment. (Note: present policy: two weeks vacation upon completing three years of continuous employment.) That all employees receive four weeks vacation after four years of continuous service. (Note: present policy: three weeks vacation for service of more than three years.)
9. That the probation period for employees shall be three months. (Note: present policy is probation for six months.)
10. That any employee who is dismissed from the department shall have the right to appeal his case directly to the mayor and council. (Note: present policy: any employee who wishes to appeal his dismissal to the mayor and council must request permission in writing from the director of parks and recreation within two weeks after his dismissal.)

Employees covered in this agreement include: mechanic foreman, mechanic, maintenance foreman, maintenance repairmen, gardener, horticulturist, greenskeeper, assistant greenskeeper, equipment operator, operations foreman, forestry foreman, tree trimmer, electrical foreman, electrician, maintenance custodian, and custodian. Office personnel and supervisory personnel are not part of this contract.

Problem

What recommendations would you make to the mayor that might assist in the negotiations with the union? What specific compromises would you suggest? How would you approach the union officials? Do you feel that the requests made by the union are legitimate? In lieu of the present cost of living increase, is the $60 per month for all employees a reasonable request? Discuss the pros and cons of permitting employees to go directly to the mayor and council with their grievances. Should an employee's birthday be declared a holiday for him? What are the present trends regarding vacations? What do you think union officials mean when they say "this request is not negotiable"? What requests do you feel are most negotiable? Why? Develop the plan of action you would use in negotiating this contract with union officials.

Suggested Key Words and Phrases for
Literature Search for Case 208

Collective bargaining	Contract
Grievance procedure	Labor relations
Negotiating	Personnel policies
Probationary period	Public relations
Union demands	Unions
Vacation	

Selected References for Case Study 208

DeMaria, A. (1980). *How management wins union organizing campaigns.* New York: Executive Enterprises.

Dilts, D., and Walsh, W. (1988). *Collective bargaining and impasse resolution in the public sector.* New York: Quorum.

Holley, W., and Jennings, K. (1984). *The labor relations process.* Second ed. Chicago: Dryden.

Kilgour, J. (1981). *Preventive labor relations.* New York: AMACOM.

Kniveton, B. (1989). *The psychology of bargaining.* Hong Kong: Avebury.

Lewin, D., Feuille, P., and Kockan, T. (1981). *Public sector labor relations: Analysis and readings.* Second ed. Sun Lakes, AZ: Horton.

McNally, J. (1989, Feb.). The care and feeding of aquatic personnel. *Parks and Recreation,* 36-40, 80.

Morse, B. (1988). *How to negotiate a labor agreement: An outline summary of tested bargaining practices expanded from earlier editions.* Eleventh ed. San Diego, CA: Trends.

Quinn, C., Hill, T., and Nichols, J. (1982). *Maintaining nonunion status.* Boston: CBI.

Repas, B. (1984). *Contract administration.* Washington, D.C.: Bureau of National Affairs.

Richardson, R. (1985). *Collective bargaining by objectives: A positive approach.* Second ed. Englewood Cliffs, NJ: Prentice-Hall.

Sluane, A., and Witney, F. (1985). *Labor relations.* Fifth ed. Englewood Cliffs, NJ: Prentice-Hall.

Toalson, R., and Herchenberger, P. (1985). *Developing community support for parks and recreation.* Champaign, IL: Champaign Park District.

209
Planning Recreation Facilities

Situation

A city with a population of 100,000 is divided into three large neighborhoods or small districts, each with its own distinctive characteristics and needs. They are known as the North Side, West Side, and South Side areas, respectively. The situation in these areas is as follows:

North Side:
1. Has 36 percent of the existing public recreation areas.
2. Has 25 percent of the city-wide attendance and registration at public recreation centers.

3.   Has the smallest number of voluntary agency programs (Boy Scouts, Girl Scouts, YMCA, and the like) in the city.
4.   Has a fair amount of commercial recreation facilities (bowling alleys, movies, and the like).
5.   Population
       a. Has 31 percent of the population.
       b. Has in proportion to its population the highest percent-age of teenagers.
       c. Has just a handful of minority group families.
6.   Has a high rate of juvenile delinquency.
7.   Has a high economic and employment level.
8.   Has a relatively low illness and mortality rate.

West Side:
1.   Has 34 percent of the existing public recreation areas.
2.   Has 35 percent of the city-wide attendance and registration at public recreation centers.
3.   Has an average number of voluntary agency programs (Boy Scouts, Campfire Girls, YMCA, and the like) in the city.
4.   Has an overabundance of the commercial recreation facilities (bowling alleys, movies, and the like).
5.   Population
       a. Has 33 percent of the population.
       b. Has average number of teenagers.
       c. Has average but increasing number of minority group families.
6.   Has an average rate of juvenile delinquency.
7.   Has a low economic and employment level.
8.   Has a relatively high illness and mortality rate.

South Side:
1.   Has 30 percent of the existing public recreation areas.
2.   Has 40 percent of the city-wide attendance and registration at public recreation centers.
3.   Has the most voluntary agency programs in the city.
4.   Has few commercial recreation facilities.
5.   Population
       a. Has 36 percent of the population.
       b. Has lowest number of teenagers.
       c. Has largest proportion of minority groups.
6.   Has a very low rate of juvenile delinquency.
7.   Has an average economic and employment level.
8.   Has a low illness and mortality rate.

Problem

The city has voted a limited amount of money—sufficient to provide additional public recreation area facilities in only one of the three areas. In which area should the new facilities be placed? What other factors not mentioned here need to be taken into consideration? What recommendations should be made in establishing a long-range recreation facilities plan for this community? What important elements should be kept in mind?

Suggested Key Words and Phrases for
Literature Search for Case 209

Commercial recreation	Comprehensive planning
Construction	Equity
Facility management	Long-range planning
Master plan	Nonprofit organization
Short-range planning	Urban planning
Voluntary agency program	

Selected References for Case Study 209

Adrian, J. (1981). *CM: The construction management process.* Reston, VA: Reston.

Branch, M. (1983). *Comprehensive planning: General theory and principles.* Pacific Palisades, CA: Palisades.

Castaldi, B. (1987). *Educational facilities: Planning, modernizing, and management.* Boston: Allyn and Bacon.

Cook, L., Osterholt, B., and Riley, E., Jr. (1988). *Anticipating tomorrow's issues: A handbook for policymakers.* Washington, D.C. Council of State Policy and Planning Agencies.

Connors, T., (ed.) (1988). *The nonprofit organization handbook.* New York: McGraw-Hill.

Crompton, J. (1987). Are your leisure services distributed equitably? In *Current issues in leisure services: Looking ahead in a time of transition.* J. Bannon, (ed.) Washington, D.C.: International City Management Association, 108-118.

Fogg, G., and Shivers, J. (1981). *Management planning for park and recreation areas.* Arlington, VA: National Recreation and Park Association.

Gold, S. (1987). A human service approach to recreation planning. In *Current issues in leisure services: Looking ahead in a time of transition.* J. Bannon,(ed.) Washington, D.C.: International City Management Association, 5-16.

Hunt, S., and Brooks, K. (1987). A planning model for public recreation agencies. In *Current issues in leisure services: Looking ahead in a time of transition.* J. Bannon, (ed.) Washington, D.C.: International City Management Association, 5-16.

Kelsey, C., and Gray, H. (1985). *Master plan process for parks and recreation.* Reston, VA: American Alliance for Health, Physical Education, Recreation, and Dance.

Kelsey, C., and Gray, H. (1986). *The feasibility study process for parks and recreation.* Reston, VA: American Alliance for Health, Physical Education, Recreation, and Dance.

Mueller, F. (1986). *Integrated cost and schedule control for construction projects.* New York: Van Reinhold.

Tobin, G., ed. (1985). *Social planning and human service delivery in the voluntary sector.* New York: Greenwood.

Tumblin, C. (1980). *Construction cost estimates.* New York: Wiley.

210
Grand Jury Investigates the Park Board

Situation

President of the Park Board Seeley Thompson opened the morning newspaper and read the headline, "Grand Jury to Investigate Park Board." Naturally he was surprised, since he was unaware of any problem with the park board's operations. He immediately called an emergency meeting of the five-man board to discuss the situation.

Mr. Thompson appealed to Howard Cascade, a new board member, for cooperation instead of criticism while the board was trying to get going on a greatly expanded park program. Thompson's remarks came after Cascade reported that he requested the state's attorney general to look into the activities of the board.

In a letter, Cascade told the attorney general that a board member was receiving compensation for conflict of interest. His reference was to payment of $281.20 to Burt Sloan, an attorney and member of the board, for legal services in negotiations for an option on an eighty-acre tract of land west of the city. Sloan performed this service for the board while the regular board attorney was out of town on vacation. Thompson stated, "Sloan helped us out in a tight spot and he certainly did not overcharge us for the service. I don't know why there is any fuss; nobody made any big money on this transaction."

Cascade further said that he asked the attorney general to investigate nine items relative to the park board's activities. They included the following facts:

1. Minutes of board proceedings are very seldom kept.
2. Board equipment and employees have been used for board members' personal gain.
3. Checks are being written before the board meets to approve or disapprove the bills.
4. Board members are receiving compensation for conflict of interest.
5. A board employee has been arrested in another city at 3 a.m. driving a park district truck.
6. The board does not keep a regular book or record of all ordinances.
7. Board funds are in the First National Bank and the Savings Bank; two park board members are presently serving on the board of directors at these banks.
8. The board does not use any formal bidding procedures.
9. Debts are being created without first issuing purchase orders.

Other board members were very upset that Mr. Cascade did not discuss his accusations with the board prior to his writing a letter to the attorney general. However, all of them indicated they would welcome the investigation and would cooperate fully.

Problem

Should Mr. Cascade have discussed his letter with the board prior to sending it to the attorney general? Why do you think Mr. Cascade is requesting an investigation? Do you feel that Burt Sloan has a conflict of interest? Should a board member be permitted to provide a service to the board for which he will receive compensation? What is the state law regarding this? What kind of records should be kept by the park board? Should employees be permitted to use board equipment for their personal use? What procedure should be established to permit the payment of bills? What bidding procedures would you recommend to the park board? Are there any state laws that affect bidding procedures? Recommend a purchase order and voucher system that would adequately facilitate park board business.

Suggested Key Words and Phrases for
Literature Search for Case 210

Bidding procedures	Conflict of interest
Ethics	Equipment policies
Fiscal policies	Inventory control
Ordinances	Purchase orders
Record keeping	

Selected References for Case Study 210

Barlow, C., and Eisen, G. (1983). *Purchasing negotiations*. Boston: CBI.

Burke, J. (1986). *Bureaucratic responsibility*. Baltimore: Johns Hopkins University Press.

Cooper, T. (1984). *The responsible administrator: An approach to ethics for the administrative role*. Third printing. Port Washington, NY: Associated Faculty Press.

Crossley, J. (1990, March). Multi-tier programming in commercial recreation. *Parks and Recreation*, 69-73.

Dearstyne, B. (1988). *The management of local government records: A guide for local officials.* Nashville: American Association for State and Local History.

Heinritz, S., and Farrell, P. (1981). *Purchasing: Principles and application.* Sixth ed. Englewood Cliffs, NJ: Prentice-Hall.

Kaplan, M. (1988). *Acquiring major systems contracts: Bidding methods and winning strategies.* New York: Wiley.

Leenders, M., Fearon, H., and England, W. (1980). *Purchasing and materials management.* Seventh ed. Homewood, IL: Irwin.

Prabhu, V., and Baker, M., (eds.) (1986). *Materials management.* London: McGraw-Hill.

Silver, A., and Peterson, R. (1985). *Decision systems for inventory management and production planning.* Second ed. New York: Wiley.

Tersine, R. (1982). *Principals of inventory and materials management.* Second ed. New York: North-Holland.

Williams, S. (1985). *Conflict of interest: The ethical dilemma in politics.* Brookfield, VT: Gower.

Zenz, G. (1987). *Purchasing and the management of materials.* Sixth ed. New York: Wiley.

211
Should We Hire From Within the Organization?

Situation

The Lincolnshire Park District, which has been in existence for three years, is a suburb of a thriving metropolis in the Midwest. The park district itself has grown larger proportionally than have the surrounding areas. The budget is large, acquisition of land has been increasing, programs are growing at a rapid pace, and development of special facilities and large neighborhood parks has been on the upswing for the past three years. This park district is classified as one of the most aggressive and progressive in the state. The staff organization currently consists of a director of parks and recreation, a superintendent of recreation who has also been assisting the director for three or four years, a supervisor of recreation, and a facilities supervisor who is currently responsible for the indoor tennis facility. The facilities supervisor and the program supervisor report to the superintendent of recreation. There is also a superintendent of parks supervising five full-time maintenance people. (See organization chart below.)

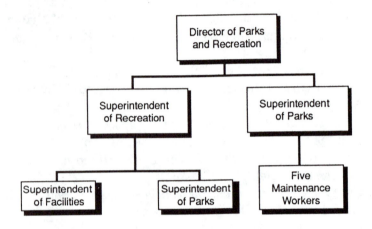

The director of parks and recreation recently announced that he is leaving the Lincolnshire Park District for a new position. He will be leaving in one week. The board of park commissioners has been interviewing for his replacement for some time now. It is their intention to promote the superintendent of recreation to the director of parks and recreation. You, as superintendent of recreation for the past four years, look forward to the new challenges and opportunities with a tremendous amount of enthusiastic spirit and board support.

One of the most important items on your list of goals for the next several weeks is to hold the personnel on a level that will enable you to continue the business of the district as usual. Although you may be short handed, you still have to provide the services expected of a park and recreation department. You have no problems with the superintendent of parks. He was not interested in securing the position of director, and he is fully supporting you in your new endeavors. As superintendent of recreation, you had an astute program supervisor and a capable facilities supervisor.

The key position that now must be filled is that of the superintendent of recreation. Needless to say, you have several thoughts running through your mind. Among them are the following:

1. Should you recruit from outside the park district for the position of superintendent of recreation?;
2. Should you promote the present program supervisor to the position of superintendent or?;
3. Should you promote the facilities supervisor to the superintendent's position?

Both of these supervisors have excellent credentials. You pride yourself on the fact that your recruitment for these two positions was a successful part of your job as superintendent of recreation. Either one would do an admirable job. There is one small problem, however, and that is if you promote one over the other, will the one not promoted remain?

Problem

1. Which move as the new director of parks and recreation would be in the best interest of all concerned in keeping the business of the park district going? What are the affirmative action procedures that must be followed?
2. If you promote someone from within the organization, what are the problems that would ensue?
3. If you recruit and select an individual from the outside, what consequences would that have on dealing with the two supervisors as well as with other personnel?
4. With the current amount of growth of this park district, would a reorganization be worthwhile? You already know that the plans for the district call for additional special facilities such as ice rinks, swimming pools, outdoor tennis courts, indoor handball courts and golf courses. If a reorganization plan is to be developed, how would you justify this to your board of park commissioners and how would you sell this to the rest of your staff?
5. If you promote one supervisor from within and the other leaves, what would be your short-term plan to fill that void?

6.   Are there economic factors that might be considered to help you reach a decision?
7.   If you are going to select someone outside, what qualifications will you be seeking?
8.   Do you feel that as the new director of parks and recreation for the Lincolnshire Park District that this may be one of your most important decisions?

Suggested Key Words and Phrases for
Literature Search for Case 211

Job search   Personnel selection
Personnel assessment center   Personnel policies
Staff relations

Selected References for Case Study 211

Arvey, R., and Faley, R. (1988). *Fairness in selecting employees.* Second ed. Reading, MA: Addison-Wesley.

Cook, M. (1988). *Personnel selection and productivity.* New York: Wiley.

Dreker, G., and Sackett, P. (1983). *Perspectives on employee staffing and selection: Readings and commentary.* Homewood, IL: Irwin.

Grossman, A., (ed.) (1989). *Personnel management in recreation and leisure services.* Second ed. South Plainfield, NJ: Groupwork Today.

Kleiner, M., McLean, R., and Dreber, G. (1988). *Labor markets and human resource management.* Glenview, IL: Scott, Foresman.

Kochan, T., and Barocci, T. (1990). *Human resource management and industrial relations: Text, readings, and cases.* Boston: Little, Brown.

Lewis, C. (1985). *Employee selection.* London: Hutchinson.

McCullock, K. (1981). *Selecting employees safely under the law.* Englewood Cliffs, NJ: Prentice-Hall.

Nigro, F., and Nigro, L. (1981). *The new public personnel administration.* Second ed. Itasca, IL: Peacock.

Smith, M., and Robertson, I., (ed.) (1989). *Advances in selection and assessment.* New York: Wiley.

212
J. Porter Causes Problems in the Maintenance Shop

Situation

J. Porter, sixty-two years old, is currently a mechanic for the Minerva Park and Recreation Department. He has served in this capacity for the last six years. Before his employment with the department, he owned and operated a large garage for thirty years. He was responsible for major repairs to all types of autos and trucks. Attempts were made to hire additional mechanics, but Mr. Porter was so uncooperative and critical of their work that they quit or had to be transferred to other types of work. Mr. Porter feels strongly that the only way a job can be done right is for him to do it himself. These feelings stem from and are reinforced by his many years in private business. His resistance to working with others indicates that he fears being replaced. He is set in his own ways and does not want to do anything differently. He feels that the park and recreation department should be grateful and that he does not have to cooperate with other employees.

Six months ago, the park district moved into a new maintenance shop, at which time two additional mechanics were hired. The repair work was divided into three categories: major repairs, field repairs, and motor repairs. J. Porter was given the primary responsibility for field repairs. The mechanics were instructed to coordinate their work with each other but would receive their instructions for repair priorities and methods from the maintenance supervisor. (See organizational chart.)

J. Porter has refused to coordinate his work with the other mechanics and has chosen to ignore instructions from the maintenance supervisor. Not wishing to share joint responsibility for repair work, he has made complete repairs in the field, or when equipment had to be sent into the shop, he has made no attempt to advise the mechanic in charge of major repairs of the probable cause or reasons for mechanical breakdowns. Furthermore, on days when field repair work was not pressing, he still has made the rounds of the large parks and golf courses. This has angered

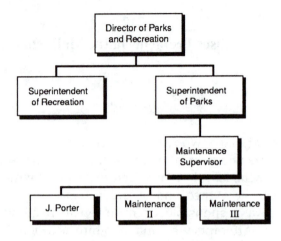

the other mechanics, who felt that he should have been helping them with their duties.

The superintendent of parks has been hesitant to discharge J. Porter because of his many years of service to the department. Even though the working conditions were extremely poor (lack of space, poor lighting, insufficient tools, and so forth) before increasing the maintenance staff, J. Porter still made every effort to complete all repair work promptly. Further, because of his superior mechanical ability, he was able to keep 90 percent of the equipment in operation. The maintenance supervisor often has mentioned the strong bond of friendship between the superintendent of parks and J. Porter.

Problem

How would you deal with J. Porter? Should he be relieved of his responsibilities? How could you involve the other two mechanics in solving this problem? Should the director of recreation and parks become involved in the problem? Superintendent of parks? Maintenance foreman? What effect will this have on the morale of the other employees?

Suggested Key Words and Phrases for
Literature Search for Case 212

Personnel management   Maintenance procedures
Staff coordination   Mechanic

Job satisfaction
Organizational development
New employees
Industrial relations

Employee-employer
    relations
Reorganization
Workers

Selected References for Case Study 212

Coulson, R. (1981). *The termination handbook.* New York: Free.

Culkin, D. (1988, Feb.). The right way to discipline. *Parks and Recreation,* 44-45.

Gambrill, E., and Stein, T. (1983). *Supervision: A decision-making approach.* Beverly Hills, CA: Sage.

Hampton, D., Sumner, C., and Webber, R. (1987). *Organizational behavior and the practice of management.* Fifth ed. Glenview, IL: Scott, Foresman.

Hawkins, P., and Shohet, R. (1989). *Supervision in the helping professions: An individual, group, and organizational approach.* Philadelphia: Open University.

Holloway, S., and Brager, G. (1989). *Supervising in the human services: The politics of practice.* New York: Free.

Holloway, W., and Leech, M. (1985). *Employment termination: Rights and remedies.* Washington, D.C.: Bureau of National Affairs.

Kelly, J. (1982). *Scientific management, job redesign, and work performance.* London: Academic.

Knights, D., Willmott, H., and Collinson, D. (1985). *Job redesign: Critical perspectives on the labour process.* Brookfield, VT: Gower.

Manese, W. (1988). *Occupational job evaluation: A research-based approach to job classification.* New York: Quorum.

McNally, J. (1989, Feb.). The care and feeding of aquatic personnel. *Parks and Recreation,* 36-40, 80.

Miller, K. (1988, Jan.). Can we bridge the gap between managers and workers? *Parks and Recreation,* 46-47.

Nelson, D. (1990, May). Good management practices. *Park Maintenance and Grounds Management,* 17-19.

Redeker, J. (1983). *Discipline: Policies and procedures.* Washington, D.C.: Bureau of National Affairs.

Wren, D. (1987). *The evolution of management thought.* Third ed. New York: Wiley.

213
Greenfield Village User-Fee Policy Creates Hassle

Situation

The village of Greenfield recently enacted a policy of charging 100 percent higher fees to persons outside the village for programs. This is causing misunderstanding and financial burdens to some people, according to opinions expressed at Tuesday's recreation and park board meeting.

John Stangle, director of the Lots for Tots, a preschool day care program, said that the policy will drive out some long-term users of the program because they cannot afford the extra money. Stangle said seven children from six families may be forced to drop out of the program. The enrollment in summer usually has a waiting list, but filling those vacancies in the fall and spring may be difficult.

The board agreed to consider a modified policy for the preschool program. One board member, Sue Petri, said that it might not be practical to make an exception for just one program. This issue has been before the board before, but not much has been done to enforce the policy. Since the news media are giving it more attention, community opinion has been both for and against the policy. Some taxpayers feel that it is unfair for them to carry the burden for the public recreation program: "If persons outside the village want to participate in the recreation program, let them pay their fair share." Opponents of the ordinance argue that the recreation program attracts people from other communities and that this helps theirs. As one citizen stated, "On weekends over two thousand persons from outside the city go to the zoo—they spend an entire day in our community—this sure helps our economy."

The commission has asked the recreation and park staff to prepare a report on this issue. They have requested that a recommendation for future action be included.

Problem

Is charging double fees to citizens outside the village legitimate? What kind of policy would you suggest to the recreation and park board? Should the citizens living in the village be responsible for paying the greater cost of the recreation program? If so, why? If not, why? Are there other solutions to this problem? Would you consider this a fair policy if the "100 percent" was reduced? What kind of modified policy could be recommended? Are there any legal problems in this policy?

Suggested Key Words and Phrases for
Literature Search for Case 213

Fees and charges
Budget and finance
Zero-base budgeting
Financial regulations
Recreation administration

Federal grants to local
  government
Fee legislation
Program fees

Selected References for Case Study 213

Bovaird, A., Tricker, M., and Stoakes, R. (1984). *Recreation management and pricing: The effect of charging policy on demand at countryside recreation sites.* Brookfield, VT: Gower.

Camillus, J. (1984). *Budgeting for profit: How to exploit the potential of your business.* Randor, PA: Chilton.

Crompton, J. (1987). How to establish a price for park and recreation services. In *Current issues in leisure services: Looking ahead in a time of transition.* J. Bannon, (ed.) Washington, D.C.: International City Management Association, 93-107.

Crompton, J. (1988, March). Are you ready to implement a comprehensive revenue-generating program? *Parks and Recreation,* 54-60.

Garbutt, D. (1985). *How to budget and control cash.* Brookfield, VT: Gower.

Moore, B., (ed.) (1983). *The entrepreneur in local government.* Washington, D.C.: International City Management Association.

More municipal public fee courses as golf boom continues in '90s. (1990, June). *Park Maintenance and Grounds Management,* 3.

Mulford, C. (1984). *Interorganizational relations: Implications for community development.* New York: Human Sciences.

Ramsey, J., and Ramsey, I. (1985). *Budgeting basics: How to survive the budgeting process.* New York: Franklin Watts.

Rossman, J. (1989). *Recreation programming: Designing leisure experiences.* Champaign, IL: Sagamore.

Thomsett, M. (1988). *The little black book of budgets and forecasts.* New York: AMACOM.

Walters, J. (1987). Fees and charges: Underutilized revenues. In *Current issues in leisure services: Looking ahead in a time of transition.* J. Bannon, (ed.) Washington, D.C.: International City Management Association, 88-92.

Wood, A. (1990, May). Golf and government: A partnership that works. *Parks and Recreation,* 48-51.

214

Admission Charge Urged at City Parks

Situation

Plagued by little money, inadequate maintenance, vandalism, over-use, and litter, park officials should institute an admission charge at the city's 238 parks. "It is certainly conceivable," said George Monti, president of Westchester's recreation council, "that people would be willing to pay a nominal charge to visit a park simply to sit or picnic, if that park was clean and well maintained, if noise was controlled, and if admissions were limited to a certain number of people at one time."

Mr. Monti made his proposal yesterday at the annual meeting of the recreation council. The council is a private organization that functions as a recreation, parks, and conservation advocate. The group has just finished a report on the problems facing the city's recreation and park department.

In a report entitled "The Prospect for Parks," Mr. Monti said that it was recognized that the "notion of fees for the use of public parks, popular in other countries, somehow bothers the citizens of Westchester." Immediately bothered was George Bolton, director of Westchester's recreation and park department. "I am astonished," Mr. Bolton said when asked to comment, "that the council should propose such an idea. I am 100 percent against the proposal to have a general admission charge to any city park. This is entirely against the whole theory of city-maintained parks."

Ron Buchanan, an assistant administrator for public information, said that the legal office of the park and recreation department asserted that the admission charge was "highly questionable from the legal point of view."

"There are admission fees to skating rinks, wading and swimming pools, and boating facilities. A $15-dollar tennis permit is required for an individual to play on city-owned courts—more for control than for revenue," Mr. Buchanan said. "But there is no cost to use the grass or for the use of a bench."

Mr. Monti's suggestion was one of four offered in the report. The others were: a decentralization of the parks' day-to-day operation, the use of streets and temporarily available space for park-related activities, and public pressure to protect parks from encroachment by "those who are looking for land for other purposes." Mr. Monti's premise was that "the prospect for the parks of our city is poor." He predicted that the city park system "as it now generally operates and exists cannot last until the end of this century. Lack of money is a major woe," he said. "It results in a loss of staff and makes all but impossible preventative maintenance and prompt repair of damaged or worn-out facilities."

Vandalism, overuse, and litter are, according to Mr. Monti, "euphemistically called 'signs' of the times." He also stated that the park system needed three million dollars a year for the next ten years "just to keep the present park facilities intact and in operable condition." Yet, he said, "they would be fortunate to have one million dollars annually."

Problem

Should a fee be charged for the general use of the parks in Westchester? Under what conditions would you charge a fee? Is it fair to charge a fee for special facilities in the park and not for its general use? Other than increasing taxes, what can the officials do to increase revenues for the recreation and park department? Should parks be limited to a "certain number of people at any one time"? If so, how would you control this? Regarding Mr. Monti's other suggestions, what are the advantages and disadvantages of decentralizing the parks' day-to-day operations? Is the use of streets for recreation purposes a good idea? If so, what is the city's liability? What laws and ordinances can be created to protect the city from encroachment on park lands? Assume you are the director of recreation and parks, Mr. George Bolton. Draft a reply to the report presented by Mr. Monti that will respond to the issues he has suggested.

Suggested Key Words and Phrases for
Literature Search for Case 214

Fee and charges	Decentralization versus
Public relations	centralization
Use of public parks	Tax revenues
Local taxation	Municipal
Legal responsibility	Governmental function
Proprietary functions	Recreation streets
Park encroachment	Disadvantages

Selected References for Case Study 214

Bovaird, A., Tricker, M., and Stoakes, R. (1984). *Recreation management and pricing: The effect of charging policy on demand at countryside recreation sites.* Brookfield, VT: Gower.
Christianson, M. (1983). *Vandalism control management for parks and recreation areas.* State College, PA: Venture.

Crompton, J. (1987). How to establish a price for park and recreation services. In *Current issues in leisure services: Looking ahead in a time of transition.* J. Bannon, (ed.) Washington, D.C.: International City Management Association, 93-107.

Crompton, J. (1988, March). Are you ready to implement a comprehensive revenue-generating program? *Parks and Recreation*, 54-60.

Culhane, P. (1981). *Public lands politics: Interest group influence on the forest and the bureau of land management.* Baltimore: Johns Hopkins University.

Moore, B., (ed.) (1983). *The entrepreneur in local government.* Washington, D.C.: International City Management Association.

More municipal public fee courses as golf boom continues in the '90s. (1990, June). *Park Maintenance and Grounds Management*, 3.

Ramsey, J., and Ramsey, I. (1985). *Budgeting basics: How to survive the budgeting process.* New York: Franklin Watts.

Shattuck, J. (1988, July). Vandal-proof your park. *Parks and Recreation*, 32-37.

Toalson, R., and Herchenberger, P. (1985). *Developing community support for parks and recreation.* Champaign, IL: Champaign Park District.

Underwood, R. (1990, Jan.). Education and vandalism. *Park Maintenance and Grounds Management*, 10-13.

Waters, J. (1987). Fees and charges: Underutilized revenues. In *Current issues in leisure services: Looking ahead in a time of transition.* J. Bannon, (ed.) Washington, D.C.: International City Management Association, 88-92.

Wood, A. (1990, May). Golf and government: A partnership that works. *Parks and Recreation*, 48-51.

215
Who Should be the Director of Recreation and Parks?

Situation

At the request of the mayor, you are serving as chairperson of the search committee for the position of director of parks and recreation for Cederville, New York. James Orcutt, the current director, will retire on December 31 after 21 years of service. Serving with you on this committee is the city's personnel officer, Tom Gaines; Tom Bolen, superintendent of parks; Nancy Ottis, a member of the department of parks and recreation advisory committee; and James Metric, a council member. The position has been advertised through the National Recreation and Park Association. In order to describe the position to prospective candidates, the following job description and information about the city of Cederville has been publicized with the job announcement:

Director of Parks & Recreation
Cederville, N.Y.
Job Description

Under the general guidance of, and within policies, regulations, and plans set by the mayor, council, and the recreation and park board, the director of parks and recreation is responsible for the planning, organizing, directing, and evaluating a comprehensive program of recreation and parks for the city of Cederville. The director of parks and recreation serves as the chief executive officer of the department. It is further the responsibility of the director to:

1.   Coordinate department programs with those of other local and regional organizations.
2.   Prepare and oversee the preparation of proposed actions for intermediate- and long-range recreation and park plans.
3.   Keep the mayor, council, and the recreation board informed of all policy and major program matters as well as administrative and operating problems that affect the department's performance.
4.   Serve actively as the department's representative within the community.
5.   Direct the development of communications within the department and between it and the general public.
6.   Attend and actively participate in meetings on the local, state, and national levels.

About Cederville, N.Y.

The city of Cederville, population approximately two million people, is in central New York State. Lake Katrine forms its western boundary. The eastern and southern boundaries have no outstanding characteristics. The city covers about seventy-five square miles. Located in the community is a major depot of the New York Central Railroad and a newly developed airport. The New York State Throughway also covers the southwest corner of Cederville. Recent studies completed by County Planning Associates indicate that the population of Cederville will increase to 2,800,000 by 1990.

Both the Chrysler and Bendix Corporations have announced plans to construct two plants within the next three years, which will employ almost two thousand people.

Cederville, like thousands of other American cities, has "pockets of poverty." Racially, Cederville's population is about 91 percent white. The remaining 9 percent of the population is made up of minority groups with blacks representing about 6.5 percent of the total population. As in most large cities, people living in low-income areas are making their voices heard at city hall. Recently, the recreation and park department denied a request for East Cederville Civic Association to renovate the recreation center and to add recreational programs. It was reported that funds were not available for these requests. Approximately 4 percent of the black population lives in the East Cederville area.

In 1928, the city charter established a strong mayor-council form of government. Elective offices are those of mayor, comptroller, president of the council, five council members at large, and nine district council members. The mayor prepares the budget and controls executive powers, with the council balancing them through powers of taxation, appropriation, and confirmation. With the exception of the mayor, the president of the council and the council members at large may not succeed themselves after their four-year terms. District council members may be reelected to a second term.

The recreation and park board is an administrative unit appointed by the mayor with the approval of the council. It has the power to employ personnel and to carry out the recreation

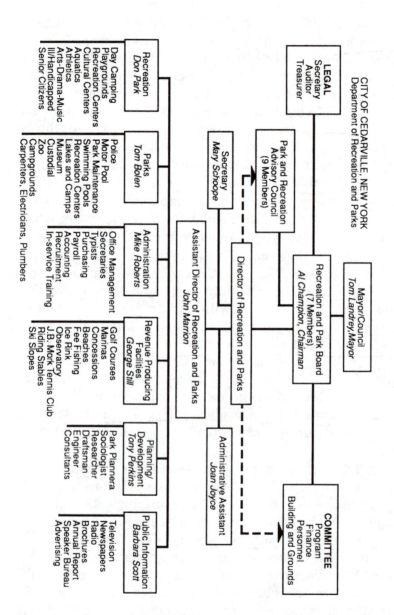

CITY OF CEDARVILLE, NEW YORK
Department of Recreation and Parks

Mayor/Council
Tom Landrey, Mayor

LEGAL
Secretary
Auditor
Treasurer

Recreation and Park Board
(7 Members)
Al Champion, Chairman

COMMITTEE
Program
Finance
Personnel
Building and Grounds

Park and Recreation
Advisory Council
(9 Members)

Secretary
Mary Schope

Director of Recreation and Parks

Administrative Assistant
Joan Joyce

Assistant Director of Recreation and Parks
John Marrion

Recreation
Don Park

Day Camping
Playgrounds
Recreation Centers
Cultural Centers
Aquatics
Athletics
Arts-Drama-Music
Ill/Handicapped
Senior Citizens

Parks
Tom Bolen

Police
Motor Pool
Park Maintenance
Swimming Pools
Recreation Centers
Lakes and Camps
Museum
Custodial
Zoo
Campgrounds
Carpenters, Electricians, Plumbers

Administration
Mike Roberts

Office Management
Secretaries
Typists
Purchasing
Payroll
Accounting
Recruitment
In-service Training

Revenue Producing
Facilities
George Still

Golf Courses
Marinas
Concessions
Beaches
Fee Fishing
Ice Rink
Observatory
J.B. Mork Tennis Club
Riding Stables
Ski Slopes

Planning/
Development
Tony Perkins

Park Planners
Sociologist
Researcher
Draftsman
Engineer
Consultants

Public Information
Barbara Scott

Television
Newspapers
Radio
Brochures
Annual Report
Speaker Bureau
Advertising

and park services. Personnel in this unit are directly responsible to the recreation and park board. However, the mayor has always maintained influence in recreation matters because recreation and park funds are appropriated by the mayor and council from the city's general revenue fund. All capital improvements for recreation, land, and facilities must also be approved by the mayor and council.

For the most efficiency, the recreation and park board has appointed a nine-member advisory council (see organization chart on page 190). The purpose of this council is to advise the recreation and park staff in matters concerning programs and activities offered by the department.

At present, there are five senior high schools, twelve junior high schools, and sixty-two elementary schools. Within two years, the Cederville Community College will be established; the board of education has shown great foresight in acquiring land for school development. There have been some difficulties in establishing joint use and development of school, park, and recreation sites. Recreation and park board members feel this problem exists because of the attitude by the school board that "schools are for education not recreation." However, the new superintendent is doing much to change this attitude.

One of the principal influences in community decision making is the Downtown Chamber of Commerce. This group has supported the park and recreation program. It cooperates in a number of events during the year. One of the major attractions is the Leisure Day Parade held each June. Merchants throughout the downtown area offer "dollar sidewalk sales" on the day of the parade. It is estimated that over fifty thousand people come to this event.

Both the Democratic and Republican parties are active in Cederville. At present, approximately 60 percent of the registered voters are Democrats, the remaining 40 percent of the registered voters Republicans. Tom Landrey is the first Republican to be elected mayor in over twenty years. The coming election hinges on a number of issues. One high on the agenda is the proliferating budget of the recreation and park department. Mayor Landrey has become very sensitive to these issues.

Cederville is served by two independent newspapers, the *Times* and the *Post Star*. The *Post Star* also owns a radio station,

WPAR, and WREC-TV. The news media are always alert to problems that affect city government. The *Post Star's* city hall reporter, Gene Hartman, tours the administrative offices of the city department each day looking for news. Only two weeks ago Gene wrote a feature story in the *Post Star* pointing out the five-year growth of the recreation and park department. Until this appeared, many people were not aware of the department's budget growth during the five-year period.

The search committee has received over 75 applications for the position and has reviewed all of them. Four candidates have shown excellent potential for becoming the next director of parks and recreation. By Tuesday, your committee must submit the four potential candidates, in priority ranking, to the mayor, council and the recreation and park board. Below is a brief description of the four finalists.

John Marrion

Present Position—Assistant director of parks and recreation for Cederville, New York, for the last eight years.

Present Responsibility— To assist the director of parks and recreation in the operation of the department.

Total Years of Experience—21

Age—44

Married— Yes—wife sells real estate

No. of Children—3—Ages 10,16, and 20

Education—B.S., Recreation and Park Administration, M.S., City Management

Career Goal—Has said that he would like to become director when James Orcutt retires

Health—Diabetic, but under control

Recommendations— All excellent

Professional Involvement—Active on New York State Recreation Society Committees; served on the Curriculum review Committee for Recreation at Ithaca College; popular speaker at "high school career days"; member of the NRPA Mid-Atlantic District Council, its vice-chairperson; member of NRPA's Legislative Committee; served for three years on the Kennedy Foundation's Review Board for Special Olympics.

Informal Feedback—Very well liked by the present staff; has their respect and affection; well organized; may be too comfortable in the number two spot, but this may be due to serving in this position for too long; member of the Rotary Club and is now its president; held in high regard by both Democrats and Republicans; has support from the community for becoming the next director of parks and recreation;has expressed interest in the job.

George Stein

Present Position—Assistant director of recreation and parks, Metroville, California, for seven years.

Present Responsibility—Administration of the recreation program; secretary to the park board and acts in the absence of the director of parks and recreation.

Total Years of Experience—11

Age— 33

Married—Yes— wife is a TV news reporter

No. of Children—Four— ages 1,4,7,9

Education—B.S. in Recreation and Park Administration, M.S. in Business Administration and M.S. in City Management

Career Goal—Not stated

Health—Was treated for heart murmur as a child; however, doctor has indicated that this is no problem.

Recommendations—All excellent.

Professional Involvement—Past president of the California State Park and Recreation Society; NRPA Legislative Committee; served as State Conference chairperson; served as the state's first professional certification chairperson; two years ago was named California's "most outstanding young professional."

Informal Feedback—Very well liked in the community; is held in high regard by staff; will not "play ball" with those who want political favors; is part owner of a commercial ice rink; excellent public speaker; while in college was an All-American football player; sold insurance and real estate after graduating from college; recently became active in Republican politics as ward committee member; excellent administrator.

About Metroville, Calif.— Metroville is in northwestern California and has a population of about 2 million. It operates under a strong mayor council form of government, with the mayor serving as the chief executive officer and administrator. The Director of parks and recreation reports directly to the mayor and serves in his "advisory cabinet." Under the jurisdiction of the Director of parks and recreation are 106 playgrounds, 4 golf courses, 33 recreation centers, 21 swimming pools, 3 national beaches, 1 botanical garden, 1 zoo, 3 marinas, 1 riding academy, 2 ice rinks, 1 tennis club, and 1 observatory. There are 75 recreation and park professionals with a staff of 630 employees. The annual operating budget is $9,267,844 with a capital improvement budget of $3 million. Three years ago the citizens defeated a $10 million bond issue referendum for recreation and land acquisition. Last year, the city was selected as a Gold Medal Winner for having an outstanding recreation and park system for a city of its size.

Peter Stickney

Present Position—Director of recreation and parks, Ellensville, Iowa for three years.

Present Responsibility—Direction of the recreation and park department.

Total Years of Experience—12

Age—35

Married—Yes—wife English teacher at Land High School

No. of Children—Two—ages 7 and 9

Education—B.S. and M.S. in Recreation and Park Administration

Career Goal—To become director of a large metropolitan recreation and park department.

Health—Excellent

Recommendations—All excellent

Professional Involvement—Past president of State Recreation and Park Society; active on committee of the National Recreation and Park Association.

Informal Feedback—Peter is an excellent administrator, good public speaker, very aggressive, works hard to accomplish his goals—a determined individual—well liked by the professionals in his state. Sometimes gets a letter about being overcommitted with responsibilities. According to one former staff member, "sometimes does not give his staff enough credit for what they do." Probably would do an excellent job as the director.

About Ellensville, IA.—Ellensville, Iowa, is a community of approximately 50,000. The mayor appoints an advisory board to the recreation and park department. There are four major divisions within the department; recreation center, aquatics, day camps, and maintenance. There are 12 professional staff members with a total staff of 46 employees. Under the direction of the recreation and park department are 4 swimming pools, 6 recreation centers, 3 day camps, 2 municipal golf courses, and over 600 acres of park land. The annual operating budget of Ellensville is $725,000 with a capital improvement budget of $2.6 million. Recreation programs are well attended, and the department has a good reputation among its citizens.

Nancy Watson

Present Position—Deputy director of parks and recreation in Bennetville, New York, for the past 4 1/2 years.

Present Responsibility—Primarily responsible for the direction of the recreation programs.

Total Years of Experience—14

Age—38

Married—Yes—husband is salesman for IBM

No. of Children—3—ages 9,12,14

Education—B.S. in Recreation and Park Administration, M.S. in Business Administration. Nearly completed Ph.D. in Political Science.

Career Goal—To be chief administrator in one of the leading recreation and park departments in the U.S.

Health—Had polio as a child, but causes no problems in adulthood.

Recommendations—All excellent

Professional Involvement—Now serving as treasurer of the New York Park and Recreation Society; vice-chairperson of NRPA Mid-Atlantic Regional Council; active in legislative committee of the Municipal League; service on the board of trustees of a small women's college in upstate New York; recently appointed by the governor of New York to the state's urban problem committee.

Informal Feedback—Nancy has a great deal of energy and is very ambitious; emphasizes training and education; sometimes appears to be a little pushy; capable and knowledgeable; good administrator; gets along with the staff "most of the time"; understands the policies of city hall; a no-nonsense type of person; is capable of being an outstanding administrator and is highly respected by her peers.

About Bennetville, N.Y.— Bennetville is a community of approximately 1 million people in central New York. The city operates under a strong mayoral form of government. An administrator is employed to oversee municipal functions. The director of parks and recreation reports to the mayor through the city administrator. The deputy director reports to the director of parks and recreation. The Department of Parks and Recreation is responsible for the operation of 14 municipal pools, 24 recreation centers, 2 day camps and 1 resident camp, 4 golf courses, a harbor, zoo, museum, and ice rink and 3 tennis facilities. There are 52 professional staff members with a total staff of 425 employees. The total annual operating budget is $6,255,000 with a capital improvement budget of $1.5 million. The city has also been the recipient of a number of federal grants for park land acquisition. The city has a national reputation of attempting to provide a worthwhile recreation and park program. However, like most metropolitan areas it has had its problems— financial difficulty and racial strife.

Problem

How would you rank the candidates for the position of director of parks and recreation in Cederville? What criteria would you use? With the information you now have, which of the four candidates do you think would be the best director? Why? Is there any information about the candidates not presented that would be helpful? Describe the information that is lacking.

*Suggested Key Words and Phrases for
Literature Search for Case 215*

Personnel assessment center   Personnel recruitment
Personnel selection   Interview techniques
Personnel administration

Selected References for Case Study 215

Arvey, R., and Faley, R. (1988). *Fairness in selecting employees.* Second ed. Reading, MA: Addison-Wesley.

Booth, W. (1987, Jan.). Putting your best foot forward at an assessment center. *Parks and Recreation,* 86-89.

Cook, M. (1988). *Personnel selection and productivity.* New York: Wiley.

Dreker, G., and Sackett, P. (1983). *Perspectives on employee staffing and selection: Readings and commentary.* Homewood, IL: Irwin.

Eder, R., and Ferris, G., (ed.) (1989). *The employment interview: Theory, research, and practice.* Newbury Park, CA: Sage.

Hawkins, T. (1988, May). Parks: For the people, by the people. *Parks and Recreation,* 39-43.

Haworth, J., (ed.) (1979). *Community involvement and leisure.* London: Lepus.

Kaplan, M. (1988). *Acquiring major systems contracts: Bidding methods and winning strategies.* New York: Wiley.

Kelsey, C., and Gray, H. (1986). *The citizen survey process in parks and recreation.* Reston, VA: American Alliance for Health, Physical Education, Recreation, and Dance.

Lewis, C. (1985). *Employee selection.* London: Hutchinson.

Manese, W. (1986). *Fair and effective employment testing: Administrative, psychometric, and legal issues for the human resources professional.* New York: Quorum.

McCullock, K. (1981). *Selecting employees safely under the law.* Englewood Cliffs, NJ: Prentice-Hall.

Potter, E., (ed.) (1986). *Employee selection: Legal and practical alternatives to compliance and litigation.* Second ed. Washington, D.C.: National Foundation for the Study of Equal Employment Policy.

Smith, M., and Robertson, I.,(ed.) (1989). *Advances in selection and assessment*. New York: Wiley.

Tindell, J. (1987). "Grass Roots" community development of leisure opportunity. In *Current issues in leisure services: Looking ahead in a time of transition*. J. Bannon, (ed.) Washington, D.C.: International City Management Association, 159-167.

216
Evaluation—A Problem in Leisure Services

Situation

Almost everyone has questioned at some point the efficiency and effectiveness of government services. Responses to these questions usually have been subjective at best.

The city of Belos, Montana and many other progressive local governments are now establishing objective criteria and measurements to answer such questions. A formal program to measure and improve productivity is now under way, funded by a federal agent. The Intergovernmental Personnel Administration Act of 1970, administered by the state of Montana, is providing $20,500 for the effort. The money is being used for research and office expenses.

Like most other cities, Belos maintains statistical data on all of its operations, including park and recreation services. This information is useful but lacks quality and does not allow reliable comparative analysis. The one-year investigation of identifying and measuring service productivity will provide this information and enable more cost-effective policy and management decisions. Such efforts in other cities have been quite successful. A recent report of the National Commission on Productivity and Work Quality states: "To our knowledge, productivity has increased in every known instance in which concerted planning, scheduling, and dispatching procedures were implemented in local jurisdiction using work-measurement techniques."

With the increasing pressures to maintain existing or improve services in an inflated economy, productivity is emphasized by the government, as well as by private businesses. Once established, monitoring can be performed through an impartial review similar to an annual financial audit.

Problem

What criteria can you use to determine the effectiveness of local park and recreation services? Design an evaluation program for the city of Belos at a cost not to exceed $20,500. Explain in detail how you would design this evaluation process. What type of data would be important for you to collect? How would you validate this data? How would you measure the "productivity" of the professional recreation and park staff? What other cities in the United States have developed an evaluation scheme? What are the strong and weak points of these evaluation systems? Review the national commission's report on productivity and work quality and relate how this affects evaluation of park and recreation services.

Suggested Key Words and Phrases for Literature Search for Case 216

Program evaluation	Employee productivity
Evaluation of leisure services	Evaluation of municipal services
Evaluation of public service	Local government evaluation
Management by objectives	Community planning (city)
Recreation evaluation	Research evaluation
Community survey	Measurement data effectiveness

Selected References for Case Study 216

Busson, T., and Coulter, P.,(eds.) (1987). *Policy evaluation for local government*. New York: Greenwood.

Culkin, D., and Kirsch, S. (1986). *Managing human resources in recreation, parks, and leisure services*. New York: Macmillan.

Farley, M. (1987). Program evaluation as a political tool. In *Current issues in leisure services: Looking ahead in a time of transition*. J. Bannon, (ed.) Washington, D.C.: International City Management Association, 36-44.

Hendon, W. (1981). *Evaluating urban parks and recreation*. New York: Praeger.

Howe, C. (1987). Evaluating for accountability. In *Current issues in leisure services: Looking ahead in a time of transition*. J. Bannon, (ed.) Washington, D.C.: International City Management Association, 27-35.

Klingner, D., and Nolbandian, J. (1985). *Public personnel management: Context and strategies*. Englewood Cliffs, NJ: Prentice-Hall.

Lundegren, H., and Farrell, P. (1985). *Evaluation for leisure service managers: A dynamic approach*. Philadelphia: Saunders.

McCurdy, D. (1985). *Park management*. Carbondale: Southern Illinois University Press.

Morrisey, G. (1976). *Management by objectives and results in the public sector*. Reading, MA: Addison-Wesley.

Slavin, S., (ed.) (1985). *Managing finances, personnel, and information in human services*. New York: Haworth.

Torkildsen, G. (1986). *Leisure and recreation management*. Second ed. London: E & F.N. Spoon.

217
Dunes County Credibility Gap

Situation

A report critical of the Dunes County Recreation and Park Authority is like "Alice in Wonderland," commented Dale Summers, chairperson of the recreation and park commission. The chairperson said the sixty-two page report, "has too many opinions of what somebody thinks, but not enough concrete facts." The report, completed in November and made public by *The Dunes Reporter*, was compiled by a three-member team from the Dunes County Planning Authority.

The report criticized the Dunes County Recreation and Park Authority and laid much of the blame for the problems on the former authority executive director, John Simmons, who resigned under pressure.

Summers, at yesterday's meeting of the commissioners, said,"a lot of this report is good but there's a lot of myth because it's opinion." He said the commissioners became aware that the Recreation and Park Authority was "not up to Dunes County's general performance standards," and as a result, four of the Authority's five commissioners have been replaced by the county chairperson. The appointment of a new board led to the forced resignation of John Simmons. He said that no one had denied there was a need for restructuring the authority, and it is now being done. Key abuses alleged by the report were:

A. The files of the central office of the authority are virtually worthless.
B. All records of the authority are missing, to the extent that the past has been lost, the present is basically without explanation, and the future is undefined.
C. The authority under John Simmons awarded some contracts without the legally required advertising and awarded others without putting them up for bid.
D. The authority kept no central list of persons participating in the activities for which a fee was charged.
E. Authority funds are kept in the First National Bank and in a savings and loan association where two of the Authority's board members currently serve on the loan's board of directors.
F. Some debts are being created without first issuing purchase orders.
G. Authority equipment and employees have been used for board members' personal gain.
H. Federal civil rights laws were being violated as they relate to fair employment practices.

The chairperson of the county board of commissioners has requested that the Dunes Park and Recreation Authority submit a report responding to the alleged violations and to list what measures they are taking to correct any wrongdoing, if, in fact, any occurs.

Problem

Who should assume the responsibility of the alleged violations—the former executive director or the board of the park and
recreation authority? What action would you take to determine
if the alleged accusations were correct? Is it a conflict of interest
for money of the authority to be held in deposit at a savings and
loan at which board members serve in an official capacity? What
is the state law regarding this? Should employees and/or board
members be permitted to use authority equipment for personal
use? What bidding procedure would you recommend? What
procedures should be established for the deposit of authority
funds in local banks? Recommend a purchase order and voucher
system that would adequately facilitate the authority's business.
What affirmative action guidelines would you recommend for
the employment of new personnel at the authority?

*Suggested Key Words and Phrases for
Literature Search for Case 217*

Affirmative action	Banking practices
Bidding procedures	Civil rights
Contract awards	Building contracts
Discrimination (employment)	Employee fringe benefits
Ethical practices	Hiring practices
Law finance (per state)	Media relations
Recruiting employees	Non-wage payments

Selected References for Case 217

Barlow, C., and Eisen, G. (1983). *Purchasing negotiations*. Boston:
    CBI.
Burke, J. (1986). *Bureaucratic responsibility*. Baltimore: Johns
    Hopkins University Press.
Cooper, T. (1984). *The responsible administrator: An approach to
    ethics for the administrative role*. Third printing. Port Wash-
    ington, NY: Associated Faculty Press.

Crossley, J. (1990, March). Multi-tier programming in commercial recreation. *Parks and Recreation*, 69-73.

Dearstyne, B. (1988). *The management of local government records: A guide for local officials.* Nashville: American Association for State and Local History.

Dreker, G., and Sackett, P. (1983). *Perspectives on employee staffing and selection: Readings and commentary.* Homewood, IL: Irwin.

Fleishman, J., Liebman, L., and Moore, M., (eds.) (1981). *Public duties: The moral obligations of government officials.* Cambridge, MA: Harvard.

Fleishman, J. (1981). Self-interest and political integrity. In *Public duties: The moral obligations of government officials.* J. Fleishman, L. Liebman., and M. Moore, (eds.) Cambridge, MA: Harvard University Press, 52-92.

Kaplan, M. (1988). *Acquiring major systems contracts: Bidding methods and winning strategies.* New York: Wiley.

Potter, E., (ed.) (1986). *Employee selection: Legal and practical alternatives to compliance and litigation.* Second ed. Washington, D.C.: National Foundation for the Study of Equal Employment Policy.

Silver, A., and Peterson, R. (1985). *Decision systems for inventory management and production planning.* Second ed. New York: Wiley.

Tersine, R. (1982). *Principals of inventory and materials management.* Second ed. New York: North-Holland.

Toalson, R., and Herchenberger, P. (1985). *Developing community support for parks and recreation.* Champaign, IL: Champaign Park District.

Zenz, G. (1987). *Purchasing and the management of materials.* Sixth ed. New York: Wiley.

218
Promotion Will Determine Success of the Racquet Club

Situation

You have just been employed as a consultant to the Saratoga Racquet Club, a private commercial recreation facility. Your principal responsibility is to design a public relations and information campaign that will attract new members six months from now, when the facility will open.

Saratoga is a community of approximately fifty thousand with a median family income of $15,600. At present there are no other indoor racquetball facilities in the community. Tennis is very popular because of the instructional program and tournaments offered by the city's recreation department. The only exposure that the community has had to racquetball is through the use of three courts at the local YMCA. There are four radio stations in the community, one of which devotes most of its programming to teenagers, a morning and evening newspaper, and three television stations, one of which is a public education station affiliated with the local university.

Upon accepting this assignment, the owner and builder inform you that the following facilities will be included in this new recreation development: six indoor tennis courts, twelve air-conditioned racquetball/handball courts, a supervised nursery, a well-equipped exercise room, carpeted locker rooms, a furnished lounge area, a pro-shop with the latest tennis, handball, and racquetball equipment, and a steam room, whirlpool, and sauna. A large room with a kitchenette for social activities is also being included. Annual membership fees have been established at sixty dollars for an individual and eighty dollars for a family membership. Persons wishing to use the tennis courts or the racquetball courts must pay an hourly rental fee of ten dollars. The club will be open daily from 6:00 A.M. to 11:00 P.M.

You have been told that the maximum amount of money that can be spent during the next six months on the campaign is nine thousand dollars. Advertising on radio, TV, and in newspapers, and any promotional brochures must come from this amount.

Problem

Plan a detailed promotional campaign for the opening of the racquet club, not to exceed nine thousand dollars. What would be the most effective way to spend the allotted money? Which of the media mentioned would be the most effective in publicizing the program? Develop a promotional brochure describing the club's facilities and why individuals should join. What promotional gimmicks can you suggest that would encourage individuals to join before the club opens? Are there any public relations and information programs that require little or no expenditure of funds? What assistance would you need to carry out your proposed program? Outline your entire campaign.

Suggested Key Words and Phrases for
Literature Search for Case 218

Advertising	Barriers to buying
Budgeting	Buying motives
Buyer motivation	Consumer benefit
Marketing	Media promotion
Merchandising	Sales promotion
Sales promotion	Sales tactics

Selected References for Case Study 218

Camillus, J. (1984). *Budgeting for profit: How to exploit the potential of your business.* Randor, PA: Chilton.

Crompton, J., and Lamb, Jr., C. (1986). *Marketing government and social services.* New York: Wiley.

Cunningham, W., Cunningham, I., and Swift, C. (1987). *Marketing: A managerial approach.* Cincinnati, OH: South-Western.

Garbutt, D. (1985). *How to budget and control cash.* Brookfield, VT: Gower.

Holloway, J., and Plant, R. (1989). *Marketing for tourism.* London: Pitman.

Knopf, R. (1990, March). Marketing public land: Is it the right thing to do? *Parks and Recreation*, 57-60.

McEwen, D., and Paterson, R. (1986, Nov.) The move to marketing: Land between the lakes. *Parks and Recreation*, 36-41.

Prus, R. (1989). *Pursuing customers: An ethnography of marketing activities*. Newbury Park, CA: Sage.

Soderberg, J. (1989, June). Marketing recreation right. *Parks and Recreation*, 38-41.

Toalson, R., and Herchenberger, P. (1985). *Developing community support for parks and recreation*. Champaign, IL: Champaign Park District.

Uysal, M. (1986, Oct.). Marketing for tourism - A growing field. *Parks and Recreation*, 57-66.

Venkatesan, M., Schmalensee, D., and Marshall, C., (eds.) (1986). *Creativity in services marketing: What's new, what works, and what's developing*. Chicago, IL: American Marketing Association.

219
Redbud Park Reapproval
Splits Neighborhood into Factions

Situation

Construction of Redbud Park, an object of pride and example of progress in the black community a year ago, was reapproved by area residents last night—but not before a deep split between neighborhood groups showed that the project had become a symbol of division in the community west of Third Street, south of Peebles.

The Barton Heights Civic Club approved the project at the end of a meeting last night at the Greater Harvest Church of God. Although the recorded vote was thirty-two to twenty-three in favor of continued construction of the park, opponents of the project staged a walkout when it became apparent as the vote was taken that they were outnumbered.

Rev. McRay Doss, who owns a home facing the park site—

a linear park running down the center of Redbud between Brooks and Mitchell—declared as the group walked out,"You can vote whatever way you want,but there will be no park on Redbud."

Doss said that he and other homeowners on Redbud plan to seek a federal court injunction blocking the project. He said a petition for an injunction probably would be sought Tuesday. "We're going to get a court order and tie it up for the next five years, if that's what it takes," he said.

Doss and homeowners on Redbud maintain that the park will bring vandals and juvenile delinquents into the neighborhood.

The project is financed by community development funds granted to the city by the Department of Housing and Urban Development. About $400,000 has been spent on the project. Park architect, Mitch Hall, said that curbs and gutters for the project were in. Marquest Taylor, president of the civic club, said that if construction were not halted, it could be completed in three months. Taylor charged that Doss, who has indicated he plans to run for the city council, has inflamed the dispute to get his name known in the area.

"We had three public hearings, and everything was approved by the residents," Taylor said. "There were no objections then, and everybody had plenty of opportunities to speak." Despite pleas by some neighborhood residents for a compromise, Taylor said, "We're here for one reason: to vote in favor of this or not."

Ellis Booker, a resident, pleaded, "Let's not go downtown, and let the white folks make our decisions for us." Taylor said, however, that the results of the vote will be given to Mrs. Gwen Awsumb, director of the city housing and community development division, and "she will have to handle any problems now."

He also said that opponents of the park rejected any modifications at the meetings last month with Rep. Harold Ford of Memphis and Mrs. Awsumb, making construction of the park an all-or-nothing issue.

Marilyn Bowers, a Redbud resident who maintained that a basketball court is being built in front of her house, charged that Taylor did not adequately inform opponents of the park of scheduled meetings and park construction plans. She and other residents also maintained that they will have no control over rough youths who come into the area to use park facilities such as basketball courts.

Miss Bowers said that Redbud residents are unanimously opposed to the project. She said support for it comes from residents in the neighborhood who do not live on Redbud and will not have to contend with noise and other problems.

Geraldine Patton, a Redbud resident, said, "I want the park, but I don't want it in front of my house. But if I have to choose between a place for my children to play and not having a park, I'll choose (having) the park."

Taylor, speaking for residents in favor of the park, said, "You can't say that rough kinds of kids won't come here without a park."

Clifton Brown, representing the Greater Harvest Church near Redbud added, "We'll suffer more if we don't have a park. We need a better place for the children. They're playing on the church grounds now, and they have caused damage and have broken in several times."

Problem

What responsibility do the municipal officials have in allowing the community to participate in the decision-making process? Should the Redbud Park construction be completed despite the citizens' objections? Should homeowners have a right to veto the construction of a city park because of its potential dangers? What responsibility does the federal Department of Housing and Urban Development have? What should be the federal government's position on funding local projects? From what other city departments would you request information? Draft a statement of your views on the completion of Redbud Park. Create a procedure that will allow citizen involvement in the planning and decision-making process.

Suggested Key Words and Phrases for
Literature Search for Case 219

Citizen involvement   Community decision making

Community involvement   Federal funding
Grantsmanship   Park location and design
Park planning

Selected References for Case Study 219

Bazerman, M. (1986). *Judgment in managerial decision making*. New York: Wiley.

Branch, M. (1983). *Comprehensive planning: General theory and principles*. Pacific Palisades, CA: Palisades.

Cook, L., Osterholt, B., and Riley, E., Jr. (1988). *Anticipating tomorrow's issues: A handbook for policymakers*. Washington, D.C. Council of State Policy and Planning Agencies.

Fick, G., and Sprague, Jr., R., (eds.) (1980). *Decision support systems: Issues and challenges*. Oxford: Pergamon.

Gold, S. (1987). A human service approach to recreation planning. In *Current issues in leisure services: Looking ahead in a time of transition*. J. Bannon, (ed.) Washington, D.C.: International City Management Association, 5-16.

Hailey, M. (1990, May). Fighting urban apathy with tennis. *Parks and Recreation*, 24-29.

Hunt, S., and Brooks, K. (1987). A planning model for public recreation agencies. In *Current issues in leisure services: Looking ahead in a time of transition*. J. Bannon, (ed.) Washington, D.C.: International City Management Association, 5-16.

Kelsey, C., and Gray, H. (1985). *Master plan process for parks and recreation*. Reston, VA: American Alliance for Health, Physical Education, Recreation, and Dance.

Kelsey, C., and Gray, H. (1986). *The feasibility study process for parks and recreation*. Reston, VA: American Alliance for Health, Physical Education, Recreation, and Dance.

Molnar, D., and Rutledge, A. (1986). *Anatomy of a park: The essentials of recreation area planning and design*. New York: McGraw-Hill.

Pratt, S. (1988, Dec.). Urban fishing: It's catching on. *Parks and Recreation*, 32-34.

Willis-Kistler, P. (1988, Nov.) Fighting gangs with recreation. *Parks and Recreation*, 44-49.

220
Off-Road Vehicle Park in Doubt

Situation

The county planning commission soon will be asked to give its final verdict on a proposed off-road vehicle park near here— and supporters and opponents alike are sure the commission will reject the project.

Woodie Miller, chairperson of the Santee Planning Committee, said yesterday he believes that the commission will affirm its earlier four-to-nothing vote against the planned regional park. Although the commission's vote against the park in February was tentative, Miller said that he expects it to stand at the commission meeting on March 31.

"I'm not against off-road vehicles," maintains Miller, who said his children number among the legions of off-road vehicle enthusiasts. "But there is a place for everything, and in this instance it's not in an urban area."

Miller is not alone in his belief that the planners will veto the plan. The same opinion is held by Peter Cuthbert, a county park planner and a supporter of the county's off-road vehicle park proposal. "The die is cast as far as the planning commission is concerned, and it was cast at their first meeting" (when the tentative four to nothing vote was cast), said Cuthbert. "I'm not even going to go to the meeting (March 31); I think it's all going to be routine."

Although the planning commission is expected to reject the Santee off-road vehicle plan, Cuthbert said he still believes that concerns over park noise can be resolved. Cuthbert did admit that there may be problems with air pollution, specifically the amount of dust generated from the park. Nevertheless, Cuthbert said emotionalism may have played a major role in turning the tide against the proposed Santee regional park. A recent letter to the planning commission was one indication of the concerns and feelings of supporters of the proposed park. "Your commission has been deceived into believing that the Santee park is worse than the Russian flu," wrote Ivan McDermott, chairperson of the

County Off-Road Vehicle Citizens Advisor Committee. "Problems suggested by staff are not nearly as bad as they are represented to be . . . It is very hard for me and a few other people on the committee to compete with perhaps as many as fifty persons in IPO (county-integrated planning office) who are working full-time to do away with the ORV (off-road vehicle) program," said McDermott, who called the Santee site "one of the best sites in the county."

Although April 17 and 24 have been set as the tentative dates for the county board of supervisors to decide the matter, Cuthbert said the board may not receive the matter until May or June. But regardless of when the supervisors hear the matter, supporters and opponents of the park are planning for the next confrontation.

Although he did not identify them, Cuthbert said some "local heavyweights" are being lined up to appear before the supervisors. Meanwhile, Miller said he expects residents of the nearby Eucalyptus Hills area to come to the board chambers "with their guns loaded."

The Eucalyptus Hills section is situated east of the planned Santee Regional Park, to be built in northern Santee in an area just east of proposed U.S. 125. About 400 of the planned 1500 acres would be set aside for off-road vehicle use.

Problem

What provisions should be made for off-road vehicles in the park development plan? Should parks of this nature be allowed within the city limits? Why? What amount of land in relation to community total park land should be set aside for this type of activity? What criteria should be established for selecting sites for this type of activity? To what extent should the planning commission seek citizen involvement in this decision? How could they do this? Assuming that you are Woodie Miller, chairperson of the planning committee, develop a strategy for this problem.

Suggested Key Words and Phrases for
Literature Search for Case 220

Citizen involvement	Comprehensive planning
Guidelines for planning	Land acquisition
Off-road vehicles	Park standards
Recreation demand	Special facilities
Special use parks	Motor vehicles—All terrain

Selected References for Case Study 220

Cook, L., Osterholt, B., and Riley, E., Jr. (1988). *Anticipating tomorrow's issues: A handbook for policymakers.* Washington, D.C. Council of State Policy and Planning Agencies.

Culhane, P. (1981). *Public lands politics: Interest group influence on the forest and the bureau of land management.* Baltimore: Johns Hopkins University.

Dysart, III, B., and Clawson, M. (1989). *Public interest in the use of private lands.* New York: Praeger.

Gold, S. (1987). A human service approach to recreation planning. In *Current issues in leisure services: Looking ahead in a time of transition.* J. Bannon, (ed.) Washington, D.C.: International City Management.

Hawkins, T. (1988, May). Parks: For the people, by the people. *Parks and Recreation*, 39-43.

Haworth, J., (ed.) (1979). *Community involvement and leisure.* London: Lepus.

Hunt, S., and Brooks, K. (1987). A planning model for public recreation agencies. In *Current issues in leisure services: Looking ahead in a time of transition.* J. Bannon, (ed.) Washington, D.C.: International City Management Association, 5-16.

Kelsey, C., and Gray, H. (1986). *The citizen survey process in parks and recreation.* Reston, VA: American Alliance for Health, Physical Education, Recreation, and Dance.

Lacey, R., and Severinghaus, W. (1981). *Evaluation of lands for off-road recreational four-wheel drive vehicle use.* Springfield, VA: National Technical Information Center.

O'Bama, B. (1988, Aug.-Sept.). Why organize? Problems and promise in the inner city. *Illinois Issues,* 40-42.

Shelby, B., and Heberlein, T. (1986). *Carrying capacity in recreation settings.* Corvallis, OR: Oregon State University.

Stambler, I. (1984). *Off-roading: Racing and riding.* New York: Putman.

Tindell, J. (1987). "Grass Roots" community development of leisure opportunity. In *Current issues in leisure services: Looking ahead in a time of transition.* J. Bannon, (ed.) Washington, D.C.: International City Management Association, 159-167.

Warren, R. (1990, June). Land stewardship: Your professional responsibility. *Park Maintenance and Grounds Management,* 14-16.

Webb, R., and Wilshire, H. (1983). *Environmental effects of off-road vehicles: Impact and management in arid regions.* New York: Springer Verlog.

221
City Makes War on Old Eyesores

Situation

Hardly anyone here thinks Speedway is a beautiful street. In addition to being a major east-west thoroughfare and a main route to the university, it is a caricature of the effects of rapid, unplanned growth.

A person walking along Speedway is assaulted by automobile fumes and secondhand smells from fast-food stands, as well as by a blitz of neon lights and billboards hawking everything from motorcycles to female "escorts."

If Speedway is a manifestation of new and instant decay, downtown can qualify as vintage decay with a touch of charm. The old part of the city, once the home of Hohokam Indians and Spanish colonialists, is now the daytime center of governmental activity. At night, with its barren streets and sleazy bars, it becomes a good place to roll a drunk.

Apparently, however, it is not too late to change all this. After years of talking about developing policies that would recognize the value of esthetics, the city government lately has taken a few tentative steps toward putting its money where its mouth is.

Because governments tend to move more slowly, only one of the three ideas being discussed has actually progressed from the drawing board to the cement mixer.

Work has begun on the 14-mile Santa Cruz Riverpark, a ribbon of bike and horse paths, walkways, golf course, houses, and tasteful concessions that will mark the western edge of the downtown area, passing by the sites of the city's earliest settlements along the Santa Cruz River. The park is modeled somewhat after Scottsdale's Indian Bend Wash.

Construction of the park began last summer. Officials estimate it will take ten years and $20 million to complete. When it is done, it will accommodate two golf courses, about 1,700 apartments and condominiums, and about 1,200 new homes.

In addition, for about four miles, the river—which is nearly always dry—will be flowing with highly treated sewage. The experts say the water will be clean enough for boating and fishing.

As of today, much of the debris that has accumulated in the dry riverbed has been removed, some landscaping has been done, a portion of the bicycle path has been paved, and signs have been erected. There is still much to be done, but at this point there is at least the appearance of less talk and more action.

The opposite still is true, however, for the city's second major undertaking: the beautification and resurrection of the downtown, an area now officially described, with symbolic significance, as the central business district. The term "downtown" became a melancholy artifact when the city sprawled so drastically that it had to build a second city hall to serve the suburban far east side.

For over a year, the Downtown Advisory Committee, a group of business persons, professionals, and some city department heads, has been discussing the failure of plans to revive the downtown with the hope of coming up with a new, realistic approach—realistic meaning that it offends neither the money makers, the esthetes, nor the politicians.

The committee brought its report to the mayor and council last week and noted, among other points, that "from the economic viewpoint, downtown represents a public and private investment that is simply so substantial that it cannot be permitted to deteriorate." The theory of investment as justifying preservation was followed by the theory of preservation as a psychological need. The report continues:

"Psychologists point out that human beings living in urban areas need various geographic and social points of reference to provide them with a sense of identity and equilibrium in what can be a very impersonal lonely environment."

The committee observed that the downtown can be revived by building houses there, places where the retired, the single, or the childless might want to live alongside those who would move there because they work there and want to save gas money. What the downtown needs is housing, more parking, and a design "to facilitate pedestrian and automobile traffic circulation."

The committee made tentative suggestions on how all of these elements can be achieved and linked to the Santa Cruz Riverpark, and the mayor and council agreed to set up a public hearing date for the proposal in mid-May. A spokesperson for the advisory committee said that $25 million was a ballpark figure.

The last ideas are aimed at controlling signs: neon, freestanding, wall painting, and billboard, and similar impediments. Like the Riverpark and the model of Indian Bend Wash, Scottsdale again is one of the places the downtown may imitate. Generally speaking, during the next decade, the city wants to avoid the catastrophe of Speedway, and a variety of new approaches will be sought for an ordinance to control the types of signs allowable.

The new ordinance, however, will not be developed overnight. Instead, the council ordered the city manager to organize a fifteen-member committee, which will spend six months coming up with ideas for a new way to control billboards and other signs. At that time, the city council may adopt a new ordinance—clearly, that process is a sign in itself.

Problem

What position, if any, should the recreation and park

department take in improving the physical environment in the city? Should the city control the activities in the downtown area? Is it practical to build golf courses, bike paths, and horse paths in the downtown area? To what extent should the downtown area improve residential housing? What methods can be used to finance the redevelopment of the downtown area? Describe these methods in detail. How important is it for a city to have a well-developed and well-planned downtown area? Why? Should the downtown area be the principal place for business enterprises? Why? How else can the downtown area be used? What is meant by the psychologist's reference to "geographic and social points" of reference? Assuming that you are the director of parks and recreation in the city, define your role in the community development plan.

*Suggested Key Words and Phrases for
Literature Search for Case 221*

City economics	City planning
Comprehensive planning	Condominiums
Downtown development	Environmental planning
(Business districts)	Freeways
Sign ordinances	Urban planning

Selected References for Case Study 221

Davidson, J. (1989, May). Cycling in the city: An urban race course plan. *Parks and Recreation*, 32-36.

Evans, C. (1987, Oct.). Bringing walkways to your doorstep. *Parks and Recreation*, 30-35.

Frieden, B., and Sagalyn, L. (1989). *Downtown, inc.: How America rebuilds cities*. Cambridge, MA: MIT University Press.

Lai, R. (1988). *Law in urban design and planning: The invisible web*. New York: Van Reinhold.

Macdonald, S. (1987, Nov.). Building support for urban trails. *Parks and Recreation*, 26-33.

Marciniak, E. (1986). *Reclaiming the inner city*. Washington, D.C.: National Center for Urban Ethnic Affairs.

222
Is the Vendor Carting Off Profits?

Situation

The case presented below was actually reported in the *Chicago Tribune* on March 9, 1978, by Ronald Koziol and William Crawford, Jr.:

A top aide to Cook County Board President George W. Dunne has held a sweetheart concession contract with the Chicago Park District for 30 years at a loss of millions of dollars to the taxpayers, a *Tribune* investigation has disclosed.

William J. Burns, a $34,000 per year administrative assistant to Dunne, has held the exclusive, no-bid contract since he wrested it from another concessionaire after a bitter court battle in 1948. The contract gives Burns and his company, Consolidated Concessions, Inc., which occupies free office space in Soldier Field, the exclusive right to sell food, beverages, and other confections at Soldier Field and all public parks, beaches, and golf courses south of the Chicago River. The current three-year Consolidated contract, which expires January 31, 1979, grossed the company a record $1.3 million in 1976. The company is expected to set a new record for 1977 after all the receipts are counted.

Like Walter J. Henley, president of Airline Canteen Corporation, who held a monopoly on O'Hare International Airport concessions, Burns has won perfunctory renewal of his contract from the park district board every three to five years without public bidding.

In addition, the terms of the contract—which guarantee the park district $105,000 annually or 15 percent of revenues, whichever is greater—have remained unchanged for more than three decades. Sports complexes in other cities receive up to 42 percent of the revenues from concessions. The favorable treatment to Consolidated has cost the financially strapped park district between $1 million and $2 million since 1970 alone, the Tribune found. Though figures are incomplete, the loss for prior years could exceed $4 million. Since 1971, with the addition of Chicago Bear football games, professional soccer matches, and rock concerts at the lakefront stadium, attendance has gone up and revenues have risen by more than $500,000 annually. But the park district has not reopened negotiations on terms of the Consolidated contract.

The *Tribune* investigation also found:

- Consolidated was formed in 1947 by Burns, Jerry Devine, Ashley Richets, and the late Andy Frain of Usher Company fame for the purpose of landing the lucrative contract. The company has never had another client.
- A survey of publicly owned sports stadiums around the country disclosed that with one exception the park district struck the worst bargain with its 15 percent of sales. For example, the sports complexes in Milwaukee and Philadelphia are taking home 33.5 percent and 42.2 percent of revenues respectively.
- Midwest based concessionaires interviewed by the *Tribune* said they never had been asked to bid on the contract, which they regard as a plum. All said they would offer 30 percent of sales if the bidding were open to the public.
- Because of a jurisdictional dispute between the city and the park district, Consolidated's food dispensing facilities, which include a cafeteria in the district's administration building, have never been inspected or licensed by the Chicago Board of Health. A Board of Health spokesman told the *Tribune* he believed Consolidated's mobile food trailers wouldn't pass the Board's licensing inspection.
- The park district provides Consolidated with 12 free storage rooms and offices in Soldier Field. It also picks up the tab for electricity, heat, and maintenance.

When confronted with these findings, Burns and park district officials said district regulations did not require that personal service contracts, such as Consolidated's, be publicly bid.

Nevertheless, when Consolidated took the contract away from Fred and Catherine Dillon, who had held it for 12 years, Dillon filed suit in Circuit Court. The presiding judge suggested that the bids should be opened to the public, saying, "this is a contract with a public body, not with a private firm or individual."

Burns, an attorney who served as an assistant under Democratic State's Attorneys John Stamos and Daniel Ward, defended
his contract with the park board, saying he has provided excellent service through the years. "We've always tried to do a good
job and evidently we have because the board continues to renew
our agreement," said Burns, who became president of Consolidated when Frain died in 1964. "Over the years we've made
heavy capital improvements at Soldier Field and the parks,
buying new refreshment stands, trucks, and dispensing machin-
ery. We've pioneered in the business," he said.

Though he declined to reveal his salary as president of
Consolidated, Burns denied the contract was a lucrative one. He
said that Consolidated actually lost money during 10 years it had
the agreement and that overall, yearly company profits were
averaging only between 1 and 2 percent of gross sales.

He also said the cafeteria in the administration building has
never made money, even though Consolidated receives a 15
percent credit or deduction from its gross revenues each year.
Last year, Burns said the cafeteria for park district employees lost
$45,000.

Burns saw no conflict between his role with Consolidated
and his work as an administrative assistant to Dunne. "My work
with Consolidated is a weekend business. There's no need for me
to be at Soldier Field during the week," he said.

Although most area concessionaires interviewed by the
Tribune said they had never been asked to bid on the park district
contract, some said they attempted to bid on the work, but got
"nothing but the runaround."   Sheldon Silver, spokesman for
Interstate United Corporation, one of the country's biggest concessionaires, said, "Our company has never been asked to submit
a bid, but we'd love to." Interstate, which has contracts with the
Los Angeles Coliseum and Tampa Stadium, is remitting between 35 and 40 percent of gross receipts, said Silver. Another
food vendor, who asked not to be identified, said, "I'd love to
offer them 30 percent. I went to the park board in 1971 to find out
how to bid on the work. I was told to come back in 1972. But when
I did, I got the runaround."

Joseph A. Power, former chief judge of the Criminal Courts,
who now represents the park district, said he was unaware of any
concessionaire being interested in the Soldier Field contract. "If
a person comes in here and demonstrates he is able to perform on

the contract and comes up with a better proposal than Consolidated, I am certain the board would give that person the contract. All he has to do is submit a written letter to the park board."

Problem

What procedures should be established for awarding the concession contracts in the Chicago Park District? Outline these procedures in detail. What is your opinion of the involvement of William J. Burns, the administrative aide to the county board chairperson, in Consolidated Concessions, Inc.? Is this a conflict of interest? What would be a reasonable percentage of return to the park district on concession business? Give reasons for your answer. Should public bidding be required for this contract? Should Consolidated Concession be required to pay rent for the twelve storage rooms at Soldier Field? Should city health inspectors be required to inspect the concession stands at Soldier Field? To what extent should the financial records of Consolidated Concessions be available to the park district?

Suggested Key Words and Phrases for Literature Search for Case 222

Concessions	Conflict of interest
Contract bidding	User fees and charges
Food service contract	Public bidding procedures
Public finance	Sport complex administration

Selected References for Case Study 222

Barlow, C., and Eisen, G. (1983). *Purchasing negotiations*. Boston: CBI.

Busson, T., and Coulter, P., (eds.) (1987). *Policy evaluation for local government*. New York: Greenwood.

Dowd, L. (1990, April). Sport facility management. *Park Maintenance and Grounds Management*, 9-12.

Gottlieb, L. (1980). *The best of Gottlieb's bottom line: A practical profit guide for today's foodservice operator*. New York: Lebhar-Friedman.

Hawthorne, D. (1987, Oct.). Administrating concessioner services in public parks. *Parks and Recreation*, 36-39, 40.

Howe, C. (1987). Evaluating for accountability. In *Current issues in leisure services: Looking ahead in a time of transition*. J. Bannon, (ed.) Washington, D.C.: International City Management Association, 27-35.

Kaplan, M. (1988). *Acquiring major systems contracts: Bidding methods and winning strategies*. New York: Wiley.

Lundegren, H., and Farrell, P. (1985). *Evaluation for leisure service managers: A dynamic approach*. Philadelphia: Saunders.

Powers, T., and Powers, J. (1984). *Food service operations: Planning and control*. New York: Wiley.

Sammet, Jr., G., and Kelly, C. (1980). *Do's and Don'ts in subcontract management*. New York: AMACOM.

Sammet, Jr., G., and Kelly, C. (1981). *Subcontract management handbook*. New York: AMACOM.

Thorner, M., and Manning, P. (1983). *Quality control in foodservice*. Westport, CT: Avi.

Williams, S. (1985). *Conflict of interest: The ethical dilemma in politics*. Brookfield, VT: Gower.

223
Halloween Fracas Causes a Disturbance

Situation

You are the director in the division of campus recreation at a large midwestern state university with an enrollment of over 30,000 students. Many of the students have established a tradition of going out to the campus town bars dressed up in Halloween costumes. Perhaps as a release from mid-semester tension or as an opportunity to shed their student image, the Saturday night Halloween observance has grown in popularity and attracts thousands of masked students into campus town.

When the bars close at 1 a.m., many students are not ready to retire for the evening and leave the festive atmosphere behind. So most of the masqueraders linger in the streets with really nothing to do. A few students seeking entertainment begin to block traffic in the street and "rock" cars. The resulting traffic jam attracts not only an even larger crowd, but also the police. When the students refuse to disperse upon request from the police, a small-scale riot begins. Police bring out riot sticks and dogs. Students reply with bottle and can throwing and verbal abuse. Before the area is cleared, there has been a substantial amount of vandalism, several minor injuries to both students and police, and 10 to 20 students are arrested. This confrontation between students and police has been repeated for the last two years.

A special university committee for campuswide programming representatives and administrators has been formed to discuss the problem. The decision has been made to plan a special nighttime program that will preserve the festive ritual of dressing up but will avoid another police-student confrontation. You and your campus recreation staff have been given the responsibility of creating a challenging program that will provide activity for the Halloween enthusiasts.

Problem

What do you think are the main causes of the Halloween disturbances? Outline your idea for the programmed activities for the evening, and be ready to present this plan to the committee. Do you feel that scheduled activity alone can solve the problem? What form of police patrol would you recommend for the evening? What special arrangements could you make with the campus town businesses? Do you feel it will be necessary to close off the streets—why or why not?

*Suggested Key Words and Phrases for
Literature Search for Case 223*

Campus recreation   Committee planning
Crowd control   Halloween events
Police relations   College students
Program planning   Recreation programming
Special events   Student involvement
Holidays

Selected References for Case 223

Allen, G., Bastaiani, J., Martin, I., and Richards, J., (eds.) (1987). *Community education: An agenda for educational reform.* Philadelphia: Open University.

Block, J., and King, N. (1987). *School play: A source book.* New York: Garland.

Bullaro, J., and Edginton, C. (1986). *Commercial Leisure Services: Managing for profit, service, and personal satisfaction.* New York: Macmillan.

Cook, L., Osterholt, B., and Riley, E., Jr. (1988). *Anticipating tomorrow's issues: A handbook for policymakers.* Washington, D.C. Council of State Policy and Planning Agencies.

Davis, D., ed. (1981). *Communities and their schools.* New York: McGraw-Hill.

Dwyer, W., and Murrell, D. (1988, July). Park law: Fourteen points to ponder. *Parks and Recreation,* 50-52.

Dwyer, W., and Murrell, D. (1990, April). The ins and outs of park law enforcement. *Parks and Recreation,* 50-53.

Kamberg, M. (1989, Sept.) *The three R's in Overland Park, KS: Reading, 'riting, and recreation,* 92-93.

Lewis, A. (1986). *Partnerships connecting school and community.* Arlington, VA: American Association of School Administrators.

Miller, M., and Galey, D. (1988). *Administration and operation of the college union.* Bloomington, IN: Association of College Unions-International.

Schoem, D., and Knox, W.,(eds.) (1988). *Students talk about college: Essays from the pilot program.* Ann Arbor, MI: Prakken.

Walsh, E. (1989, Aug.). Programming a ghostly good Halloween. *Parks and Recreation,* 33-37.

224
Should Insensitivity Charge be Shrugged Off?

Situation

Eight months after you were hired to shape up the long-troubled Liverpool Park and Recreation Department, you are facing many problems of your own. In a four-page letter sent to you this week, the executive committee of the parks and recreation advisory commission charged that you and your staff have misrepresented information to the City Council, have used parks issues to widen racial divisions, and have been unresponsive and insensitive to the commission and its duties. The letter complained that a commission memorandum on city playgrounds had been "aggressively and falsely characterized as an attempt by white, female outsiders to curtail or eliminate adult basketball for black neighborhoods." The same memorandum was misrepresented to the City Council's parks committee, the letter said.

In addition, this letter claimed that you as director have not established good relations with the commission, and you have not kept members informed of community meetings and other activities. Commission Chair Paul West, in a published interview with a local journalist, acknowledged that the letter is critical, but it was meant to help resolve difficulties, not exacerbate them. He said that the full commission supported the letter, although only three of the commission members signed it.

In the letter, West acknowledges that there has been a history of communication problems between the commission and the department. The relationship between the commission and the previous parks director had deteriorated considerably before the embattled director resigned last year.

You showed the commission's letter to your assistant for his comments, and he replied, "We're following the City Council's orders, which are to clean up the parks system. We have nothing to be ashamed of. My thought is that somebody's relative lost a job in the reorganization, and that person is now seeking revenge."

Parks Commission Member Stan Egbert has also talked to you in private. He said the letter is "an outreach from the commission. I want you to pay attention to these concerns. I'm disappointed that we can't hire a parks and recreation director who can work with our commission."

Problem

What do you say in response to this letter? What are the concerns that are overtly expressed in the letter? What are the concerns that may be covertly expressed? Does one issue underlie all of these problems?; if so, what is it? How would you address each of the concerns stated in the letter? Would you address the concerns covertly stated?, if so, how?

Through what means should you respond? What are the advantages and disadvantages of (a) calling a press conference; (b) writing a letter in return; (c) calling an emergency board session; or (d) ignoring the letter. Should a response be immediate, or should you wait a few days?

Is eight months enough time for the board to make a fair evaluation of the director? What must the board show to prove that the evaluation is unbiased? What criteria should be used in judging the effectiveness of the director? Should the director be held responsible for a "mistake" that a subordinate made? Why or why not?

Define communication. Diagram a model of effective communication taking place between two parties. Suggest ways that communication could be strengthened between the director and the board. Which of the parties should be responsible for making sure that good communication exists?

Suggested Key Words and Phrases for
Literature Search for Case 224

Board relations	Communication
Evaluation	Memorandums
Parks department	Prejudice
Public relations	Race relations
Recreation program planning	Span of control

Selected References for Case Study 224

Busson, T., and Coulter, P., (eds.) (1987). *Policy evaluation for local government*. New York: Greenwood.

DuBois, P. (1981). *Modern administrative practices in human services*. Dubuque, IA: Kendall/Hunt.

Farley, M. (1987). Program evaluation as a political tool. In *Current issues in leisure services: Looking ahead in a time of transition*. J. Bannon, (ed.) Washington, D.C.: International City Management Association, 36-44.

Grossman, A., (ed.) (1989). *Personnel management in recreation and leisure services*. Second ed. South Plainfield, NJ: Groupwork Today.

Hendon, W. (1981). *Evaluating urban parks and recreation*. New York: Praeger.

Herman, R., and Til, J., (eds.) (1989). *Nonprofit board of directors: Analyses and applications*. New Brunswick, NJ: Transaction.

Howe, C. (1987). Evaluating for accountability. In *Current issues in leisure services: Looking ahead in a time of transition*. J. Bannon, (ed.) Washington, D.C.: International City Management Association, 27-35.

Ibrahim, H., Banes, R., and Gerson, G. (1987). *Effective parks and recreation boards and commissions*. Reston, VA: American Alliance for Health, Physical Education, Recreation, and Dance.

Kraus, R. (1985). *Recreation program planning today*. Glenview, IL: Scott, Foresman.

Lundegren, H., and Farrell, P. (1985). *Evaluation for leisure service managers: A dynamic approach*. Philadelphia: Saunders.

Nisbet, R. (1982). *Prejudices*. Cambridge, MA: Harvard Stoops, J., and Edginton, C. (1988, April). Needed: Effective park and recreation boards and commissions. *Parks and Recreation*, 51-55.

Robin, J., and Steinhauer, M. (1988). *Handbook on human services administration*. New York: Marcell Iekker.

Rockwood, L. (1980). *Public parks and recreation administration: Behavior and dynamics*. Salt Lake City: Brighton.

Shivers, J. (1987). *Introduction to recreation service administration*. Philadelphia: Lea & Febiger.

Steiss, A. (1982). *Management control in government*. Lexington, MA: Lexington.

225
Weeds Choke Funds

Situation

You are a member of the White Castle Forest Preserve District. At a recent board meeting, it was noted that additional funds are needed for operations for the district. To raise these funds, Commissioner Joey Jones has said that if the taxpayers paid 2.5 cents per hundred dollars assessed valuation over and above the present tax rate, about $200,000 could be raised.

Board member Tom Johnson opposes the tax increase. He notes that for the past few years the District, with the use of two power driven grass mowers, has maintained State Route 67 adjacent to the District property. The same service has been extended to County Road 34 to the East. These services should be performed by the state and county, thereby freeing sufficient funds of the forest preserve to eradicate the weeds that have been allowed to mar the beauty of the preserve's parks, he says.

"It is important for our image to be in a well-kept area," countered Vern Ricker. "Besides, we are part of the community, and we have a responsibility of keeping the area free from weeds."

Problem

Are Ricker's arguments logical? What other arguments can you think of for mowing the weeds? What arguments can you think of for not mowing the weeds?

Should mowing the weeds on the highways' edge be a high priority for the district? Why or why not? Who is ultimately responsible for the weeds along the highways?

Is the tax increase necessary? If so, how could you present it to the citizens? If not, what sort of additional funding cuts do you recommend? If the burden of mowing the weeds is placed on another agency and the agency does not do it, how do you cope with the negative public relations?

Suggested Key Words and Phrases for
Literature Search for Case 225

Assessed evaluation	Civic responsibility
County highways	Fiscal responsibility
Forest preserve	Mowing
Policy evaluation	Public relations
Subcontracting	Tax increases
Trespass	

Selected References for Case Study 225

Busson, T., and Coulter, P., (eds.) (1987). *Policy evaluation for local government.* New York: Greenwood.

Hansen, S. (1983). *The politics of taxation: Revenue without represen-tation.* New York: Praeger.

Hirschman, A. (1981). *Essays in trespassing: Economics to politics and beyond.* New York: Cambridge University Press.

Klemens, M. (1988, May). Taxes and the economy: Searching for cause and effect. *Illinois Issues,* 10-12.

Klemens, M. (1990, Feb.). Property tax: Hot potato between local and state politicians. *Illinois Issues,* 11-13.

Lewis, Jr., S. (1984). *Taxation for development: Principles and applications.* New York: Oxford University Press.

Sammet, Jr., G., and Kelly, C. (1980). *Do's and Don'ts in subcon-tract management.* New York: AMACOM.

Sammet, Jr., G., and Kelly, C. (1981). *Subcontract management handbook.* New York: AMACOM.

Ramsey, J., and Ramsey, I. (1985). *Budgeting basics: How to survive the budgeting process.* New York: Franklin Watts.

Slavin, S., (ed.) (1985). *Managing finances, personnel, and informa-tion in human services.* New York: Haworth.

Stein, H., (ed.) (1988). *Tax policy in the twenty-first century.* New York: Wiley.

Summers, L., (ed.) (1989). *Tax policy and the economy: Volume three.* Cambridge, MA: MIT University Press.

226
Tourism Project Threatens Town's Attraction

Situation

You have been hired by the Westernburg City Council to advise it about whether to approve a commercial recreation project. Mayor Dale Elks, the person who recommended hiring you, says he remembers the "good ol' days" in this riverside town. Nearly thirty years ago — just a few years before he was first elected mayor — he was chief of police. His own car served as the town's squad car and he had no radio. A flashing beer sign at a local tavern meant trouble; ditto if the light was flashing in the town's telephone office.

"It was like Mayberry here," he told you. "People used to sit on the corner and spit and whittle. But it can't stay that way. Times change, and you have to change with the times."

Right now, the biggest change facing this town of 1,050 people is a proposal to develop 1,200 acres of bluff-lined riverfront into a massive tourist attraction, complete with a water theme park, resort hotel, condominiums, private homes, and an 18-hole golf course.

The project is proposed by businessman Sam Jones, on land his family owns. The first part scheduled to be completed is a 20-acre water park.

The Chamber of Commerce unanimously approved Jones' plan last autumn, saying it could boost the city's sagging treasury by adding as much as $60,000 to the town's tax base — no small change to a town with a total budget of $230,000. The Chamber of Commerce hopes that Jones' plan is the first in a series of bluff-front developments that could ultimately include a small museum, another hotel, a discount shopping center, and medical offices.

"What happens if the project doesn't go through?" supporters asked. "Nothing. Absolutely nothing. And we sit here like we have been for the past twenty years."

However, local environmentalists say the water park and the ensuing development will only denigrate the town's prime asset — its natural beauty. "We are extremely concerned about what this means for the scenic beauty of the area," said Shirley Wright, who heads a local chapter of the Sierra Club. "It's the most scenic section of the entire Mississippi. Sure, we understand it's on private land, but the state and the community have fought to preserve the area the way it is now. Jones may own the property, but the heritage belongs to everyone."

Jones dismissed the importance of a Sierra Club petition of 8,500 signatures opposing the project, saying that many of the signatures are from tourists only passing through. Wright acknowledges this, but suggests that Jones should heed the wishes of those who are drawn to the area for its beauty and who see development as a detriment.

Wright claims that the construction will also have a tremendous, adverse wildlife impact because "a lot of species which currently inhabit the area, including the bald eagle, will be driven out." Jones counters this claim, saying that two-thirds of the area under development will remain "green."

Problem

What would you recommend to the City Council? Is Jones realistic about how little environmental damage his project will cause? Who should have the rights to determine the fate of scenic land, the owner or the public? Could the town better market its current assets rather than seek to bring in new attractions?; if so, devise a marketing strategy. Does the fact that you are being paid by the City Council influence your decision on whether you recommend the project; does it influence how you word your presentation?

Suggested Key Words and Phrases for Literature Search for Case 226

Chamber of Commerce	Consulting
Commercial recreation	Environmental impact
"green space"	Marketing
Outdoor recreation	Public land
Rural development	Special interest groups
Tourism	

Selected References for Case 226

Bar-El, R., Bendavid, A., and Karaska, G. (1988). *Patterns of change in developing rural regions.* Boulder, CO: Westview.

Britt, S., and Guess, N. (1983). *The Dartnell marketing manager's handbook.* Chicago: Dartnell.

Bullaro, J., and Edginton, C. (1986). *Commercial Leisure Services: Managing for profit, service, and personal satisfaction.* New York: Macmillan.

Crompton, J., and Richardson, S. (1986, Oct.). The tourism connection: When public and private leisure services merge. *Parks and Recreation, 38-44, 67.*

Crossley, J. (1988). *Public/Commercial cooperation in parks and recreation.* Columbus, OH: Publishing Horizons.

Crossley, J., and Jamieson, L. (1988). *Introduction to commercial and entrepreneurial recreation.* Champaign, IL: Sagamore.

Knudson, D. (1980). *Outdoor recreation.* New York: Macmillan.

Pigram, J. (1983). *Outdoor recreation and resource management.* New York: St. Martin.

Russell, C., and Nicholson, N. (1982). *Public choice and rural development.* Washington, D.C.: Resources for the future.

Warren, R. (1990, June). Land stewardship: Your professional responsibility. *Park Maintenance and Grounds Management,* 14-16.

Zook, L. (1986, Jan.). Outdoor adventure programs build character in five ways. *Parks and Recreation, 54-57.*

227
Board Looks at User Fee for Park

Situation

You are a member of the Grant County Forest Preserve Board. Tonight, as part of the June meeting, the president of the board is expected to attempt to enact a one-month-trial user fee. The special fee, which would be in effect Saturdays and Sundays in July and on the Fourth of July, would be $1 per car and would be collected at all of the park's entrances.

"Our costs have just skyrocketed and we are trying to put some of the cost on the user rather than on the general public," explained the president at the previous board meeting. "We already have golfers paying $7 a round and swimmers and boaters paying. What's wrong with a dollar a car anyway? Everyone else is paying for a service. This may be the only way to prevent a tax increase."

The president emphasized that the user fee would only be collected on weekends and on the single July holiday. He said it might help to "spread out" the use of the park, which has been described as "very heavy" in recent weekends and "light" during the week.

The entrance user fee would be established in such a way so golfers, swimmers, and boaters do not have to pay an additional fee as well as the special facility charge they pay to use the golf course, beach, or rental boats. The fee will be collected from car and motorcycle riders but not from bicyclists.

Assuming typical July attendance patterns, the president projected that the district will be able to raise approximately $20,000 with the user fee.

Problem

Do you vote in favor of the proposed fee? Is it fair to charge the public if they have already paid for it with their taxes? Develop an argument for voting for the fee. Develop an argument for voting against the fee. Why does the board distinguish between "cars and motorcycles" and "bicyclists"? How will the board avoid charging the golfers, swimmers and boaters twice? Is such a proposed fee workable? Discuss problems that must be overcome if such a fee is to be implemented. How should the board evaluate whether the fee is successful?

Suggested Key Words and Phrases for
Literature Search for Case 227

Budgeting	Charging policy
Double taxation	Fees
Evaluation	Forest preserve board
Pricing	User fee

Selected References for Case Study 227

Bovaird, A., Tricker, M., and Stoakes, R. (1984). *Recreation management and pricing: The effect of charging policy on demand at countryside recreation sites.* Brookfield, VT: Gower.

Camillus, J. (1984). *Budgeting for profit: How to exploit the potential of your business.* Randor, PA: Chilton.

Crompton, J. (1987). How to establish a price for park and recreation services. In *Current issues in leisure services: Looking ahead in a time of transition.* J. Bannon, (ed.) Washington, D.C.: International City Management Association, 93-107.

Dworak, R. (1980). *Taxpayers, taxes, and government spending: Perspectives on the taxpayer revolt.* New York: Praeger.

Garbutt, D. (1985). *How to budget and control cash.* Brookfield, VT: Gower.

Hansen, S. (1983). *The politics of taxation: Revenue without representation.* New York: Praeger.

Lewis, Jr., S. (1984). *Taxation for development: Principles and applications.* New York: Oxford University Press.

Moore, B., (ed.) (1983). *The entrepreneur in local government.* Washington, D.C.: International City Management Association.

More municipal public fee courses as golf boom continues in '90s. (1990, June). *Park Maintenance and Grounds Management, 3.*

Ramsey, J., and Ramsey, I. (1985). *Budgeting basics: How to survive the budgeting process.* New York: Franklin Watts.

Stein, H., (ed.) (1988). *Tax policy in the twenty-first century.* New York: Wiley.

Waters, J. (1987). Fees and charges: Underutilized revenues. In *Current issues in leisure services: Looking ahead in a time of transition.* J. Bannon, (ed.) Washington, D.C.: International City Management Association, 88-92.

Wood, A. (1990, May). Golf and government: A partnership that works. *Parks and Recreation*, 48-51.

228
Improvement from Proposition Thirteen?

Situation

You are the financial consultant to Wayne Higgs, director of the Grantsville Parks and Recreation Department. Although Wayne does not like to see seasonal workers cut or staff salaries frozen, he is convinced that one good effect of Proposition Thirteen and similar legislation is to "get us off our duffs and make the majority of us become better managers."

Wayne is optimistic the district can survive the loss of tax revenue by somehow tightening its belt. One encouraging sign is that the "pay as you play" programs now being offered by the district are proving to be very successful. In fact, Wayne claims that participation has doubled, even tripled in some cases, even though people are now paying a fee for their recreation.

The West Lake Aquatic Recreation Area should continue to pay for itself, said Wayne. However, because of the budget cuts, the number of summer seasonal personnel at the lake have been cut from 22 to nine. Wayne admits this cutting may adversely affect the maintenance of the lake.

Wayne also fears that other programs may not be able to pay for themselves. He is troubled that needed maintenance on the campsites and picnic areas can not be done because of a lack of personnel. He is also bothered by the fact that the money targeted to light a ballpark must now be rerouted. Therefore, he has asked you to suggest ways to generate revenue and/or make budget cuts for his parks department.

Problem

What would you recommend that Wayne do? What options does Wayne have for generating money? Could the parks department sell bonds? Would applying for a grant be a reasonable solution? Would it be wise to use volunteers? Should the parks department continue charging fees for its services? Would you suggest any budget controls to make sure the money being spent is used wisely? If so, describe them. What sort of belt-tightening could a parks department do? Is freezing salaries a wise move? Discuss the pros and cons of it.

Suggested Key Words and Phrases for
Literature Search for Case 228

Bonds	Budgeting
Consulting	Cutbacks
Financing	Grants
Personnel cuts	Proposition 13
Volunteers	Wage Freeze

Selected References for Case Study 228

Crompton, J. (1988, March). Are you ready to implement a comprehensive revenue-generating program? *Parks and Recreation*, 54-60.

Dworak, R. (1980). *Taxpayers, taxes, and government spending: Perspectives on the taxpayer revolt.* New York: Praeger.

Finsterbusch, K. (1980). *Understanding social impacts: Assessing the effects of public projects.* Beverly Hills, CA: Sage.

Foley, J., and Benest, F. (1988, Aug.). Rx for agency blues: A dose of entrepreneurship. *Parks and Recreation*, 42-46.

Green, M., and Berry, J. (1985). *The challenge of hidden profits: Reducing corporate bureaucracy and waste.* New York: Morrow.

Hansen, S. (1983). *The politics of taxation: Revenue without representation.* New York: Praeger.

Henderson, K. (1988, Nov.). Are volunteers worth their weight in gold? *Parks and Recreation*, 40-43.

King, S. (1990, June). Planning a low maintenance playground. *Park Maintenance and Grounds Management*, 6-8.

Lewis, Jr., S. (1984). *Taxation for development: Principles and applications.* New York: Oxford University Press.

Reynolds, J., and Hormachea, M. (1976). Budgeting for public recreation and park agencies. *Public recreation administration*, 272-300.

Stein, H., (ed.) (1988). *Tax policy in the twenty-first century.* New York: Wiley.

Summers, L., (ed.) (1989). *Tax policy and the economy: Volume three.* Cambridge, MA: MIT University Press.

Umapathy, S. (1987). *Current budgeting practices in U.S. industry.* New York: Quorum.

229
Skating into Trouble

Situation

You are a member of the Bailey City Council. One of the problems in the community is skateboarders who attempt reckless stunts at the parks and who have harassed pedestrians on public sidewalks. The issue was brought up by police officer Joe Riley at the City Council meeting. "If you are a resident and you are trying to walk down the street, all it takes is one skateboarder for it to be a nuisance," said Riley. He also noted the property damage done by skateboarders, the injuries that had resulted by youths flipping off of public steps, and the liability the parks currently assumed for skateboard accidents. He proposed several solutions, including:

1. Pass legislation requiring that skateboarders wear protective gear.
2. Assess fines for breaking laws that restrict skateboarding. Riley suggested that the fines start at $10 and run as high as $500.
3. Restrict skateboarders from the streets and steps but build them a challenging course. The estimated cost for the course would be $8,000.

4. Confiscate skateboards of those skateboarders who violate the law.
5. Pass a law that would limit the use of skateboards to particular streets and facilities.

Also at the meeting, however, were members of the group SKATE, Students Keeping American Transportation Efficient. The group claimed that skateboards were the only way that many students had to travel and that restricting the use of skateboards restricted their freedom.

The SKATE president was especially defiant. "Kids love to do whatever they can't do . . . the bans are not one bit a threat."

"Skateboarding is a sport. We should be free to participate in the sport if we choose," said another SKATE representative. "I'm not a criminal; I'm an athlete."

Problem

Which, if any, of Officer Riley's suggestions do you think the board should pursue? If you do adopt one of Riley's suggestions, how would you answer each of the objections submitted by SKATE? If someone does violate a skateboard ordinance, should the person be treated "like a criminal" — arrested, jailed, and forced to stand trial? If fines were to be assessed, would you argue with Riley that they should range depending on the circumstance, or that they should apply to everyone at all times?

Suggested Key Words and Phrases for
Literature Search for Case 229

Carrying capacity	City ordinances
Liability	Nuisance laws
Police relations	Public streets
Property damage	Skateboard facilities
Skateboarding	Urban recreation
Youth culture	Zoning

Selected References for Case Study 229

Burke, W. (1987, Sept.). Designing safer playgrounds. *Parks and Recreation*, 38-43, 73.

Christiansen, M. (1987). Safety is no accident. In *Current issues in leisure services: Looking ahead in a time of transition*. J. Bannon, (ed.) Washington, D.C.: International City Management Association.

Crawford, Jr., C. (1979). *Strategy and tactics in municipal zoning.* Second ed. Englewood Cliffs, NJ: Prentice-Hall.

Direnfeld-Michael, B. (1989, March). A risk management primer for recreators. *Parks and Recreation*, 40-45.

Fairfax, J., Wright, L., and Maupin, M. (1988, Dec.). At-risk youth: Special needs. *Parks and Recreation*, 40-43.

Fogg, G., and Shivers, J. (1981). *Management planning for park and recreation areas.* Arlington, VA: National Recreation and Park Association.

Graham, P., and Kalar, L., Jr. (1979). *Planning and delivering leisure services.* Dubuque, IA: Brown.

Kauffman, R. (1989, Sept.). Recognizing the accident chain. *Parks and Recreation*, 68-73.

Lai, R. (1988). *Law in urban design and planning: The invisible web.* New York: Van Reinhold.

Macdonald, S. (1987, Nov.). Building support for urban trails. *Parks and Recreation*, 26-33.

Peterson, D. (1984). *Analyzing safety performance.* Deer Park, NY: Alaray.

Powell, L. (1989, Sept.). Safety and success: Who's responsible? *Parks and Recreation*, 74-77.

Shivers, J. (1986). *Recreational safety: The standard of care.* Cranbury, NJ: Associated University Presses.

Shelby, B., and Heberlein, T. (1986). *Carrying capacity in recreation settings.* Corvallis, OR: Oregon State University Press.

Simpson, N. (1988, Oct.). Playgrounds: Safety and fun by design. *Parks and Recreation*, 21-32, 63.

230
Snow Dumping Procedure has Residents in Dumps

Situation

You are a member of the Jonesburg City Council. For years, the city has been using the city's parks as wholesale dumping grounds during blizzards. However, at tonight's meeting, residents have commented that the piles of garbage and ice in the parks have begun to attract rats, and they fear that the parks are a health hazard for children. The residents claim that the baseball and softball fields have been gouged by snowplows, which have left rivers of melted snow, chunks of earth, asphalt, and other debris in their wake. In addition, a local newspaper has just run a photo essay showing the parks to be marshlands of garbage and melting ice, with debris-packed snow mounds as high as six feet surrounding several baseball diamonds.

Park District Director Ivan Turpin claims that the park district does not have the necessary heavy equipment to clean up the mess. The district has only one giant vacuum truck available for clean-up work, he said. He insists that the city should supply the labor and equipment to clean up the mess or else provide him the funds for more trucks, and salaries for extra personnel. "The city caused the predicament and it must take the necessary steps to clean it up!"

The director also said that the park district would no longer allow the city to dump snow in the parks. "The city should begin planning now where to dump snow —other than in the parks— in the event of another emergency situation."

Problem

Does the city have an obligation to help the park district clean up the debris? If so, what should the city do to help? What alternatives would you suggest for the placement of removed snow if the parks cannot be used as dumping grounds? What sort of compromise might the city and the park district reach regarding the dumping of snow? How would you handle the residents'

complaints of rats resulting from the snow-dumping incident?
What would you say about the editor of the newspaper who
published the degrading but truthful photo essay of the parks'
condition? Should an ordinance be drawn up by the park board
to prohibit snow being dumped in the parks? If so, should the
ordinance mention anything besides snow?

*Suggested Key Words and Phrases for
Literature Search for Case 230*

City-park district relations   City ordinances
Ecology   Landscaping
Liability   Off-season park usage
Press relations   Public relations
Safety   Snow dumping
Zoning

Selected References for Case Study 230

Cook, L., Osterholt, B., and Riley, E., Jr. (1988). *Anticipating
   tomorrow's issues: A handbook for policymakers.* Washington,
   D.C.: Council of State Policy and Planning Agencies.
Crawford, Jr., C. (1979). *Strategy and tactics in municipal zoning.*
   Second ed. Englewood Cliffs, NJ: Prentice-Hall.
Gold, S. (1980). *Recreation planning and design.* New York:
   McGraw-Hill.
Gold, S. (1987). A human service approach to recreation plan-
   ning. In *Current issues in leisure services: Looking ahead in a
   time of transition.* J. Bannon,(ed.) Washington, D.C.: Inter-
   national City Management Association, 5-16.
Ibrahim, H., Banes, R., and Gerson, G. (1987). *Effective parks and
   recreation boards and commissions.* Reston, VA: American
   Alliance for Health, Physical Education, Recreation, and
   Dance
Lai, R. (1988). *Law in urban design and planning: The invisible web.*
   New York: Van Reinhold.

Molnar, D., and Rutledge, A. (1986). *Anatomy of a park: The essentials of recreation area planning and design.* New York: McGraw-Hill.

Marsh, W. (1983). *Landscape planning: Environmental applications.* Reading, MA: Addison-Wesley.

Peterson, C., and McCarthy, C. (1982). *Handling zoning and land use litigation: A practical guide.* Charlottesville, VA: Michie.

Powell, L. (1989, Sept.). Safety and success: Who's responsible? *Parks and Recreation,* 74-77.

Reynolds, J., and Hormachea, M. (1976). Legal authority for public recreation. *Public recreation administration.* Reston, VA: Reston, 39-54.

Reynolds, J., and Hormachea, M. (1976). Public relations. *Public recreation administration.* Reston, VA: Reston, 372-394.

Warren, R. (1990, June). Land stewardship: Your professional responsibility. *Park Maintenance and Grounds Management,* 14-16.

231
Is Free Trip a Theft of Public Funds?

Situation

You are the assistant director of the Smithville Public Parks and Recreation Department. As part of your duties, you fly across the United States as a member of a team to promote Smithville. Because of your travels, you have accumulated the mileage necessary to qualify for a free "frequent flyer" air fare to Paris. Should you take the trip?

Dave Clark, city attorney, says no. He claims that the previous trips were made at taxpayer expense and therefore should not be for personal use. City funds were used to earn the mileage, and the benefit should belong to the city, he said.

However, Recreation Director Ron Myers says that such "perks" are considered normal practice, and that during the last legislative session many legislators — as well as city representatives at the Legislature — took advantage of airline programs that provided them with free rental cars and other fringe benefits. He claims that the parks department personnel are paid low salaries but receive many benefits, thereby keeping most of them content with their pay.

Problem

Should you accept the trip? If you do not accept the trip, what would you do with the trip? If you do accept it, would you make it public or try to keep it a secret? Although the trip is free, there will be expenses such as hotels, food and entertainment — who should pay for these? Would it make a difference if your boss was saying not to take the trip but the city attorney was encouraging you to take it? What are the legalities about accepting such a trip? What are the ethical issues?

Suggested Key Words and Phrases for Literature
Search for Case 231

Bonuses	Commercial recreation
Ethics	Fringe benefits
Junket	Perks
Public funds	Right to know
Vacation	

Selected References for Case Study 231

Culkin, D. (1988, Feb.). The right way to discipline. *Parks and Recreation*, 44-45.

Dworak, R. (1980). *Taxpayers, taxes, and government spending: Perspectives on the taxpayer revolt.* New York: Praeger.

Grossman, A., (ed.) (1989). *Personnel management in recreation and leisure services.* Second ed. South Plainfield, NJ: Groupwork Today.

Hansen, S. (1983). *The politics of taxation: Revenue without representation.* New York: Praeger.

Husband, T. (1976). *Work analysis and pay structure.* London: McGraw-Hill.

Kleinbeck, U., Quast, H., Thierry, H., and Hacker, H., (eds.) (1990). *Work motivation.* Hillsdale, NJ: Lawrence Erlbaum.

Milkovich, G., and Newman, J. (1984). *Compensation.* Third ed. Homewood, IL: BPI/Irwin.

Morf, M. (1986). *Optimizing work performance: A look beyond the bottom line.* New York: Quorum.

Nash, M. (1985). *Making people productive.* San Francisco: Jossey-Bass.

Patten, T. (1977). *Pay: Employee compensation and incentive plans.* New York: Free.

Patten, T. (1988). *Fair pay.* San Francisco: Jossey-Bass.

Redeker, J. (1983). *Discipline: Policies and procedures.* Washington, D.C.: Bureau of National Affairs.

232
Should Kids' Ideas Become Reality?

Situation

You are the assistant director of the Butcher Park District. Butcher needs a new park built on the edge of town. To help inspire interest in the project, a local newspaper ran a "perfect playground" contest in the elementary school. Each child drew the "perfect playground" and submitted the idea to the class teacher. The class teacher, in turn, gave them to the local newspaper.

The local newspaper ran a story about the proposed new park and illustrated it with pictures that the children had drawn. The following day, the newspaper turned the pictures over to you with the suggestion that you go through them to get ideas about what to put in the park.

The director, though, already knows what he wants to build into the park. He has made his budget request and plans to present a detailed proposal at the next board meeting. His ideas, though, are considerably different from what the children drew.

When you confront him with this problem, he tells you not to worry. He explains that children only ask for what they know and that he knows best. Although he has not constructed a city survey, he has read recent literature about trends in playground facilities. Who is the expert in recreation, he asks — me or them?

Problem

Should you incorporate the children's ideas into the new park? Should a survey be taken of community needs or is relying on national trends okay? If you were to take a survey in the town, whom should you question? — children, parents, or everyone? Was the newspaper justified in sponsoring the contest? Was the newspaper obligated to turn the pictures over to you, or was this a special favor? From the pictures, how could you identify what the majority of the children wanted? To what extent can a recreation specialist utilize a "I know what is best for you" approach for decision making?

Suggested Key Words and Phrases for Literature Search for Case 232

Community input	Decision making
Facility construction	Market demand analysis
Playgrounds	Press relations
Public relations	Specialization
Survey research	

Selected References for Case Study 232

Adrian, J. (1981). *CM: The construction management process.* Reston, VA: Reston.

Burke, W. (1987, Sept.). Designing safer playgrounds. *Parks and Recreation*, 38-43, 73.

Flynn, P. (1987, April). Small parks projects: Getting citizens involved. *Parks and Recreation*, 34-36.

Frost, J. (1990, June). Tips on lighting park playgrounds. *Park Maintenance and Grounds Management*, 10-12.

Hain, P. (1980). Neighborhood participation. London: Billing.

Hawkins, T. (1988, May). Parks: For the people, by the people. *Parks and Recreation*, 39-43.

Haworth, J., (ed.) (1979). *Community involvement and leisure.* London: Lepus.

Kelsey, C., and Gray, H. (1986). *The citizen survey process in parks and recreation.* Reston, VA: American Alliance for Health, Physical Education, Recreation, and Dance.

King, S. (1990, June). Planning a low-maintenance playground.

233
Is "One Circus Policy" One Policy Too Many?

Situation

You are the marketing director at a large public coliseum in a Midwestern town of approximately 100,000 people. On your desk is an application from Circus-Circus Circus Products requesting permission to stage a circus in your auditorium.

Your first reaction is no. A 30-year-old policy exists that says only one circus, ice show, rodeo, and tractor-pull can be booked each year because booking more than one such show would likely lose money for the coliseum. For this year, the coliseum has already booked the Ringling Bros. and Barnum & Bailey Circus.

In the cover letter, you note that the applicant believes that your policy is unfair. He writes that the coliseum is a public facility and that it should be able to be used by the public. He notes that other facilities in the area are too small to seat the crowd capacity or else have ceilings to low too allow the high-wire acts to be performed. He claims that he loses money when using other area facilities and insists that he be allowed to use yours. If he is not granted permission, he says he may have to resort to a lawsuit.

Your predecessor explained the policy to you before she left for her next job. She said that the market could not adequately support two circuses a year. "We don't deal in politics, we deal in show business," she said. The coliseum charges 12 percent of the gross proceeds after state taxes and must be guaranteed a minimum of $3,000 at each event it sponsors. She said that higher grosses could be made by sponsoring more rock concerts rather than sponsoring an additional circus.

Problem

Write a reply to the Circus-Circus Circus representative. Should you allow him to stage his circus? Can private groups be excluded from a public arena? Is a 30-year-old policy outdated? If so, what could be done to update it? Is it fair for one circus to have a monopoly on the arena for a year; should the monopoly be renewed if there is a positive relationship even though another group would like a turn at using the arena? Should you call your lawyer about the possibility of a lawsuit? Should you call other arenas about their current policies? Should the financial goal of a public arena be to make a profit, break even, or lose money, but provide culture?

Suggested Key Words and Phrases for
Literature Search for Case 233

Arena management	Commercial recreation
Contract negotiation	Financial philosophy
Market demand	Monopoly
Networking	Policies
Public arenas	

Selected References for Case Study 233

Bailey, K. (1982). *Methods of social research.* New York: Free.
Baker, T. (1988). *Doing social research.* New York: McGraw-Hill.
Crompton, J., and Lamb, Jr., C. (1986). *Marketing government and social services.* New York: Wiley.

Crompton, J., and Richardson, S. (1986, Oct.). The tourism connection: When public and private leisure services merge. *Parks and Recreation,* 38-44, 67.

Crossley, J. (1988). *Public/Commercial cooperation in parks and recreation.* Columbus, OH: Publishing Horizons.

Cunningham, W., Cunningham, I., and Swift, C. (1987). *Marketing: A managerial approach.* Cincinnati, OH: South-Western.

deVaus, D. (1986). *Surveys in social research.* London: Allen & Unwin.

Heydt, M. (1986, Feb.). Ten principles for contract administration. *Parks and Recreation,* 48, 51.

Hipps, S. (1990, March). Partners in profit. *The Leisure Manager,* 14-18.

Melillo, J. (1983). *Market the arts!* New York: Foundation for the Extension and Development of the American Professional Theatre.

Mulford, C. (1984). *Interorganizational relations: Implications for community development.* New York: Human Sciences.

Prus, R. (1989). *Pursuing customers: An ethnography of marketing activities.* Newbury Park, CA: Sage.

Soderberg, J. (1989, June). Marketing recreation right. *Parks and Recreation,* 38-41.

Uysal, M. (1986, Oct.). Marketing for tourism - A growing field. *Parks and Recreation,* 57-66.

234
Should Guard be Fired for Firing Pistol?

Situation

You are the assistant director of recreation in a large metropolitan area. One of your duties is to listen to discipline cases and decide a verdict. This morning, you are to review the case of Felix Hand, a guard at the zoological park. Hand fired his service revolver at a stray dog, just twenty yards from two bird watchers whom he did not realize were there. He was suspended for ten days without pay by his immediate supervisor for "discharging his firearm without authority and not reporting the incident to his supervisor."

You are quite well acquainted with the problem of stray dogs roaming in the park. Three of the dogs killed a blesbok, a rare African antelope, this past Monday, and six to ten dogs are still running loose. The health department reports that these dogs are very dangerous.

Hand fired the gun at least once around dusk Tuesday evening. The shooting occurred in the park's experimental meadow, a 14-acre site of dense foliage west of the zoo. Hand claimed he had not hit the animal. Park regulations forbid guards from firing guns unless a person's life or zoo animal's life is threatened. Hand and a friend had fired at the dogs in the blesbok attack. Two of the dogs were injured from the shots and were later captured and killed. Many guards have been combing the park Tuesday, but the dogs eluded all of the searchers except Hand. Hand considered the shooting incident not out of the ordinary, considering the circumstances, and therefore did not report it to his supervisor.

"As far as can be determined, this was not a life-and-death situation," his supervisor told you. "Possessing a firearm is a very serious responsibility. We expect our employees who are authorized to carry firearms to act responsibly."

The bird watchers did not let Hand know that they were there before he shot at them or even after he inadvertently shot at them. However, they did report the incident to the recreation department. They explained why they did not tell Hand they were there: "We thought he might start shooting. If he saw us moving in the bushes, he might have thought we had tails and opened fire. We were screened by the bushes; he couldn't see us, and we didn't see him until he started shooting."

Problem

Should Hand be reinstated? Was Hand correct in firing on the dogs? Should Hand have reported shooting at the dogs to his supervisor? Did the guard have an obligation to watch for bird watchers—did the bird watchers have an obligation to watch for guards? Was the supervisor justified for suspending Hand without pay? Would you discipline the supervisor? What would you do to rid the park of the dogs?

Suggested Key Words and Phrases for
Literature Search for Case 234

Animal rights   Contracting services
Disciplinary procedures   Firearms
Formal organization   Safety
Security procedures   Security services
Situational ethics   Suspension
Termination   Zoological parks

Selected References for Case Study 234

Christiansen, M. (1987). Safety is no accident. In *Current issues in leisure services: Looking ahead in a time of transition*. J. Bannon, (ed.) Washington, D.C.: International City Management Association.

Coulson, R. (1981). *The termination handbook.* New York: Free.

Culkin, D. (1988, Feb.). The right way to discipline. *Parks and Recreation*, 44-45.

DeHoog, R. (1984). *Contracting out for human services: Economic, political, and organizational perspectives.* Albany, NY: State University of New York Press.

Direnfeld-Michael, B. (1989, March). A risk management primer for recreators. *Parks and Recreation*, 40-45.

Holloway, W., and Leech, M. (1985). *Employment termination: Rights and remedies.* Washington, D.C.: Bureau of National Affairs.

Kauffman, R. (1989, Sept.). Recognizing the accident chain. *Parks and Recreation*, 68-73.

Peterson, D. (1984). *Analyzing safety performance.* Deer Park, NY: Alaray.

Powell, L. (1989, Sept.). Safety and success: Who's responsible? *Parks and Recreation*, 74-77.

Redeker, J. (1983). *Discipline: Policies and procedures.* Washington, D.C.: Bureau of National Affairs.

Shivers, J. (1986). *Recreational safety: The standard of care.* Cranbury, NJ: Associated University Presses.
Zwerin, K. (1986, March). Zoos: A blueprint for fiscal survival. *Parks and Recreation*, 42-45, 67.

235
Curfew Considered to Curb Vandalism

Situation

You are the parks and recreation director in the town of Warrensville, a community of 150,000 people. The Warrensville City Council is considering two actions to reduce vandalism in the town: establishing a curfew and closing a park.

"We are giving serious thought to closing the park," said Council spokesman Steve Peterson. "Although the park has been open for nearly ten years, it has recently been the site of rough and rowdy teenage parties. Police have been called to handle fighting, noise pollution, and teenage drinking on many occasions during the past two years, especially on weekends. Broken beer bottles are more prevalent than flowers in the park. We have recently received petitions from residents asking that the park be closed. Ironically, we have also received a petition from a group of teenagers who asked that the park be refurbished. The youth want new equipment because the current equipment has been destroyed. Although I would like to help our youth, the town can't be babysitting for people's children."

A City Council vote is necessary to close the park. Peterson said the vote is likely to come at next month's Council meeting. He also said that the attorney would present a list of streets to be included in a curfew ordinance at the meeting.

Problem

Should the park be closed permanently? If not, should the City Council refurbish it? Is a curfew likely to keep teenagers out of the park? Is either the curfew or the closing of the park a good alternative; can you think of a better one? Do residents living near a park deserve a voice in what happens in the park? Should the youth petition be ignored since it was submitted by "just a bunch of kids"? How can you balance the wants and needs of the residents near the park, the youth who party in the park, and the youth who merely utilize the park?

Suggested Key Words and Phrases for
Literature Search for Case 235

Alcohol	Citizen input
Curfew	Gangs
Problem patrons	Refurbishing
Resident complaints	Vandalism
Youth	

Selected References for Case Study 235

Christianson, M. (1983). *Vandalism control management for parks and recreation areas.* State College, PA: Venture.

Fairfax, J., Wright, L., and Maupin, M. (1988, Dec.). At-risk youth: Special needs. *Parks and Recreation*, 40-43.

Fogg, G., and Shivers, J. (1981). *Management planning for park and recreation areas.* Arlington, VA: National Recreation and Park Association.

Hain, P. (1980). Neighborhood participation. London: Billing.

Hawkins, T. (1988, May). Parks: For the people, by the people. *Parks and Recreation*, 39-43.

Haworth, J., (ed.) (1979). *Community involvement and leisure.* London: Lepus.

Kelsey, C., and Gray, H. (1986). *The citizen survey process in parks and recreation.* Reston, VA: American Alliance for Health, Physical Education, Recreation, and Dance.

O'Bama, B. (1988, Aug.-Sept.). Why organize? Problems and promise in the inner city. *Illinois Issues*, 40-42.

Sewell, W., and Coppock, J., (eds.) (1977). *Public participation in planning.* London: Wiley.

Shattuck, J. (1988, July). Vandal-proof your park. *Parks and Recreation*, 32-37.

Stewart, W., Jr. (1976). *Citizen participation in public administration*. Birmingham, AL: University of Alabama, Bureau of Public Administration.

Tindell, J. (1987). "Grass Roots" community development of leisure opportunity. In *Current issues in leisure services: Looking ahead in a time of transition*. J. Bannon, (ed.) Washington, D.C.: International City Management Association, 159-167.

Underwood, R. (1990, Jan.). Education and vandalism. *Park Maintenance and Grounds Management*, 10-13.

236
Insubordinate Worker Feared For His Life

Situation

You are on the Civil Service Commission for a large metropolitan area. Today, you are asked to decide the case of John Timmy, a community center director. Timmy was fired by his supervisor for insubordination when he failed to report to work in a downtown community city.

Timmy claims that he had received death threats after he enforced an unpopular policy late one evening. The threat came from some teenagers, reputed to be gang members. The teenagers said that they were going home to get their knives and, if he was ever seen in the area again, he would not leave it alive. The center is in a rough area of town, and Timmy believes that the death threats are genuine. He claims that his life was/is in danger, and therefore did not report for work the next day. Instead, he notified his supervisor of the situation. His supervisor, however, insisted that he report to work. Timmy refused to go and was fired on the spot.

Problem

Should Timmy be reinstated? Do employees have the right to refuse to work in certain parks/community centers? Is the parks and recreation department responsible for its employees' safety? If so, what should be done about Timmy's safety concerns? How would you investigate whether Timmy is overreacting to what the teens said? If Timmy is reinstated, should he be allowed to collect back pay? If reinstated, should he be sent to the same center or a different center as director? If he is reinstated, should his job assignment be kept a secret since his life is in danger? Do supervisors have the right to remove an employee for insubordination?

Suggested Key Words and Phrases for Literature Search for Case 236

Civil service commission	Community center
Death threats	Employee safety
Gangs	Grievance procedures
Insubordination	Reinstatement
Supervision	Teenagers

Selected References for Case Study 236

Coulson, R. (1981). *The termination handbook.* New York: Free.

Culkin, D. (1988, Feb.). The right way to discipline. *Parks and Recreation*, 44-45.

Gambrill, E., and Stein, T. (1983). *Supervision: A decision-making approach.* Beverly Hills, CA: Sage.

Hawkins, P., and Shohet, R. (1989). *Supervision in the helping professions: An individual, group, and organizational approach.* Philadelphia: Open University.

Holloway, S., and Brager, G. (1989). *Supervising in the human services: The politics of practice.* New York: Free.

Holloway, W., and Leech, M. (1985). *Employment termination: Rights and remedies.* Washington, D.C.: Bureau of National Affairs.

Huntington, S. (1985). *Planning a community center*. Ames, IA: North Central Regional Extension Publications.

Jackson, J. (1984). *Leisure and sports center management*. Springfield, IL: Thomas.

Matteson, M., and Ivancevich, J. (1987). *Controlling work stress: Effective human resource and management strategies*. San Francisco: Jossey-Bass.

Powell, L. (1989, Sept.). Safety and success: Who's responsible? *Parks and Recreation*, 74-77.

Redeker, J. (1983). *Discipline: Policies and procedures*. Washington, D.C.: Bureau of National Affairs.

Willis-Kistler, P. (1988, Nov.) Fighting gangs with recreation. *Parks and Recreation*, 44-49.

237
Stadium Violence: Athletes Used as Live Targets

Situation

You are the recreation director responsible for supervising the public arena and public stadiums in a large metropolitan area. Your security director, as well as star baseball players, have reported that things are getting out of hand at the stadium.

In the eighth inning of a tight game, George Polk, the all-star left-fielder, was nearly maimed by a 9-volt radio transistor battery launched at him by an anonymous "fan" while Polk patrolled left field. A few days earlier, Polk barely escaped serious injury when a sock full of bolts weighing five pounds just missed him as he chased a fly ball. Infuriated by being a live target for grandstand terrorists, Polk insists that such incidents be stopped, or that he be traded to another team where playing baseball is safer.

Tim Stalks, security director, reports that he closed a section of bleachers during a recent game after bottles and other trash were heaved at players walking onto the field. He promised that the one game closing would be followed by closing the bleachers for the season if such behavior happened again. The team owners, though, are opposed to following through with the threat, fearing a large amount of revenue will be lost.

Problem

What would you recommend to solve the problem? Was Stalks right in closing a section of bleachers for a game? Since he made the threat to close the bleachers permanently for the season, should he follow through with it if the need arises, even though the owners oppose the idea? Should fans be placed further from the playing field? Is more security needed to monitor what the fans bring into the stadium? Create a list of items that fans could be allowed to bring. Would you recommend that Polk, the popular superstar responsible for bringing out most of the well-behaved fans as well as the trouble-makers, be traded? How would you deal with this situation if it were at the collegiate level instead of the professional level?

Suggested Key Words and Phrases for Literature Search for Case 237

Athletic administration	Arena management
Collegiate athletics	Crowd control
Professional sports	Safety
Security personnel	Spectators
Stadium security	Violence

Selected References for Case Study 237

Evans, J. (1974). *Blowing the whistle on intercollegiate sports.* Chicago: Nelson-Hall.

Dwyer, W., and Murrell, D. (1988, July). Park law: Fourteen points to ponder. *Parks and Recreation*, 50-52.

Dwyer, W., and Murrell, D. (1990, April). The ins and outs of park law enforcement. *Parks and Recreation*, 50-53.

Hillery, G., and Lincoln, A. (1982). *Leisure, freedom, and crowd behavior*. Durham, NH: Library Crime Research Project.

Pooley, J. (1980). *The sport fan: A social-psychology of misbehavior*. Vanier City, Ontario: Canadian Association for Health, Physical Education, and Recreation.

Rose, J. (1982). *Outbreaks, the sociology of collective behavior*. New York: Free.

Russell, R. (1986). *Leadership in recreation*. St. Louis: Times Mirror/Mosby.

Skalko, T., and Ellard, J. (1987, June). Applied situational leadership. *Parks and Recreation*, 28-33.

Stillman, Jr., R. (1976). *Public administration: Concepts and cases*. Boston: Houghton-Mifflin.

Tropman, J. (1984). *Policy management in the human services*. New York: Columbia University Press.

Twardzik, L. (1986, March). Intercollegiate athletics: A clash of values. *Parks and Recreation*, 54, 57-59.

Wright, S. (1978). *Crowds and riots: A study in social organization*. Beverly Hills, CA: Sage.

238
"Locker Room Lacks Privacy"

Situation

You are the recreation supervisor in charge of aquatics. One afternoon, as you tour one of the city's revenue generating swimming pools, a lifeguard points to you, and the man she was talking to starts walking toward you.

"I'd like to talk to you," he said. "I'm Roland Henry, a 31-year-old swimmer. Yesterday I went swimming at this pool. While I was in the locker room changing into my swimming trunks, I turned around to find a five-year-old girl staring at me! I later learned that she had been brought there by her father, who was calmly drying himself after showering.

"The locker room was crowded with men in various stages of dress and undress. Some were completely naked. All were unaware that we were being observed by a wide-eyed girl.

"I found the pool manager and complained. She went to the father and asked him not to bring the child into the men's locker room again. The father got extremely angry. He said he had no one to leave his little girl with, and he wasn't about to let her wait for him outside alone. When the father was informed that the other men in the locker room might not appreciate being observed by a young girl, he said that any man who is embarrassed to be seen naked in front of a five-year-old girl must have something wrong with him.

"So I ask you — who has something wrong with him? Me? Or a man who would bring his daughter into a men's locker room? Also, what are you going to do about this situation? And, while you're at it, what are you going to do about the lifeguard who did nothing about the situation except talk to the man, and then point me toward you?"

Problem

What do you say to the man? Should a five-year-old girl be allowed in the men's locker room? What other alternatives are there? Would your decision be affected if you were told that the man was a season pass holder? Why or why not? Would it make any difference if the girl was four or six-years-old instead of five? Was the man right in going to the pool manager, or should he have confronted the other man directly? How much privacy should be guaranteed in a locker room? Would similar rules apply if a female lifeguard entered the locker room to chase out male patrons after the pool had closed?

What could be done to increase the father's trust in pool security so that he would feel comfortable leaving his child outside the locker room? Where should he leave her? Would you discipline the lifeguard for the way she handled the situation? What discipline would be justified?

Suggested Key Words and Phrases for
Literature Search for Case 238

Adult participation	Aquatics
Complaints	Discipline
Fees	Locker room
Membership	Nudity
Privacy	Safe
Security	Segregated settings
Swimming pools	

Selected References for Case Study 238

Biondo, A. (1990, May). How to have happy customers - guaranteed. *Parks and Recreation*, 34-35, 38-40.

Bisno, H. (1988). *Managing conflict*. Newbury Park, CA: Sage.

Culkin, D. (1988, Feb.). The right way to discipline. *Parks and Recreation*, 44-45.

Harker, G. (1987, August). Nude bathing, no controversy. *Parks and Recreation*, 58-61.

O'Sullivan, E. (1986, Jan.). Facilitating adult participation in organized recreation programs. *Parks and Recreation*, 58-60.

Peterson, D. (1984). *Analyzing safety performance*. Deer Park, NY: Alaray.

Powell, L. (1989, Sept.). Safety and success: Who's responsible? *Parks and Recreation*, 74-77.

Redeker, J. (1983). *Discipline: Policies and procedures*. Washington, D.C.: Bureau of National Affairs.

Shivers, J. (1986). *Recreational safety: The standard of care*. Cranbury, NJ: Associated University Presses.

Thompson, C. (1986, April). Safety management for water play facilities. *Parks and Recreation*, 36-40, 74.

Waters, J. (1987). Fees and charges: Underutilized revenues. In *Current issues in leisure services: Looking ahead in a time of transition*. J. Bannon, (ed.) Washington, D.C.: International City Management Association, 88-92.

Wood, A. (1990, May). Golf and government: A partnership that works. *Parks and Recreation*, 48-51.

239
Yoga Class Stretches Limits

Situation

You are the recreation supervisor at a large community center. In your brochure of upcoming activities, you have listed a weekly yoga class. A week before the class is to begin, a group of picketers forms outside your building to protest the class.

"Yoga is a form of New Age mysticism that can lead to devil worship," said Larry McCoy, the organizer of the protest. "The people who signed up for the class are just walking into it like cattle to a slaughter. Half of yoga is a branch of Eastern mysticism and it has strong occult influences. As Christians, we must protest what you are doing."

While the protests continued, you called a professor of religion at a nearby university to see if what McCoy said was true. The professor replied that yoga has become a secularized form of exercise and relaxation. He admitted that yoga did have ties to Eastern religions, but stressed that Eastern religions and devil worship are far from being the same thing.

The superintendent of recreation wants to know if you still plan to offer the class. He claims that the parks department cannot promote religion but that it should definitely promote health. He has given you until this afternoon to decide what to do.

Problem

Should the yoga class be presented? Why or why not? Does the fact that it has already been listed in a printed brochure influence your decision? Should the community have been surveyed prior to offering such a class? If so, discuss the survey procedure.

Should the protesters be allowed to influence your choice? How do you propose to deal with the protesters? What kind of power do protesters have? Compare this power to the power that the elected park district board has, and the power the park district director has.

Is yoga a form of religion? What does "separation of church and state" mean? How does this apply to the park district? Draft an outline of a "yoga class" lesson plan that could be presented to the park board.

Suggested Key Words and Phrases for
Literature Search for Case 239

Church-state issues	Citizen involvement
Crowd control	Lesson plans
Market demand analysis	New age movement
Printed material	Protests
Protestors	Religion
Survey	Yoga

Selected References for Case Study 239

Hawkins, T. (1988, May). Parks: For the people, by the people. *Parks and Recreation*, 39-43.

Haworth, J., (ed.) (1979). *Community involvement and leisure*. London: Lepus.

Hillery, G., and Lincoln, A. (1982). *Leisure, freedom, and crowd behavior*. Durham, NH: Library Crime Research Project.

Hirschman, A. (1982). *Shifting involvements: Private interest and public action*. Princeton, NJ: Princeton University Press.

Kelsey, C., and Gray, H. (1986). *The citizen survey process in parks and recreation*. Reston, VA: American Alliance for Health, Physical Education, Recreation, and Dance.

O'Bama, B. (1988, Aug.-Sept.). Why organize? Problems and promise in the inner city. *Illinois Issues*, 40-42.

Rose, J. (1982). *Outbreaks, the sociology of collective behavior*. New York: Free.

Sewell, W., and Coppock, J., (eds.) (1977). *Public participation in planning*. London: Wiley.

Stewart, W., Jr. (1976). *Citizen participation in public administration*. Birmingham, AL: University of Alabama, Bureau of Public Administration.

Tindell, J. (1987). "Grass Roots" community development of leisure opportunity. In *Current issues in leisure services: Looking ahead in a time of transition*. J. Bannon, (ed.) Washington, D.C.: International City Management Association, 159-167.

Useem, M. (1975). *Protest movements in America*. Indianapolis: Bobbs-Merrill.

Vasu, S. (1975). *An introduction to the Yoga philosophy*. Second ed. New Delhi: Oriental Book Reprint Corporation.

240
Swimmer Claims He was Humiliated

Situation

You are a recreation supervisor in charge of an aquatics program. One day as you routinely inspect the facilities, your pool manager calls you aside and asks you to read a "letter to the editor," which appeared in last evening's newspaper.

The letter reads: "If you want to be degraded, humiliated, and embarrassed, then by all means go to Denver City Pool. I guarantee you will have a whistle blown blatantly at you and be yelled at through a megaphone as if you were a ten-year-old by young, immature people who call themselves lifeguards.

"I have been going to the Denver pool for years, but I have never been yelled at and humiliated as many times as I have these past two weeks. I feel it is my civic duty as a season pass holder to warn the entire public that the rules are not posted anywhere nor are they available in any written form.

"Whistle one came about when one of my children grabbed me around the shoulders. No holding around the shoulders, the lifeguard said. I followed the rule, but do they really think that this child whom I have protected and guarded since birth is going to drown on my shoulders? I am an adult, not an eight-year-old playing with a baby.

"Whistle two was when I decided to go off the diving board. Standing by the ladder, I decided to take one step up the ladder. No one on the ladder while someone is on the diving board, the lifeguard said. Once I got on the board, I tried the perfect dive, bouncing twice, and ending in a bellyflop. Whistle three sounded, and the lifeguard said, no bouncing off the board twice.

"Whistle four happened when I saw my three-year-old heading into deep water. As I took off after her, the lifeguard said, no running.

"I won't even bother telling you about the rest of the rules I broke. I violated nine non-posted rules and was whistled at ten different times in thirty minutes. As many silly non-posted rules as I broke, I'm amazed they didn't kick me and my family out."

After reading the letter, you hand it back to the pool manager. She waits patiently for your comment.

Problem

What do you say to the pool manager? Should rules be posted? If so, create the poster. Should people with season passes receive a copy of the rules when they apply for season passes? Should all rules apply equally to all people, or should adults be treated differently than children?

Should the lifeguards be using both whistles and magaphones? How could they discipline without humiliating people and creating resentment? How would you suggest that the lifeguards handle patrons such as the letter writer? How would you suggest that the pool manager handle lifeguards who develop a "power" syndrome?

Should you write a "letter to the editor" for the newspaper to explain your side of the situation? If so, draft the article. Are there other ways to correct any public relations damage this article may have caused?

Suggested Key Words and Phrases for
Literature Search for Case 240

Adult participation	Aquatics
Complaints	Crowd control
Discipline	Facility management
Fee	Lifeguards
Pool management	Public relations
Rules	Safety
Supervision	

Selected References for Case Study 240

Biondo, A. (1990, May). How to have happy customers - guaranteed. *Parks and Recreation*, 34-35, 38-40.

Bisno, H. (1988). *Managing conflict*. Newbury Park, CA: Sage.

Culkin, D. (1988, Feb.). The right way to discipline. *Parks and Recreation*, 44-45.

O'Sullivan, E. (1986, Jan.). Facilitating adult participation in organized recreation programs. *Parks and Recreation*, 58-60.

Peterson, D. (1984). *Analyzing safety performance*. Deer Park, NY: Alaray.

Powell, L. (1989, Sept.). Safety and success: Who's responsible? *Parks and Recreation*, 74-77.

Redeker, J. (1983). *Discipline: Policies and procedures*. Washington, D.C.: Bureau of National Affairs.

Reynolds, J., and Hormachea, M. (1976). Public relations. *Public recreation administration*. Reston, VA: Reston, 372-394.

Shivers, J. (1986). *Recreational safety: The standard of care*. Cranbury, NJ: Associated University Presses.

Thompson, C. (1986, April). Safety management for water play facilities. *Parks and Recreation*, 36-40, 74.

Toalson, R., and Herchenberger, P. (1985). *Developing community support for parks and recreation*. Champaign, IL: Champaign Park District.

Waters, J. (1987). Fees and charges: Underutilized revenues. In *Current issues in leisure services: Looking ahead in a time of transition*. J. Bannon, (ed.) Washington, D.C.: International City Management Association, 88-92.

Wood, A. (1990, May). Golf and government: A partnership that works. *Parks and Recreation*, 48-51.

241
Should Reality Enter "Fantasy World"?

Situation

You are the director of the large theme park, American Fantasy World. On the news this morning as you drove to work, you heard that 250 soldiers were killed in a terrorist attack. The President of the United States urged that all flags should be lowered. Your park, though, has a policy of only lowering its flags when a President dies. You decide to question your public relations representatives about what to do.

"We don't want to remind visitors of the tragedies outside the gates," said Eva, the senior park publicist. "American Fantasy World is a place of fantasy. People come here to escape, and they couldn't do that if we remind them of the problems in the real world. It's always been our policy, and we must keep it our policy to maintain our market."

The assistant publicist disagreed. "If we don't lower the flags, people will say that we are un-American. This is the United States; we are supposed to be proud of our soldiers. This park is a tribute to America, and the least we can do is honor our soldiers."

The other publicist suggested a compromise. "Let the flags that the patrons see fly at full-staff. The high-flying flags are an important part of our theme. However, let's fly the flag at the administration building, the 'official flag,' at half-mast. Because the administration building is tucked unobtrusively into a corner of the park, this will not affect the customers' moods and yet will make the point that we are patriotic."

Problem

Which flags, if any, should be flown at half-staff? Why? What is the main issue here — patriotism, respect for the dead, or something else? Is patriotism more important than making a profit for a commercial theme park? Is it possible for flags to be mere decorations, or are they always symbolic? Are there other ways/better ways — of showing patriotism other than lowering the flag? If you did lower all of the flags, how would you justify breaking the policy to your superiors?

What "realities" should be allowed into a fantasy park? Should public relations specialists be providing input into these decisions? Should anyone else? Should flags be lowered at a founder's death?

Suggested Key Words and Phrases for
Literature Search for Case 241

Commercial recreation	Escapism
Flags	Marketing
Patriotism	Public relations
Respect for dead	Symbolism
Theme parks	

Selected References for Case Study 241

Bullaro, J., and Edginton, C. (1986). *Commercial Leisure Services: Managing for profit, service, and personal satisfaction.* New York: Macmillan.

Burkart, A., and Medlik, S. (1981). *Tourism: Past, present, and future.* Second ed. London: Heinemann.

Cooper, A. (1976). *World of logotypes.* Volume 1. New York: Art Direction.

Crompton, J. (1990, March). Claiming our share of the tourism dollar. *Parks and Recreation*, 42-47, 88.

Crossley, J., and Jamieson, L. (1988). *Introduction to commercial and entrepreneurial recreation.* Champaign, IL: Sagamore.

Cunningham, W., Cunningham, I., and Swift, C. (1987). *Marketing: A managerial approach*. Cincinnati, OH: South-Western.

Davidoff, P., and Davidoff, D. (1983). *Sales and marketing for travel and tourism*. Rapid City, SD: National Publishers of the Black Hills.

Ellis, T., and Norton, R. (1988). *Commercial recreation*. St. Louis: Times Mirror/Mosby.

Epperson, A. (1986). *Private and commercial recreation*. State College, PA: Venture.

Gunn, C. (1988). *Tourism planning*. New York: Taylor & Francis.

Holloway, J., and Plant, R. (1989). *Marketing for tourism*. London: Pitman.

Hunt, J. (1986, Oct.). Tourism comes of age in the 1980s. *Parks and Recreation*, 30-36, 66.

Igarashi, T., (ed.) (1987). *World trademarks and logotypes II: A collection of international symbols and their applications*. Tokyo: Graphic-Sha.

Prus, R. (1989). *Pursuing customers: An ethnography of marketing activities*. Newbury Park, CA: Sage.

Travis, A. (1985). *Collected papers in leisure and tourism - volume one*. Birmingham, Canada: Center for Urban and Regional Studies, University of Birmingham.

242
Caricature Causes Controversy

Situation

You are the director of a public parks and recreation agency. In your hurry to meet a deadline, you allowed a questionable caricature to be placed into a brochure. To have replaced the item would have taken several hours and involved considerable money. You realized that this caricature — a black woman with bones in her hair cooking a white hunter — which you used to introduce a foreign cooking class might be controversial, but you decided to run it anyway.

Rev. Thomas Clark, a local pastor of a predominantly black church, was appalled when he received his copy in the mail and observed that the drawing was used. In conjunction with the Urban League, the Ministerial Alliance, and the NAACP, he has organized a considerable mass demonstration outside the park district office with plans to speak at tonight's park board meeting. He claims that the caricature carries all of the connotations of cannibalism. "White slave traders used the rationale that blacks were somehow subhuman to start enslaving them," he said, "and this cartoon is based on such a stereotype."

Over 27,000 copies of the publication have been mailed, one per household in the community. Rev. Clark says that he wants this to be a win-win situation for everybody, but the all-white park board is leery of the pending problem. They believe that the caricature is harmless and was not done with the intention of hurting anyone. They think Rev. Clark is making a big deal out of nothing.

"It is for these people — the educated, the middle class, the supposedly enlightened — that the issue must be pressed," Rev. Clark says. "Too many people, including blacks, have forgotten black history. We cannot allow this lack of education to be tolerated."

Although his figures may be exaggerated, Rev. Clark predicted at a Chamber of Commerce meeting earlier today that over 400 people of all races are going to participate in the demonstration. Board members are afraid that a demonstration this large may get out of their control.

Problem

How would you attempt to put your board members at ease? What would you say to Rev. Clark? Should you apologize for the use of the art? What could have been some other alternatives to the art piece? Should the board adopt a resolution admitting errors in the handling of the brochure? Should prejudice reduction workshops be scheduled? Is it ever okay to "step on toes" to meet a deadline or to meet a budget? Was it okay in this situation?

If you were Rev. Clark, what options would be open to you to suppress the brochure? If you wanted to enlighten the community, including the park board, about prejudice, what would you do?

Suggested Key Words and Phrases for
Literature Search for Case 242

Black history   Brochure
Caricature   Citizen involvement
Clip art   Community relations
Mass mailings   Prejudice
Protest marches

Selected References for Case Study 242

Berwitz, C. (1975). *The job analysis approach to affirmative action.* New York: Wiley.
Billings, C. (1976). *Racism and prejudice.* Rochelle Park, NJ: Hayden.
Hillery, G., and Lincoln, A. (1982). *Leisure, freedom, and crowd behavior.* Durham, NH: Library Crime Research Project.

Hirschman, A. (1982). *Shifting involvements: Private interest and public action.* Princeton, NJ: Princeton University Press.

Nisbet, R. (1982). *Prejudices.* Cambridge, MA: Harvard University Press.

Rochman, J., Teresa, J., Kay, T., and Morningstar, G. (1983). *Marketing human service innovations.* Beverly Hills, CA: Sage.

Sewell, W., and Coppock, J., (eds.) (1977). *Public participation in planning.* London: Wiley.

Snowden, F. (1983). Before color prejudice: The ancient view of Blacks. Cambridge, MA: Harvard University Press.

Soderberg, J. (1989, June). Marketing recreation right. *Parks and Recreation*, 38-41.

Starr, R., and Deteveiler, R., (eds.) (1975). *Race, prejudice, and the origins of slavery in America.* Cambridge, MA: Schenkman.

Useem, M. (1975). *Protest movements in America.* Indianapolis: Bobbs-Merrill.

Zimet, S. (1976). *Print and prejudice.* London: Hodder and Stoughton.

243
Playing by the Rules

Situation

You are the director of parks and recreation in a medium-sized city. One night at a board meeting, an irate resident demands to know why her fun must be regulated. "I go to the park to break free of constraints and restrictions, but I find that I cannot enjoy myself because of the numerous rules."

Upon the request of a board member, she specified rules that infuriated her:

- no parking on the grass
- no alcohol consumption on park grounds
- no dogs without a waste disposal bag

- no entering the park after 11 p.m.
- no parking vehicles in the park after 11 p.m.
- no picking flowers
- no standing on swings
- no fishing except in designated areas

"Everywhere you turn, there are rules, rules, rules. There's a sign here, a sign there, a sign everywhere. How can we enjoy the beauty of the park with so many signs? How can we enjoy life with so many rules?"

Problem

Explain why rules are needed if a park is to be enjoyed by everyone. Is it possible to have too many rules? Should all rules be posted, or should some be assumed? Is it better to have one huge sign indicating all of the rules or many signs with one rule each?

For each rule that she objected to, provide a rationale for why that specific rule is needed. Do you think that providing a rationale for a rule makes it more palatable? If so, should the rationale be available on a brochure for park patrons?

What is the real problem here? Is it the clutter of signs? Is it the numerous rules? Is it the desire to have input about things that affect one's life?

Suggested Key Words and Phrases for Literature Search for Case 243

Citizen involvement   Landscaping
Parks   Policing
Public good   Regulations
Rules   Safety
Security   Signs

Selected References for Case Study 243

Booth, N. (1983). *Basic elements of landscape architectural design.* New York: Elsevier.

Christiansen, M. (1987). Safety is no accident. In *Current issues in leisure services: Looking ahead in a time of transition.* J. Bannon, (ed.) Washington, D.C.: International City Management Association.

Direnfeld-Michael, B. (1989, March). A risk management primer for recreators. *Parks and Recreation,* 40-45.

Dwyer, W., and Murrell, D. (1988, July). Park law: Fourteen points to ponder. *Parks and Recreation,* 50-52.

Dwyer, W., and Murrell, D. (1990, April). The ins and outs of park law enforcement. *Parks and Recreation,* 50-53.

Espeseth, R. (1977). *Site planning of park areas.* Champaign, IL: Office of Recreation and Park Resources, Department of Leisure Studies, Cooperative Extension Service, University of Illinois at Urbana-Champaign.

Hjelte, G., and Shivers, J. (1978). *Public administration of recreational services.* Second ed. Philadelphia: Lea and Febiger.

Kauffman, R. (1989, Sept.). Recognizing the accident chain. *Parks and Recreation,* 68-73.

Mandelker, D., and Ewald, W. (1988). *Street graphics and the law.* Washington, D.C.: Planners.

Marsh, W. (1983). *Landscape planning: Environmental applications.* Reading, MA: Addison-Wesley.

Molnar, D., and Rutledge, A. (1986). *Anatomy of a park: The essentials of recreation area planning and design.* New York: McGraw-Hill.

Ries, M. (1973). *Design standards to accommodate people with physical disabilities in park and open space planning.* Madison, WI: Cooperative Extension Programs, Recreation Resources Center, University of Wisconsin at Madison.

Shivers, J., and Hjelte, G. (1971). *Planning recreational places.* Rutherford, NJ: Fairleigh Dickinson University Press.

Urban Research Development Corporation. (1977). *Guidelines for understanding and determining optimum recreation carrying capacity.* Washington, D.C.: U.S. Department of Interior, Bureau of Outdoor Recreation.

244
Golfers Teed Off Over Fee Use

Situation

You are a recreation supervisor in charge of the community golf course. Your golf course takes in over $300,000 annually; however, it only spends about $200,000. The difference is used to supplement the city's general recreation fund. Golfers, though, are not happy about the arrangement.

"I want the money I pay for my membership to be spent on the golf course," said Sam Soa, president of the local golfer's club. "I paid taxes to take care of the general recreation fund. I paid $330 to take care of this golf course."

The golf course made a net profit of more than $223,000 last year. The profit was 27 percent of operating costs. Not only do golfers believe that this is too high; they believe that the money should have been reinvested into the grounds of the golf course.

"The golf course needs to be maintained," Soa said. "The city has the philosophy that they fix something only if it is broken; they don't believe in preventive maintenance. Sure, they are making a profit now and subsidizing many programs that cannot stand on their own merit; but before long they are going to have to pay huge repair bills here at the golf course. Such costly bills could be avoided by shelling out a few of those dollars for routine maintenance now."

Problem

Should money designated for one form of recreation be used for another form of recreation? Should high profit recreation centers support recreation centers that lose money? What is a "reasonable" profit percentage for a golf course? What percentage of money should be reinvested back into the golf course? What considerations must you make when setting a fee? —should you look at supply and demand, competition from the private sector, and/or something else; why?

Should public recreation agencies seek to make a profit? Develop pro and con arguments. Should public recreation agencies contract golf course management to a private firm that specializes in golf course maintenance? Develop pro and con arguments.

Suggested Key Words and Phrases for
Literature Search for Case 244

Contracting	Fee structure
General fund	Greens fees
Golf course management	Financing
Leasing	Profit making
Public-private relationship	Reinvesting
Taxes	

Selected References for Case Study 244

Allen, S. (1979). *Private financing in public parks: A handbook.* Washington, D.C.: Hawkins.

Bierman, Jr., H. (1982). *The lease versus buy decision.* Englewood Cliffs, NJ: Prentice-Hall.

Crompton, J., and Lamb, Jr., C. (1986). *Marketing government and social services.* New York: Wiley.

Crossley, J. (1988). *Public/Commercial cooperation in parks and recreation.* Columbus, OH: Publishing Horizons.

DeHoog, R. (1984). *Contracting out for human services: Economic, political, and organizational perspectives.* Albany, NY: State University of New York Press.

Fitchard, R., and Hindelang, T. (1980). *The lease/buy decision.* New York: AMACOM.

Greenberg, B. (1988, May). Contract management can help your golf course. *Parks and Recreation,* 28-30, 59.

Herst, A. (1984). *Lease or purchase: Theory and practice.* Boston: Kluwer-Nijhoff.

Heydt, M. (1986, Feb.). Ten principles for contract administration. *Parks and Recreation,* 48, 51.

Hipps, S. (1990, March). Partners in profit. *The Leisure Manager*, 14-18.

Marlin, J. (1984). *Contracting municipal services: A guide for purchases from the private sector*. New York: Wiley.

Venkatesan, M., Schmalensee, D., and Marshall, C., (eds.) (1986). *Creativity in services marketing: What's new, what works, and what's developing.* Chicago, IL: American Marketing Association.

Waters, J. (1987). Fees and charges: Underutilized revenues. In *Current issues in leisure services: Looking ahead in a time of transition.* J. Bannon, (ed.) Washington, D.C.: International City Management Association, 88-92.

Wood, A. (1990, May). Golf and government: A partnership that works. *Parks and Recreation*, 48-51.

245
"Range War" Threatens Trail Park

Situation

You have been hired as a consultant by your state's Department of Conservation. The Department has proposed that the abandoned railroad line's roadbed be turned into a state park, a trail of natural prairie to be used by hikers and bikers. According to the plan, the railroad right-of-way would be converted into a crooked ribbon of oak trees and prairie plants.

Landowners, fearing increased liability, noise, and litter from the city crowds who would likely use the park, have protested against it. Most landowners could accept the railroad bisecting their property, but they oppose the presence of the trail. "When the railroad was here, it brought us a service. The trail, meanwhile, will do nothing for us," summarized one landowner.

Landowners are especially concerned about who would be liable if someone should wander from the trail onto their property. One alternative the Conservation Department has suggested is fencing the land, but the proposal was nixed by both sides — landowners don't want to incur the expenses and environmentalists don't want the wire to ruin the view.

"I don't see how the matter can be so complex," the Conservation director tells you. "Some farmers think only of themselves individually. Everyone should be able to see the miles of ancient plains and natural wildlife, the bubbling creeks, the tiny villages, and the green patchwork of farm country which line this trail. Everybody should have the opportunity to enjoy the prairie."

Problem

Should the state build a trail on the railroad's bed? What approaches could be used to convince landowners of the value of the trail? Should rare prairie land be in the hands of farmers or in the hands of the state? Should farmers be required to share the expense of installing fences? Who should be held liable if someone does climb over a fence onto a farmer's property? Is there a difference between accidentally wandering off the trail and trespassing? If no fences were used, how could the trail boundaries be designated? How would the trail be patrolled for unauthorized hunters and beer parties?

Suggested Key Words and Phrases for Literature Search for Case 245

Bikers	Citizen input
Department of Conservation	Environmentalist
Hikers	Liability
Public land	Rails-to-trails
State park	Trespassing

Selected References for Case Study 245

Baron, R. (1988, Sept.). Risk management: The defensive game plan. *Parks and Recreation*, 53-55.

Direnfield-Michael, B., and Michael, D. (1987, Jan.). Everything you ought to know about the liability insurance crisis but didn't know how to ask. *Parks and Recreation*, 74-80.

Holford, E., and Geyer, L. (1990, March). Torts on your turf. *Park Maintenance and Grounds Management*, 13-15.

Kaiser, R. (1986). *Liability and law in recreation, parks, and sports.* Englewood Cliffs, NJ: Prentice-Hall.

Kozlowski, J. (1988, Sept.). A common sense view of liability. *Parks and Recreation*, 56-59.

Macdonald, S. (1987, Nov.). Building support for urban trails. *Parks and Recreation*, 26-33.

Molnar, D., and Rutledge, A. (1986). *Anatomy of a park: The essentials of recreation area planning and design.* New York: McGraw-Hill.

Reynolds, J., and Hormachea, M. (1976). Legal authority for public recreation. *Public recreation administration.* Reston, VA: Reston, 39-54.

Russell, C., and Nicholson, N. (1982). Public choice and rural development. Washington, D.C.: Resources for the future.

Scott, M. (1985). *The law of public leisure services.* London: Sweet and Maxwell.

Scott, M. (1988). *Law and leisure services management.* Essex, England: Longman.

Tiffany, A. (1987, Jan.). How to tame the liability monster. *Parks and Recreation*, 64-69, 103.

246
Red Ink in Budget

Situation

You are the director for the Jonestown Explorer Boy Scout Council, which is expected to serve more than 5,000 young people in your county and two adjoining counties.

The Council desires to keep itself financially solvent and to keep up with increasing costs and expansion plans at the Council's downtown headquarters and at its campsite outside of town. Currently, projected expenditures for the upcoming year total $246,000, while income from the United Way, sustaining membership, trust funds, the summer golf tournament, and the bowla-thon are projected to bring in $230,900. The board believes that a deficit may become an annual event unless you take action.

Several proposals have been offered: 1) To create an endowment fund, with the interest earnings going into the operating fund; 2) To sponsor an annual city-wide popcorn sales drive, with all profits going into the operating fund; 3) To actively recruit more young people, increasing the amount of revenue derived from dues; 4) To reduce the length of camping sessions, allowing more boys to utilize the camp; and 5) to freeze all expansion and capital improvement projects for a year.

Problem

Evaluate each of the five proposals; what are their strengths and weaknesses? Which proposal or combination of proposals is the best? What other options can you suggest?

What is the purpose of a budget? Is a budget a contract, a guideline, or merely a formality? What types of budgets are available? Which type would you recommend that this agency utilize?

What legal problems can arise if an agency is consistently in the red? What advantages might there be to going into the red for one year?

Suggested Key Words and Phrases for
Literature Search for Case 246

Budget	Capital improvements
Deficit	Dues
Endowments	Financial law
Fund raising	Trust funds
Voluntary agencies	Zero-based budgeting

Selected References for Case 246

Boy Scouts of America. (1978). *Boy Scout Fieldbook*. New York: Workman.

Camillus, J., 1984. *Budgeting for profit: how to exploit the potential of your business*. Randor, PA: Chilton.

Garbutt, D. (1985). *How to budget and control cash*. Brookfield, VT: Gower.

Ramsey, J., and Ramsey, I., (1985). *Budgeting basics: How to survive the budgeting process*. New York: Franklin Watts.

Reynolds, J., and Hormachea, M., (1976). Budgeting for public recreation and park agencies. *Public recreation administration*, 272-300.

Rosenthal, M., (1986). *The character factory: Baden-Powell and the origins of the Boy Scout movement*. New York: Pantheon.

Schnidman, F., and Bloch, S., (1977). *Real estate development: Legal and business regulation*. New York: Practicing Law Institute.

Slavin, S., (ed.) (1985). *Managing finances, personnel, and information in human services*. New York: Haworth.

Stoner, J., and Wankel, C., (1986). *Management*. Third ed. Englewood Cliffs, NJ: Prentice-Hall.

Thomsett, M. (1988). *The little black book of budgets and forecasts*. New York: AMACOM.

Umapathy, S., (1987). *Current budgeting practices in U.S. industry*. New York: Quorum.

Walsh, E., (1990, Oct.). Fund raising made easy. *Parks and Recreation*, 60-63, 78.

247
Is the Town Ready to Rock 'n' Roll?

Situation

You are the public arena manager of a town of 100,000. For years your 80,000-seat arena has been used for circuses, country music shows, and sporting events. The arena has rarely been more than half filled, and in recent years it has lost considerable money. Concert promoters Grant & West believe that you could make a fortune from rock and roll shows. They claim that such shows would bring a lot of people into town and would help the town's sagging economy, not to mention the arena's financial condition.

Police Chief Johnson also thinks it would bring a lot of people into town — but he calls it a bad idea. He claims that the additional visitors will mean that he will need additional personnel. He suspects that brawls will likely erupt and questions if there is enough jail space for hotheads. He points out that the extra people coming into town could cause severe traffic jams. When Grant & West point out that people might come throughout the day rather than all at once, he argues that crowd control might become a problem. He also notes that the town's sanitary system could not handle a large influx of people.

Maggie Marple, representing the Senior Center in town, is also against the proposed concert. She claims that rock music is from the devil. She says that the concert would indeed revive the town's economy, but adds "who wants to sell their soul?" She suspects that the concert would attract "acid-heads," "freaks," and "New Age devil worshipers," and she asks the city council to please keep such people out of town.

Problem

How would you answer each of Chief Johnson's objections? Is it possible to overcome each of these practical considerations?; if so, suggest how. Is one problem he suggested dominant over all of the others?

Should the concert promoters be expected to "chip in" to help get the project underway? Should the financial goal of a public arena be to make money, break even, or lose money?

How do you answer each of Maggie Marple's concerns and fears? Is she objecting primarily from religious reasons or for security reasons? What could be done to "bridge the generation gap"? What, if anything, would be unacceptable for presentation in a public arena?

Suggested Key Words and Phrases for
Literature Search for Case 247

Arena management	Citizen input
Concert	Crowd control
New age philosophy	Profit margin
Promoter	Religion
Rock 'n' roll	Safety
Sanitation	Security
Traffic	

Selected References for Case Study 247

Bovaird, A., Tricker, M., and Stoakes, R. (1984). *Recreation management and pricing: The effect of charging policy on demand at countryside recreation sites.* Brookfield, VT: Gower.

Crompton, J. (1987). How to establish a price for park and recreation services. In *Current issues in leisure services: Looking ahead in a time of transition.* J. Bannon, (ed.) Washington, D.C.: International City Management Association, 93-107.

Hillery, G., and Lincoln, A. (1982). *Leisure, freedom, and crowd behavior.* Durham, NH: Library Crime Research Project.

Hoyt, K., and Yamanota, J. (1987). *The new age rage.* Old Tappas, NJ: Revell.

Melton, J., Clark, J., and Kelly, A. (1990). *New age encyclopedia: A guide to the beliefs, concepts, terms, people, and organizations that make up the new global movement toward spiritual development, health, and healing, higher consciousness, and related subjects.* Detroit: Gale Research.

Pooley, J. (1980). *The sport fan: A social-psychology of misbehavior.* Vanier City, Ontario: Canadian Association for Health, Physical Education, and Recreation.

Rose, J. (1982). *Outbreaks, the sociology of collective behavior.* New York: Free.

Rossman, J. (1989). *Recreation programming: Designing leisure experiences.* Champaign, IL: Sagamore.

Russell, R. (1982). *Planning programs in recreation.* St. Louis: Mosby.

Schultz, J., McAvoy, L., and Dustin, D. (1988, Jan.). What are we in business for? *Parks and Recreation*, 52-54.

Waters, J. (1987). Fees and charges: Underutilized revenues. In *Current issues in leisure services: Looking ahead in a time of transition.* J. Bannon, (ed.) Washington, D.C.: International City Management Association, 88-92.

Wright, S. (1978). *Crowds and riots: A study in social organization.* Beverly Hills, CA: Sage.

248
Overt Culvert Repairs Raise Questions

Situation

You have been hired as a consultant by your state's Department of Conservation. Your assignment is to determine whether the state should spend over $44,000 for repairs in a park that nobody can use.

The 27-mile-long hiker-biker trail has been closed for several years in a squabble between landowners and conservationists. Farmers who live along the trail claim that the increased use by hikers and bikers would increase liability, litter, and noise, and they worry that the state might condemn adjacent farmland in the future if it chose to enlarge the park. The 27-mile-strip had been a railroad right-of-way before being acquired by the Rails-to-Trails Foundation and then turned over to the Department of Conservation for use as a park.

A section of a stone arch drainage culvert fifteen miles into the trail recently collapsed, partly blocking the flow of a tributary of Wesley Creek. The lowest bid solicited to repair the damage is $44,000.

Farmers argue that the fallen bridge is a potential safety hazard and the cause of a drainage problem. They claim that the bridge belongs to the state and therefore the state has an obligation to maintain the bridge. The farmers insist, however, that no further development of the park take place.

Problem

Who is responsible for the bridge repairs? Is it legally and morally correct for public money to be spent on land the public cannot use? Should the bridge repair be a high priority? If the state allows the water to back up onto a farmer's land, could the state be sued?

Suggest ways of obtaining the farmers' backing for the rails-to-trails project. Are the farmers' objections reasonable? What could be done to overcome these objections? What benefits might the farmers find in a rails-to-trails park?

Suggested Key Words and Phrases for Literature Search for Case 248

Citizen input	Conservation department
Donated land	Liability
Park development	Prioritizing
Public funds	Rails-to-trails
State parks	

Selected References for Case Study 248

Anderson, R., Leitch, J., and Mittleider, J. (1986, Oct.). Contribution of state parks to state economies. *Parks and Recreation*, 62-63.

Baron, R. (1988, Sept.). Risk management: The defensive game plan. *Parks and Recreation*, 53-55.

Culhane, P. (1981). *Public lands politics: Interest group influence on the forest and the bureau of land management.* Baltimore: Johns Hopkins University Press.

Direnfield-Michael, B., and Michael, D. (1987, Jan.). Everything you ought to know about the liability insurance crisis but didn't know how to ask. *Parks and Recreation*, 74-80.

Dysart, III, B., and Clawson, M. (1989). *Public interest in the use of private lands.* New York: Praeger.

Holford, E., and Geyer, L. (1990, March). Torts on your turf. *Park Maintenance and Grounds Management*, 13-15.

Kaiser, R. (1986). *Liability and law in recreation, parks, and sports.* Englewood Cliffs, NJ: Prentice-Hall.

Kozlowski, J. (1988, Sept.). A common sense view of liability. *Parks and Recreation*, 56-59.

Myers, P. (1990, April). State parks in a new era. *Parks and Recreation*, 28-32.

Scott, M. (1985). *The law of public leisure services.* London: Sweet and Maxwell.

Scott, M. (1988). *Law and leisure services management.* Essex, England: Longman.

Tiffany, A. (1987, Jan.). How to tame the liability monster. *Parks and Recreation*, 64-69, 103.

249
Wanted: Lifeguards

Situation

You have been hired as the personnel recruiter for the aquatics division of the Department of Recreation. Your job is to attract the best lifeguards possible. The job is not as easy as it sounds, however. Currently there are three job applications on file and over 130 public vacancies to fill. The reasons for the few number of applicants has been explained in four ways:

- private pools pay three times as much as the public pools.
- the population of young people is smaller than in past years.
- other employment opportunities provide the same pay, but with better hours and fewer responsibilities.
- potential lifeguards fear getting AIDS during a rescue.

A consultant has offered some suggestions for increasing the pool of applicants. His suggestions include (1) seek to attract teachers and other adults who might seek seasonal summer employment, (2) restructure the pay scale and include it with all job announcements, and (3) offer lifeguard training programs free of charge to anyone in the hopes that class members will later apply for jobs.

Problem

Design a recruitment campaign for lifeguards. Overcome each of the objections to becoming a lifeguard. Evaluate the consultant's advice. Are his ideas good ones in view of the reasons people give for not becoming lifeguards? Can you think of ideas to add to, or replace ideas on the consultant's list? How could you enrich the jobs of those lifeguards returning from last year?

Lifeguards are traditionally young people. What advantages and disadvantages are there in hiring young people? What are the advantages and disadvantages of hiring a middle-aged adult? Is it legal to discriminate based on age? How could you protect yourself from a lawsuit by a disgruntled adult who was not hired because you selected a young person for the position?

Suggested Key Words and Phrases for
Literature Search for Case 249

AIDS	Job description
Job enrichment	Lifeguards
Pay structure	Personnel administration
Recruitment	Retention
Seasonal employment	Training
Wage reviews	

Selected References for Case Study 249

Arvey, R., and Faley, R. (1988). *Fairness in selecting employees.* Second ed. Reading, MA: Addison-Wesley.

Brademas, D., Lowrey, G., and Wallin, D. (1980). *Hiring practices for part-time and seasonal leisure services personnel.* Champaign, IL: Department of Leisure Studies, Cooperative Extension Service, University of Illinois at Urbana-Champaign.

Brademas, D., and Lowrey, G. (1982). *Manual for systematically developing job descriptions.* Champaign, IL: Department of Leisure Studies, Cooperative Extension Service, University of Illinois at Urbana-Champaign.

Cook, M. (1988). *Personnel selection and productivity.* New York: Wiley.

Dreker, G., and Sackett, P. (1983). *Perspectives on employee staffing and selection: Readings and commentary.* Homewood, IL: Irwin.

Elizur, D. (1987). *Systematic job evaluation and comparable worth.* Brookfield, VT: Gower.

Kenney, J., Donnelly, E., and Reid, M. (1979). *Manpower training and development.* Second ed. London: Institute of Personnel Management.

Lewis, C. (1985). *Employee selection.* London: Hutchinson.

London, M. (1989). *Managing the training enterprise: High-quality, cost-effective employee training in organizations.* San Francisco: Jossey-Bass.

McKinney, W., and Lowrey, G. (1989). *Staff training and development for park, recreation, and leisure service organizations.* Second ed. Alexandria, VA: National Recreation and Parks Association.

Potter, E., (ed.) (1986). *Employee selection: Legal and practical alternatives to compliance and litigation.* Second ed. Washington, D.C.: National Foundation for the Study of Equal Employment Policy.

Smith, M., and Robertson, I., (ed.) (1989). *Advances in selection and assessment.* New York: Wiley.

250
City Parks Panel to Review Priorities

Situation

You are a member of the Grover City Park District Advisory Committee. At tonight's meeting of the Grover City Park District, the Grover City recreation director has just stated that your committee — first as individuals and then as a group — will be asked to review a list of fifty possible projects and rank them in order of importance. He said this would help to determine the direction of the district's capital improvement program over the next five years.

At the Park Advisory Committee earlier this week, members of the capital improvements subcommittee announced that they planned to prepare a survey, with the aid of the park district staff, to be sent to the full advisory committee. The project spoken about tonight is the result of their work.

The director says that in addition to ranking the items, you should designate each of the fifty suggested projects as either (1) projects of immediate concern, (2) projects that could be completed within two to four years, or (3) long-range projects. The last category includes projects the district will not be able to begin for at least five years.

After presenting the instrument to the committee members, the director asks if you have any questions or concerns about it or about the purposes behind it.

Problem

What do you say to the director? Does being in a public board meeting affect how you word your answer? Is it possible to be able to rate fifty projects in importance, or are there the "top-five, bottom-five, and others"? Is survey research something advisory board members should be willing to accept without objection, or is it more than they agreed to when they assumed a position on the advisory board? Are the feelings of the advisory board representative of everyone in the town?

Should the director have waited until the meeting to unveil the instrument? Should a research authority have been consulted in the making of the instrument or, since this is "by the park district, for the park district" should scientific research principles be only loosely followed?

Is long-range planning a good idea? What are the pros and cons of long-range planning? What other styles of planning are there? What style of planning is the most ideal for a capital improvements program?

Suggested Key Words and Phrases for
Literature Search for Case 250

Advisory committees	Capital improvements
Citizen input	Five-year plan
Long-range planning	Park boards
Prioritizing	Public meeting
Research	Survey research

Selected References for Case Study 250

Branch, M. (1983). *Comprehensive planning: General theory and principles.* Pacific Palisades, CA: Palisades.

Herman, R., and Til, J., (eds.) (1989). *Nonprofit board of directors: Analyses and applications.* New Brunswick, NJ: Transaction.

Ibrahim, H., Banes, R., and Gerson, G. (1987). *Effective parks and recreation boards and commissions.* Reston, VA: American Alliance for Health, Physical Education, Recreation, and Dance.

Kelsey, C., and Gray, H. (1985). *Master plan process for parks and recreation.* Reston, VA: American Alliance for Health, Physical Education, Recreation, and Dance.

Kelsey, C., and Gray, H. (1986). *The feasibility study process for parks and recreation.* Reston, VA: American Alliance for Health, Physical Education, Recreation, and Dance.

Kraus, R., and Allen, L. (1987). *Research and evaluation in recreation, parks, and leisure studies.* Columbus, OH: Publishing Horizons.

Mann, P. (1985). *Methods of social investigation.* Second ed. New York: Blackwell.

McNeill, P. (1985). *Research methods.* London: Tavistock.

Pelegrino, D. (1979). *Research methods for recreation and leisure: A theoretical and practical guide.* Dubuque, IA: Brown.

Stoops, J., and Edginton, C. (1988, April). Needed: Effective park and recreation boards and commissions. *Parks and Recreation,* 51-55.

Tobin, G., and Peacock, T. (1981). *Problems and issues in comprehensive planning for a small community: The case of Soldier's Grove, Wisconsin.* Iowa City, Iowa: Institute of Urban and Regional Planning, University of Iowa at Iowa City.

Vogt, A. (1977). *Capital improvement programming: A handbook for local government officials.* Chapel Hill, NC: Institute of Government, University of North Carolina at Chapel Hill.

251
Forest Preserve Board Debates Cuts

Situation

You are the assistant director of the Franklin County Forest Preserve District. Due to property tax cuts, fewer lake permits, less boat rentals, and a drastic reduction in the use of the golf course, you are facing a huge budget deficit of over $60,000, with one month to go in the current fiscal year.

As the recreation director, the board has asked you to determine what should be done to keep the Franklin County

Forest Preserve District financially sound. Several board members have ideas:

- drop the environmental education coordinator position.
- decrease the number of maintenance workers and simply perform routine maintenance less frequently.
- reorganize the job hierarchy so that expensive middle management positions are eliminated.
- freeze wages until further notice, even though wage reviews and pay raises have been promised.
- develop a long-term plan.

The board believes that declining revenues are a fact of life, not a temporary setback. Due to financial pressure, the board insists that you present a proposal to cut the budget losses and to provide a surplus in next year's budget.

Problem

Which of the board's ideas would you suggest be implemented? Is education an important part of the mission of a county forest preserve agency? Are there minimum maintenance standards that must be upheld? Is it ethical to freeze wages after wage reviews have been promised? Is a long-term plan an extra expense or a worthwhile investment?

What other ideas can you suggest to help remedy the situation? Would hiring a marketing coordinator likely increase usage of the golf course and boats, thereby bringing in more revenue? Would leasing the boating facility to a private company be a viable option? Could bonds be sold to meet the debt?

Suggested Key Words and Phrases for
Literature Search for Case 251

Budget	Forest preserve board
Funding cuts	Leasing
Leisure education	Marketing
Organizational hierarchy	Park upkeep

Personnel   Standards
Wage freezes   Wage reviews

Selected References for Case Study 251

Culkin, D., and Kirsch, S. (1986). *Managing human resources in recreation, parks, and leisure services.* New York: Macmillan.

Edginton, C., and Griffith, C. (1983). *The recreation and leisure service delivery system.* Philadelphia: Saunders.

Graham, P., and Kalar, L., Jr. (1979). *Planning and delivering leisure services.* Dubuque, IA: Brown.

Klingner, D., and Nolbandian, J. (1985). *Public personnel management: Context and strategies.* Englewood Cliffs, NJ: Prentice-Hall.

McCurdy, D. (1985). *Park management.* Carbondale: Southern Illinois University Press.

Mundt, B., Olsen, R., and Steinberg, H. (1982). *Managing public resources.* Peat Marwick International.

Reynolds, J., and Hormachea, M. (1976). Budgeting for public recreation and park agencies. *Public recreation administration*, 272-300.

Slavin, S., (ed.) (1985). Managing finances, personnel, and information in human services. New York: Haworth.

Stoner, J., and Wankel, C. (1986). *Management.* Third ed. Englewood Cliffs, NJ: Prentice-Hall.

Thomsett, M. (1988). *The little black book of budgets and forecasts.* New York: AMACOM.

Torkildsen, G. (1986). *Leisure and recreation management.* Second ed. London: E & F.N. Spoon.

Umapathy, S. (1987). *Current budgeting practices in U.S. industry.* New York: Quorum.

252
Is Developer's Fee Fair?

Situation

You are the parks and recreation director for the city of Flintsville. The Flintsville Board of Recreation has recently proposed that a new law be adopted that would require developers of subdivisions or multi-family dwellings to give either 1,000 square feet of usable land or $1,000 per housing unit in lieu of the land for the establishment of parks and other recreational facilities. The proposal comes at a time when the board, and many residents, are concerned with the shortage of recreational areas in the rapidly growing town.

At a recent public hearing on these proposals at the town board meeting, local developers and builders expressed their objections to them. While agreeing that the recreational space was needed, objections centered around the steep requirements. Developers said that the proposals can hurt the building industry in town by chasing away potential developers, and that they discriminate against new residents coming to Flintsville by forcing them to bear the brunt of recreation costs for all residents. Developers were also concerned with the structure of the proposals, particularly that the fee would have to be paid "up front" before any of the units had been occupied.

With the public hearing concluded, the board has asked you to make recommendations concerning the developer's fee.

Problem

Is the concept of a developer's fee workable? If so, what should be the amount of the fee? Develop arguments stating why the gift of land is better than the gift of cash, and then suggest why cash might be preferred to land. Should developers be required to pay all of the fee up front? Is the fee likely to discourage development? Are developers likely to pass the costs on to the new residents? If so, is it ethical to have new residents pay an unfair share for recreation facilities? As director, would you recommend that the developer's fee be implemented?

Suggested Key Words and Phrases for
Literature Search for Case 252

Developer's fee   Funding
Landscaping   Public hearings
Public-private relationship   Subdivision regulations
Real estate development   Taxes

Selected References for Case Study 252

Crawford, Jr., C. (1979). *Strategy and tactics in municipal zoning.* Second ed. Englewood Cliffs, NJ: Prentice-Hall.

Dowall, D. (1989). *Public real estate development: A new role for planners.* Berkeley, CA: Institute of Urban and Regional Development, University of California at Berkeley.

Dworak, R. (1980). *Taxpayers, taxes, and government spending: Perspectives on the taxpayer revolt.* New York: Praeger.

Hansen, S. (1983). *The politics of taxation: Revenue without representation.* New York: Praeger.

Klemens, M. (1988, May). Taxes and the economy: Searching for cause and effect. *Illinois Issues,* 10-12.

Lai, R. (1988). *Law in urban design and planning: The invisible web.* New York: Van Reinhold.

Lewis, Jr., S. (1984). *Taxation for development: Principles and applications.* New York: Oxford University Press.

Meyers, E. (1988). *Rebuilding America's cities.* Cambridge, MA: Ballinger.

Peterson, C., and McCarthy, C. (1982). *Handling zoning and land use litigation: A practical guide.* Charlottesville, VA: Michie.

Schnidman, F., and Block, S. (1977). *Real estate development: Legal and business regulation.* New York: Practicing Law Institute.

Stein, H., (ed.) (1988). *Tax policy in the twenty-first century.* New York: Wiley.

Summers, L., (ed.) (1989). *Tax policy and the economy: Volume three.* Cambridge, MA: MIT University Press.

Urban Land Institute. (1985). *Working with the community: A developer's guide.* Washington, D.C.: Urban Land Institute.

White, M. (1980). *Urban renewal and the changing residential structure of the city.* Chicago: Community and Family Study Center, University of Chicago.

253
Little Leaguers Face "Lockout"

Situation

You are the athletic director for a public parks and recreation department in Blueberry, a town of 100,000. As part of your duties, you provide the facilities used by the local Little League Baseball organization. However, you have no jurisdiction over the Little League Baseball administration. A dispute between two boards of directors, each claiming control of the local Little League, is threatening the start of this year's season for nearly 300 youngsters.

The dispute began last autumn when a group of parents charged that the board of directors was violating Little League regulations by refusing to conduct annual elections. After much bickering, each player's family received ballots in the mail under the supervision of LeRoy Vanderville, a county regional administrator for Little League. When Vanderville counted the votes, three long-term board members lost their positions.

Joe Wintworth, who founded the league in 1977, was among those who were re-elected, but he refused to recognize the new board. He split from Little League Baseball and started his own league. He also refused to surrender the Little League's bats, balls, gloves, and homeplate. In addition, he sued in state Supreme Court seeking to prohibit the new board from using the name Blueberry Little League; however, his request was denied.

Wintworth contends that he founded the Blueberry Little League, incorporated it, and was therefore not bound by Little League rules governing the operation of the board. "Little League can just dictate things such as size of playing field, weight of ball, and circumference of the bat," he maintained.

The national Little League backs the new board, but has taken the position that the dispute is a local matter to be resolved by the parents. Fourteen year-old Travis Miller, meanwhile, summed up the reaction of his teammates saying, "They should get all this ridiculous stuff out of the way and let us play ball. We just want to have some fun."

Problem

Should you become involved in the dispute as the city's recreation director? If so, what should your role be? How do you personally think that the crisis ought to be resolved? Do the feelings of the children matter? How much control should Little League maintain? What are the advantages and disadvantages of retaining the Little League logo and affiliation? Can the parents resolve the issue or should it be resolved elsewhere — in court, with an arbitrator, or by the national Little League office?

What is the central issue here? Why do you think the original board was against elections? If elections had been held annually, do you think the current crisis would have occurred? Does democracy have a place in sports administration? Does administration take the "fun" out of the game or does it make the game more efficient and "more fun"?

Suggested Key Words and Phrases for
Literature Search for Case 253

Autocratic administration   Crowd behavior
Hierarchy   Humanistic administration
Little League   Logo
National-local relationships   Parental input
Sports administration   Trademarks
Youth sports

Selected References for Case Study 253

Benest, F., Foley, J., and Welton, G. (1984). *Organizing leisure and human services.* Dubuque, IA: Kendall/Hunt.

Cooper, A. (1976). *World of logotypes.* Volume 1. New York: Art Direction.

DuBois, P. (1981). *Modern administrative practices in human services.* Dubuque, IA: Kendall/Hunt.

Hillery, G., and Lincoln, A. (1982). *Leisure, freedom, and crowd behavior.* Durham, NH: Library Crime Research Project.

Igarashi, T., (ed.) (1987). *World trademarks and logotypes II: A collection of international symbols and their applications.* Tokyo: Graphic-Sha.

Iso-Ahola, S. (1980). The social psychology of leisure and recreation. Dubuque, IA: Brown.

Kraus, R., and Curtis, J. *Creative administration in recreation, parks, and leisure services.* Fourth ed. St. Louis: Times Mirror/ Mosby.

Loy, J., McPherson, B., and Kenyin, G. (1978). *Sport and social systems: A guide to the analysis, problems, and literature.* Reading, MA: Addison-Wesley.

Pfeffer, J. (1978). *Organizational design.* Second printing. Arlington Heights, IL: AHM.

Pooley, J. (1980). *The sport fan: A social-psychology of misbehavior.* Vanier City, Ontario: Canadian Association for Health, Physical Education, and Recreation.

Robin, J., and Steinhauer, M. (1988). *Handbook on human services administration.* New York: Marcell Iekker.

Rockwood, L. (1980). *Public parks and recreation administration: Behavior and dynamics.* Salt Lake City: Brighton.

Snyder, E., and Spreitzer, E. (1983). *Social aspects of sport.* Second ed. Englewood Cliffs, NJ: Prentice-Hall.

254
Lobbying Campaign Seeks Guidance

Situation

You have been hired to evaluate the advice a lobbying group was recently given by a consultant. The group, Keep Our Downtown Green (KODG) wishes to preserve a scenic area of town traditionally used as a meeting place for truck gardeners and consumers. That area of town has become run-down in recent years, however, and many businesses favor installing a parking garage, hotel, and apartments in its place. The group asked a consultant for advice on how to lobby city hall, and the consultant offered the following:

- Give politicians credit when they have accomplished something you favor.
- Improve communication with the council members. Be concise, organized, and factual. Use statistics and economics. Provide the information several days in advance of the meeting so it can be reviewed thoroughly.
- Identify your allies and use them.
- Ask politicians for advice. Often they can tell you what they think will sell the project.
- Help other groups with their pet causes and they will likely help your group with its cause.
- Find out how the opposition is trying to influence the politicians and try to counter their attempts.
- Present a united front.
- Utilize the opportunity to vote out people who do not support your project. Also, be sure to support the people who might get in trouble by voting for your project.

Problem

Which pieces of advice are good ones? Can you think of any other advice to offer a lobbying group? If you had to identify one piece of advice as being the best, which would it be? Take each point and elaborate on how it could be applied to this specific situation. Describe a lobbying campaign to preserve the downtown.

Does lobbying have a place in a democracy? Support the case that "lobbying is more than just the squeaky wheel getting the grease."

Suggested Key Words and Phrases for
Literature Search for Case 254

Citizen input	Downtown revitalization
Ecology	Green space
Lobbying	Politicians
Preservation	Public officials
Public relations	Relationship with city hall
Restoration	

Selected References for Case Study 254

Culhane, P. (1981). *Public lands politics: Interest group influence on the forest and the bureau of land management*. Baltimore: Johns Hopkins University Press.

Cunningham, P. (1988, Sept.). How to win clients and influence co-workers. *Parks and Recreation*, 68-70, 83.

Gilbert, W., (ed.) (1975). *Public relations in local government*. Washington, D.C.: International City Management Association.

Hawkins, T. (1988, May). Parks: For the people, by the people. *Parks and Recreation*, 39-43.

Haworth, J., (ed.) (1979). *Community involvement and leisure*. London: Lepus.

Hirschman, A. (1982). *Shifting involvements: Private interest and public action*. Princeton, NJ: Princeton University Press.

McAvoy, L. (1990, Sept.). An environmental ethic for parks and recreation. *Parks and Recreation*, 68-72.

McAdam, G. (1990, Oct.). Environmental protection through citizen action. *Parks and Recreation*, 46-51.

Reynolds, J., and Hormachea, M. (1976). Public relations. *Public recreation administration*. Reston, VA: Reston, 372-394.

Toalson, R., and Herchenberger, P. (1985). *Developing community support for parks and recreation*. Champaign, IL: Champaign Park District.

Useem, M. (1975). *Protest movements in America*. Indianapolis: Bobbs-Merrill.

Wallace, G., Tierney, P., and Hass, G. (1990, Sept.). The right link between wilderness and tourism. *Parks and Recreation*, 62-66, 111.

255
Is the Proposed Park District an Economic Disaster?

Situation

You have been hired to promote the formation of a controversial park district. To gather evidence for your presentation, you listen to a speech given by Linda Taylor, a leading opponent of the district. She says that she has had experiences working with park districts previously — and blames them for the economic troubles in her home town.

"A park district is more than just a park. We had three fieldhouses and a library. The district also had pavilions and even an olympic-sized pool. There's more to the park district than what the name implies. A park district has the legal power to enter into contracts, to purchase, lease and condemn land, to build streets, boating facilities, airports, playgrounds, and museums. All of this requires large amounts of money.

"My park district was funded primarily by the property taxes leveled against a huge electrical plant. Unfortunately, the power plant, which supplied 90 percent of the tax base, suffered an economic setback and closed. Tax rates began to increase for everybody else, and pretty soon other businesses also had to leave, as well as many residents.

"Park districts have a habit of expanding. There are all kinds of activities in which a park district becomes involved. We had three fieldhouses and three full-time directors to run activities for children. There was a manager, assistant manager and ten lifeguards at the pool. We had a park maintenance department, which oversaw safety, repairs, and routine tasks such as cutting grass. As the district expands, it hires more people, which means it needs more revenue for salaries. More revenue for salaries, meanwhile, means money must be taken from capital projects. When these capital projects need money, a new bond is financed. The financing of a new bond then leads to higher taxes. Higher taxes ultimately lead to the ruin of the economy."

Problem

What do you say in reply to Linda's speech? Where was she right? Where was she wrong? What were the facts? What were only her opinions? Discuss the role of enabling legislation; what boundaries does it place upon a park district? Create a speech to promote the district, trying to counter every negative statement that she made.

What are the advantages and disadvantages of park districts? Are park districts significantly different from general-fund municipal government recreation departments, and if so, how? As a recreation director, would you prefer a park district or a recreation department? As a community citizen, would you prefer a park district or a recreation department?

Should park districts become involved in library facilities? Should park districts build museums? Create the ideal park district, indicating the program areas in which you think the district should be involved. Justify each area. Create the ideal park district organizational chart that would provide the personnel for the programs you indicated an ideal park district should have.

Suggested Key Words and Phrases for
Literature Search for Case 255

Economy	Enabling legislation
Fieldhouses	Library
Park district	Personnel
Public relations	Recreation department
Special districts	Tax base
Tax payment	

Selected References for Case Study 255

Board of Economic Development, State of Illinois. (1962, Feb.). *Illinois enabling legislation for municipal planning and zoning as amended by the 72nd Illinois General Assembly.* Springfield, IL: Board of Economic Development, State of Illinois.

Dworak, R. (1980). *Taxpayers, taxes, and government spending: Perspectives on the taxpayer revolt.* New York: Praeger.

Hansen, S. (1983). *The politics of taxation: Revenue without representation.* New York: Praeger.

Herman, R., and Til, J., (eds.) (1989). *Nonprofit board of directors: Analyses and applications.* New Brunswick, NJ: Transaction.

Ibrahim, H., Banes, R., and Gerson, G. (1987). *Effective parks and recreation boards and commissions.* Reston, VA: American Alliance for Health, Physical Education, Recreation, and Dance.

Illinois Department of Local Government Affairs, Office of Community Services. (1979). *Simplified financial management manual for Illinois park districts.* Springfield, IL: Department of Local Government Affairs, Office of Community Services.

Klemens, M. (1988, May). Taxes and the economy: Searching for cause and effect. *Illinois Issues,* 10-12.

Klemens, M. (1990, Feb.). Property tax: Hot potato between local and state politicians. *Illinois Issues,* 11-13.

Lewis, Jr., S. (1984). *Taxation for development: Principles and applications.* New York: Oxford University Press.

Perrenod, V. (1984). *Special districts, special purposes: Fringe governments and urban problems in the Houston area.* College Station, TX: Texas A & M University Press.

Porter, D., Lin, B., and Peiser, R. (1987). *Special districts: A useful technique for financing infrastructure.* Washington, D.C.: Urban Land Institute.

Russell, R. (1982). *Planning programs in recreation.* St. Louis: Mosby.

Stein, H., ed. (1988). *Tax policy in the twenty-first century.* New York: Wiley.

Stoops, J., and Edginton, C. (1988, April). Needed: Effective park and recreation boards and commissions. *Parks and Recreation*, 51-55.

Summers, L., (ed.) (1989). *Tax policy and the economy: Volume three.* Cambridge, MA: MIT University Press.

256
Access for Disabled Debated

Situation

You are the director for a state park. Of the park land, 53 percent is classified as "wild forest", 43 percent is classified as "wilderness," and four percent is classified as "developed." While there are numerous distinctions between "wild forest" and "wilderness," a significant difference relates to motorized access. Vehicles are permitted in the wild forest areas, but not in wilderness areas. However, wilderness areas are accessible where they border roads or waterways.

The handicapped and elderly have complained that they do not have access to the wilderness areas because their motorized vehicles are not allowed in these areas. They have proposed that a road be built through the wilderness so that they can enjoy nature.

An environmental group, Mountain Men of America, claim it is important to preserve certain wild lands. They claim that this conservation includes making certain that these lands will always be free of blacktop and vehicles. They argue that the goal of the park should be to preserve the natural land for future generations, not to destroy it in an attempt to pacify a lobbying group.

The Handicapped Environmentalists Lobby Program (HELP) has threatened to take the park to court if access is not provided.

Problem

Should certain lands remain completely undeveloped; why or why not? Is air and water access as important as road access? What is the legal process of changing land classification? Why is there such a mix of state land classifications? If you were sued, how would you defend the park's refusal to build the road? What can be done to meet the needs of the handicapped and/or elderly in this situation without destroying the wilderness?

Suggested Key Words and Phrases for
Literature Search for Case 256

Conflict demands   Handicap access
Land classification   Land development
Land usage   Lawsuit
Lobby   Wild forest
Wilderness

Selected References for Case Study 256

Bear, F.; Pritchard, H.; and Akin, W. (1986). *Earth: The stuff of life*. Normal, OK: University of Oklahoma Press.

Harlow, W. (1979). *Ways of the woods: A guide to the skills and spirit of the woodland experience*. Washington, D.C.: American Forestry Association.

Jubenville, A. (1978). *Outdoor recreation management*. Philadelphia: Saunders.

Knudson, D. (1980). *Outdoor recreation*. New York: Macmillan.

McAvoy, L. (1990, Sept.). An environmental ethic for parks and recreation. *Parks and Recreation*, 68-72.

McAdam, G. (1990, Oct.). Environmental protection through citizen action. *Parks and Recreation*, 46-51.

Olsen, L. (1976). *Outdoor survival skills*. 4th ed. Second printing. Provo, UT: Brigham Young University Press.

Pigram, J. (1983). *Outdoor recreation and resource management*. New York: St. Martin.

Stein, J. (1986, Jan.). Including disabled participants: Four goals for recreation management. *Parks and Recreation*, 49-52, 79.

Wallace, G., Tierney, P., and Hass, G. (1990, Sept.). The right link between wilderness and tourism. *Parks and Recreation*, 62-66, 111.

Warren, R. (1990, June). Land stewardship: Your professional responsibility. *Park Maintenance and Grounds Management*, 14-16.

Wekman, P., and Schleien, S. (1981). *Leisure programs for handicapped persons: Adaptations, techniques, and curriculum*. Baltimore: University Park.

Zook, L. (1986, Jan.). Outdoor adventure programs build character in five ways. *Parks and Recreation*, 54-57.

257
Toxic Waste Leakage Threatens Softball Season

Situation

You are the athletic supervisor and recreation director for a municipal parks and recreation department in a town of 70,000. It is late August, and the annual softball season is almost complete. Things appeared to be going well. However, this afternoon the state Environmental Protection Agency announced that it has found toxic waste in one of the four city parks. An EPA representative said the EPA believes that the park is built on a hazardous waste site and former landfill. Because of possible long-term health hazards to players, spectators, and children at the park, the EPA has recommended that you close the park, including both the playground and the softball diamonds.

The mayor has stated that he personally is against closing the park. "There is nothing in the report that indicates to me that there are any reasons to close the ballpark. There is not enough evidence to warrant closing the park; most of their report is speculation."

"I think the report is a joke," said one ballplayer. "We've played here all year. What's another three or four games going to hurt? If we've been exposed to anything, it's too late now." Other ballplayers do not agree, and six teams have already announced that they plan to drop out of the fifty-team league if the games are played on the former landfill.

Problem

Should the park be closed immediately? Should the park be closed at all? If the park is closed, should the remaining softball season be cancelled or should the games be moved to another field? Is it dangerous to the health of the players and spectators to keep the field open only until the end of the season? Is it dangerous to public relations if the fields are kept open? What should be done about the six teams that have already dropped out — should they be ignored, invited to play, or have their money refunded?

Is it typical for parks to be built on landfills? Are parks built on landfills likely to experience problems with waste? What do you suggest that the future of the park should be?

Suggested Key Words and Phrases for Literature Search for Case 257

Athletic administration
Hazardous material
Landfill
Public relations
Softball league
Toxic waste

Environmental Protection Agency
Park development
Scheduling
Sociology of sports

Selected References for Case Study 257

Espeseth, R. (1977). *Site planning of park areas.* Champaign, IL: Office of Recreation and Park Resources, Department of Leisure Studies, Cooperative Extension Service, University of Illinois at Urbana-Champaign.

Glancy, M., and Donnelly, G. (1988, March). How to manage chemicals in your department. *Parks and Recreation*, 34-36, 103.

Gilbert, W., (ed.) (1975). *Public relations in local government.* Washington, D.C.: International City Management Association.

Hjelte, G., and Shivers, J. (1978). *Public administration of recreational services.* Second ed. Philadelphia: Lea and Febiger.

Loy, J.; McPherson, B.; and Kenyin, G. (1978). *Sport and social systems: A guide to the analysis, problems, and literature.* Reading, MA: Addison-Wesley.

Molnar, D., and Rutledge, A. (1986). *Anatomy of a park: The essentials of recreation area planning and design.* New York: McGraw-Hill.

Reynolds, J., and Hormachea, M. (1976). Public relations. *Public recreation administration.* Reston, VA: Reston, 372-394.

Ries, M. (1973). *Design standards to accommodate people with physical disabilities in park and open space planning.* Madison, WI: Cooperative Extension Programs, Recreation Resources Center, University of Wisconsin at Madison Press.

Shivers, J., and Hjelte, G. (1971). *Planning recreational places.* Rutherford, NJ: Fairleigh Dickinson University Press.

Snyder, E., and Spreitzer, E. (1983). *Social aspects of sport.* Second ed. Englewood Cliffs, NJ: Prentice-Hall.

Toalson, R., and Herchenberger, P. (1985). *Developing community support for parks and recreation.* Champaign, IL: Champaign Park District.

Urban Research Development Corporation. (1977). *Guidelines for understanding and determining optimum recreation carrying capacity.* Washington, D.C.: U.S. Department of Interior, Bureau of Outdoor Recreation.

258
Sport Sales Jog to Record High

Situation

You are the public parks and recreation director for a large metropolitan park district. As you browse through your mail, you see that Swanson Shoes has sent you a news release. This news release presents findings from a national survey. The survey indicates that jogging shoes helped to push retail sales in sporting goods to a record high of $15.1 billion. Jogging shoes, included for the first time in an annual consumer survey prepared by the National Sporting Goods Association, showed an increase in sales of 110 percent over the previous year.

Another trend observed by the survey is that women constitute nearly one-third of the market for jogging shoes, snow skis, and hiking boots. Female participation was also cited for substantial sales increases in exercise equipment, racquet sports, and softball. Almost half the bowling balls and tennis rackets purchased are for women. Twenty percent of all baseball gloves sold were intended for a female hand. Thirty percent of all skateboards were intended for female feet. The survey also noted that the number of high-level female administrators at recreational facilities had tripled in the past year.

The letter from Swanson Shoes concludes by stating that the company thought that you might find the information useful. The letter does not overtly state that you should purchase Swanson shoes, although it does suggest that your clients might like to read the survey and that perhaps it should be posted in local locker rooms. Permission is given to duplicate the survey. No reply is requested.

Problem

What should you do with the survey? Should you post it? Should you duplicate it? Should you use the information to justify offering more sports for women? If not, what other information would you need to make such a justification?

Does it make a difference that the survey was done by a national organization rather than by a shoe company? Why would a shoe company mail the results of the survey? Is the survey a marketing ploy or a public relations ploy? What is the difference between "public relations" and "marketing"?

Do you trust the information presented? What could bias the information? How could you determine if the survey is valid?

*Suggested Key Words and Phrases for
Literature Search for Case 258*

Commercial recreation	Demand analysis
Marketing	Needs assessment
Population sampling	Posting policies
Public recreation	Public relations
Reliability	Research methods
Sporting goods	Survey
Trends	Validity
Women in sports	

Selected References for Case Study 258

Bell, C., and Roberts, H., (eds.) (1984). *Social researching: Politics, problems, practice.* London: Routledge and Kegan Paul.

Boutilier, M., and SanGiovanni, L. (1983). *The sporting woman.* Champaign, IL: Human Kinetics.

Bovaird, A., Tricker, M., and Stoakes, R. (1984). *Recreation management and pricing: The effect of charging policy on demand at countryside recreation sites.* Brookfield, VT: Gower.

Crompton, J. (1987). How to establish a price for park and recreation services. In *Current issues in leisure services: Looking ahead in a time of transition.* J. Bannon, (ed.) Washington, D.C.: International City Management Association, 93-107.

Crossley, J. (1990, March). Multi-tier programming in commercial recreation. *Parks and Recreation,* 69-73.

Hudson, S. (1988). *How to conduct community needs assessment surveys in public parks and recreation.* Columbus, OH: Publishing Horizons.

Johnson, D., Meiller, L., and Summers, G. (1987). *Needs assess-ment: Theory and methods.* Ames, IA: Iowa State University Press.

Klafs, C., and Lyon, M. (1978). *The female athlete: A coaches guide to conditioning and training.* St. Louis: Mosby.

Kelly, J. (1985). *Recreation business.* New York: Wiley.

Prus, R. (1989). *Pursuing customers: An ethnography of marketing activities.* Newbury Park, CA: Sage.

Rochman, J., Teresa, J., Kay, T., and Morningstar, G. (1983). *Marketing human service innovations.* Beverly Hills, CA: Sage.

Soderberg, J. (1989, June). Marketing recreation right. *Parks and Recreation*, 38-41.

Witt, P. (1987, March). Women in recreation management: A man's perspective on understanding and change. *Parks and Recreation*, 42-44, 102.

Venkatesan, M., Schmalensee, D., and Marshall, C., (eds.) (1986). *Creativity in services marketing: What's new, what works, and what's developing.* Chicago, IL: American Marketing Association.

259
"This Place is a Zoo"

Situation

You have been hired as a consultant by the Grantsville Department of Parks, Recreation, and Cultural Affairs. You are to review the evidence from a recent series of animal mishaps at the zoo. From these incidents, you have to determine administrative changes, and present them in a positive manner to the public.

The problems at the zoo began reaching public attention when the department reported the death of an elephant named Twinkie in a press release last May. The press release indicated Twinkie died on a farm outside town; however, it was later announced that the elephant apparently died while traveling with a circus.

Last week, a lioness and a tiger from the zoo were put to death at Bighorn University, where they had been taken for treatment. The zoo's own clinic was ordered shut down by the federal government last autumn. Authorities are also investigating the deaths of two kodiak bears that had been transferred from the zoo to a game ranch.

Amid disclosures of these deaths, the Skyline Zoo asked for the return of a rare Mona monkey and a Siamang ape that were on loan, only to be told that the Mona monkey had died. However, the general curator believes the Mona monkey is alive, although he is not sure where the monkey is.

The city's mayor has announced that the city is launching an investigation of the zoo's treatment of its animals and the claims of poor management and deteriorating facilities. "I don't think anybody's condemned the zoo more than we have ourselves," he said. "In the present push of all the things that we as a city have been trying to do, I have not given the time to the zoo I should have."

Problem

What changes would you suggest that the zoo make? Should zoo animals be loaned to circuses? Should elderly animals be taken to a ranch for privacy in their last days? Should the zoo strive to maintain an animal clinic, or can it rely on other clinics in town?

What type of paperwork should accompany each animal's stay to prevent the animal from becoming "lost"? Create a system of checks and balances so that an accurate inventory can be obtained.

Is management to blame for the recent problems? If so, do you suggest that the management be fired or retrained; why? Do the mayor's remarks influence your consulting presentation? Outline a retraining program that could meet the needs of management.

Suggested Key Words and Phrases for
Literature Search for Case 259

Commercial recreation-   Consulting
  public recreation relationship   Employee relations
Evaluation   Inventory
Job descriptions   Personnel management
Public relations   Purchasing
Training   Zoo

Selected References for Case Study 259

Bell, C., and Nadler, L., (eds.) (1985). *Clients and consultants: Meeting and exceeding expectations.* Houston: Gulf.

Brademas, D. (1981). *A model job analysis procedure for the park and recreation profession.* Champaign, IL: Department of Leisure Studies, Cooperative Extension Service, University of Illinois at Urbana-Champaign.

Easton, T., and Conant, R. (1985). *Using consultants: A consumer's guide for managers.* Chicago, IL: Probus.

Hendon, W. (1981). *Evaluating urban parks and recreation.* New York: Praeger.

Howe, C. (1987). Evaluating for accountability. In *Current issues in leisure services: Looking ahead in a time of transition.* J. Bannon, (ed.) Washington, D.C.: International City Management Association, 27-35.

Leenders, M., Fearon, H., and England, W. (1980). *Purchasing and materials management.* Seventh ed. Homewood, IL: Irwin.

Lundegren, H., and Farrell, P. (1985). *Evaluation for leisure service managers: A dynamic approach.* Philadelphia: Saunders.

Rosow, J., and Zager, R. (1988). *Training —the competitive edge.* San Francisco: Jossey-Bass.

Silver, A., and Peterson, R. (1985). *Decision systems for inventory management and production planning.* Second ed. New York: Wiley.

Tersine, R. (1982). *Principals of inventory and materials management.* Second ed. New York: North-Holland.

ment programs: An organizational approach. Westport, CT: Quorum.

Zwerin, K. (1986, March). Zoos: A blueprint for fiscal survival. *Parks and Recreation,* 42-45, 67.

260
Are Kickbacks Acceptable Overtime Pay?

Situation

You are the director of a public parks and recreation department in a large metropolitan community. Early on Monday morning, the city manager, Joe Lewis, calls you into his office and announces that he is beginning a full-scale investigation of the city's recreation department after he learned that a number of park employees were accepting unauthorized compensation for the use of city recreational facilities.

Three people have already been suspended without pay — a supervisor, a recreation aide, and a utility worker — and you will be the fourth. The suspensions are based on an investigation by the city's internal auditing department and the local police. The investigation alleges that the employees took money for switching on the baseball lights at Grant Park and assisting in other activities at the park. The investigation also found that unauthorized compensation was accepted in lieu of park rental fees. The monies, though, were never turned into the city's cashier.

The employees indicated they pocketed the money in lieu of overtime pay and said the practice had existed for many years. One employee even said that he possessed a memo instructing him to take the money he should be collecting and treat it as his overtime pay. City Manager Lewis said he had no way of determining how long the practice has existed or how much money the city may have lost as a result. Because the practice has been "common," no formal charges have been filed, even though criminal charges could legally be filed. "I am troubled by what seems to be an attitude of a few employees that under-the-table-deals are okay. Deliberate violations of city ordinances and using employment for personal gain are not going to be tolerated any longer," Lewis said.

Lewis claims that the investigation is far from over. The fate of those people suspended will not be determined until the investigation is completed. The suspended supervisor, meanwhile, claims that he will take the matter to court in hopes of being reinstated.

Problem

What do you tell the city manager? If you were aware that the employees were keeping the money, should you have told him about it previously? Is it fair that you are suspended for something those below you in the administrative hierarchy did? Is it okay for an employee to break a city law if a city employer says it is okay? Why would a previous recreation director have started the practice of letting employees keep city fee money rather than insist they draw overtime pay? Aside from breaking city rules, why is it a bad idea not to keep accurate records? Is there a significant difference between a "policy" and a "procedure"?

Was the city manager right in suspending the employees? Should the suspension have been with pay instead of without pay; why or why not? Would you have recommended that the supervisor go to court to be reinstated? Would you suggest that criminal charges be filed against those thought to be guilty, even though such practice has continued for years? As the suspended recreation director, what will you do with your time for the next few weeks?

Suggested Key Words and Phrases for
Literature Search for Case 260

Administrative hierarchy	City manager
Criminal charges	Ethics
Kickbacks	Organizational hierarchy
Personnel	Policies
Public recreation	Procedures
Suspension	Termination

Selected References for Case Study 260

Bok, S. (1981). Blowing the whistle. *Public duties: The moral obligations of government officials.* J. Fleishman, L. Liebman., and M. Moore, (eds.) Cambridge, MA: Harvard, 204-220.

Burke, J. (1986). *Bureaucratic responsibility.* Baltimore: Johns Hopkins University Press.

Cooper, T. (1984). *The responsible administrator: An approach to ethics for the administrative role.* Third printing. Port Washington, NY: Associated Faculty Press.

Coulson, R. (1981). *The termination handbook.* New York: Free.

Culkin, D. (1988, Feb.). The right way to discipline. *Parks and Recreation*, 44-45.

Fleishman, J., Liebman, L., and Moore, M., (eds.) (1981). *Public duties: The moral obligations of government officials.* Cambridge, MA: Harvard University Press.

Fleishman, J. (1981). Self-interest and political integrity. In *Public duties: The moral obligations of government officials.* J. Fleishman, L. Liebman., and M. Moore, (eds.) Cambridge, MA: Harvard University Press, 52-92.

Haughey, J., (ed.) (1979). *Personal values in public policy: Conversations on government decision making.* New York: Paulist.

Holloway, W., and Leech, M. (1985). *Employment termination: Rights and remedies.* Washington, D.C.: Bureau of National Affairs.

Kernaghan, K. (1975). *Ethical conduct: Guidelines for government employees.* Toronto: Institute of Public Administration of Canada.

Moore, M. (1981). Realms of obligation and virtue. In *Public duties: The moral obligations of government officials.* J. Fleishman, L. Liebman., and M. Moore, (eds.) Cambridge, MA: Harvard University Press, 3-31.

Patten, T. (1988). *Fair pay.* San Francisco: Jossey-Bass.

Payne, B. (1981). Devices and desires: Corruption and ethical seriousness. In *Public duties: The moral obligations of government officials.* J. Fleishman, L. Liebman., and M. Moore, (eds.) Cambridge, MA: Harvard University Press, 175-203.

Price, D. (1981). Assessing policy: Conceptual point of departure. In *Public duties: The moral obligations of government officials.* J. Fleishman, L. Liebman., and M. Moore, (eds.) Cambridge, MA: Harvard University Press, 142-174.

Redeker, J. (1983). *Discipline: Policies and procedures.* Washington, D.C.: Bureau of National Affairs.

Warwick, D. (1981). The ethics of administrative discretion. In *Public duties: The moral obligations of government officials.* J. Fleishman, L. Liebman., and M. Moore, (eds.) Cambridge, MA: Harvard University Press, 93-130.

Wolf, Jr., C. (1981). Ethics and policy analysis. In *Public duties: The moral obligations of government officials.*   J. Fleishman, L. Liebman., and M. Moore, (eds.) Cambridge, MA: Harvard University Press, 131-141.

261
Mayor Forces Ouster of Community Center Leader

Situation

You are an executive director of a community center in Gladstone, a large metropolitan area. An executive director of another community center, Happy Rock, has recently come under fire from the City Council, particularly the mayor. Happy Rock has collected numerous unpaid bills during the past few months, and these have all been paid begrudgingly by the City Council. The City Council has tried to legislate fiscal efficiency at the center, but the center interprets the action as a takeover attempt.

Last night, the mayor delivered an ultimatum to Happy Rock: Remove your executive director or close your doors. The mayor said there would be no more funds given to the center unless the director was removed. "If you keep your director, the center will close. If you oust your director, the center will continue to receive funding while a search is conducted for a new director."

The vote was 11 to 6, and a search committee was formed to find a new director. However, board president Dick James believes that the vote was not in accordance with the body's by-laws, so it is not binding. He quoted a section of the by-laws stating that a two-thirds majority of the board, not a simple majority of the members present at a meeting, is required to approve a new executive director. He interprets that clause as also meaning that a two-thirds vote is needed to remove a director. He said the current director will continue operating the center.

Problem

Should the executive director continue his duties? Would the City Council's decision to require the director to step down stand in court? If the director is removed, who should run the center while a new director is sought? Should community centers be financially self-supporting? How much input should a City Council have in a community center? What are the advantages and disadvantages of the City Council being deeply involved in the day-to-day operations of the center? Are there advantages to having the Council loosely involved with the center? If so, what are they?

As the director of a similar community center in the same town, how would this affair affect how you ran your center? Do you believe the mayor is trying to seize control of Happy Rock or that he just wants efficiency? What do you believe will be the outcome for Happy Rock's executive director?

What legal requirements must the search committee follow? If the mayor puts his brother-in-law's name in the pool of candidates, what must the search committee do? Under what conditions could the City Council legally hire the mayor's brother-in-law? Under what conditions could it not legally hire the mayor's brother-in-law?

Suggested Key Words and Phrases for
Literature Search for Case 261

Budgeting	By-laws
Community center	City council relations
Funding	Managerial hierarchy
Performance appraisal	Personnel
Public recreation	Search committee
Termination	

Selected References for Case Study 261

Arvey, R., and Faley, R. (1988). *Fairness in selecting employees.* Second ed. Reading, MA: Addison-Wesley.

Bovaird, A., Tricker, M., and Stoakes, R. (1984). *Recreation management and pricing: The effect of charging policy on demand at countryside recreation sites.* Brookfield, VT: Gower.

Crompton, J. (1987). How to establish a price for park and recreation services. In *Current issues in leisure services: Looking ahead in a time of transition.* J. Bannon, (ed.) Washington, D.C.: International City Management Association, 93-107.

Chatiham, D. (1989, Oct.). Taking the fear out of performance appraisals. *Parks and Recreation*, 45-48.

Coulson, R. (1981). *The termination handbook.* New York: Free.

Dreker, G., and Sackett, P. (1983). *Perspectives on employee staffing and selection: Readings and commentary.* Homewood, IL: Irwin.

Holloway, W., and Leech, M. (1985). *Employment termination: Rights and remedies.* Washington, D.C.: Bureau of National Affairs.

Kellogg, M. (1975). *What to do about performance appraisal.* New York: AMACOM.

Lewis, C. (1985). *Employee selection.* London: Hutchinson.

Potter, E., ed. (1986). *Employee selection: Legal and practical alternatives to compliance and litigation.* Second ed. Washington, D.C.: National Foundation for the Study of Equal Employment Policy.

Reynolds, J., and Hormachea, M. (1976). Financing public recreation and park agencies. *Public recreation administration*, 246-271.

Smith, W. (1985). *The art of raising money.* New York: AMACOM.

262
Board Seeks to Restrict Employee Use of Facilities

Situation

You are the director of a public parks and recreation district in a medium-sized metropolitan area. The recreation advisory board has suggested that a policy be implemented that would curb employee use of facilities, materials, and equipment. The proposal would permit employee use on the same basis as that authorized for the general public. The proposal also tightens language regarding the loan of equipment to other agencies and personnel.

Board members contend that this proposal is necessary to protect the board against lawsuits. "Our current policy has too many loopholes," said one board member. "We don't mean this to be a witch hunt against employees, nor is it a reaction to any specific employee. However, we have been taken to court by previous employees, and our policy simply does not stand up in court."

Teachers in the park district, though, oppose the proposal. Automobile repairs instructor Jody Kelly said, "If an instructor used his own car to show how to make repairs or adjustments, it would be in violation of the rules because his personal property would be improved and he would personally gain from the use of park facilities." Many other personnel, part-time and full-time, agree with Kelly. The board has asked you to make recommendations.

Problem

Should a policy regarding the use of equipment be implemented? Is it possible to obtain a policy that is inclusive but not too restrictive? Should personnel have a voice in the forming of this policy? If you were to favor the policy, would you implement the policy immediately or give the personnel a chance to adapt? Could a park board legislate a policy even if the director did not approve of it? Is the use of equipment for personal gain a legitimate benefit of working within the agency? Should there be exceptions to the policy, such as people with certain ranks or instructors of certain courses? Draft a policy that covers loaning equipment to other agencies and using equipment for personal gain.

Suggested Key Words and Phrases for
Literature Search for Case 262

Benefits	Board-director relations
Compensation	Equipment usage
Inventory	Job analysis
Lawsuits	Materials management
Park districts	Personnel
Policies	Procedures

Selected References for Case Study 262

Cunningham, P. (1988, Sept.). How to win clients and influence co-workers. *Parks and Recreation*, 68-70, 83.

Hopkins, A. (1983). *Work and job satisfaction in the public sector.* Totowa, NJ: Rowman and Allanheld.

Husband, T. (1976). *Work analysis and pay structure.* London: McGraw-Hill.

Kelly, J. (1982). *Scientific management, job redesign, and work performance.* London: Academic.

Knights, D., Willmott, H., and Collinson, D. (1985). *Job redesign: Critical perspectives on the labour process.* Brookfield, VT: Gower.

Leenders, M., Fearon, H., and England, W. (1980). *Purchasing and materials management.* Seventh ed. Homewood, IL: Irwin.

Milkovich, G., and Newman, J. (1984). *Compensation.* Third ed. Homewood, IL: BPI/Irwin.

Patten, T. (1977). *Pay: Employee compensation and incentive plans.* New York: Free.

Patten, T. (1988). *Fair pay.* San Francisco: Jossey-Bass.

Silver, A., and Peterson, R. (1985). *Decision systems for inventory management and production planning.* Second ed. New York: Wiley.

Prabhu, V., and Baker, M., (eds.) (1986). *Materials management.* London: McGraw-Hill.

Tersine, R. (1976). *Materials management and inventory systems.* New York: North-Holland.

Tersine, R. (1982). *Principals of inventory and materials management.* Second ed. New York: North-Holland.

Zenz, G. (1987). *Purchasing and the management of materials*. Sixth ed. New York: Wiley.

263
Candidate Seeks Endorsement from Incumbent

Situation

You are a commissioner on a forest preserve board. You have been asked by Jimmy Jones, a candidate for the forest preserve board, to endorse him in the upcoming election. Jones claims that he loves nature. To prove it, he shows you his office, which is filled with stuffed bears, elk, and deer. Huge fish are proudly mounted on his wall. "I'm not a destroyer of wildlife," he contends, "I simply keep nature in balance."

"Sportsmen have contributed over $5 billion during the past 50 years for wildlife management and habitat through excise taxes. In addition, these funds were supplemented by the license fees paid for the privilege of sharing in the management and conservation of game. Hunters like myself provide a great service to nature and to society."

Jones says that if he is elected he would like to see classes organized featuring fly fishing, muzzle loading, archery, hunter safety, backpacking, and hunting with dogs. "These classes would be educational. They would be about outdoor recreation at its best."

Problem

Do you give Jones your endorsement? Should incumbents endorse candidates—why or why not? Is Jones a worthwhile candidate to endorse—why or why not? Do you think Jones could carry enough votes to win based on his statements? Is Jones wise in seeking the endorsement of an incumbent? What are the advantages and disadvantages of the endorsement? What benefits and consequences are at stake for you if you endorse or do not endorse Jones?

What is the purpose of a Forest Preserve District? Are Jones' goals appropriate for it? If elected, would he be able to implement his idea of having classes; why or why not?

What might cost Jones the election? Are his statements factual? Is the sexist term "sportsman" appropriate since most hunters are males? Should hunters be involved in conservation? What purpose do licenses serve besides bringing in revenue for the conservation department? Who should finance Jones' election campaign?

Suggested Key Words and Phrases for
Literature Search for Case 263

Campaigning	Conservation department
Ecology	Education
Endorsement	Forest preserve board
Hunter safety training	Hunting
License	Public relations
Sexist language	Wildlife conservation

Selected References for Case Study 263

Bear, F.; Pritchard, H.; and Akin, W. (1986). *Earth: The stuff of life.* Normal, OK: University of Oklahoma Press.

Cunningham, P. (1988, Sept.). How to win clients and influence co-workers. *Parks and Recreation,* 68-70, 83.

Harlow, W. (1979). *Ways of the woods: A guide to the skills and spirit of the woodland experience.* Washington, D.C.: American Forestry Association.

Knudson, D. (1980). *Outdoor recreation.* New York: Macmillan.

Lydenberg, S. (1981). *Bankrolling ballots: Update 1980: The role of business in financing ballot question campaigns.* New York: Council on Economic Priorities.

McAdam, G. (1990, Oct.). Environmental protection through citizen action. *Parks and Recreation,* 46-51.

McAvoy, L. (1990, Sept.). An environmental ethic for parks and recreation. *Parks and Recreation,* 68-72.

Olsen, L. (1976). *Outdoor survival skills.* 4th ed. Second printing. Provo, UT: Brigham Young University Press.

Pigram, J. (1983). *Outdoor recreation and resource management.* New York: St. Martin.

Wallace, G., Tierney, P., and Hass, G. (1990, Sept.). The right link between wilderness and tourism. *Parks and Recreation,* 62-66, 111.

Warren, R. (1990, June). Land stewardship: Your professional responsibility. *Park Maintenance and Grounds Management,* 14-16.

Zook, L. (1986, Jan.). Outdoor adventure programs build character in five ways. *Parks and Recreation,* 54-57.

264
Executive Director's Impulsive
Moment of Gratitude Questioned

Situation

You are the director of a medium-sized park district. As a way of saying thank you to the district's three best employees — your secretary, the director of parks and planning, and your business manager — your assistant director gave each of them a $750 bonus on their December 22 paycheck. Like many governmental agencies, the park district disburses checks before they are approved by the elected board. To your surprise, the board did not approve.

"The bonuses were appropriate, timely, and deserved," your assistant director told the board when questioned. "If I was too generous with park district funds, I will repay the district the $3,000 personally."

Board President Stan Eckoff admits that the district's policy manual does not directly mention such incidents. However, he claims that there is an unwritten policy of making salary adjustments in April, which become effective May 1. He also claims that the staff members are not entitled to the bonuses and that the board should make every effort to retrieve the money. However, he places no direct blame on the people who accepted the checks. In addition to having the money returned, Eckoff wants to remove your assistant recreation director.

Problem

How do you recommend that the crisis be resolved? Should the incident simply be dropped? Should the board accept the assistant director's check of $3,000? Should those who received the bonus be required to return the money? Should the assistant director be terminated? Should the policy manual be revised? How will the incident affect morale?

Are the statements in the policy manual to be taken literally or to be used as suggested guidelines? If something is not in the policy manual, should a director assume that it is not okay to do it? If a director does something not disapproved of in the policy manual, but not specifically okayed, should he inform the board? How much authority over personnel should a director be given?

Suggested Key Words and Phrases for Literature Search for Case 264

Benefits	Board relations
Bonuses	Morale
Payroll	Personnel
Policies	Policy manual
Termination	

Selected References for Case Study 264

Coulson, R. (1981). *The termination handbook.* New York: Free.

Culkin, D. (1988, Feb.). The right way to discipline. *Parks and Recreation*, 44-45.

Holloway, W., and Leech, M. (1985). *Employment termination: Rights and remedies.* Washington, D.C.: Bureau of National Affairs.

Husband, T. (1976). *Work analysis and pay structure*. London: McGraw-Hill.

Kleinbeck, U., Quast, H., Thierry, H., and Hacker, H., (eds.) (1990). *Work motivation*. Hillsdale, NJ: Lawrence Erlbaum.

Milkovich, G., and Newman, J. (1984). *Compensation*. Third ed. Homewood, IL: BPI/Irwin.

Morf, M. (1986). *Optimizing work performance: A look beyond the bottom line*. New York: Quorum.

Nash, M. (1985). *Making people productive*. San Francisco: Jossey-Bass.

Olson, V. (1983). *White collar waste: Gain the productivity edge*. Englewood Cliffs, NJ: Prentice-Hall.

Patten, T. (1977). *Pay: Employee compensation and incentive plans*. New York: Free.

Patten, T. (1988). *Fair pay*. San Francisco: Jossey-Bass.

Redeker, J. (1983). *Discipline: Policies and procedures*. Washington, D.C.: Bureau of National Affairs.

Schappi, J. (1988). *Improving job attendance*. Washington, D.C.: Bureau of National Affairs.

265
Mayor Seeks Political Allies in Parks Department

Situation

You are an applicant for a position as public parks and recreation director serving a city department of recreation for a medium-sized metropolitan area, which has a very heated mayoral election underway. The mayor, who is running for re-election has a choice of two good job candidates, one of which is you. He says he will back hiring you, provided you will support him in the election. He cites the following activities of the former director.

The director oversaw the parks department, as 180 park and recreation employees contributed more than $16,000 last August to his campaign for re-election as mayor. The employees, most of whom were beholden to the mayor for their jobs, bought ads in a yearbook, which was sponsored by the mayor's party. The yearbook was distributed at a fundraising dinner at a major hotel—a $50-a-plate event, which raised thousands of dollars from park workers and others who attended.

Parks department personnel staffed a wide variety of Democratic-sponsored community affairs in the town. This included a film of neighborhood spring-cleaning brigades, heavily attended bingo parties, a children's costume party, and events for senior citizens. Conspicuously involved, even in the middle of the workday, were park executives such as the personnel director and the sports information director.

The previous parks director let park employees take time off with pay so that they could campaign for the mayor in an area of town where the mayor's opponent was dominating. The mayor expects this type of loyalty from all of the city offices — from the street department to the parks department. Having told you this, he asks if you are willing to accept the job.

Problem

Should you take the job? Is your opinion influenced by whether the mayor is popular or unpopular in the community? Does the parks department owe an obligation to the city? Does the parks department owe an obligation to the mayor's political welfare? Is what the mayor is doing legal?

Should parks employees be given time off to campaign? Is the freedom to campaign a First Amendment right? If parks employees do take time off to campaign, should they receive payment for their missed hours? Should parks employees use their celebrity status to endorse candidates? Is there a significant difference between campaigning for a specific candidate and campaigning for a political party in general? Is there a distinction between campaigning for a person/party and campaigning for an issue? In which, if any of these campaigns, could/should a park employee ethically be involved? Should park districts co-sponsor activities with a political party? If an event is co-sponsored with a political party, should the parks department also co-sponsor an activity with the competing party?

Suggested Key Words and Phrases for
Literature Search for Case 265

Benefits   Campaigning
"Good old boy" system   Job hunting
Mayor-administrator relationship   Networking
Paid time off   Political parties
Political appointee   Recruitment of
Selection of employees   employees

Selected References for Case Study 265

Arvey, R., and Faley, R. (1988). *Fairness in selecting employees.* Second ed. Reading, MA: Addison-Wesley.

Brademas, D., Lowrey, G., and Wallin, D. (1980). *Hiring practices for part-time and seasonal leisure services personnel.* Champaign, IL: Department of Leisure Studies, Cooperative Extension Service, University of Illinois at Urbana-Champaign.

Cook, M. (1988). *Personnel selection and productivity.* New York: Wiley.

Cunningham, P. (1988, Sept.). How to win clients and influence co-workers. *Parks and Recreation,* 68-70, 83.

Dreker, G., and Sackett, P. (1983). *Perspectives on employee staffing and selection: Readings and commentary.* Homewood, IL: Irwin.

Krannich, R., and Krannich, C. (1989). *Network your way to job and career success: The complete guide to creating new opportunities.* Manassas, VA: Impact.

Lewis, C. (1985). *Employee selection.* London: Hutchinson.

McCullock, K. (1981). *Selecting employees safely under the law.* Englewood Cliffs, NJ: Prentice-Hall.

Milkovich, G., and Newman, J. (1984). *Compensation.* Third ed. Homewood, IL: BPI/Irwin.

Mulford, C. (1984). *Interorganizational relations: Implications for community development.* New York: Human Sciences.

Patten, T. (1977). *Pay: Employee compensation and incentive plans.* New York: Free.

Patten, T. (1988). *Fair pay.* San Francisco: Jossey-Bass.

Potter, E., (ed.) (1986). *Employee selection: Legal and practical alternatives to compliance and litigation.* Second ed. Washington, D.C.: National Foundation for the Study of Equal Employment Policy.

Smith, M., and Robertson, I., (ed.) (1989). *Advances in selection and assessment.* New York: Wiley.

266
"Temporary Appointee" Could be Around for Years

Situation

You are a university professor who has been asked by a nearby park district to examine its administrative hierarchy. The problem centers on the fact that nearly all of the people in charge of major and minor facilities in the park district operate as "temporary appointees" under a policy that many claim forces them into political activity. The policy stems from the fact that there has not been a civil service examination for park supervisors in more than a quarter of a century. This means that the heads of all parks must be reappointed by officials each year.

To be reappointed, a park supervisor is sent a letter each October stipulating that a job—physical instructor, drama teacher, or other position — is open in the civil service category that he or she occupies. Since the civil service jobs pay less than the position of park supervisor, employees routinely sign the letter "waiving" their civil service status for that year and are then reappointed to their existing jobs.

"This is how they keep us under lock and chain," claims Tom Petty, a bitter park supervisor. "They keep you dangling year by year with the threat always hanging over your head that you won't be reappointed."

Betty Cooper, another employee, goes one step further. "When the ward boss asks you to work a precinct, come to meetings, or swallow dinner tickets, you sure better respond or else you're out. The whole system stinks."

Park district officials defend the practice. They claim that civil service rules require them to offer a job each year to all employees on civil service status and that "the job must be in the category the employee is certified in." The park district claims that by having yearly evaluations, they are able to see how employees are progressing. They stress that the evaluations should not be seen as threatening, but should be seen as helpful.

Problem

Should the system of "temporary appointees" be kept? What are the advantages of such a system? If you think a new system should be adopted, describe it. Does the position of "temporary appointee" lead to political campaigning?

What is the political relationship between a "park district" and a "city government"? How could a city government influence a park district?

Should job evaluations be done yearly? Are job evaluations something to fear? Should job evaluations be linked to pay increases? What criteria should be used in evaluating an employee? How is this criteria established to make certain it is valid?

Suggested Key Words and Phrases for Literature Search for Case 266

Campaigning	City government
Civil service exams	Evaluations
Hiring	Job analysis
Job description	Park district
Performance appraisal	Personnel administration
Temporary appointee	Wage increases
Work motivation	

Selected References for Case Study 266

Bailey, C. (1983). *The measurement of job performance.* Aldershot, England: Gower.

Berwitz, C. (1975). *The job analysis approach to affirmative action.* New York: Wiley.

Booth, W. (1987, Jan.). Putting your best foot forward at an assessment center. *Parks and Recreation,* 86-89.

Chatiahm, D. (1989, Oct.). Taking the fear out of performance appraisals. *Parks and Recreation,* 45-48.

Dreker, G., and Sackett, P. (1983). *Perspectives on employee staffing and selection: Readings and commentary.* Homewood, IL: Irwin.

Husband, T. (1976). *Work analysis and pay structure.* London: McGraw-Hill.

Kleinbeck, U., Quast, H., Thierry, H., and Hacker, H., (eds.) (1990). *Work motivation.* Hillsdale, NJ: Lawrence Erlbaum.

Manese, W. (1986). *Fair and effective employment testing: Administrative, psychometric, and legal issues for the human resources professional.* New York: Quorum.

McCullock, K. (1981). *Selecting employees safely under the law.* Englewood Cliffs, NJ: Prentice-Hall.

Milkovich, G., and Newman, J. (1984). *Compensation.* Third ed. Homewood, IL: BPI/Irwin.

Morf, M. (1986). *Optimizing work performance: A look beyond the bottom line.* New York: Quorum.

Nash, M. (1985). *Making people productive.* San Francisco: Jossey-Bass.

Patten, T. (1977). *Pay: Employee compensation and incentive plans.* New York: Free.

Patten, T. (1988). *Fair pay.* San Francisco: Jossey-Bass.

267
High School's Earth Day Celebration
Interpreted as Religious Ritual

Situation

You are the public parks and recreation director for a medium-sized community. One afternoon, a principal from one of the four local high schools telephones asking for your assistance to help him deal with the aftermath of the school's Earth Day celebration. To celebrate Earth Day, the high school dimmed its lights and asked for a moment of silence in memory of the earth.

Citizens for Educational Accountability are calling the event "a humanistic New Age celebration to the Mother Goddess Earth." They claim that this celebration "tends toward a religious practice that is not allowed for other religions."

"I don't believe in the school manipulating our children. Children at the high school age are very persuadable," said one activist. "I'm not saying I'm against all Earth Day activities. However, I think the kind of celebration that took place in the high school can lead to other similar celebrations of a less palatable theme than conservation. I believe in God, but I also believe in a separation of church and state. The school conducted a religious ritual, and that was inappropriate."

The principal informs you that the idea to turn down the lights came from a national environmental group. He adds that "We did not make a big deal about the moment of silence; we just sort of let the kids sit there and think. We didn't want to make it a religious activity. It was intended to be a reminder that energy conservation was a dimension of Earth Day. It was nothing more than that."

Problem

What do you tell the principal; how can you help him? If he suspected that some people might claim that his celebration was a religious ritual, should he have gone ahead with it? Can a ritual take place outside of religion; can there be religion without ritual? What is the purpose of Earth Day?

How would you have advised the principal to celebrate Earth Day? Should local schools follow national trends if local citizens are likely to object? What can be done to passify the activists? Will the issue die if no action is taken? Is no action sometimes better than action?

Suggested Key Words and Phrases for
Literature Search for Case 267

Celebrations	Church-state issues
Conservation	Earth Day
Life cycle development	Protest groups
Public schools	Public relations
Religion	Ritual
Youth	

Selected References for Case Study 267

Bear, F.; Pritchard, H.; and Akin, W. (1986). *Earth: The stuff of life.* Normal, OK: University of Oklahoma Press.

Carpenter, S., and Kennedy, W. (1988). *Managing public disputes: A practical guide to handling conflict and reaching agreements.* San Francisco: Jossey-Bass.

Csikszentmihalyi, M.; and Larson, R. (1984). *Being adolescent: Conflict and growth in the teenage years.* New York: Basic.

Hirschman, A. (1982). *Shifting involvements: Private interest and public action.* Princeton, NJ: Princeton University Press.

Hoyt, K., and Yamanota, J. (1987). *The new age rage.* Old Tappas, NJ: Revell.

McAdam, G. (1990, Oct.). Environmental protection through citizen action. *Parks and Recreation,* 46-51.

McAvoy, L. (1990, Sept.). An environmental ethic for parks and recreation. *Parks and Recreation,* 68-72.

Melton, J., Clark, J., and Kelly, A. (1990). *New age encyclopedia: A guide to the beliefs, concepts, terms, people, and organizations that make up the new global movement toward spiritual development, health, and healing, higher consciousness, and related subjects.* Detroit: Gale Research.

Murray, A. (1982). *The church and the state in a free society.* Second printing. New York: AMS Press.

Roberts, K. (1983). *Youth and leisure.* London: George Allen & Unwin.

Sorauf, F. (1976). *The wall of separation: The constitutional politics of church and state.* Princeton, NJ: Princeton University Press.

Useem, M. (1975). *Protest movements in America.* Indianapolis: Bobbs-Merrill.

Wallace, G., Tierney, P., and Hass, G. (1990, Sept.). The right link between wilderness and tourism. *Parks and Recreation,* 62-66, 111.

Warren, R. (1990, June). Land stewardship: Your professional responsibility. *Park Maintenance and Grounds Management,* 14-16.

Weiss, A. (1982). *God and government: The separation of church and state.* Boston: Houghton-Mifflin.

268
Nativity Scene Barred From Public Park

Situation

You are the public parks and recreation director of a large metropolitan area. For three weeks before Christmas each year, your staff sets up a sparkling Christmas tree in the park downtown. In addition, you also fence off a quarter of the park and allow reindeer to graze in that portion of it. The scene is breathtaking, and thousands of people come to view it each year. The local Chamber of Commerce, recognizing the numerous people your department attracts into town with the exhibit, underwrites most of the costs.

Because you are a public agency, you have attempted to avoid any reference to the religious connotations of the holiday season in the park. To make sure that groups that might promote controversial religious ideas do not have access to the park during December, your agency has adopted a policy that no group should be allowed to use the park during the holiday season. All groups are treated equally by the parks department by the policy of not allowing any group access.

Jessee Fredericks, president of the Prince of Peace Foundation, wants to install a nativity scene in the park. He claims that the three-fourths of the park that is not being used for the town display is public land and that he has a right to utilize it. He contends that to forbid him from using the land denies a First Amendment right to free speech on public ground.

Problem

Does Frederick have a right to use the park to set up a nativity scene? Would he have the right to use the park if he wanted to set up a scene that had no religious overtones? Is the park policy of denying all groups access even-handed? Is not being able to use the park as a group a form of censorship? Can the parks department legally tie up public land for an extended period of time with a display? Can private citizens tie up public land for an extended period of time with a display?

Do your personal religious values play any part in this situation; if so, how? How can you vouch for the fact that you are being fair, realizing that your own religious views color your interpretation of the situation?

Suggested Key Words and Phrases for
Literature Search for Case 268

Censorship	Church-state relations
Ethics	First Amendment rights
Holiday decorations	Nativity scene
Policies	Public land
Public-private sector partnership	Public rights
Religious celebrations	

Selected References for Case Study 268

Allen, S. (1979). *Private financing in public parks: A handbook.* Washington, D.C.: Hawkins.

Chomsky, N. (1989). *Necessary illusions: Thought control in democratic societies.* Boston: South End Press.

Crompton, J., and Richardson, S. (1986, Oct.). The tourism connection: When public and private leisure services merge. *Parks and Recreation*, 38-44, 67.

Crossley, J. (1988). *Public/Commercial cooperation in parks and recreation.* Columbus, OH: Publishing Horizons.

Crowley, K. (1988, Aug.). Teamwork: Resorts and the forest service. *Parks and Recreation*, 38-40.

Haughey, J., (ed.) (1979). *Personal values in public policy: Conversations on government decision making.* New York: Paulist.

Hirschman, A. (1982). *Shifting involvements: Private interest and public action.* Princeton, NJ: Princeton University Press.

Hollenback, D. (1979). Plural loyalties and moral agency in government. *Personal values in public policy: Conversations on government decision making.* J. Haughey, (ed.) New York: Paulist, 74-100.

Kernaghan, K. (1975). *Ethical conduct: Guidelines for government employees.* Toronto: Institute of Public Administration of Canada.

La Haze, T. (1984). *The hidden censors.* Old Tappon, NJ: Revell.

Moore, M. (1981). Realms of obligation and virtue. In *Public duties: The moral obligations of government officials.* J. Fleishman, L. Liebman., and M. Moore, (eds.) Cambridge, MA: Harvard University Press, 3-31.

Murray, A. (1982). *The church and the state in a free society.* Second printing. New York: AMS Press.

Sorauf, F. (1976). *The wall of separation: The constitutional politics of church and state.* Princeton, NJ: Princeton University Press.

Weiss, A. (1982). *God and government: The separation of church and state.* Boston: Houghton-Mifflin.

269
Oaths Annoy Atheists

Situation

You are a regional director for the Boy Scouts of America. The Boy Scouts are noted for being a lot of things — trustworthy, loyal, helpful, and friendly, to name a few. They are also known for their reverence to God. A ten-year-old atheist who wishes to join the Boy Scouts has refused to take the oath, however. He claims that he cannot say "On my honor I will do my best to do my duty to God and my country and to obey the Scout law; to help other people at all times; to keep myself physically strong, mentally awake, and morally straight" because he does not profess a belief in God. His parents have volunteered to be sponsors of the local club, but they have been turned down because they refused to sign a pledge which read "...no member can grow into the best kind of citizen without recognizing an obligation to God."

His father has gone to court contending that the Scouts' religious requirement violates the 1964 Civil Rights Act, particularly the part that bans religious discrimination in public accommodations. He has also held a news conference demanding that the United Way cut off its $1.5 million of annual funding to the area Boy Scouts since the donations violate the United Way's policy of prohibiting gifts to organizations that discriminate on the basis of religion.

The national Scouting agency contends that their units are like private clubs, which are excluded from that provision of the Civil Rights Act and are allowed to set their own membership requirements. However, the atheist contends that the Scouts are a public body since they invite every child in the public school to attend by giving each child a flyer about scouting.

Problem

Would you allow the atheist to join provided he signed the oath? Would you waive the oath requirement for him?

Would you encourage him to seek other groups to join? Would you waive the oath for the child but not the pledge for the adults; why or why not? Knowing that the volunteer was an atheist, would you accept him if his atheistic beliefs were not expressed; why or why not?

What makes an organization a "public" organization? What makes an organization a "private" organization? Are the Boy Scouts a "private" organization? Why do the Boy Scouts rely on the United Way for funds? Does a sponsor influence the decisions an agency makes? What are the advantages and disadvantages of being funded by an outside source?

Is religion an important part of Boy Scouting or can it be dropped? Is "God" a vague or a specific term? Is atheism a religion? Could Christians, Catholics, Muslims, and Buddhists all become Boy Scouts? If so, do the Scouts discriminate on the basis of religion?

Suggested Key Words and Phrases for
Literature Search for Case 269

Atheism	Boy Scouts
Civil Rights Act of 1964	Funding organizations
Membership recruitment	Oaths
Pledges	Private organizations
Public organizations	Religious discrimination
Religious freedom	United Way
Volunteers	

Selected References for Case Study 269

Boy Scouts of America. (1978). *Boy Scout fieldbook.* New York: Workman.

Dreker, G., and Sackett, P. (1983). *Perspectives on employee staffing and selection: Readings and commentary.* Homewood, IL: Irwin.

Lewis, C. (1985). *Employee selection.* London: Hutchinson.

McCullock, K. (1981). *Selecting employees safely under the law.* Englewood Cliffs, NJ: Prentice-Hall.

Murray, A. (1982). *The church and the state in a free society.* Second printing. New York: AMS Press.

Pack, J. (1983). *Meaning well is not enough: Perspectives on volunteering.* South Plainfield, NJ: Groupwork Today.

Potter, E., (ed.) (1986). *Employee selection: Legal and practical alternatives to compliance and litigation.* Second ed. Washington, D.C.: National Foundation for the Study of Equal Employment Policy.

Rosenthal, M. (1986). *The character factory: Baden-Powell and the origins of the Boy Scout movement.* New York: Pantheon.

Smith, M., and Robertson, I., (ed.) (1989). *Advances in selection and assessment.* New York: Wiley.

Sorauf, F. (1976). *The wall of separation: The constitutional politics of church and state.* Princeton, NJ: Princeton University Press.

Tedrick, T., and Henderson, K. (1989). *Volunteers in leisure: A management perspective.* Reston, VA: American Alliance for Health, Physical Education, Recreation, and Dance.

Tedrick, T. (1990, June). How to have the help you need. *Parks and Recreation,* 64-67, 86.

Toalson, R. (1990, June). Volunteers make programs work. *Parks and Recreation,* 6-8.

Toalson, R. (1990, June). Volunteers: A must in parks and recreation. *Parks and Recreation,* 28.

Weiss, A. (1982). *God and government: The separation of church and state.* Boston: Houghton-Mifflin.

270
Consultant Outlines Plan to Halt Vandalism

Situation

You are the public parks and recreation director for a large metropolitan area. Vandalism currently costs $150,000 per year, a figure you believe could be reduced. Vandalism includes graffiti, glass and lock breakage, plumbing damage, tennis nets and basketball hoops destroyed, swings and playground equipment destroyed, and landscaping mauled. The list remains the same when the damage is listed in terms of the dollar cost to the city, with the exception of graffiti moving from the head of the list to the end. You hired Betsy Miller, a private consultant, to investigate the problem. She offered the following advice:

1. Create a sense of identity but not too much ownership. If people believe that a particular facility is "theirs," they will destroy it rather than let others use it. On the other hand, if nobody identifies with it, then nobody cares if it is vandalized.
2. Make sure that all park facilities are frequently utilized. If an area is not utilized on a regular basis, it is more likely to be a target of vandalism.
3. Try to get potential vandals to take pride in the park. Instead of viewing the situation as staff versus potential vandals, encourage everyone to appreciate the park.
4. Get the cooperation of the police department. The police should not view the parks as a convenient storage place for criminals overnight.

Problem

Is the advice reasonable? Is it practical advice or naive advice? What other possibilities to curb vandalism can you think of? Suggest steps for implementing each of the four ideas provided by Miller. Which of the four, if any, is the most important?

Why hire a consultant to develop the list? Could a person in the parks department have done an equally good or better job? What are the political considerations? What are the practical considerations? When is an outside consultant better than an internal investigation?

Suggested Key Words and Phrases for
Literature Search for Case 270

Consultant	Facility usage
Glass breakage	Graffiti
Priorities	Public relations

Repairs   Security
Staff-public relations   Vandalism

Selected References for Case 270

Barcus, III, S., and Wilkinson, J.,(eds.) (1986). *Managing consulting services.* New York: McGraw-Hill.

Bell, C., and Nadler, L., (eds.) (1985). *Clients and consultants: Meeting and exceeding expectations.* Houston: Gulf.

Christianson, M. (1983). *Vandalism control management for parks and recreation areas.* State College, PA: Venture.

Dwyer, W., and Murrell, D. (1988, July). Park law: Fourteen points to ponder. *Parks and Recreation,* 50-52.

Dwyer, W., and Murrell, D. (1990, April). The ins and outs of park law enforcement. *Parks and Recreation,* 50-53.

Easton, T., and Conant, R. (1985). *Using consultants: A consumer's guide for managers.* Chicago, IL: Probus.

Fairfax, J., Wright, L., and Maupin, M. (1988, Dec.). At-risk youth: Special needs. *Parks and Recreation,* 40-43.

Golightly, H. (1985). *Consultants: Selecting, using, and evaluating business consultants.* New York: Franklin Watts.

Holtz, H. (1986). *Advice, a high profit business: A guide for consultants and other entrepreneurs.* Englewood Cliffs, NJ: Prentice-Hall.

McGonagle, Jr., J. (1981). *Managing the consultant: A corporate guide.* Radnor, PA: Chilton.

Moore, G. (1984). *The politics of management consulting.* New York: Praeger.

Shattuck, J. (1988, July). Vandal-proof your park. *Parks and Recreation,* 32-37.

Shenson, H. (1990). *How to select and manage consultants: A guide to getting what you pay for.* Lexington, MA: Lexington.

Steele, F. (1982). *The role of the internal consultant: Effective role-shaping for staff positions.* Boston: CBI.

Underwood, R. (1990, Jan.). Education and vandalism. *Park Maintenance and Grounds Management,* 10-13.

271
Fish Hunt a Whale of a Problem

Situation

You are the director of See the Sea, a huge theme park. A major attraction of the park is the live killer whales. Your staff currently has six of these whales on display at the theme park. Of these six whales, four are trained for public shows that environmentalists call "humiliating to whales," and educators call "very informative."

The whales, though, are getting old. You have initiated an effort to capture 100 killer whales in a five-year program. Ten of the whales would be kept and used for breeding purposes and public display at your theme park aquarium. The remaining 90 would be used for "non-harmful research" then released. The board of directors approved this plan. However, the governor of Alaska and environmentalists are against the plan. The governor has tried to stop the capture of the whales, but the court gave you permission to proceed.

The governor contends that both he and the citizens of Alaska are still against the plan. One of your understudies promised that as long as there was opposition to the capture, no whales would be taken. The governor says he hopes See the Sea will keep its word.

Problem

Should you authorize the capture of the whales? What will you tell the governor? Would capturing or not capturing the whales affect theme park attendance; why? Why might you want to work closely with the governor? How can you show that you are concerned about the environment and yet continue to run the theme park?

Does an understudy have the right to speak in an official capacity? Since the understudy gave his word representing the company, can you legally capture the whales? Can you ethically capture the whales?

*Suggested Key Words and Phrases for
Literature Search for Case 271*

Chain of command	Commercial recreation
Court decisions	Environmentalists
Organizational hierarchy	Public-private relationship
State authority	Theme parks
Understudies	Zoo

Selected References for Case Study 271

Bullaro, J., and Edginton, C. (1986). *Commercial Leisure Services: Managing for profit, service, and personal satisfaction.* New York: Macmillan.

Burkart, A., and Medlik, S. (1981). *Tourism: Past, present, and future.* Second ed. London: Heinemann.

Crompton, J., and Richardson, S. (1986, Oct.). The tourism connection: When public and private leisure services merge. *Parks and Recreation,* 38-44, 67.

Crompton, J. (1990, March). Claiming our share of the tourism dollar. *Parks and Recreation,* 42-47, 88.

Crossley, J., and Jamieson, L. (1988). *Introduction to commercial and entrepreneurial recreation.* Champaign, IL: Sagamore.

Crossley, J. (1988). *Public/Commercial cooperation in parks and recreation.* Columbus, OH: Publishing Horizons.

Crowley, K. (1988, Aug.). Teamwork: Resorts and the forest service. *Parks and Recreation,* 38-40.

Ellis, T., and Norton, R. (1988). *Commercial recreation.* St. Louis: Times Mirror/Mosby.

Epperson, A. (1986). *Private and commercial recreation.* State College, PA: Venture.

Gunn, C. (1988). *Tourism planning.* New York: Taylor & Francis.

Hampton, D., Sumner, C., and Webber, R. (1987). *Organizational behavior and the practice of management.* Fifth ed. Glenview, IL: Scott, Foresman.

Hunt, J. (1986, Oct.). Tourism comes of age in the 1980s. *Parks and Recreation,* 30-36, 66.

McAdam, G. (1990, Oct.). Environmental protection through citizen action. *Parks and Recreation,* 46-51.

McAvoy, L. (1990, Sept.). An environmental ethic for parks and recreation. *Parks and Recreation*, 68-72.

Longan, M. (1988, Sept.). Smokey the Bear meets Ronald McDonald. *Parks and Recreation*, 62-66, 82.

Wallace, G., Tierney, P., and Hass, G. (1990, Sept.). The right link between wilderness and tourism. *Parks and Recreation*, 62-66, 111.

Zwerin, K. (1986, March). Zoos: A blueprint for fiscal survival. *Parks and Recreation*, 42-45, 67.

272
"Where Can We Air Our Grievances?"

Situation

You are the public information director of a large metropolitan parks and recreation department. Dissatisfaction in the Quandite Parks and Recreation Department has grown to such a level that ranking officials within the department have appealed to City Manager Georgia Jones for a resolution to the problem. On Friday, according to a press report, three assistant directors met for three hours in Jones' office and discussed a lengthy list of complaints about the leadership of Sam Wilkerson, chief administrator of the department. Jones, who expressed regret that the matter had become public, reluctantly confirmed the meeting had been held and described the dispute as "a matter of employees against the chief."

Wilkerson, named chief executive officer by Jones five years ago, said he was aware the meeting had been held but had not been told the contents of the conversation. He declined to discuss any of the complaints lodged against him by the assistants, who rank just below him in the department hierarchy. "I'm not going to get into any departmental problems in the newspaper. I don't think that's the proper place."

Wilkerson said that he is deeply concerned about morale and recognizes that it is a problem. Dissent within the department reportedly has been brewing for months. However, it was the low state of employees' morale that led the three executive assistants to request the meeting with the city manager. Wilkerson had no comments for the press about the three complaints lodged against him: (1) he is unwilling to delegate authority, (2) he displays frequent flashes of temper in front of employees, and (3) he uses questionable judgment. In a recent newspaper interview, City Manager Jones said that she was also concerned about the allegations, but added, "I think that we just have some employees who are after the chief's job."

Problem

Should the allegations be investigated? If so, who should conduct the investigation? Should there be an internal investigation by the park department? Should there be an external investigation by the city? What sort of information gathering techniques should be used in an investigation? What should happen if the allegations are true?; what if they are false?

How should conflict be worked out in a parks department? Should the employees go directly to the chief? Were the employees within their rights to go to the city manager? Was the director right in saying that the newspaper is not the place to discuss internal department conflict? If you were the director, how would you seek to resolve the conflict?

What is the purpose of a newspaper? Is it to provide "community spirit" or to be a "watchdog"? Is the press providing a community service by covering the scandal? Should the scandal have been covered up, as the city manager originally wanted, or do citizens have a right to know what is happening in government offices? Should the city manager have expressed her opinion about the motives of the three assistants, or should she have stuck to the facts when providing information to the newspaper? As public information director, should you be mailing the newspaper press releases to keep the press updated about the situation? Are press releases a form of news bias? Why might a newspaper use a press release rather than assign a reporter to check the facts?

Suggested Key Words and Phrases for
Literature Search for Case 272

Allegations	City manager
Internal conflict	Grievance procedures
Mismanagement	Morale
Public information director	Press relations
Press release	Staff hierarchy

Selected References for Case Study 272

Cunningham, P. (1988, Sept.). How to win clients and influence co-workers. *Parks and Recreation*, 68-70, 83.

Gilbert, W., (ed.) (1975). *Public relations in local government.* Washington, D.C.: International City Management Association.

Kleinbeck, U., Quast, H., Thierry, H., and Hacker, H., (eds.) (1990). *Work motivation.* Hillsdale, NJ: Lawrence Erlbaum.

Kleiner, M., McLean, R., and Dreber, G. (1988). *Labor markets and human resource management.* Glenview, IL: Scott, Foresman.

Kochan, T., and Barocci, T. (1990). *Human resource management and industrial relations: Text, readings, and cases.* Boston: Little, Brown.

McNally, J. (1989, Feb.). The care and feeding of aquatic personnel. *Parks and Recreation*, 36-40, 80.

Miller, K. (1988, Jan.). Can we bridge the gap between managers and workers? *Parks and Recreation*, 46-47.

Morf, M. (1986). *Optimizing work performance: A look beyond the bottom line.* New York: Quorum.

Nash, M. (1985). *Making people productive.* San Francisco: Jossey-Bass.

Nelson, D. (1990, May). Good management practices. *Park Maintenance and Grounds Management*, 17-19.

Nigro, F., and Nigro, L. (1981). *The new public personnel administration.* Second ed. Itasca, IL: Peacock.

Olson, V. (1983). *White collar waste: Gain the productivity edge.* Englewood Cliffs, NJ: Prentice-Hall.

Reynolds, J., and Hormachea, M. (1976). Public relations. *Public recreation administration.* Reston, VA: Reston, 372-394.

Schappi, J. (1988). *Improving job attendance*. Washington, D.C.: Bureau of National Affairs.

Toalson, R., and Herchenberger, P. (1985). *Developing community support for parks and recreation*. Champaign, IL: Champaign Park District.

273
Basketball League Features "The Gang"

Situation

You are the superintendent in charge of overseeing seven public parks and recreation community centers. One of the programs that you decide to try at an inner city center is a basketball league for teenagers. The goal of the league is to keep the young public housing residents off of the streets and on the basketball courts between the peak crime hours of 10 p.m. and 2 a.m. Players practice two nights per week, and play games on two other nights during the week. The league has sixteen teams with names taken from the National Basketball League.

As you evaluate the program by witnessing a game, the community center director scans the players and spectators, pointing out which people belong to which gangs. "I'd guess that about one-third of the players are in gangs. Some teams have players from two different gangs. It's very strange—the gangs are getting along really well. I can't explain it."

After each game, players are required to attend workshops on subjects such as job training, drug abuse, and parenting. Role models talk to the young men. Although she has no proof, the director says that crime is decreasing in the area. As you complete your evening, she assures you that the program is making a difference and begs you to let her keep operating it.

Problem

What is your impression of the program? What sort of concrete evidence could the director give you to support her "gut feeling" that the program works? Should community centers be "gang hangouts"? Should members from the same gang be allowed to play on the same team, or does this cause more "us" versus "them" feelings? What security precautions can you take to prevent gang fights?

Is it fair to insist that the players attend workshops after the ballgame? Should the games/workshops be open to women? Are the workshop topics appropriate? What other topics would you include? How long should the workshops be? What sort of teaching methods should be used?

Suggested Key Words and Phrases for
Literature Search for Case 273

Community centers	Evaluation
Gangs	Public housing residents
Research methods	Security
Sex discrimination	Teaching method
Workshops	Youth

Selected References for Case Study 273

Bell, C., and Roberts, H., (eds). (1984). *Social researching: Politics, problems, practice.* London: Routledge and Kegan Paul.

Bogue, G. (1981). *Basic sociological research design.* Glenview, IL: Scott, Foresman.

Csikszentmihalyi, M., and Larson, R. (1984). *Being adolescent: Conflict and growth in the teenage years.* New York: Basic.

Fairfax, J., Wright, L., and Maupin, M. (1988, Dec.). At-risk youth: Special needs. *Parks and Recreation,* 40-43.

Huntington, S. (1985). *Planning a community center.* Ames, IA: North Central Regional Extension Publications.

Jackson, J. (1984). *Leisure and sports center management.* Springfield, IL: Thomas.

Kraus, R., and Allen, L. (1987). *Research and evaluation in recreation, parks, and leisure studies.* Columbus, OH: Publishing Horizons.

Mann, P. (1985). *Methods of social investigation.* Second ed. New York: Blackwell.

McNeill, P. (1985). *Research methods.* London: Tavistock.

Roberts, K. (1983). *Youth and leisure.* London: George Allen & Unwin.

Rothman, J. (1980). *Using research in organizations: A guide to successful application.* Beverly Hills, CA: Sage.

Schultz, J., McAvoy, L., and Dustin, D. (1988, Jan.). What are we in business for? *Parks and Recreation,* 52-54.

Sylvester, C. (1987, Jan.). The politics of leisure, freedom, and poverty. *Parks and Recreation,* 59-62.

Willis-Kistler, P. (1988, Nov.). Fighting gangs with recreation. *Parks and Recreation,* 44-49.

274

Swimmers Are Not Fully Aware of Risks, Environmentalists Claim

Situation

You are the superintendent of beachfronts in a large East Coast parks and recreation department. One day, a representative of Save Our Beaches, a radical environmental group, approaches you. She claims that you are not doing enough to discourage swimmers from entering the water. Her complaints include:

- your "Swim at own risk" signs do not specify what pollutants exist in the water nor how these pollutants affect the human body.
- your "Swim at own risk" signs do not stand out from the setting and thereby do not draw attention to themselves.

-          your parking lots that are close to the beach are open,
         providing easy access for swimmers to reach the polluted
         water.
-          you have lifeguards on duty, which in turn influences
         people to prefer the polluted waters rather than clear
         waters elsewhere, which have no lifeguards.
-          your only attempt to tell the swimmers of the danger from
         the pollutants is in your vague "Swim at own risk" signs.

She claims that if you do not make a greater effort to keep
people out of the polluted water, you will be facing a lawsuit
initiated by her group. She believes that you are endangering the
swimmers' health and that you are not making them fully aware
of the risks they are taking.

Problem

How should you respond? What should your warning
signs include on them? Draft a sample. How much responsibility
should a park assume for its visitors? How could you better
inform the swimmers of the risks than is currently being done?
How many signs should you have, and where on the beach
should they be located? Should the park keep providing lifeguards? Why or why not? Are swimmers likely to patronize the
beach if the parks department no longer maintains it? Why or
why not? Should you make it illegal to swim on the beach?
This environmental group is a radical group. To what
extent should you listen to the opinions it expresses? Where do
radical groups obtain their power to influence? How could you
counter that power? Would you treat the radical group differently if it contributed large amounts of money to your park?; why
or why not?

Suggested Key Words and Phrases for
Literature Search for Case 274

Activist   Beach
Environment   Pollution

Private interests   Risk management
Signage   Swimmers
Warning

Selected References for Case Study 274

Bannon, Jr., J., and Bannon, J. (1987). The insurance crisis: A dilemma for parks and recreation. In *Current issues in leisure services: Looking ahead in a time of transition.* J. Bannon, (ed.) Washington, D.C.: International City Management Association, 119-133.

Christiansen, M. (1987). Safety is no accident. In *Current issues in leisure services: Looking ahead in a time of transition.* J. Bannon, (ed.) Washington, D.C.: International City Management Association.

Culhane, P. (1981). *Public lands politics: Interest group influence on the forest and the bureau of land management.* Baltimore: Johns Hopkins University Press.

Direnfeld-Michael, B. (1989, March). A risk management primer for recreators. *Parks and Recreation*, 40-45.

Hirschman, A. (1982). *Shifting involvements: Private interest and public action.* Princeton, NJ: Princeton University Press.

Holland, S. (1990, Sept.). Beach parks: environmental beacons. *Parks and Recreation*, 78-82, 112.

Kauffman, R. (1989, Sept.). Recognizing the accident chain. *Parks and Recreation*, 68-73.

Mandelker, D., and Ewald, W. (1988). *Street graphics and the law.* Washington, D.C.: Planners.

McAdam, G. (1990, Oct.). Environmental protection through citizen action. *Parks and Recreation*, 46-51.

McAvoy, L. (1990, Sept.). An environmental ethic for parks and recreation. *Parks and Recreation*, 68-72.

Wallace, G., Tierney, P., and Hass, G. (1990, Sept.). The right link between wilderness and tourism. *Parks and Recreation*, 62-66, 111.

Wasserman, N., and Phelus, D. (1985). *Risk management today: A how-to guide for local government.* Washington, D.C.: International City Management Association.

275
Chemicals Prove to be a Dangerous Mixture

Situation

You are the director of the Marboro YMCA. You are sitting in your office working on the budget when an employee dashes in and says that people are being overcome by fumes at the swimming pool. She reports that the fumes smell like chlorine. The lifeguard has evacuated the pool and, with some swimmers assisting other swimmers who had already been overcome, everybody has made it out of the pool alive.

Although you are unable to verify the story until later in the day, the problem arose when a maintenance man accidentally mixed muriatic acid, a cleaning agent used on bricks and concrete, and sodium hypochlorite, a bleach used to chlorinate the pool, in a small room off the pool area. The potentially fatal gas that resulted from the mixture spread into the pool area, where swimmers were bathing. When he is interviewed, the maintenance man claims that he thought he was reaching for more sodium hypochlorite. He claims that he did not realize that he had grabbed the wrong bottle. He admits that he went to smoke a cigarette "as I always do" after preparing the bucket. He says he is very sorry and assures you that it was completely an accident.

With the YMCA building filled with poisonous gas, everybody had to be evacuated. When you arrive at the scene, you find sixty children and seven staff standing outside the building. Everybody is waiting for you to decide what to do next.

Problem

What do you do? What type of emergency vehicles should you call? Who, if anyone, should be examined by doctors? What should you do with all of the children? How can you best utilize your seven personnel? How should you dispose of the bucket of poisonous gas? Who should make an effort to contact the parents? Who else should be contacted? What should you tell the press when the reporters arrive?

Should the maintenance man be fired? Write down what you would say to the maintenance man about the incident. How could such an accident have been avoided? Describe new safety procedures that would better prevent such accidents from happening.

Suggested Key Words and Phrases for
Literature Search for Case 275

Chemicals	Crisis management
Discipline	Emergencies
Parent-staff relations	Poisonous gas
Press relations	Safety procedures
Termination	Toxic waste
YMCA	

Selected References for Case Study 275

Christiansen, M. (1987). Safety is no accident. In *Current issues in leisure services: Looking ahead in a time of transition.* J. Bannon, (ed.) Washington, D.C.: International City Management Association.

Coulson, R. (1981). *The termination handbook.* New York: Free.

Culkin, D. (1988, Feb.). The right way to discipline. *Parks and Recreation*, 44-45.

Direnfeld-Michael, B. (1989, March). A risk management primer for recreators. *Parks and Recreation*, 40-45.

Fink, S. (1986). *Crisis management: Planning for the inevitable.* New York: American Management Association.

Glancy, M., and Donnelly, G. (1988, March). How to manage chemicals in your department. *Parks and Recreation*, 34-36, 103.

Haywood, S., and Alaszewski, A. (1980). *Crisis in the health service: The politics of management.* London: Croom Helm.

Holloway, W., and Leech, M. (1985). *Employment termination: Rights and remedies*. Washington, D.C.: Bureau of National Affairs.

Kauffman, R. (1989, Sept.). Recognizing the accident chain. *Parks and Recreation*, 68-73.

Little, J. (1983). *Crisis management: A team approach*. New York: American Management Association.

Nudell, M., and Antokol, N. (1988). *The handbook for effective emergency and crisis management*. Lexington, MA: Lexington Books.

Peterson, D. (1984). *Analyzing safety performance*. Deer Park, NY: Alaray.

Powell, L. (1989, Sept.) Safety and success: Who's responsible? *Parks and Recreation*, 74-77.

Redeker, J. (1983). *Discipline: Policies and procedures*. Washington, D.C.: Bureau of National Affairs.

Shivers, J. (1986). *Recreational safety: The standard of care*. Cranbury, NJ: Associated University Presses.

276
Are Arguments Against the Water Slide All Wet?

Situation

You are the public relations director for Hampton Park District, a park district serving 100,000 people. One day the park director calls you into his office. He reminds you that the park district has recently entered into a contract with a private corporation to build and operate a water slide. In recent weeks many citizens have protested the venture. The most vocal opponents have been Citizens Against Needing the Slide (CANS). CANS has produced a brochure and mailed it to all local residents. Among the arguments against the slide outlined in the brochure are:

- The slide is likely to overburden the park that houses it, crowding other activities and facilities, especially the pool and the nearby playground.

- The slide is scarcely a substantial recreational opportunity. The only exercise it involves is walking up the steps to the top of the fiberglass troughs. The experience provided by the slide itself is not "recreational" but sheer razzle dazzle.
- The slide will transform recreational space into an amusement park. The park will be little more than a carnival, and it will attract people who are not in the best interests of the town.
- The slide is likely to be the first of many profit-making ventures in the park, all of which could be built on private capital. The park administration plans to meet its budget with revenue-producing contracts, rather than relying solely on tax- and fee-supported activities.

The brochure concludes by asking citizens to help finance the CANS goal of preventing the slide from being built. The brochure indicates that court challenges, park district meeting protests, and newspaper ads will all be undertaken to promote the CANS cause.

Problem

After showing you the arguments, the director asks that you counter each of them. How could you show that the slide will not "crowd" the park? How do you explain the "recreation experience" and how does a water slide offer that experience? What could you use as evidence that the slide will not draw undesired rowdies from other towns? Is the slide likely to cause an increased need for police protection? Will property values go up or down when the slide opens? How should a park district meet its budget? Should public property be used for private property; why or why not?

As public relations director, what kind of a campaign would you want to organize for the slide? Would you use the print media, mailings, radio, something else, or a combination of things? What audience(s) should you target? Should your appeal be the same to all audiences, or should you gear it for each audience? Describe in detail the public relations campaign you would conduct.

*Suggested Key Words and Phrases for
Literature Search for Case 276*

Budget	Crowding
Leisure motivation	Park development
Physical fitness	Profit making
Protest groups	Public information director
Public relations	Public-private relations
Recreation experience	Water slide

Selected References for Case Study 276

Allen, S. (1979). *Private financing in public parks: A handbook.* Washington, D.C.: Hawkins.

Clarke, M., Grist, R., and Mertes, J. (1987, Aug.). County nature conservancy is a unique joint venture. *Parks and Recreation,* 42-47.

Crompton, J., and Richardson, S. (1986, Oct.). The tourism connection: When public and private leisure services merge. *Parks and Recreation,* 38-44, 67.

Crompton, J., and Lamb, Jr., C. (1986). *Marketing government and social services.* New York: Wiley.

Crossley, J. (1988). *Public/Commercial cooperation in parks and recreation.* Columbus, OH: Publishing Horizons.

Crowley, K. (1988, Aug.). Teamwork: Resorts and the forest service. *Parks and Recreation,* 38-40.

Cunningham, W., Cunningham, I., and Swift, C. (1987). *Marketing: A managerial approach.* Cincinnati, OH: South-Western.

Greenberg, B. (1988, May). Contract management can help your golf course. *Parks and Recreation,* 28-30, 59.

Hatry, H. (1983). *A review of private approaches for delivery of public services.* Washington, D.C.: Urban Institute.

Hirschman, A. (1982). *Shifting involvements: Private interest and public action.* Princeton, NJ: Princeton University Press.

Jaeck, R. (1988, Aug.). Triway partnership builds sports pavilion. *Parks and Recreation,* 36-37.

Longan, M. (1988, Sept.). Smokey the Bear meets Ronald McDonald. *Parks and Recreation,* 62-66, 82.

McMullen, J. (1987, Dec.). Public recreation managers on thin ice: Maintaining a professional image. *Parks and Recreation*, 56-61.

National Center for Policy Analysis. (1985). *Privatization in the U.S.: Cities and counties*. Dallas: National Center for Policy Analysis.

Moler, C. (1990, Feb.). Make a splash with swimming programs. *Parks and Recreation*, 30-34.

Osinski, A. (1990, Feb.). *The complete aquatic guide*. Parks and Recreation, 36-43, 83.

U.S. Department of Health and Human Services. (1981). *Suggested health and safety guidelines for recreational water slide fumes*. Atlanta, GA: U.S. Department of Health and Human Services, Public Health Service Centers for Disease Control, Center for Environmental Health, Environmental Health Services Division.

277
Tower Produces High Emotions

Situation

You are the director of a state park that borders a large metropolitan community of over a million people. At a recent park meeting, a small group of protesters gathered to express their feelings about the proposal to build a weather station tower on Mister Mountain, the park's highest point. "People are coming to you with wonderful proposals," the group's spokesman said, "but years from now, as land for parks becomes scarce, officials will regret decisions to use parks for other purposes. The tower would sit in the middle of the park and be visible for miles, completely marring the scenery. Pardon the analogy, but it's like putting a cat litter box in the middle of your living room floor."

So far, the parks department has agreed to only allow the weather service to study the site. Weather service representatives have stressed that the tower, which would stand 65 feet above the mountain top, would result in 23 people being transferred to the community from nearby communities and ten completely new jobs. The tower would greatly improve weather forecasting, they stress, and the park's geographic location is the best within hundreds of miles. The weather station representatives claim that the tower will not necessarily be obtrusive.

"The parks department should not be a holding company for the land," critics of the proposed station claim. "The parks department should stress conservation, recreation, and education. The conservation concept is completely missing in this situation."

Problem

Do you think that the tower should be built? Why do you feel this way? Do private companies that benefit the public deserve to use public land? If the weather station company is allowed to build the tower, what other companies would you allow to build? If the tower is approved, should annual rent be charged for use of the land? What happens if the rent is not paid? What would be the environmental impact of building the tower?

What is the purpose of a parks department—conservation, recreation, education, something else, or all of the above? Which should be the primary purpose? Do state parks have the same purposes as city, county, and national parks? How are they different? How are they similar?

Suggested Key Words and Phrases for
Literature Search for Case 277

Conservation	Education
Environmental impact	Land stewardship
Parks' purpose	Private interest
Public-private relations	Public land
State parks	Recreation
Scenic view	Tower structures

Selected References for Case Study 277

Anderson, R., Leitch, J., and Mittleider, J. (1986, Oct.). Contribution of state parks to state economies. *Parks and Recreation*, 62-63.

Lai, R. (1988). *Law in urban design and planning: The invisible web.* New York: Van Reinhold.

McAdam, G. (1990, Oct.). Environmental protection through citizen action. *Parks and Recreation*, 46-51.

McAvoy, L. (1990, Sept.). An environmental ethic for parks and recreation. *Parks and Recreation*, 68-72.

Myers, P. (1990, April). State parks in a new era. *Parks and Recreation*, 28-32.

Peterson, C., and McCarthy, C. (1982). *Handling zoning and land use litigation: A practical guide.* Charlottesville, VA: Michie.

Price, D. (1981). Assessing policy: Conceptual point of departure. In *Public duties: The moral obligations of government officials.* J. Fleishman, L. Liebman., and M. Moore, (eds.) Cambridge, MA: Harvard, 142-174.

Sylvester, C. (1987, Jan.). The politics of leisure, freedom, and poverty. *Parks and Recreation*, 59-62.

Wallace, G., Tierney, P., and Hass, G. (1990, Sept.). The right link between wilderness and tourism. *Parks and Recreation*, 62-66, 111.

Warren, R. (1990, June). Land stewardship: Your professional responsibility. *Park Maintenance and Grounds Management*, 14-16.

Warwick, D. (1981). The ethics of administrative discretion. *Public duties: The moral obligations of government officials.* In J. Fleishman, L. Liebman, and M. Moore, (eds.) Cambridge, MA: Harvard University Press, 93-130.

Wolf, Jr., C. (1981). Ethics and policy analysis. In *Public duties: The moral obligations of government officials.* J. Fleishman, L. Liebman., and M. Moore, (eds.) Cambridge, MA: Harvard University Press, 131-141.

278
Financing of Harbor Cafe Perceived as Fishy

Situation

You are the chief executive officer of a large public park district. Your assistant director has recently proposed that a harbor cafe/fish cleaning station be built next to the lake in Flintstone Park. When asked how the department would pay for the $600,000 restaurant and fish cleaning station when only $500,000 was budgeted, she proposed that the remaining $100,000 be taken from the budget of Odie Park, a crumbling West Side park.

Her logic is that it is better to have only a few quality parks rather than several mediocre parks. "Our money is spread too thin," she contends. "If we want to provide quality recreational experiences, we are going to have to start spending our money on quality, not quantity." She also states that the boating facility will be a revenue producer for the parks department, netting over $25,000 per year in profit. Meanwhile, vandals are likely to destroy all work done to Odie Park within days of its completion, something that has happened many times before.

Your public relations advisor disagrees. "You can't take $100,000 approved for repairs of Odie Park, a park that's already underfunded, and give it to boaters to make a convenience station for them. We are not in the business of creating a White Hen Convenience Store for boaters."

Problem

Do you recommend the harbor cafe to the parks board? Why would quality be preferred over quantity of parks? Why would quantity sometimes be better than quality? What standard(s) should be used to describe how many parks are maintained by a district?

Should parks be maintained if vandals constantly destroy them? Do parks directors owe more attention to the poor, the middle class, or the rich? Should parks directors treat all citizens equally, or should they try to please those groups most likely to vote?

Should park districts operate a venture that makes a considerable profit? If so, how should that profit be utilized? Can money be taken from one park and be used in another, if it is already promised to the former park?

Suggested Key Words and Phrases for
Literature Search for Case 278

Budget	Citizen input
Convenience station	Construction projects
Funding	Ghetto parks
Marine project	Park quality
Park quantity	Philosophy of recreation
Prioritizing	Profit
Vandalism	

Selected References for Case Study 278

Adrian, J. (1981). CM: *The construction management process.* Reston, VA: Reston.

Christianson, M. (1983). *Vandalism control management for parks and recreation areas.* State College, PA: Venture.

Crompton, J. (1987). How to establish a price for park and recreation services. In *Current issues in leisure services: Looking ahead in a time of transition.* J. Bannon, (ed.) Washington, D.C.: International City Management Association, 93-107.

Downing, F., and Frank, J. (1982). *Recreation impact fees: A discussion of the issues and a survey of current practices in the United States with guidelines for Florida application.* Gainesville, FL: Policy Sciences Program, Florida State University.

Flynn, P. (1987, April). Small parks projects: Getting citizens involved. *Parks and Recreation,* 34-36.

Gold, S. (1987). A human service approach to recreation planning. In *Current issues in leisure services: Looking ahead in a time of transition.* J. Bannon, (ed.) Washington, D.C.: International City Management Association, 5-16.

Hunt, S., and Brooks, K. (1987). A planning model for public recreation agencies. In *Current issues in leisure services: Looking ahead in a time of transition.* J. Bannon, (ed.) Washington, D.C.: International City Management Association, 5-16.

Moore, B, (ed.) (1983). *The entrepreneur in local government.* Washington, D.C.: International City Management Association.

Mueller, F. (1986). *Integrated cost and schedule control for construction projects.* New York: Van Reinhold.

Schultz, J., McAvoy, L., and Dustin, D. (1988, Jan.). What are we in business for? *Parks and Recreation,* 52-54.

Sylvester, C. (1987, Jan.). The politics of leisure, freedom, and poverty. *Parks and Recreation,* 59-62.

Tumblin, C. (1980). *Construction cost estimates.* New York: Wiley.

Shattuck, J. (1988, July). Vandal-proof your park. *Parks and Recreation,* 32-37.

Underwood, R. (1990, Jan.). Education and vandalism. *Park Maintenance and Grounds Management,* 10-13.

279
General Wants to Fight Pretend War

Situation

You are the director of a medium-sized public parks and recreation department. One afternoon you are approached by "General" Clyde Drake. Drake, dressed in green and brown camouflaged fatigues, wants you to allow him and his friends to play an "adult version of Steal the Flag." He says that both teams have a flag, and that the object is to move the other team's flag onto your side. He notes that the bullets are round and plastic, the size and color of a gumball, and that they are filled with a sticky red dye that washes out with water. The bullets are shot through pistols powered by CO_2 canisters. He claims that people wear safety goggles and that the most harm the bullets do is sting "like a BB-Gun." If a bullet leaves a red mark the size of a quarter, the victim is considered dead. He assures you that there is no harm in the game.

From your journal readings, though, you know that survival games have been criticized as fostering violence and an unrealistic idea of what combat is like. Drake denies that the war game simulates real combat — "You know you aren't going to get killed" —and claims that it is truly a recreational experience. "Although the pistols and bullets are make-believe, the excitement is genuine. The adrenaline starts to flow when the pistols start popping and you are under fire. You get a rush.

"War may be hell, as General Sherman said, but war-like survival games are just plain fun," said Drake.

Problem

Should you allow the pretend war to be fought? Why or why not? If somebody was injured, who would be responsible? Would the Concerned Citizens For Peace be likely to approve of the pretend war? Would the Veterans of Foreign Wars be likely to approve of it? Should the feelings of these two groups be considered when deciding whether to allow the game to be played? If you tell him no, what material could you use to back up your reasons?

What is the purpose of a game? What is the purpose of recreation? Is the war game both a game and recreation? Does "fun" make something "recreation"? Do parks executives have a right to dictate which games can and cannot be played in a park? Why or why not? Outline a policy for which activities are acceptable in a park.

Suggested Key Words and Phrases for Literature Search for Case 279

Games	Insurance
Public land use	Public parks
Recreation	Risk assumption
Special interest groups	Survival games
War games	

Selected References for Case Study 279

Allen, T. (1987). *War games.* New York: McGraw-Hill.

Brewer, G., and Shubik, M. (1979). *The war game: A critique of military problem solving.* Cambridge, MA: Cambridge University Press.

Christiansen, M. (1987). Safety is no accident. In *Current issues in leisure services: Looking ahead in a time of transition.* J. Bannon, (ed.) Washington, D.C.: International City Management Association.

Direnfeld-Michael, B. (1989, March). A risk management primer for recreators. *Parks and Recreation*, 40-45.

Dunnigan, J. (1980). *The complete wargames handbook: How to play, design, and find them.* New York: Morrow.

Gush, G. (1984). *A guide to wargaming.* London: Croom Helm.

Hirschman, A. (1982). *Shifting involvements: Private interest and public action.* Princeton, NJ: Princeton University Press.

Kauffman, R. (1989, Sept.). Recognizing the accident chain. *Parks and Recreation*, 68-73.

Kraus, R. (1990). *Recreation and leisure in modern society.* Fourth ed. Glenview, IL: Scott, Foresman.

Peterson, D. (1984). *Analyzing safety performance.* Deer Park, NY: Alaray.

Powell, L. (1989, Sept.). Safety and success: Who's responsible? *Parks and Recreation*, 74-77.

Shivers, J. (1986). *Recreational safety: The standard of care.* Cranbury, NJ: Associated University Presses.

Wasserman, N., and Phelus, D. (1985). *Risk management today: A how-to guide for local government.* Washington, D.C.: International City Management Association.

280
Big League Dirt Creates Dream Field — Or Nightmare?

Situation

You are a public parks and recreation director for Donsville, a medium-sized midwestern city. One day you are approached by a turf sales agent who says that he wants to cover your Little League fields with Turface, a commercial dirt that is used on three-fourths of the baseball diamonds in the major leagues. He cites the following reasons:

- he wants to study the effects of the turf in a Little League setting.
- he says the field would be a model for prospective buyers of his product to examine.
- he says that his supervisor's wife came from Donsville and that his supervisor wanted to do the town a favor.
- he notes that Donsville could never afford to buy Turface.
- he says that the players will have a lot of fun playing on the surface.
- he observes that a field that is a lot of fun to play on usually attracts more players than one that is not fun to play on.

Not only will the Turface Company waive the costs of the turf, it will work closely with local volunteers to install the turf. All that you have to do for this "dream field" is to give your okay.

Problem

Do you accept the gift? Who benefits the most from the deal if you agree to it? What, if anything, do you lose by accepting the deal? Is this a decision an administrator needs to make alone or should other people be consulted? If others should be consulted, who do you recommend and why do you recommend them?

What questions should you ask before accepting the gift? Why would you want to ask questions about upkeep cost, insurance cost, risk of getting hurt on the turf, and how often the turf has to be replaced?

What is the backbone of a successful Little League program? Is it the turf or something else? What role do the grounds and maintenance aspects of a parks department play in the program aspect of the department?

Suggested Key Words and Phrases for
Literature Search for Case 280

Advertising	Citizen involvement
Gifts	Grounds personnel
Little League	Maintenance
Model fields	Risk identification
Turf	Upkeep
Volunteers	

Selected References for Case Study 280

Abraham, M., and Lodish, L. (1990, May-June). Getting the most out of advertising and promotion. *Harvard Business Review*, 50-60.

Betancourt, H. (1982). *The advertising answerbook: A guide for business and professional people.* Englewood Cliffs, NJ: Prentice-Hall.

Dyer, G. (1982). *Advertising as communication.* New York: Methuen.

Hacher, J., and Harbridge, M. (1990, Feb). Golf course maintenance - a holistic approach. *The Leisure Manager*, 14-17.

Henderson, K. (1988, Nov.) Are volunteers worth their weight in gold? *Parks and Recreation*, 40-43.

Iso-Ahola, S. (1980). The social psychology of leisure and recreation. Dubuque, IA: Brown.

Loy, J., McPherson, B., and Kenyin, G. (1978). *Sport and social systems: A guide to the analysis, problems, and literature.* Reading, MA: Addison-Wesley.

O'Connell, B., (ed.) (1983). *America's voluntary spirit: A book of readings.* New York: Foundation Center.

Pack, J. (1983). *Meaning well is not enough: Perspectives on volunteering.* South Plainfield, NJ: Groupwork Today.

Snyder, E., and Spreitzer, E. (1983). *Social aspects of sport.* Second ed. Englewood Cliffs, NJ: Prentice-Hall.

Tedrick, T., and Henderson, K. (1989). *Volunteers in leisure: A management perspective.* Reston, VA: American Alliance for Health, Physical Education, Recreation, and Dance.

Wasserman, N., and Phelus, D. (1985). *Risk management today: A how-to guide for local government.* Washington, D.C.: International City Management Association.

Young, R. (1983). *Managing cooperative advertising: A strategic approach.* Lexington, MA: Lexington.

281
Should Parks Department Organize Community Groups?

Situation

You are a senior recreation supervisor in Lastima, California. In the wake of Proposition 13, Lastima, with a population of 75,000, faced a significant reduction in its revenues. Acting upon the recommendation of the city manager, the city council seriously reduced the budget of the Recreation and Parks Department in an effort to maintain the levels of service in the public safety, physical development, and maintenance areas.

One of the most significant cutbacks approved by the city council was the elimination of the city's recreation programming at the community center and park, located in the northeast section of Lastima. The programming at the center and park had consisted of a well-rounded recreation program, including instructional classes (partially offset by fees) for youth and adults, sports, and special events.

The Proposition 13 budget proposal called for all program staff (one center coordinator and three part-time recreation leaders) to be laid off, with only one caretaker staff person authorized to supervise the facility. This action was finalized after the council perceived that the multi-ethnic and low- to moderate-income residents of the area did not actively protest the cutback proposal.

While recreation programming was reduced at the other two community centers, the community center and park in the northeast section were the hardest hit. Moreover, the community center was the only public facility located in the northeast part of town. The other recreation and social services agencies (Boys' Club, YMCA, Family Services Organization, Alcoholics Anonymous, Regional Family Planning Agency) in Lastima did not have offices in the area, and no significant outreach efforts existed.

After council action, Recreation and Parks Director Mike Foley met with the city manager to discuss the situation. The manager suggested increasing fees for instructional classes and sports leagues, so that these programs would be completely self-supporting. He also indicated that he would consider allocating a full-time CETA slot to the facility for the summer. Foley was concerned that increasing fees in that part of the community would simply reduce participation. While Foley would certainly appreciate the CETA slot, he discussed the possibility that the Recreation and Parks Department reallocate some of its limited staff resources to organize community involvement groups and activities in the area. Such an effort, if successful, would stimulate a more active participation in the facility, a greater sense of unity and cohesion in that part of the community, and possibly some volunteer and self-help programs by certain neighborhood groups. (Of course, the proposal could also generate active community support for the Department in its recreation programs, but the Director did not mention this possible outcome of his proposal.)

While not committing himself, the city manager suggested that Foley think about his proposal. He also warned Foley that, even if the Department began stimulating community involvement, under no circumstances should the Department staff assist in organizing political activist groups, which could begin making demands on the City Council.

Subsequent to the meeting, Foley called together his senior staff, consisting of three recreation supervisors, to discuss the issues posed by the situation.

Problem

Should the Department help to organize community involvement groups? Is it appropriate? If so, how should it be done? What are the implications for staff training, staff skills, and staff deployment? What would be possible roles for other agencies, if any? Is it possible to generate community involvement without organizing community groups who may at some time make political demands on the city and the Department? Is it desirable to make sure there is no political activism? If by necessity some political activism may result in the medium- to long-run, should the Department cancel its proposal or should it proceed even though the city manager would strongly resist any effort with such an outcome?

Suggested Key Words and Phrases for
Literature Search for Case 281

Activists	Budget
Charges	Citizen involvement
City-department relations	Community centers
Cutbacks	Fee
Networking	Organization
Political action committees	Proposition 13
Special interest groups	

Selected References for Case Study 281

Dworak, R. (1980). *Taxpayers, taxes, and government spending: Perspectives on the taxpayer revolt.* New York: Praeger.

Flynn, P. (1987, April). Small parks projects: Getting citizens involved. *Parks and Recreation,* 34-36.

Hain, P. (1980). Neighborhood participation. London: Billing.

Hansen, S. (1983). *The politics of taxation: Revenue without representation.* New York: Praeger.

Hawkins, T. (1988, May). Parks: For the people, by the people. *Parks and Recreation,* 39-43.

Haworth, J., (ed.) (1979). *Community involvement and leisure.* London: Lepus.

Hillery, G., and Lincoln, A. (1982). *Leisure, freedom, and crowd behavior.* Durham, NH: Library Crime Research Project.

Hirschman, A. (1982). *Shifting involvements: Private interest and public action.* Princeton, NJ: Princeton University Press.

Kelsey, C., and Gray, H. (1986). *The citizen survey process in parks and recreation.* Reston, VA: American Alliance for Health, Physical Education, Recreation, and Dance.

Lewis, Jr., S. (1984). *Taxation for development: Principles and applications.* New York: Oxford University Press.

Mulford, C. (1984). *Interorganizational relations: Implications for community development.* New York: Human Sciences.

O'Bama, B. (1988, Aug.-Sept.). Why organize? Problems and promise in the inner city. *Illinois Issues,* 40-42.

Sewell, W., and Coppock, J., (eds.) (1977). *Public participation in planning.* London: Wiley.

Stewart, W., Jr. (1976). *Citizen participation in public administration.* Birmingham, AL: University of Alabama, Bureau of Public Administration.

Stein, H., (ed.) (1988). *Tax policy in the twenty-first century.* New York: Wiley.

Summers, L., (ed.) (1989). *Tax policy and the economy: Volume three.* Cambridge, MA: MIT University Press.

Tindell, J. (1987). "Grass Roots" community development of leisure opportunity. In *Current issues in leisure services: Looking ahead in a time of transition.* J. Bannon, (ed.) Washington, D.C.: International City Management Association, 159-167.

Useem, M. (1975). *Protest movements in America.* Indianapolis: Bobbs-Merrill.

Wright, S. (1978). *Crowds and riots: A study in social organization.* Beverly Hills, CA: Sage.

282
Is a Human Services Agency the Most Humane Option?

Situation

At the request of the Human Relations Commission, the City Council formed the Human Needs Assessment Committee (HNAC). The HNAC was formed to conduct an assessment of unmet human needs within the town, which is an industrial community of 100,000 residents characterized by increasing social problems, middle-class reaction against high taxes, growing minority population, redevelopment activity, a fine park system with numerous recreation centers, and a well-developed recreation program.

The City Council appointed to the HNAC two human relations commissioners, a city council member, city planning and parks and recreation commissioners, community opinion leaders, a member of the Chamber of Commerce, and the chair of the United Way Planning Council. The City Council also invited key human services providers (members of the United Way Planning Council, Boys' Club, Salvation Army, Department of Recreation and Parks, City Library, Mental Health Center, Hospital Administration, and Older American Commission staff) to become members of a Technical Advisory Council (TAC) to assist HNAC in the assessment.

Four months after reviewing information and data on needs, resources to meet needs, and organizations that might have a responsibility in meeting such needs, the HNAC ranked fifteen categories of needs that were originally identified by TAC. The ranking provides two measures: (a) the rank order of importance/concern with which the city should view the needs, and (b) the relative severity of current unmet needs. The fifteen categories in order of importance were ranked:

1.   Housing.
2.   Community education.
3.   Crisis intervention, supportive services to families/individuals.

4. Legal aid services to seniors and low-income families.
5. Multi-service centers for seniors.
6. Child care.
7. Employment, (particularly minority youth under 25 years of age).
8. Justice, protection, and safety.
9. Financial resource development for human services.
10. Physical health care and maintenance.
11. Mental health care and maintenance.
12. Transportation (especially handicapped and elderly).
13. Housing rehabilitation.
14. Recreation.
15. Nutrition (especially elderly and minority communities).

The ten most severe unmet human services needs were ranked as follows:

1. Housing opportunities.
2. Legal information and advice.
3. Cooperation, coordination, integration of human services agencies.
4. Human need awareness by public employees.
5. Improved information on individual rights.
6. Reassessment of high school curriculum.
7. Gang violence — junior and senior high levels.
8. Care in nursing homes.
9. Recreation and life maintenance services to the handicapped.
10. Child abuse identification.

The City Council has directed the city manager to prepare an action plan with cost data as a separate report to the Council. It is known that two council members are sympathetic to creating a human services agency as a planning, resource, and coordinating agency. Funds are tight, and it is clear that if a new agency is created, funds will come from cuts in existing services, including parks and recreation. Other prospects include reorganization, consolidation, or elimination of existing city departments. As the director of parks and recreation, you have a lot at stake including a fine parks and recreation system that you helped to build. The city manager has asked for your input.

Problem

How do you respond to the city manager? What are the issues and what strategies, if any, would you develop? Would you involve your staff, and, if so, how? If you decide to pursue a stronger role in delivering and coordinating social services, what are the implications for training and deployment of staff? What options are available to you? Would you consider pursuing political solutions beyond the manager's report?

Suggested Key Words and Phrases for
Literature Search for Case 282

Action plan   City-department relationship
Consolidation   Cutbacks
Human services agency   Long-range planning
Needs assessment   Networking
Priorities   Reorganization

Selected References for Case Study 282

Branch, M. (1983). *Comprehensive planning: General theory and principles.* Pacific Palisades, CA: Palisades.

Davis, D., (ed.) (1981). *Communities and their schools.* New York: McGraw-Hill.

Hudson, S. (1988). *How to conduct community needs assessment surveys in public parks and recreation.* Columbus, OH: Publishing Horizons.

Johnson, D., Meiller, L., and Summers, G. (1987). *Needs assessment: Theory and methods.* Ames, IA: Iowa State University Press.

Kamberg, M. (1989, Sept.). *The three R's in Overland Park, KS: Reading, 'riting, and recreation*, 92-93.

Kelsey, C., and Gray, H. (1985). *Master plan process for parks and recreation*. Reston, VA: American Alliance for Health, Physical Education, Recreation, and Dance.

Kelsey, C., and Gray, H. (1986). *The feasibility study process for parks and recreation*. Reston, VA: American Alliance for Health, Physical Education, Recreation, and Dance.

Lewis, A. (1986). *Partnerships connecting school and community*. Arlington, VA: American Association of School Administrators.

Mulford, C. (1984). *Interorganizational relations: Implications for community development*. New York: Human Sciences.

Reynolds, J., and Hormachea, M. (1976). Public recreation and public schools. *Public recreation administration*. Reston, VA: Reston, 103-117.

Ruffin, Jr., S. (1989). *School-business partnerships: Why not?: Laying the foundation for successful programs*. Reston, VA: National Association of Secondary School Principals.

Wallat, C., and Goldman, R. (1979). *Home/School/Community interaction: What we know and why we don't know more*. Columbus, OH: Merrill.

Williams, M. (1989). *Neighborhood organizing for urban school reform*. New York: Teachers College Press.

283
Park Inhabited by "Dragsters, Drunks, and Drug Users"

Situation

You are the director of a county public parks and recreation department for a midwestern county that consists of seventeen towns ranging in population from 89 to 18,000. It is no secret that several years ago a group of local teenagers adopted the park pavilion in Westner Park, just outside Brownsville, a community of 18,000, as its hangout. The park soon became a drag strip, an al fresco bar, and, reportedly, a local drug-dealing center. Families and fraternal groups have deserted in droves, complaining that it is not safe to picnic and hold meetings where dragsters, drunks, and drug users congregate. However, the county's best ball diamonds are housed within the park.

A recent "streaking" incident in the park further enraged residents of Brownsville, which is located on the park's northern border. A 13 year-old girl who witnessed the scene says the park was crowded with children and parents watching a Little League game when a teenage girl started to run around the field. "She was pretty drunk or stoned or something. She kept falling down. Then she started dropping her clothes and making dirty gestures. It was disgusting. And in front of all of those little kids." Outraged parents called the city police. A city officer and county deputy apprehended the girl and evicted her from the park.

"Is that all they can do?" demanded one outraged parent at the recent city council meeting. Dissatisfaction with park policing is at the heart of citizen's complaints. County Sheriff Gregory Stone admits that his department does not patrol there as often as it would like. He points out that he has only eight men to cover the entire county, including several towns that have no police force.

"We don't tear up the park," one teen countered at the council meeting. "We come out here because there is no place else to go and nothing else to do in town. Nobody hassles you out here. It's outside the city limits."

Problem

What, if anything, should be done? What are the pros and cons of hiring a full-time security officer for the park? What would be the effects of posting more warning signs? Does the sheriff's department have an obligation to patrol the park? Could city police officers patrol a county park?

How should the "streaker" incident have been handled? What sort of message did the sheriff's department's handling of the incident send to the youths, the parents, and the nearby residents? Do people have a constitutional right to express themselves in the park, even if the expressing includes rude gestures/nudity? Why do you think proponents of the discipline crackdown in the park had a 13 year-old girl retell the incident out of the many witnesses available? What sort of charges could have been filed against the streaker? Why do you think the police merely evicted her from the park for the evening?

What opportunities could be provided for the youth in Brownsville? Would more opportunities for recreation within the town likely decrease the delinquency in the park? Does the source of the problem stem from the youth, the city, the county police, or the county parks system? How could each of these sources aid in solving the problem?

Suggested Key Words and Phrases for
Literature Search for Case 283

City-county relations	County parks
Crowd control	Discipline
Drag racing	Nudity
Public relations	Security
Security officers	Self-expression
Streaking	Youth

Selected References for Case Study 283

Csikszentmihalyi, M., and Larson, R. (1984). *Being adolescent: Conflict and growth in the teenage years.* New York: Basic.

Dwyer, W., and Murrell, D. (1988, July). Park law: Fourteen points to ponder. *Parks and Recreation*, 50-52.

Dwyer, W., and Murrell, D. (1990, April). The ins and outs of park law enforcement. *Parks and Recreation*, 50-53.

Fairfax, J., Wright, L., and Maupin, M. (1988, Dec.). At-risk youth: Special needs. *Parks and Recreation*, 40-43.

Gilbert, W., (ed.) (1975). *Public relations in local government.* Washington, D.C.: International City Management Association.

Harker, G. (1987, August). Nude bathing, no controversy. *Parks and Recreation*, 58-61.

Roberts, K. (1983). *Youth and leisure.* London: George Allen & Unwin.

Hillery, G., and Lincoln, A. (1982). *Leisure, freedom, and crowd behavior.* Durham, NH: Library Crime Research Project.

Reynolds, J., and Hormachea, M. (1976). Public relations. *Public recreation administration*. Reston, VA: Reston, 372-394.

Rose, J. (1982). *Outbreaks, the sociology of collective behavior*. New York: Free.

Stambler, I. (1984). *Off-roading: Racing and riding*. New York: Putnam.

Toalson, R., and Herchenberger, P. (1985). *Developing community support for parks and recreation*. Champaign, IL: Champaign Park District.

Wright, S. (1978). *Crowds and riots: A study in social organization*. Beverly Hills, CA: Sage.

284
"Worthwhile Group" Wants Rent Free, Not Rent Fee

Situation

You are the director of a civic center in a medium-sized Midwest community of 100,000. To offset operating costs, you have had to raise your weekend rent rates from $50 to $60 for nonprofit groups and $65 to $120 for profit making groups. Even with these rental increases, the income will likely only cover 65 percent of the operating costs.

Teen Life, a nonprofit group, has complained that your rate increase is too steep. "I think it would be a fantastic example by the city to cooperate in keeping these kids off the street and from drinking. We typically have 150 young people each Saturday evening for our disco dance. We just want the city to do its part," said volunteer chaperone Stacy Hall. "Most of those who come can barely afford to pay the $1.25 we collect as a cover charge at the door. We use that money to provide free soda and music. There is no money left over to pay the rent. We don't want to drop this worthwhile program, but the city is leaving us no choice."

In a private conference with you, Hall shows you attendance figures. She also points to police data indicating that crime in the city parks has decreased. She notes that all Teen Life sponsors and chaperones are volunteers. She explains that the group is guided by a group of teenagers who assume responsibility for program planning. Although the dance is the most popular Teen Life activity, the young people also plan numerous other activities.

Senior Citizens for Action is watching the case closely. They contend that if you let one group use the center rent-free just because it has a good cause, you must let other groups such as Senior Citizens for Action, also use the center free of charge.

Problem

Should Teen Life be allowed to use the center free of charge? If you say no, what alternatives do you propose? If you say yes, defend the decision that Senior Citizens for Action will not have free rent also. Draft guidelines of a rental policy and for acquiring a rent-fee waiver.

If Teen Life is allowed to use the center for free, does the city have more input into the group's activities than if the group paid rent? Does allowing the group to have free rent indicate that the city accepts more responsibility for the group's activities than it does for other groups?

What methods could Teen Life use to raise the money? Which, if any, of these methods would you recommend the group pursuing? Does the fact that taxes help to pay the center's bills help justify their right to use the facility for free?

Suggested Key Words and Phrases for
Literature Search for Case 284

Civic center	Fee waiver
Fees	Financing
Liability	Rent
Special interest groups	Taxes
Volunteers	Youth

Selected References for Case Study 284

Anderson, S., and Lauderdale, M. (1986). *Developing and managing volunteer programs: A guide for social service agencies.* Springfield, IL: Thomas.

Bovaird, A., Tricker, M., and Stoakes, R. (1984). *Recreation management and pricing: The effect of charging policy on demand at countryside recreation sites.* Brookfield, VT: Gower.

Crompton, J. (1987). How to establish a price for park and recreation services. In *Current issues in leisure services: Looking ahead in a time of transition.* J. Bannon, (ed.) Washington, D.C.: International City Management Association, 93-107.

Crompton, J. (1988, March). Are you ready to implement a comprehensive revenue-generating program? *Parks and Recreation,* 54-60.

Csikszentmihalyi, M.; and Larson, R. (1984). *Being adolescent: Conflict and growth in the teenage years.* New York: Basic.

Darvill, G., and Munday, B. (1984). *Volunteers in the personal social services.* London: Tavistock.

Downing, F., and Frank, J. (1982). *Recreation impact fees: A discussion of the issues and a survey of current practices in the United States with guidelines for Florida application.* Gainesville, FL: Policy Sciences Program, Florida State University.

Fairfax, J., Wright, L., and Maupin, M. (1988, Dec.). At-risk youth: Special needs. *Parks and Recreation,* 40-43.

Gross, H. (1990, May). Volunteers in Dunedin make the difference. *Park Maintenance and Grounds Management,* 14-16.

Harman, J., (ed.) (1982). *Volunteerism in the eighties: Fundamental issues in voluntary action.* New York: University Press of America.

Moore, B., (ed.) (1983). *The entrepreneur in local government.* Washington, D.C.: International City Management Association.

Roberts, K. (1983). *Youth and leisure.* London: George Allen & Unwin.

Walsh, E. (1990, Oct.). Fund raising made easy. *Parks and Recreation,* 60-63, 78.

285

Lobby Group Claims Contract Void
Since Its Views Were Not Represented

Situation

You are the park district director for a Midwestern town of 100,000. You have just signed a contract with a commercial company to build a waterslide in the biggest park in the district. Several citizens have complained that they were not informed in time to stop the signing. At this evening's board meeting, Board President Anthony Todd conceded that no opinion or marketing surveys were taken prior to the board vote. Todd said the park was chosen because of its relative size and because of its huge swimming pool.

Todd also said that the proposal was subject to several months' study by commissioners and district staff, and that it was publicly discussed at five board meetings prior to a vote. Several members of the audience then criticized the lack of publicity about the project, noting that they learned about the plan through the media, only after the board had signed the contract.

Todd proceeded to blame the media for not presenting the issue prior to the board's vote. He observed that park district meetings generally do not receive coverage, although the media was well represented this evening.

Citizens Against The Slide (CATS) demanded that the contract be voided since they were unable to be represented at earlier meetings. What is your reaction to their request?

Problem

What do you say to CATS? Are there times when a park district can legally void a contract once it is signed; if so, what must the circumstances be? Is a park district contract legal if some views were not represented prior to its being signed?

Must the park district announce its meetings to the public? What sort of business can be discussed in private? What must a park district do to consider that it has announced its meetings in public? If a newspaper desires to print something else other than park district material, does it have the right to refuse to print meeting announcements? Must a newspaper cover all park district meetings? If no reporter is assigned to the meetings, should the park district submit minutes to the newspaper the next day? If a park district leader realizes that a particular group of citizens may be upset about a decision, should she or he personally notify the group?

Should a survey have been taken? If so, who should have been surveyed — nearby residents, local citizens, regional dwellers, someone else, or all of the above? What questions should have been included on the survey? Create the survey instrument the park district should have used.

Suggested Key Words and Phrases for
Literature Search for Case 285

Citizen input	Marketing
Media coverage	Needs assessment
Open meeting laws	Public meetings
Public relations	Press relations
Research methods	Sunshine laws
Survey	

Selected References for Case Study 285

Gilbert, W., (ed.) (1975). *Public relations in local government.* Washington, D.C.: International City Management Association.

Hudson, S. (1988). *How to conduct community needs assessment surveys in public parks and recreation.* Columbus, OH: Publishing Horizons.

Johnson, D., Meiller, L., and Summers, G. (1987). *Needs assessment: Theory and methods.* Ames, IA: Iowa State University Press.

Mater, J. (1984). *Public hearings, procedures, and strategies: A guide to influencing public decisions.* Englewood Cliffs, NJ: Prentice-Hall.

Moler, C. (1990, Feb.). Make a splash with swimming programs. *Parks and Recreation*, 30-34.

Relyea, H. (1976). Government in the Sunshine Act—S. 5 (Public Law 94-409): Source book, legislative history, texts, and other documents. Washington, D.C.: U.S. Government Printing Office.

Reynolds, J., and Hormachea, M. (1976). Public relations. *Public recreation administration*. Reston, VA: Reston, 372-394.

Scott, M. (1988). *Law and leisure services management*. Essex, England: Longman.

Shaw, S., and Smith, E. (1979). *The law of meetings: Their conduct and procedure*. Fifth ed. Plymouth, England: Macdonald & Evans.

Toalson, R., and Herchenberger, P. (1985). *Developing community support for parks and recreation*. Champaign, IL: Champaign Park District.

Townley, S., and Grayson, E. (1984). *Sponsorship of sports, arts, and leisure: Law, tax, and business relationships*. London: Sweet and Maxwell.

United States Congress. House. Committee on the Judiciary. Subcommittee on Administrative Law and Governmental Relations (1976). *Government in the sunshine: Hearings before the subcommittee on administrative law and governmental relations of the committee on the judiciary, house of representatives, ninety-fourth Congress, second session, on H.R.11656, March 24 and 25, 1976*. Washington, D.C.: U.S. Government Printing Office.

United States. Congress. Senate. Committee on Governmental Affairs. (1978). *Oversight of the government in the Sunshine Act, Public Law 94-409: Hearings before the subcommittee on federal spending practices and open governments of the committee on governmental affairs. United States Senate first and second session, November 29, 1977, July 13 and Aug. 4, 1978*. Washington, D.C.: U.S. Government Printing Office.

U.S. Department of Health and Human Services. (1981). *Suggested health and safety guidelines for recreational waterslide fumes*. Atlanta, GA: U.S. Department of Health and Human Services, Public Health Service Centers for Disease Control, Center for Environmental Health, Environmental Health Services Division.

286
Board Ponders — Should Liquor Be Present in the Future?

Situation

You are the director of a public parks and recreation park district in an eastern city of 100,000. Two groups have approached the park district board about changing your liquor laws on the park grounds. One group wants alcohol allowed for "special occasions" such as weddings. The other group wants to allow alcohol at all times, especially for tailgate parties before softball games. The current policy forbids alcohol.

One board member proposes that liquor can be served provided that the group obtain a $10 permit from the park for the evening, make a $50 refundable deposit, and obtain dram shop insurance. "These restrictions will make sure they are serious about wanting to serve it. We shouldn't make it easy, but we should make it possible."

Another board member disagrees. "We've had to really clamp down on people tailgating before or after softball games. The drinking sometimes results in fights between rival teams. To be fair, we can't allow anybody to drink, regardless of the occasion."

A third board member suggests a compromise. "If they want to have a private party to celebrate a wedding or family reunion, for example, we should let them. That's a whole lot different than people tailgating before and after the game."

Problem

Should drinking alcohol be allowed in the public parks? Why or why not? Is there a difference between drinking at a wedding and tailgating? Describe the difference. Create a drinking policy. How would you enforce your drinking policy?

Is a permit system justified? How should the money that is collected be spent? What is the purpose of a refundable deposit? In what cases would the deposit not be refunded? What is dram shop insurance? Why would a board member insist that it be purchased by the liquor distributor before the permit is granted?

Suggested Key Words and Phrases for
Literature Search for Case 286

Alcohol	Charges
Dram shop insurance	Fees
Liquor ordinance	Park district law
Permit	Policies
Policy enforcement	Tailgating
Refundable deposit	

Selected References for Case Study 286

Bovaird, A., Tricker, M., and Stoakes, R. (1984). *Recreation management and pricing: The effect of charging policy on demand at countryside recreation sites.* Brookfield, VT: Gower.

Crompton, J. (1987). How to establish a price for park and recreation services. In *Current issues in leisure services: Looking ahead in a time of transition.* J. Bannon, (ed.) Washington, D.C.: International City Management Association, 93-107.

Downing, F., and Frank, J. (1982). *Recreation impact fees: A discussion of the issues and a survey of current practices in the United States with guidelines for Florida application.* Gainesville, FL: Policy Sciences Program, Florida State University.

Loy, J.; McPherson, B.; and Kenyin, G. (1978). *Sport and social systems: A guide to the analysis, problems, and literature.* Reading, MA: Addison-Wesley.

Moore, B., (ed.) (1983). *The entrepreneur in local government.* Washington, D.C.: International City Management Association.

Smart, R. (1980). *The new drinkers: Teenage use and abuse of alcohol.* Second ed. Toronto: Addiction Research Foundation of Ontario.

Snyder, E., and Spreitzer, E. (1983). *Social aspects of sport.* Second ed. Englewood Cliffs, NJ: Prentice-Hall.

Steiss, A. (1982). *Management control in government.* Lexington, MA: Lexington.

Stillman, Jr., R. (1976). *Public administration: Concepts and cases.* Boston: Houghton-Mifflin.

Tropman, J. (1984). *Policy management in the human services*. New
    York: Columbia University Press.

Waters, J. (1987). Fees and charges: Underutilized revenues. In
    *Current issues in leisure services: Looking ahead in a time of
    transition*. J. Bannon, (ed.) Washington, D.C.: International
    City Management Association, 88-92.

287
Logos Logic Confuses Liquor Liaison

Situation

You are the park district chief executive officer for a metropolitan area with a population of 100,000. As the softball season
prepares to open, a beer company distributor approaches the
park board about letting the beer company distribute free mer-
chandise to softball patrons. The company representative claims
that he will pass out t-shirts, footballs, and other miscellaneous
items with a popular brand of beer's logo imprinted on them. He
emphasizes that he will not be distributing free beer. The board
decides to turn him down ,because, as one board member put it,
"allowing beer logo distribution will encourage drinking at
softball games. He knows that or else he wouldn't be here."

After the representative has his request turned down, the
board decides to proceed with other new business. The next item
of business is approving softball sponsors. Billy's Bar has applied to be one of the sponsors for this year. The board approves
the sponsorship and agrees to let Billy's logo be printed on the
team t-shirt.

The beer company representative now claims that you are
being unfair by allowing the bar to have its logo present while
excluding his company's logo. How do you respond?

Problem

What do you say to the representative? How do you justify the decision that has been made? Is the justification likely to hold up in court? What is the park district objecting to regarding the representative's request? Would a beer company sponsoring a team be acceptable, or is there something greatly different between a national beer company with a local distributor sponsoring a team and a local tavern sponsoring a team?

Do either the beer distributor or Billy's Bar want to "do something nice for the community" or are both trying to make money through advertising? What is the purpose of a logo? Would the beer distributor's gifts be acceptable without the logo on them?

Suggested Key Words and Phrases for
Literature Search for Case 287

Advertising	Alcohol
Funding	Gifts
Logo	Product promotion
Sales incentives	Softball uniforms
Sponsors	T-shirts

Selected References for Case Study 287

Abraham, M., and Lodish, L. (1990, May-June). Getting the most out of advertising and promotion. *Harvard Business Review*, 50-60.

Betancourt, H. (1982). *The advertising answerbook: A guide for business and professional people.* Englewood Cliffs, NJ: Prentice-Hall.

Calvin, R. (1984). *Profitable management and marketing for growing businesses.* New York: Van Nostrand Reinhold.

Cooper, A. (1976). *World of logotypes.* Volume 1. New York: Art Direction.

Dfford, F. (1984). *Lite reading.* Harmondsworth, Middlesex, England: Penguin.

Dyer, G. (1982). *Advertising as communication.* New York: Methuen.

Igarashi, T., (ed.) (1987). *World trademarks and logotypes II: A collection of international symbols and their applications.* Tokyo: Graphic-Sha.

Lancaster, G. (1985). *Forecasting for sales and material management.* Houndmills, Basingstoke, Hamsphire: Macmillan.

Loy, J.; McPherson, B.; and Kenyin, G. (1978). *Sport and social systems: A guide to the analysis, problems, and literature.* Reading, MA: Addison-Wesley.

Smart, R. (1980). *The new drinkers: Teenage use and abuse of alcohol.* Second ed. Toronto: Addiction Research Foundation of Ontario.

Snyder, E., and Spreitzer, E. (1983). *Social aspects of sport.* Second ed. Englewood Cliffs, NJ: Prentice-Hall.

Young, R. (1983). *Managing cooperative advertising: A strategic approach.* Lexington, MA: Lexington.

288
Driven to Drink, Now He Wants to Drive

Situation

You are one of five sales team members for a large, prestigious health club. At the request of Stan Rodgers, the sales director, the two of you and three other sales agents go on a business trip to observe other prestigious health clubs. Rogers planned the excursion but unexpected difficulties arose. Upon entering the first facility, the receptionist informs your group that they cannot enter the club since they are from another non-affiliated health club. Rodgers claims he has complied with the $20 guest fee and is a guest of a member. He proceeds to argue with and embarrass the assistant manager, who then requests help from the club manager. Eventually, you calm Rodgers down and lead him back to the van.

Rodgers, still steaming, drives the van to the other sites without incident. However, just before leaving town for the evening, he stops at a tavern for a beer. Before long, he is intoxicated to the extent that some of the sales team are uncomfortable with letting him drive. Rodgers insists that he must drive since it is company policy that the leader of the group chauffeur. He says that if you do not get in the van that he will fire you for insubordination.

Problem

What should you say and do? Does Rodgers have the right to fire you in these circumstances? Is this a time when company policy can be broken? If so, what are other times? Does the incident at the first health club affect how you approach Rodgers now? Since Rodgers is under the influence of alcohol, can what he says or does be held against him?

If the sales director is unable to drive, who should take control of the situation, and why? How would that person exert control over the sales director?

Is it proper for one agency to scout its competition? What do you think the sales team was looking for? What would it most likely do with the information it gathered?

Suggested Key Words and Phrases for Literature Search for Case 288

Alcohol	Assessment of competition
Authoritarian leadership	Company policy
Democratic leadership	Health club
Insubordination	Organizational hierarchy
Sales team	Span of control

Selected References for Case Study 288

Calvin, R. (1984). *Profitable management and marketing for growing businesses.* New York: Van Nostrand Reinhold.

Caverly, J. (1987, July). Recreation and big business join forces in Westchester County. *Parks and Recreation,* 38-42.

Corneil, D., (ed.) (1987). *Alcohol in employment settings.* New York: Haworth.

Coulson, R. (1981). *The termination handbook.* New York: Free.

Culkin, D. (1988, Feb.). The right way to discipline. *Parks and Recreation,* 44-45.

Denenberg, T., and Denenberg, R. (1983). *Alcohol and drugs: Issues in the workplace.* Washington, D.C.: Bureau of National Affairs.

Holloway, W., and Leech, M. (1985). *Employment termination: Rights and remedies.* Washington, D.C.: Bureau of National Affairs.

Lancaster, G. (1985). *Forecasting for sales and material management.* Houndmills, Basingstoke, Hamsphire: Macmillan.

Lewis, J., and Lewis, M. (1986). *Counseling programs for employees in the workplace.* Monterey, CA: Brooks/Cole.

Pfeffer, J. (1978). *Organizational design.* Second printing. Arlington Heights, IL: AHM.

Pugh, M. (1986, Dec.). Kettering's employee wellness program - getting employees on the right track. *Parks and Recreation,* 34-35.

Scanlon, W. (1986). *Alcoholism and drug abuse in the workplace: Employee assistance programs.* New York: Praeger.

Redeker, J. (1983). *Discipline: Policies and procedures.* Washington, D.C.: Bureau of National Affairs.

White, C. (1989, August). A corporate trend: Working mind and body. *Parks and Recreation,* 28-32.

289
Squash Pro Closes Sale — But Quotes Wrong Rate

Situation

You are the sales director at a large, prestigious private health club. One afternoon, two prospects walk into your office and ask for a tour. After guiding them through the facility, you can tell that both are very impressed. On the tour, they informed you that they represent a new automobile manufacturing company moving into the city, and that they would like to consider purchasing several memberships. They also inform you that they are very good squash players.

The following day, you give their names and phone numbers to the squash pro. The pro promptly calls the prospects and invites them to come back to the facility as his guests to play some squash. Later that afternoon, the squash pro telephones your office. He says he is calling on behalf of the prospects and asks you for the corporate membership rate. He claims that he has promised that he himself would try to get the businessmen the best deal possible. The corporate rate and other sales information is not common knowledge among non-sales employees, so you refuse to give the numbers. However, you assure the pro that the businessmen have been offered the best deal possible.

A few minutes later, you discover that the squash pro is talking to the sales receptionist (a new employee), extracting what she thought was the correct corporate rate. The price she gave him, though, was far too low. The squash pro, however, quoted that price to the businessmen. The businessmen eagerly accepted the deal and have come to your office to sign the necessary paperwork.

Problem

What do you tell the businessmen, and why? Since the rate has been quoted to them by an official representative of the health club, can you legally or ethically quote a different rate? What roles do "profit" and "integrity" of the club have in this situation?

What should the role of the squash pro have been in recruiting the prospects? Why should his job involve these duties and only these duties?

How would you discipline the secretary who quoted the wrong rate? How would you discipline the squash pro? Would you discipline either of them in front of the businessmen? Would you discipline either of them personally, or would you allow someone higher in the organization to handle the matter?

Why would a health club not want its pros to know the corporate rate? Is this a good policy? Was the squash pro right in trying to break the policy? Are there times when policies must be broken? If so, provide examples of when the policy regarding the pros not knowing the corporate rate could be broken.

Suggested Key Words and Phrases for
Literature Search for Case 289

"Bait and Switch" tactics	Corporate recreation
Discounts	Health club facilities
Hierarchy	Integrity
Insubordination	Memberships
Organizational structure	Policy
Profit	Sales

Selected References for Case Study 289

Biondo, A. (1990, May). How to have happy customers - guaranteed. *Parks and Recreation*, 34-35, 38-40.

Britt, S., and Guess, N. (1983). *The Dartnell marketing manager's handbook.* Chicago: Dartnell.

Calvin, R. (1984). *Profitable management and marketing for growing businesses.* New York: Van Nostrand Reinhold.

Caverly, J. (1987, July). Recreation and big business join forces in Westchester County. *Parks and Recreation*, 38-42.

Crompton, J., and Lamb, Jr., C. (1986). *Marketing government and social services.* New York: Wiley.

Crompton, J. (1987). How to establish a price for park and recreation services. In *Current issues in leisure services: Looking ahead in a time of transition.* J. Bannon, (ed.) Washington, D.C.: International City Management Association, 93-107.

Cunningham, P. (1988, Sept.). How to win clients and influence co-workers. *Parks and Recreation,* 68-70, 83.

Cunningham, W., Cunningham, I., and Swift, C. (1987). *Marketing: A managerial approach.* Cincinnati, OH: South-Western.

Lancaster, G. (1985). *Forecasting for sales and material management.* Houndmills, Basingstoke, Hamsphire: Macmillan.

Pfeffer, J. (1978). *Organizational design.* Second printing. Arlington Heights, IL: AHM.

Prus, R. (1989). *Pursuing customers: An ethnography of marketing activities.* Newbury Park, CA: Sage.

Pugh, M. (1986, Dec.). Kettering's employee wellness program - getting employees on the right track. *Parks and Recreation,* 34-35.

Redeker, J. (1983). *Discipline: Policies and procedures.* Washington, D.C.: Bureau of National Affairs.

Rochman, J., Teresa, J., Kay, T., and Morningstar, G. (1983). *Marketing human service innovations.* Beverly Hills, CA: Sage.

Soderberg, J. (1989, June). Marketing recreation right. *Parks and Recreation,* 38-41.

Venkatesan, M., Schmalensee, D., and Marshall, C., (eds.) (1986). *Creativity in services marketing: What's new, what works, and what's developing.* Chicago, IL: American Marketing Association.

White, C. (1989, August). A corporate trend: Working mind and body. *Parks and Recreation,* 28-32.

290
If You Want to Play, You Pay—and Pay Again, Policy Says

Situation

You are the director of a park district located within the city limits of a community of 100,000. To the west is another town of 100,000, which borders your town, and it has the Tebo Park District surrounding it. To the north, south, and east are many small towns that have no recreation departments or park districts. In the past, you have agreed to charge residents of the neighboring park district the "local" rate provided they will give your residents the same break. All other people, though, have had to pay double the resident rate. The logic behind this is that residents outside of the park districts are not paying any taxes to support the districts, whereas those citizens within the districts are already partially paying for the services through taxes.

Out-of-town residents, however, have begun to complain that the non-resident rates are too high. At a recent park board meeting they note that the recreation programs are designed to break even and be self-supporting with just the resident's fee; hence, they feel gouged when they pay double that fee. They also contend that they have nowhere else to turn for public recreation services, and inquire if you "want to deny a youth a chance at a beneficial program just because he was born outside the district's boundaries."

After much discussion, several solutions to the problem are generated during the meeting. These include:

1.   Computing non-residents' fees on a program-by-program basis rather than merely doubling the residential rate.
2.   Allow non-residents the option of paying an annual fee based on what their property tax would be if they were in the district.
3.   Encourage non-residents to push for annexation into the park district.

After the solutions have been formally proposed, the chair of the board asks for your input.

Problem

What do you say? What are the advantages and disadvantages of each of the solutions suggested? What other solutions can you think of? Which solution would you recommend as the best?

Should residents pay a tax and a fee? Why or why not? What is the logic of non-residents paying twice the residents' rate? Is "twice" an arbitrary, or a realistic point? What should be the primary funding source for a park district — fees, taxes, grants, concession revenues, or something else? Rank these in order of importance.

How often should a district ponder its fee structure? By program, monthly, yearly, bi-yearly, or every five years? Why should a fee structure be reviewed periodically? Are "fee structures" and "fee amounts" related? How are they alike, and what is the distinction? Who should determine what the fee is?

*Suggested Key Words and Phrases for
Literature Search for Case 290*

Administrative hierarchy	Break-even point
Fee review	Fee structure
Financing	Non-resident fee
Resident fee	Revenue generation
Special districts	Supply and demand
Taxes	

Selected References for Case Study 290

Bovaird, A., Tricker, M., and Stoakes, R. (1984). *Recreation management and pricing: The effect of charging policy on demand at countryside recreation sites.* Brookfield, VT: Gower.

Calvin, R. (1984). *Profitable management and marketing for growing businesses.* New York: Van Nostrand Reinhold.

Crompton, J. (1987). How to establish a price for park and recreation services. In *Current issues in leisure services: Looking ahead in a time of transition.* J. Bannon, (ed.) Washington, D.C.: International City Management Association, 93-107.

Dworak, R. (1980). *Taxpayers, taxes, and government spending: Perspectives on the taxpayer revolt.* New York: Praeger.

Hansen, S. (1983). *The politics of taxation: Revenue without representation.* New York: Praeger.

Klemens, M. (1988, May). Taxes and the economy: Searching for cause and effect. *Illinois Issues,* 10-12.

Klemens, M. (1990, Feb.). Property tax: Hot potato between local and state politicians. *Illinois Issues,* 11-13.

Lancaster, G. (1985). *Forecasting for sales and material management.* Houndmills, Basingstoke, Hamsphire: Macmillan.

Lewis, Jr., S. (1984). *Taxation for development: Principles and applications.* New York: Oxford University Press.

Moore, B., ed. (1983). *The entrepreneur in local government.* Washington, D.C.: International City Management Association.

Perrenod, V. (1984). *Special districts, special purposes: Fringe governments and urban problems in the Houston area.* College Station, TX: Texas A & M University Press.

Porter, D., Lin, B., and Peiser, R. (1987). *Special districts: A useful technique for financing infrastructure.* Washington, D.C.: Urban Land Institute.

Stein, H., (ed.) (1988). *Tax policy in the twenty-first century.* New York: Wiley.

Summers, L., (ed.) (1989). *Tax policy and the economy: Volume three.* Cambridge, MA: MIT University Press.

Waters, J. (1987). Fees and charges: Underutilized revenues. In *Current issues in leisure services: Looking ahead in a time of transition.* J. Bannon, (ed.) Washington, D.C.: International City Management Association, 88-92.

291
Is Polygraph Test a Big Lie?

Situation

You are the chief administrative officer for a large public parks and recreation agency. Larry Sanders, the personnel director, has just sent you a memo requesting permission to administer a polygraph test (lie detector test) to all applicants as part of a job interview. He provides the following reasons:

1. Employee theft currently costs the department thousands of dollars each year. The $50 polygraph test would screen out likely thieves, saving thousands of dollars.
2. Reference checks currently cost about $200 each, thus the department would save $150 per applicant by administering the polygraph test rather than performing reference checks.
3. The polygraph test can be taken in minutes whereas reference checks can take days and weeks. Because the feedback is immediate, the hiring decision can be made considerably faster.

Stan Hall, labor union leader, has also sent you a memo. He is strongly against the use of polygraphs and wants to talk to you about it. He claims the following:

1. The machine is likely to err since all it does is graph how someone sweats, palpates, and pants in response to a given question.
2. The polygraph is more likely to find an innocent person guilty than a guilty person innocent. Research indicates that intelligent and/or sensitive people are more likely to fail than other people.
3. Test administrators often have low ethics, asking inappropriate questions.
4. Test administrators are often sloppy.
5. If a person fails the polygraph, he/she is likely to be branded a crook, even if later proven innocent.

Hall admits that if the test administrator and the test are both unbiased, the results of the polygraph test are correct 70 percent of the time (proponents contend that it is correct 96 percent of the time). However, he concludes his memo by asking, "Seventy percent? Who wants to play Russian roulette, being wrong about three out of every ten people tested?"

Problem

What will you say to Hall when he walks into your office? Does a polygraph test have a place in personnel administration? Should the polygraph test be used alone, as part of a battery of tests, or not at all? Would it be ethical to administer the polygraph test only to applicants for certain jobs in the department? Why or why not? Should the polygraph test be used primarily for current employees, potential employees, all employees, or no one? What sort of company/department would you recommend use the polygraph, and why?

What kind of questions can be asked in a job interview? What kind of questions cannot be asked? What legal repercussions are there if an illegal question is asked? Draw up a list of interview questions to be administered to a maintenance staff applicant.

If you were to decide to allow the personnel director to administer the polygraph test, how would you express this decision to Hall? How would you pacify Hall? What options does Hall have if he chooses to oppose the decision? Are positive labor relations important? Why or why not?

Suggested Key Words and Phrases for Literature Search for Case 291

Applicant pool	Civil Rights Act of 1964
Discrimination	Interview
Labor relations	Labor union
Lie detector	Personnel administration
Polygraph test	Testing

Selected References for Case Study 291

Arvey, R., and Faley, R. (1988). *Fairness in selecting employees.* Second ed. Reading, MA: Addison-Wesley.

Booth, W. (1987, Jan.). Putting your best foot forward at an assessment center. *Parks and Recreation*, 86-89.

Dilts, D., and Walsh, W. (1988). *Collective bargaining and impasse resolution in the public sector.* New York: Quorum.

Holley, W., and Jennings, K. (1984). *The labor relations process.* Second ed. Chicago: Dryden.

Kilgour, J. (1981). *Preventive labor relations.* New York: AMACOM.

Kniveton, B. (1989). *The psychology of bargaining.* Hong Kong: Avebury.

Lewin, D., Feuille, P., and Kockan, T. (1981). *Public sector labor relations: Analysis and readings.* Second ed. Sun Lakes, AZ: Horton.

Manese, W. (1986). *Fair and effective employment testing: Administrative, psychometric, and legal issues for the human resources professional.* New York: Quorum.

McCullock, K. (1981). *Selecting employees safely under the law.* Englewood Cliffs, NJ: Prentice-Hall.

Moberly, R., and Mulcahy, C. (1974). *Public employment labor relations.* Madison, WI: Impressions.

Morse, B. (1988). *How to negotiate a labor agreement: An outline summary of tested bargaining practices expanded from earlier editions.* Eleventh ed. San Diego, CA: Trends.

Pepper, W., and Kennedy, F. (1981). *Sex discrimination in employment: An analysis and guide for practitioner and student.* Charlottesville, VA: Michie.

Public Service Research Council. (1976). *Public sector bargaining and strikes.* Vienna, VA: Public Service Research Council.

Rappaport, S. (1989). *Age discrimination: A legal and practical guide for employers.* Washington, D.C.: Bureau of National Affairs.

Smith, M., and Robertson, I., (ed.) (1989). *Advances in selection and assessment.* New York: Wiley.

292
Lifeguards to be Replaced by Swim-at-Own-Risk Sign

Situation

You are the director of the White Fox Forest Preserve District. Your insurance has tripled in the past four years, primarily due to your lake activities. To reduce the insurance premium, board member Paul Grabel has proposed that the risks of swimming at the lake be taken from the district and placed upon the swimmers. To transfer the risks, he suggests that the lifeguards be removed and that a swim-at-your-own-risk sign be established. He said that the injury cases that may surface could be evaluated on an individual basis but that the district would not be held as responsible as it would if it had lifeguards on duty. "The more responsibility we assume for participation in a given activity, the higher our risk insurance premiums are going to be," he argues.

To reduce insurance premiums in the past, the preserve board has previously taken out the water slide, paddle boats, and diving board. The only activities that take place now at the lake are swimming, sunbathing, and sandcastle building. As the meeting progresses, some board members express the belief that the board has already made all of the cuts it can.

Grabel persists in arguing his cause, however. Finally, one board member asks him to show what he means when he refers to a sign being posted. When pressed for a description of an adequate sign, Grabel draws the following:

Beach Rules

1. Swim at your own risk. No lifeguard on duty.
2. No person may enter the water or swim alone.
3. No bather 16 years of age or under may enter the beach area without being supervised by a responsible person 17 years of age or older.
4. Swim in marked area only.
5. Stay within buoy lines.

6. All food or drink is prohibited in beach area.
7. No glass containers allowed in swimming area.
8. No diving or horseplay in the swimming area.

After Grabel has finished his presentation, the board members ask you for feedback.

Problem

What would you reply? Is Grabel right in saying that insurance would go down if you took away your lifeguards? Are more accidents likely to happen if the lifeguards are removed? Are more law suits likely to happen if you do not post lifeguards? Why or why not?

Is Grabel's sign adequate? What would you add or delete? Is the sign a good idea? How will the rules on the sign be enforced? What sort of penalties would violators be assessed?

Many of Grabel's sentences are stated negatively (with a "no"), while others are not. Should these negative sentences be reworked? Is Grabel's cutoff of a 16-year-old and a 17-year-old reasonable? Why do you think he chose the 16-17 year mark instead of something else, such as 18-19?

What alternatives can you think of that would likely reduce insurance while keeping lifeguards at the beach? What is the purpose of carrying insurance? What would happen if you dropped insurance coverage? What other options are there besides purchasing insurance from a commercial carrier, or not having any insurance at all?

Suggested Key Words and Phrases for
Literature Search for Case 292

County forest preserve	Crowd control
Injuries	Insurance
Lawsuit	Legal responsibility
Lifeguards	Public relations
Risk management	Rules
Signage	Youth

Selected References for Case Study 292

Bannon, Jr., J., and Bannon, J. (1987). The insurance crisis: A dilemma for parks and recreation. In *Current issues in leisure services: Looking ahead in a time of transition*. J. Bannon, (ed.) Washington, D.C.: International City Management Association, 119-133.

Baron, R. (1988, Sept.). Risk management: The defensive game plan. *Parks and Recreation*, 53-55.

Christiansen, M. (1987). Safety is no accident. In *Current issues in leisure services: Looking ahead in a time of transition*. J. Bannon, (ed.) Washington, D.C.: International City Management Association.

Csikszentmihalyi, M.; and Larson, R. (1984). *Being adolescent: Conflict and growth in the teenage years*. New York: Basic.

Direnfeld-Michael, B. (1989, March). A risk management primer for recreators. *Parks and Recreation*, 40-45.

Direnfield-Michael, B., and Michael, D. (1987, Jan.). Everything you ought to know about the liability insurance crisis but didn't know how to ask. *Parks and Recreation*, 74-80.

Holford, E., and Geyer, L. (1990, March). Torts on your turf. *Park Maintenance and Grounds Management*, 13-15.

Holland, S. (1990, Sept.). Beach parks: environmental beacons. *Parks and Recreation*, 78-82, 112.

Kaiser, R. (1986). *Liability and law in recreation, parks, and sports*. Englewood Cliffs, NJ: Prentice-Hall.

Kozlowski, J. (1988, Sept.). A common sense view of liability. *Parks and Recreation*, 56-59.

Mandelker, D., and Ewald, W. (1988). *Street graphics and the law*. Washington, D.C.: Planners.

Reynolds, J., and Hormachea, M. (1976). Legal authority for public recreation. *Public recreation administration*. Reston, VA: Reston, 39-54.

Roberts, K. (1983). *Youth and leisure*. London: George Allen & Unwin.

Scott, M. (1985). *The law of public leisure services*. London: Sweet and Maxwell.

Scott, M. (1988). *Law and leisure services management*. Essex, England: Longman.

Tiffany, A. (1987, Jan.). How to tame the liability monster. *Parks and Recreation*, 64-69, 103.

Townley, S., and Grayson, E. (1984). *Sponsorship of sports, arts, and leisure: Law, tax, and business relationships.* London: Sweet and Maxwell.

Wasserman, N., and Phelus, D. (1985). *Risk management today: A how-to guide for local government.* Washington, D.C.: International City Management Association.

293
YMCA Battles Membership Woes

Situation

You are the planning officer of a YMCA in a town of 100,000. Membership — not only a measure of success, but what pays the bills — has declined drastically at both your YMCA and the YWCA across town. Currently, the YMCA has 3,500 members and the YWCA has 2,262. The most steady growth at your YMCA has been people attending the senior citizen functions and people joining the Nautilus Fitness Center. Family memberships and individual adult memberships have dropped drastically.

Besides the issue of declining enrollment, you also face other problems, such as brick-and-mortar facilities that are in great need of repair. In addition, your 42-year-old building is nestled in a high-crime neighborhood, and people have expressed their fear about going to the YMCA to attend programs. To make matters worse, a high-tech health club has opened down the street.

Your director has enlisted you to turn around the fortunes of the YMCA. "The YMCA is unique," he tells you proudly. "We must rebuild lagging memberships, redefine our role in the community by emphasizing social services, downplay competition with the YWCA, and beat back the challenge of the health clubs. We have an excellent leadership team and we can turn this around."

Problem

Are these objectives realistic? Justify the YMCA's involvement in social services. Why would the director want to downplay the competition with the YWCA, while stressing the competition with the health clubs? Justify the YMCA attempting to take the market away from the health club. Should an agency that relies on United Way donations compete with a private company when the market is tight?

What is the biggest problem facing the YMCA? How would you attempt to solve it? Are there underlying problems that the director has not thought of? If so, what are they and how can they be overcome? Sketch a two-year plan that would accomplish the director's goals.

Suggested Key Words and Phrases for
Literature Search for Case 293

Competition	Decaying facilities
Health clubs	Management by objective
Marketing	Membership fees
Public relations	Role in community
Social services	United Way
Voluntary agencies	Volunteer recruitment
YMCA	YWCA

Selected References for Case Study 293

Anderson, S., and Lauderdale, M. (1986). *Developing and managing volunteer programs: A guide for social service agencies.* Springfield, IL: Thomas.

Crompton, J., and Lamb, Jr., C. (1986). *Marketing government and social services.* New York: Wiley.

Cunningham, W., Cunningham, I., and Swift, C. (1987). *Marketing: A managerial approach.* Cincinnati, OH: South-Western.

Darvill, G., and Munday, B. (1984). *Volunteers in the personal social services.* London: Tavistock.

Ellard, A., and Cundiff, L. (1989, August). How to plan a safe exercise program. *Parks and Recreation*, 44-46, 53.

Morrisey, G. (1976). *Management by objectives and results in the public sector*. Reading, MA: Addison-Wesley.

O'Sullivan, E. (1986, Jan.). Facilitating adult participation in organized recreation programs. *Parks and Recreation*, 58-60.

Prince, R. (1990, Feb.). Drug prevention through parks and recreation. *Parks and Recreation*, 10-11.

Prus, R. (1989). *Pursuing customers: An ethnography of marketing activities*. Newbury Park, CA: Sage.

Raia, A. (1974). *Managing by objectives*. Glenview, IL: Scott, Foresman.

Redman, S., Preo, L., and Brown, L. (1989, Aug.). The facts and fiction of fitness. *Parks and Recreation*, 22-27.

Rochman, J., Teresa, J., Kay, T., and Morningstar, G. (1983). *Marketing human service innovations*. Beverly Hills, CA: Sage.

Soderberg, J. (1989, June). Marketing recreation right. *Parks and Recreation*, 38-41.

Tiffany, A. (1990, Oct.). Buying fitness equipment: Why weight? *Parks and Recreation*, 36-40, 78.

Tropman, J. (1984). *Policy management in the human services*. New York: Columbia University Press.

294
Record Disarray Leads Director to Give Press
Wrong Information

Situation

You are the executive director of a YWCA whose membership records are in a state of disarray. The computer that holds the membership data crashed (i.e., broke to the extent that the information inside it cannot be recovered). The hand-kept books, meanwhile, are error-filled.

Last week you showed membership figures to the *Daily Bugle,* claiming that the agency had more members than it did a year ago. Today, though, your assistant director presents you with a tally that indicates you lost as many as 692 members — nearly 24 percent of the membership — in the last year. Her numbers indicate that the YWCA membership declined from 2,914 to 2,222.

Your gut feeling is that the membership is down somewhat, but probably not by 692. Your assistant's numbers came from the error-filled books, and therefore you question their validity.

Problem

What should you do? Should you call the *Daily Bugle*? If so, what should you say? Which set of numbers should you submit to the United Way and other funding agencies? Has an illegal/ unethical wrongdoing taken place? Will something be illegal/ unethical if you do not publicly release your assistant's findings?

What kind of membership records should an agency keep? What kind of checks and balances could have prevented errors from creeping into the books? What kind of back-ups should be made in case of a computer crash?

Suggested Key Words and Phrases for
Literature Search for Case 294

Bookkeeping	Checks and balances
Computers	Cover-up
Membership	Press relations
Record keeping	United Way
Voluntary agency	YMCA

Selected References for Case Study 294

Berkebile, J. (1986, Feb.). How computer reports can improve park management. *Parks and Recreation*, 40-44, 68.

Chatfield, D., Deans, Jr., C., and Freshwater, D. (1990, June). Computerizing parks and recreation. *Parks and Recreation*, 54-59.

Crossley, J. (1990, March). Multi-tier programming in commercial recreation. *Parks and Recreation*, 69-73.

Dearstyne, B. (1988). *The management of local government records: A guide for local officials.* Nashville: American Association for State and Local History.

Dean, D., Wellman, D., and Charles, B. (1990, June). PASSing the computer test. *Parks and Recreation*, 46-53.

Gardner, J. (1989, Jan.). Byte back: A computer guide for the professional. *Parks and Recreation*, 52-54.

Gardner, J. (1989, June). The smart way to buy your computer. *Parks and Recreation*, 53-56.

Godbey, G. (1978). *Recreation, park, and leisure services: Foundations, organization, administration.* Philadelphia: Saunders.

Kelly, J. (1990). *Leisure.* Second ed. Englewood Cliffs, NJ: Prentice-Hall.

Kraus, R. (1990). *Recreation and leisure in modern society.* Fourth ed. Glenview, IL: Scott, Foresman.

O'Sullivan, E. (1986, Jan.). Facilitating adult participation in organized recreation programs. *Parks and Recreation*, 58-60.

Wirth, L. (1980). *Parks, politics, and the people.* Norman, OK: University of Oklahoma Press.

295
Proposed Bill Limits Operator's Liability

Situation

You are the executive director of Charlie's Ski Resort, a large commercial recreation enterprise in the Catskill Mountains. Last year a man smashed into a tree on an expert trail at your resort. He sued and was awarded $1.2 million by the jury, and his wife received $400,000 for loss of services. Because of this case, ski insurance premiums jumped across the state. At Charlie's Ski Resort, lift prices jumped twenty percent because of insurance premium costs.

Taxpayers, upset at the higher slope fees, appealed to their state congressional representatives. The representatives have created a bill that would (a) mandate ski operators keep lifts and slopes in safe conditions, and (b) require ski operators to clearly mark all hazards. In addition, the bill would require that skiers know their abilities and ski in control. Congressional authorities claim that the proposed law would give juries guidelines by which to judge the merit of the suit.

A reporter for WXYZ Television has arranged to interview you for a statement on the national news. Although he has about thirty minutes of questions, he admits that only about a minute of the interview will be shown. He says that the majority of the interview will focus on your reaction to the proposed law.

Problem

What will you say to the reporter? Since the law outlines areas of responsibility, is the law likely to discourage suits or will it encourage suits? Should a bill focus only on the ski industry, or should it be expanded to encompass ice skating, white water rafting, horseback riding, and other dangerous sports? Why or why not?

Are the bill's restrictions placed on the ski resort fair? Are the bill's restrictions placed on the skier fair? What changes would you make on the bill, and why?

As director of Charlie's Ski Resort, what options are available to avoid paying high insurance costs? Is it important to carry insurance? Why or why not? Besides raising lift fees, what other options would a ski resort have to generate the money necessary for an insurance premium?

Are props important for a television interview? What should you wear to the interview? Where would be the ideal place on the ski property to film the interview; why? What impression do you want to convey?

*Suggested Key Words and Phrases for
Literature Search for Case 295*

Commercial recreation	Congressional bill
Insurance premium	Lawsuit
Legal responsibility	Legislation
Profit margin	Public relations
Risk management	Signage
Skiing	

Selected References for Case Study 295

Bannon, Jr., J., and Bannon, J. (1987). The insurance crisis: A dilemma for parks and recreation. In *Current issues in leisure services: Looking ahead in a time of transition.* J. Bannon, (ed.) Washington, D.C.: International City Management Association, 119-133.

Baron, R. (1988, Sept.). Risk management: The defensive game plan. *Parks and Recreation,* 53-55.

Christiansen, M. (1987). Safety is no accident. In *Current issues in leisure services: Looking ahead in a time of transition.* J. Bannon, (ed.) Washington, D.C.: International City Management Association.

Direnfeld-Michael, B. (1989, March). A risk management primer for recreators. *Parks and Recreation,* 40-45.

Direnfield-Michael, B., and Michael, D. (1987, Jan.). Everything you ought to know about the liability insurance crisis but didn't know how to ask. *Parks and Recreation,* 74-80.

Holford, E., and Geyer, L. (1990, March). Torts on your turf. *Park Maintenance and Grounds Management,* 13-15.

Kaiser, R. (1986). *Liability and law in recreation, parks, and sports.* Englewood Cliffs, NJ: Prentice-Hall.

Kozlowski, J. (1988, Sept..). A common sense view of liability. *Parks and Recreation,* 56-59.

Reynolds, J., and Hormachea, M. (1976). Legal authority for public recreation. *Public recreation administration.* Reston, VA: Reston, 39-54.

Scott, M. (1985). *The law of public leisure services.* London: Sweet and Maxwell.

Scott, M. (1988). *Law and leisure services management*. Essex, England: Longman.

Tiffany, A. (1987, Jan.). How to tame the liability monster. *Parks and Recreation*, 64-69, 103.

Townley, S., and Grayson, E. (1984). *Sponsorship of sports, arts, and leisure: Law, tax, and business relationships*. London: Sweet and Maxwell.

Wasserman, N., and Phelus, D. (1985). *Risk management today: A how-to guide for local government*. Washington, D.C.: International City Management Association.

296
Supervisor Uncovers Liability Scam

Situation

You are the supervisor of lifeguards in a large metropolitan parks and recreation department. Even though your pools and beaches have been packed for years without a major liability incident, your insurance premiums have increased greatly over the last five years because of national lawsuits. If your agency had a lawsuit filed against it and lost, your premiums would be likely to increase three to four times more next year.

One day, as you walk along a crowded beach inspecting it, you overhear four young men. They are plotting to scratch each others' backs until they bleed so they can claim that they have been injured at the beach. One of the young men assures the other three that because of the claims and settlements paid for any type of liability, they can make lots of money quickly. He claims that an out-of-court settlement is likely, and therefore no trial will ever take place.

As you continue to walk by, one of the young men takes off his t-shirt, lays down on a beach towel, and lets his three friends begin to claw at his back.

Problem

What should you do? Should you try to stop the young men from mutilating each other? Why or why not? Should you tell anyone what you heard? Is the young men's plan likely to work? Is an out of court settlement likely? Why or why not? If the case did go to court, would the young men be likely to win? What would the beach have to prove to defend itself?

How could liability insurance costs on beaches be reduced? How much risk should swimmers assume? If swimmers assume more responsibility for their own safety, will insurance premiums go down? How could you prove that swimmers are taking more responsibility?

How much responsibility should a public parks department assume for swimmers' safety? Why should it assume such responsibility? Are there some responsibilities that an administrating agency must always assume, and if so, what are they?

Suggested Key Words and Phrases for
Literature Search for Case 296

Beachfront operations	Injuries
Liability insurance	Liability settlements
Lifeguards	Negligence
Public beaches	Public safety
Risk management	Self-inflicted injury
Youth	

Selected References for Case Study 296

Bannon, Jr., J., and Bannon, J. (1987). The insurance crisis: A dilemma for parks and recreation. In *Current issues in leisure services: Looking ahead in a time of transition.* J. Bannon, (ed.) Washington, D.C.: International City Management Association, 119-133.

Baron, R. (1988, Sept.). Risk management: The defensive game plan. *Parks and Recreation*, 53-55.

Christiansen, M. (1987). Safety is no accident. In *Current issues in leisure services: Looking ahead in a time of transition*. J. Bannon, (ed.) Washington, D.C.: International City Management Association.

Direnfeld-Michael, B. (1989, March). A risk management primer for recreators. *Parks and Recreation*, 40-45.

Direnfield-Michael, B., and Michael, D. (1987, Jan.). Everything you ought to know about the liability insurance crisis but didn't know how to ask. *Parks and Recreation*, 74-80.

Holford, E., and Geyer, L. (1990, March). Torts on your turf. *Park Maintenance and Grounds Management*, 13-15.

Holland, S. (1990, Sept.). Beach parks: environmental beacons. *Parks and Recreation*, 78-82, 112.

Kaiser, R. (1986). *Liability and law in recreation, parks, and sports*. Englewood Cliffs, NJ: Prentice-Hall.

Kozlowski, J. (1988, Sept.). A common sense view of liability. *Parks and Recreation*, 56-59.

Reynolds, J., and Hormachea, M. (1976). Legal authority for public recreation. *Public recreation administration*. Reston, VA: Reston, 39-54.

Scott, M. (1985). *The law of public leisure services*. London: Sweet and Maxwell.

Scott, M. (1988). *Law and leisure services management*. Essex, England: Longman.

Tiffany, A. (1987, Jan.). How to tame the liability monster. *Parks and Recreation*, 64-69, 103.

Wallach, F. (1990, Aug.). Playground safety update. *Parks and Recreation*, 46-50.

Wasserman, N., and Phelus, D. (1985). *Risk management today: A how-to guide for local government*. Washington, D.C.: International City Management Association.

297
Jet Ski Dealer Offers to Make Splash With Board

Situation

You are the marine manager for the Lake Charlie Park Commission. At today's commission meeting, the topic is what to do about jet skis at Lake Charlie. Everybody present agrees that some regulation is needed. Many people, though, would prefer to ban them. The public has been invited to comment about a proposed Personal Water Craft (PWC) Ordinance. A proponent of jet skiing, a local Honda dealer, presents the following speech:

"In the debate over the future of PWC such as jet skis on Lake Charlie, we should strive to be reasonable and not overreact. Some have suggested an outright ban of jet skis, but what is needed is regulation, not elimination. The PWC business has grown very quickly, becoming a very large recreational sport within three years. The sport has experienced growing pains that are both normal and correctable.

"Yes, the use of jet skis has irritated many people, and some people have used the craft incorrectly, but that alone is no reason to ban them from Lake Charlie. New York State has come up with rules and regulations for PWC's. The state's approach is to regulate, not ban, and that's what our approach should be also.

"The PWC industry has developed educational material that every manufacturer makes available to new purchasers. In my own business, handling the three major PWC brands, I expose all buyers to the educational materials and to general boating rules on Lake Charlie. The proposed ordinance could require instruction for renters. Education and regulation need to be given a chance to work.

"Regarding noise levels, PWC's meet the existing state and federal regulations. Nevertheless, manufacturers are responding to the concern by making the machines quieter. The proposed regulations would also require jet skis to operate farther from shore than other boats.

"Regarding safety, according to the U.S. Coast Guard, there are no inherent safety deficiencies in PWC's. As far as potential damage to wetlands, jet skis use water-jet propulsion. Traveling through shallow, marshy areas will clog the water intake with vegetation, stopping the machine—not the kind of experience riders seek.

"I believe that many people who are opposed to PWC's are not familiar with them. I invite any of you to contact me, and I will arrange a personal demonstration to help you better understand the craft."

Problem

Having heard the argument, draft an ordinance that regulates jet ski activities on Lake Charlie. Be able to support and justify each sentence. Also be able to justify why certain items are not covered in the ordinance.

What is your reaction to the dealer's argument? Did he appeal to emotions, to logic, or to both? How did he support his argument? Is the evidence he used selected from a minority of material or is it typical for the field? If you wanted to undertake a study to determine the feelings of the residents and boaters of Lake Charlie, what would you need to do? Are the radical proponents and the opponents of the jet skiers at the meeting typical of the majority of people in the community? Can they be called a fair sample of the community?

Suggested Key Words and Phrases for
Literature Search for Case 297

Commercial recreation	Jet ski
Marine management	Noise restrictions
Outdoor education	Outdoor recreation
Personal water craft	Research methods
Safety	Regulations
Water safety	Wetlands

Selected References for Case Study 297

Bear, F., Pritchard, H., and Akin, W. (1986). *Earth: The stuff of life*. Normal, OK: University of Oklahoma Press.

Brimmer, L. (1989). *Snowboarding*. New York: Watts.

Brown, B. (1990, Jan. 18). Snowmobile!: Machines of winter a necessity for some, a nuisance to others. *USA Today*, 8C.

Brown, B. (1990, Jan. 18). Wisconsin town transforms into mecca for racing fans. *USA Today*, 8C.

Harris, J. (1988). *Personal watercraft*. Mankato, MN: Crestwood.

Jubenville, A. (1978). *Outdoor recreation management*. Philadelphia: Saunders.

Knudson, D. (1980). *Outdoor recreation*. New York: Macmillan.

McAvoy, L. (1990, Sept.). An environmental ethic for parks and recreation. *Parks and Recreation*, 68-72.

McAdam, G. (1990, Oct.). Environmental protection through citizen action. *Parks and Recreation*, 46-51.

Olsen, L. (1976). *Outdoor survival skills*. 4th ed. Second printing. Provo, UT: Brigham Young University Press.

Pigram, J. (1983). *Outdoor recreation and resource management*. New York: St. Martin.

Wallace, G., Tierney, P., and Hass, G. (1990, Sept.). The right link between wilderness and tourism. *Parks and Recreation*, 62-66, 111.

Warren, R. (1990, June). Land stewardship: Your professional responsibility. *Park Maintenance and Grounds Management*, 14-16.

Zook, L. (1986, Jan.). Outdoor adventure programs build character in five ways. *Parks and Recreation*, 54-57.

298
Park Visitors Warm to Winter Wonderland

Situation

You are the chief naturalist for the Forest Service at a large national park located in the heart of Wyoming. Winter has fallen on the park, and many problems associated with summer tourists are gone. However, recent national newscasts have promoted the winter beauty of the park, and tourists have begun to flock to the park despite it being January.

The tourists are not prepared for what they encounter. Although the six feet of snow is beautiful to see, the tourists are ill-prepared to cross it. The parks department has special snowmobiles — snowcoaches, which are similar to regular snowmobiles but have an enclosed cab —but the park's shuttle service is having trouble keeping up with the demand. In addition, animals have a very limited amount of food, and the extra human population is destroying their food supply. The animals also have limited energy, and many have literally been scared to death by tourists hot-rodding on snowmobiles.

One afternoon, the program director calls a special meeting of all ranking park personnel. He explains that access to citizens is important, but so is preservation. He asks for feedback on how to best handle the situation.

Problem

What do you suggest? What kind of access should people have? Who should determine who can have access to the park? Does a public park have the right to deny access to anyone wanting to use the public land? What sort of guidelines should be established to preserve the winter experience? Draft a sample of guidelines. Who should enforce these guidelines and what sort of penalties should be administered? What is a national park's primary goal — conservation, education, research, or recreation? Why is this goal the most important?

Does it make a difference that this is wilderness management instead of forest management, and if so, why? What is the purpose of preserving a wilderness? What techniques are used to preserve the wilderness? What is the naturalist's role in promoting the wilderness?

Suggested Key Words and Phrases for
Literature Search for Case 298

Carrying capacity   Conservation
Education   National parks
Naturalist   Public access
Research   Snowcoaches
Snowmobiles   Wilderness management
Winter management

Selected References for Case Study 298

Bear, F., Pritchard, H., and Akin, W. (1986). *Earth: The stuff of life.* Normal, OK: University of Oklahoma Press.

Brimmer, L. (1989). *Snowboarding.* New York: Watts.

Brown, B. (1990, Jan. 18). Snowmobile!: Machines of winter a necessity for some, a nuisance to others. *USA Today*, 8C.

Brown, B. (1990, Jan. 18). Wisconsin town transforms into mecca for racing fans. *USA Today*, 8C.

Harlow, W. (1979). *Ways of the woods: A guide to the skills and spirit of the woodland experience.* Washington, D.C.: American Forestry Association.

Jubenville, A. (1978). *Outdoor recreation management.* Philadelphia: Saunders.

Knudson, D. (1980). *Outdoor recreation.* New York: Macmillan.

McAvoy, L. (1990, Sept.). An environmental ethic for parks and recreation. *Parks and Recreation*, 68-72.

McAdam, G. (1990, Oct.). Environmental protection through citizen action. *Parks and Recreation*, 46-51.

Olsen, L. (1976). *Outdoor survival skills.* Second printing. Provo, UT: Brigham Young University Press.

Pigram, J. (1983). *Outdoor recreation and resource management.* New York: St. Martin.

Shelby, B., and Heberlein, T. (1986). *Carrying capacity in recreation settings.* Corvallis, OR: Oregon State University.

Wallace, G., Tierney, P., and Hass, G. (1990, Sept.). The right link between wilderness and tourism. *Parks and Recreation*, 62-66, 111.

Warren, R. (1990, June). Land stewardship: Your professional responsibility. *Park Maintenance and Grounds Management*, 14-16.

Zook, L. (1986, Jan.). Outdoor adventure programs build character in five ways. *Parks and Recreation*, 54-57.

299

Mayor Announces Developmentally Disabled
Youth Program

Situation

You are the recreation director for a large municipal parks and recreation department. This morning, at a special press conference, the mayor announced that the recreation department will participate this summer in a unique program involving developmentally disabled children. "We have been given a $20,000 grant from the Developmentally Disabled Council of Louisiana and we are the only city in the state to be so funded," the mayor said at a press conference in his office. "In fact, we are one of the few municipal governments in the nation to get this type of funding. Normally, such funding has gone into educational opportunity for these children, not recreational activities.

"The recreation department will open a day camp program for the children June 19. The camps will be located at four schools. The program will select for each center ten children who are developmentally disabled because of mental retardation, cerebral palsy, epilepsy, or other afflictions. The program will strive to have 50 percent of the children come from disadvantaged families. Transportation to and from the day camp sites is provided in the grant.

"The program will serve as a model for future development and expansion of similar projects for the handicapped citywide. Working closely with our recreation department will be the Louisiana State University Development Disability Center, the Tulane School of Social Work, and the Council of the Arts for Children."

After the mayor's speech, a reporter stops by your office to inquire if you have any comments about the mayor's handling of the situation or about the program itself.

Problem

What do you say? Is it typical for a mayor to call a press conference to announce receiving a grant of $20,000? Do you think he was using the grant as an excuse to recruit votes? If so, is this ethical? If you thought it was unethical, would you tell the reporter?

What is the relationship between recreation departments and schools? What advantages and disadvantages are there to using school facilities for recreation programs? Should public money marked for the developmentally disabled be spent primarily on recreation?

Should special attempts be made to provide recreation for the underprivileged and/or the developmentally disabled? Why or why not? Should such programs be limited to the special clientele? What are major differences between a therapeutic recreational activity and a nontherapeutic recreational activity?

Suggested Key Words and Phrases for
Literature Search for Case 299

City-department relations
Disadvantaged families
Handicap access
Public relations
Therapeutic recreation
Youth

Developmentally disabled
Grants
Press relations
School-public recreation
  partnership

Selected References for Case Study 299

Carter, M. (1988, Dec.). Defining therapeutic standards. *Parks and Recreation*, 28-31.

Coffey, F. (1988, Dec.). Developing a disabled resource directory: A good investment. *Parks and Recreation*, 44-50, 54.

Davis, D., (ed.) (1981). *Communities and their schools*. New York: McGraw-Hill.

Gilbert, W., (ed.) (1975). *Public relations in local government*. Washington, D.C.: International City Management Association.

Kamberg, M. (1989, Sept.). *The three R's in Overland Park, KS: Reading, 'riting, and recreation*, 92-93.

Kraus, R. (1973). *Therapeutic recreation service: Principles and practices*. Philadelphia: Saunders.

Lewis, A. (1986). *Partnerships connecting school and community*. Arlington, VA: American Association of School Administrators.

Reynolds, J., and Hormachea, M. (1976). Public recreation and public schools. *Public recreation administration*. Reston, VA: Reston, 103-117.

Reynolds, J., and Hormachea, M. (1976). Public relations. *Public recreation administration*. Reston, VA: Reston, 372-394.

Ruffin, Jr., S. (1989). *School-business partnerships: Why not?: Laying the foundation for successful programs*. Reston, VA: National Association of Secondary School Principals.

Stein, J. (1986, Jan.). Including disabled participants: Four goals for recreation management. *Parks and Recreation*, 49-52, 79.

Toalson, R., and Herchenberger, P. (1985). *Developing community support for parks and recreation*. Champaign, IL: Champaign Park District.

Wallat, C., and Goldman, R. (1979). *Home/School/Community interaction: What we know and why we don't know more*. Columbus, OH: Merrill.

Wekman, P., and Schleien, S. (1981). *Leisure programs for handicapped persons: Adaptations, techniques, and curriculum*. Baltimore: University Park.

300
Is An Indoor Park Equal to an Outdoor Park?

Situation

You are the director of a public parks and recreation agency in a large metropolitan community. The City Council has the opportunity to sell a one-acre downtown park to Moonlight Travel, an international upper-class hotel chain. In exchange for the right to build over the park, developers have offered to pay the city $568,000, and to build a public plaza of 29,500 square feet in the heart of their office-hotel-shopping complex. According to legal documents, the new plaza would be open to the public and offer all constitutional privileges accorded citizens, such as freedom of speech and assembly, as are allowed in city-owned parks.

"The city is not losing a park, but gaining another, better-designed public space," Developer David Ditmer told the Council. He proceeded to present an elaborate slide show narrated by the landscape architect. Most Council members were awed.

Having held two public hearings and having encountered only minimal objection, the City Council wants to know if you have any personal feelings, or know of any legal concerns that you think should be mentioned.

Problem

How do you reply to the City Council? Is an indoor plaza equal to an outdoor park? Why or why not? Should a private company be in charge of a "public" park? What problems do you see arising?

What legal problems are involved with the sale? Must the city get an objective appraisal of the land value of the park or may it use the figure offered by Moonlight Travel? Does the city have "good cause" (in the legal sense) to sell the land? What might it have to prove if challenged in a lawsuit?

Suggested Key Words and Phrases for
Literature Search for Case 300

Appraisal of land	Citizen participation
Conservation	Downtown development
Developers	"Good cause"
Indoor plaza	Land sales
Legal documents	Public hearings
Private parks	Urban renewal

Selected References for Case Study 300

Black, J., Howland, L., and Rogel, S. (1983). *Downtown retail development: Conditions for success and project profiles.* Washington, D.C.: Urban Land Institute.

Crawford, Jr., C. (1979). *Strategy and tactics in municipal zoning.* Second ed. Englewood Cliffs, NJ: Prentice-Hall.

Frieden, B., and Sagalyn, L. (1989). *Downtown, inc.: How America rebuilds cities.* Cambridge, MA: MIT University Press.

Hawkins, T. (1988, May). Parks: For the people, by the people. *Parks and Recreation*, 39-43.

Kaiser, R. (1986). *Liability and law in recreation, parks, and sports.* Englewood Cliffs, NJ: Prentice-Hall.

Marciniak, E. (1986). *Reclaiming the inner city.* Washington, D.C.: National Center for Urban Ethnic Affairs.

McNulty, R., Penne, R., and Jacobson, D. (1986). *The return of the livable city: Learning from America's best.* Washington, D.C.: Acropolis.

Meyers, E. (1988). *Rebuilding America's cities.* Cambridge, MA: Ballinger.

Lai, R. (1988). *Law in urban design and planning: The invisible web.* New York: Van Reinhold.

Peterson, C., and McCarthy, C. (1982). *Handling zoning and land use litigation: A practical guide.* Charlottesville, VA: Michie.

Urban Land Institute. (1985). *Working with the community: A developer's guide.* Washington, D.C.: Urban Land Institute.

White, M. (1980). *Urban renewal and the changing residential structure of the city.* Chicago: Community and Family Study Center, University of Chicago.

Williams, B. (1988). *Upscaling downtown: Stalled gentrification in Washington, D.C.* Ithaca, NY: Cornell University.

INDEX

P

Q

R

SUBJECT MATTER INDEX TO CASES

Number refers to case number.